EMPIRE OF SALONS

Empire of Salons

CONQUEST AND COMMUNITY IN EARLY MODERN OTTOMAN LANDS

Helen Pfeifer

PRINCETON UNIVERSITY PRESS
PRINCETON & OXFORD

Published by Princeton University Press
41 William Street, Princeton, New Jersey 08540
99 Banbury Road, Oxford OX2 6JX

press.princeton.edu

First paperback printing, 2024
Paperback ISBN 9780691224947
Cloth ISBN 9780691195230
ISBN (e-book) 9780691224954

British Library Cataloging-in-Publication Data is available

Editorial: Ben Tate and Josh Drake
Production Editorial: Nathan Carr
Jacket/Cover Design: Layla Mac Rory
Production: Danielle Amatucci
Publicity: Alyssa Sanford and Charlotte Coyne
Copyeditor: Michelle Garceau Hawkins

Jacket/Cover art: From Aşık Çelebi, *Meşāʿirü's-Şuʿarā'*, c. 1600.
Ali Emiri-tarih No. 772, fol. 80. Courtesy of Millet Library, Fatih, Turkey.

This book has been composed in Miller

CONTENTS

LIST OF FIGURES

0.1. The poet Baki converses with two Ottoman gentlemen. 4
0.2. The Aleppo Chamber. 5
0.3. The expansion of the Ottoman Empire. 14
1.1. Ottoman, Mamluk, Aqquyunlu, and Timurid territories in the second half of the fifteenth century. 28
1.2. Scholars working in Ottoman lands with experience abroad, 1299–1512. 48
2.1. ʿAbd al-Rahim al-ʿAbbasi's *Clusters of Pearls*. 81
2.2. Saʿdi Çelebi meets another scholar in a room lined with books. 86
2.3. Decoration in the Aleppo Chamber. 88
2.4. The chief military judge of Anatolia, Kadiri Çelebi. 92
3.1. The Janbulat house in Aleppo. 102
3.2. Reception hall in the ʿAzm palace in Damascus. 110
3.3. A courtyard reception area in the Zahrawi residence in Homs. 111
3.4. The Great Mosque of Damascus in the late Mamluk era. 112
3.5. The scholar Ebu's-Suʿud presides over a scholarly gathering. 114
3.6. A man kisses the hand of a Sufi shaykh. 117
5.1. ʿAli, the father of the biographer ʿAşık Çelebi, receives another scholar next to shelves containing books. 170
5.2. An excerpt from Badr al-Din al-Ghazzi's versified Qurʾan commentary. 174
5.3. Badr al-Din al-Ghazzi's endorsement of Fevri Efendi's *Gloss on The Sura of the Believers*. 196
6.1. The mufti Fevri Efendi meets with another scholar. 207

ACKNOWLEDGMENTS

AT HEART, this book is about the personal and collaborative nature of Ottoman scholarship. My own research has been no less shaped by the generosity, wisdom, and guidance of others.

The book began as a dissertation at Princeton University. My adviser, Molly Greene, furnished the razor-sharp questions and unflagging support upon which this project was built. I thank her for having given me the freedom to write the dissertation I wanted to write, and the direction that allowed me to write the best dissertation I was able to write. Anthony Grafton kindly accepted me into his own flock as well, and has never ceased being a source of support and inspiration since. Finally, Michael Cook raised all of the big questions and found all of the small mistakes (though many surely remain). I would have never dared to become a historian without the inspiration and guidance of my undergraduate advisers, Margaret Garb and Gerald Izenberg. Heba Fekry taught me Arabic and a great many other things. Emma Kafalenos, Phillip Overeem, Timothy Parsons, Mark Pegg, and Nancy Reynolds were others who convinced me that I could and wanted to be a scholar.

Many friends and colleagues took the time to read and comment on drafts, including Andrew Arsan, Arthur Asseraf, Cumhur Bekar, Maria-Magdalena Pruß, Simon Fuchs, Valeria Lopez-Fadul, Christopher Markiewicz, David Reynolds, Nir Shafir, Baki Tezcan, and Sara Nur Yıldız. Melissa Calaresu, David Reynolds, Ulinka Rublack, and Alexandra Walsham provided endless encouragement. Andrei Pesic asked the key questions on a park bench early on, and persevered until the bitter end. My biggest debt is to Alexander Bevilacqua. His generosity knows no bounds, and he has taught me as much about friendship as he has about history.

The thoughts of friends and fellow wayfarers have entered this book in a thousand visible and invisible ways. My thanks for the conversations and companionship of Seth Anziska, Ori Beck, Alissa Bellotti, Angèle Christin, Ramazan Demir, Matthew Ellis, John-Paul Ghobrial, Martin Greve, Azad Ibrahim, Gabriele Jancke, Sooyong Kim, Tijana Krstić, Harriet Lyon, Owen Miller, Mehmet Sait Özervarlı, Jenna Phillips, Ronny Regev, Liliana Reyes, Ünver Rüstem, Delia Solomons, Henry Spelman, Michael Sonenscher, Derin Terzioğlu, Yasemin Ural, Caroline Vout, Ruth Watson, Danielle Wessler, and Nurfadzilah Yahya. The Canfora family has been just that to me, as have Abdul Nasser Yassin and Nawal Masri. My sister Annie has been a constant source of inspiration to me, and she and Amir have offered me more support—tangible and intangible—than they can ever know.

Like the scholars I study, I have relied on the patronage of many individuals and institutions. This project was supported at various stages by the Beinecke Scholarship Program, the Bernadotte E. Schmitt Grant, the Centre for Research in the Social Sciences and Humanities at Cambridge, the German Orient-Institut in Istanbul, the Princeton Institute for International and Regional Studies, the Princeton University Center for the Study of Religion, the Princeton University History Department, and the U.S. Department of Education's Foreign Language and Area Studies Program. I would like to thank the staff of the British Library, the Escorial Library, the Kastamonu Public Library, the Princeton University Library, the Staatsbibliothek zu Berlin, the Topkapı Palace Museum Library, and the Süleymaniye Library for their efficiency, patience, and, in the last case, tea.

Some of the material presented in Chapter 5 has been published in *The International Journal of Middle East Studies* and in *Historicizing Sunni Islam in the Ottoman Empire, c. 1450–c. 1750*, edited by Tijana Krstić and Derin Terzioğlu.

At Princeton University Press, I would like to extend my thanks to Ben Tate, whose patience and sense of humor got me through this project, as well as to Nathan Carr, Josh Drake, and Michelle Hawkins. Many thanks also to the anonymous reviewers for their invaluable feedback.

I owe the greatest debt to my parents, who believed that I could become anything and supported me as I tried everything. I hope they find within this book the integrity and humanity they both possess so strongly and worked so hard to instill in me.

To Christian I offer my love and give my thanks, for his humor, loyalty, support, and patience. I have learned as much from him as I have from writing this book, and his companionship has been my single greatest source of joy and fulfillment. Many new thresholds await us.

NOTE ON USAGE

ARABIC WORDS that appear in this book are transliterated according to a modified version of the system recommended by the *International Journal of Middle East Studies*. Ottoman Turkish words are rendered according to modern Turkish orthography, though the *hamza* (ʾ) and *ʿayn* (ʿ) have been retained. For the sake of readability, diacritics have been omitted in the body of the text, except when quoting from a historical source. Author names and book titles appear both in the footnotes and in the bibliography with diacritics.

I use English terms whenever possible, though Arabic and Turkish originals are given at their first use. Arabic-origin words used in both Arabic and Ottoman Turkish follow their primary linguistic context—hence *kadıasker* for the chief military judge, based at the imperial center, and *qadi al-qudat* for the chief judge of Damascus. Personal names are rendered according to an individual's primary language of daily communication. Place names are referred to by their English equivalents whenever possible, and dates are given according to the Common Era (as are measurements of years).

Translations are mine unless stated otherwise. Many of the sources consulted for this book were written in rhyme, and I have sought to translate these in a way that approximates not only their content but also their style. Rhymed prose has also been rendered in rhyme, and distinguished from poetry by its presentation in paragraph format.

EMPIRE OF SALONS

Introduction

STEPPING ACROSS THE threshold into the literary salon, many an Ottoman gentleman must have felt the excitement and fear of the boxer entering the ring. To be sure, there were countless physical comforts: gold-threaded sofa spreads lined with velvet cushions; gilded platters loaded with honeyed sweets; marble walls rosied by the glow of candlelight. Such sensory pleasures could help to bring men into heady communion with one another, spurring spontaneous recitations of verse and impassioned expressions of love. But equally often, the mood was combative. In a rapidly expanding empire, the salon was a theater for fierce disputes over status and power whose echoes resounded across far-flung Ottoman lands. This was the Ottoman Empire on twenty square meters of carpet: the salon of empire in an empire of salons.

Informal gatherings of gentlemen were an indispensible part of Ottoman political, social, and intellectual life in the early modern period (c. 1400–1800 CE). In cities and towns stretching from Albania to Arabia, elite salons brought leading figures from diverse ethnic and geographical backgrounds into close contact. Part business, part pleasure, and highly flexible in their form, these gatherings yielded to whatever the needs of the era were. In times of plenty, they served an incorporative function, drawing outsiders in and helping knowledge to circulate. When belts were tightened, however, so too were the boundaries of the salon, keeping newcomers out and resources in. In either case, salons functioned as key institutions of empire, contributing substantially to the Ottoman system of governance.

Salons were especially important in the wake of the Ottoman expansion into the Arab Middle East in the early part of the sixteenth century. Since the medieval period, salons had offered a forum for socializing that was shared, at least in its roughest outlines, all across the Islamic world.[1] With the Ottoman conquest of Greater Syria, Egypt, and parts of the Arabian Peninsula in 1516–7, such assemblies offered a venue in which encounters between the Turkish-speaking Ottoman ruling elite and local Arab notables could take place. Although in many ways the salon reproduced the asymmetrical relations between conqueror and conquered, in other key ways the imperatives of salon conversation generated their own social hierarchies, hierarchies that were a function not of political office but of eloquence, learning, and wit.

This book views the salon in this transformative era as it looked from the Syrian city of Damascus through the perspective of one Arab notable, Badr al-Din al-Ghazzi (d. 1577). Born in Damascus in 1499 during the last decades of the expiring Mamluk Sultanate, Ghazzi adjusted quickly to the new imperial order; he became friendly with the Ottoman functionaries that now passed through his hometown and eventually developed into one of the city's leading scholars. Ghazzi possessed all of the traits required to shine in the salon, including a powerful intellect, a deep erudition, and a seemingly endless repertoire of anecdotes and poems. But he, too, had his weaknesses, especially his stutter, which thwarted his ability to partake in the kind of verbal acrobatics that were the hallmark of elite sociability. Though his knowledge and stature meant that few ever dared to oppose him, by the end of his life Ghazzi was fending off a growing number of challengers from home and afar.

Ottoman Salons

The most recognizable and widely studied forum for early modern Ottoman sociability is the coffeehouse. Ever since Jürgen Habermas made the coffeehouse a cornerstone of his theory of the public sphere, scholars eager to incorporate non-Western lands into histories of modernity have shown how this distinctly Ottoman invention promoted new, more public lifestyles and offered a more inclusive space for social and political action.[2] The most recognizable and widely-studied forum for Ottoman intellectual

1. Samer Ali argues that "one of the primary mechanisms for forming Abbasid society and literature was the literary gathering or salon"; Maria Subtelny describes the *majlis* as "the main forum for literary, particularly poetical, expression in the late Tīmūrid period"; and Dominic Brookshaw maintains that "it was largely within the framework of *majālis* that much of the intellectual, cultural and social life of medieval Muslims took place." Ali, *Salons*, 13; Subtelny, "Scenes," 144; Brookshaw, "Palaces," 199. For more on medieval salons, see Lazarus-Yafeh et al., *The Majlis*; Kraemer, *Humanism*, 55–60; Madelung et al., "Madjlis."

2. Habermas, *Strukturwandel*, esp. 90–116. For Ottoman coffeehouses, see Kafadar, "Night"; Yaşar, *Osmanlı Kahvehaneleri*; Çaksu, "Coffee Houses"; Mikhail, "Desire";

activity, in turn, is the classic Islamic institution of higher education, the madrasa (Tur. *medrese*). Primarily designed to train students in the religious sciences, madrasas were also dynamic social centers, since they were often attached to larger mosque complexes and offered accommodation to many pupils.[3] Finally, the most recognizable and widely studied forum for sixteenth-century Ottoman state-building is the formal bureaucracy, with a strong sultan at the top and administrative support structures cascading down like so many domes and arches on an Ottoman imperial mosque.

The renown of these institutions is well deserved, especially in light of the markedly weaker institutionalization common amongst most of the empire's Eurasian contemporaries.[4] However, historians' focus on these structures also reflects modern expectations of separation between state and society, work and leisure, as well as private and public spheres. In fact, these institutions coexisted with, and in part developed out of, another social form more difficult to classify according to such divisions: the salon. When the coffeehouse first emerged in the sixteenth century, it was viewed by many Ottoman elites as a competitor to, and indeed usurper of, domestic forms of hospitality. The madrasa was just one theater for a wider culture of instruction and intellectual debate that flourished equally in mosques or at home. As for the Ottoman bureaucratic system, much of the daily business of governing was performed in the houses of imperial officials. However institutionalized the Ottoman Empire became, loosely defined gatherings held in multifunctional spaces continued to play an important societal role.

All members of early modern Ottoman society had opportunities to socialize. Ottoman sultans conversed with courtiers in pavilions overlooking the Bosphorus or in royal tents while on campaign.[5] Women congregated in bathhouses or in the family quarters of the home.[6] Neither did religious

---

Özkoçak, "Coffeehouses"; Kömeçoğlu, "Publicness"; Işın, "Conversation"; Hattox, *Coffee*. A comprehensive overview of the historiography can be found in Yaşar, "Şehir Mekânları."

3. Atçıl, *Scholars;* Baltacı, *Osmanlı Medreseleri;* Uzunçarşılı, *İlmiye Teşkilatı*; Repp, *The Müfti of Istanbul.*

4. Coffeehouses did not spread to Europe until the seventeenth century, and states there were rarely able to exert the same kind of centralized control over higher education and administration. Sturmberger, "Vorbildhaftigkeit"; Çizakça, "Ottoman Government," esp. 241–52.

5. Ertuğ, "Entertaining the Sultan"; İnalcık, *Tarab*; Ertuğ, "Meclis"; İnalcık, "Klasik edebiyat menşei"; Necipoğlu, "Garden Culture"; Mahir, *Minyatür Sanatı*, 117–8.

6. For bathhouses, see Ergin, *Bathing Culture*; Boyar and Fleet, *Ottoman Istanbul*, chapter 7; Rafeq, "Diversion." For women socializing in the home in sixteenth-century Ottoman lands, see Peirce, *Morality Tales*, chapter 7; Necipoğlu, "Garden Culture," 40. Eighteenth-century Ottoman miniatures depict gatherings of women as well, and evidence

دیمزمرکه سلمان سپهر کلام بلاغت انجامدن درجهٔ علیاسی واردر بلکه
منطق وکلامدن دم مسیحا وار ایدی مکتبه وارلدن منظوری لوح سینهٔ
پیمبران ومنتهی همتی الف لی مثال سرو قدان ایدی

مطمح نظری تشبیه نرکس خوبان ونصب عینی خیال نقطه خال ایدی
زلف دلبر وصفی اداسنه قدی فکاردن دال ایدی نون والقلم اوقورکن
ابرو وانکشت دلبر مدحنده غزللر سولدی یاسینه چقدقده ابرو دلداران

وصف

FIGURE 0.1. AND FIGURE 0.2. Figure 0.1 (*left*): The poet Baki, who sits on the right, converses with two Ottoman gentlemen in a reception area accessible by steps. From ʿAşık Çelebi, *Meşaʿirü's-şuʿaraʾ* (c. 1600). (Reproduced by permission from the Directorate of the Turkish Institution for Manuscripts, Millet Library Istanbul, MS Ali Emiri Tarih 772, 80.) Figure 0.2 (*above*): The Aleppo Chamber (c. 1600–1). Once owned by a Christian family in Aleppo, this wood-paneled chamber was part of a domed *qaʿa* structure with three raised platforms for sitting, two of which are visible in the photograph. (Reproduced with permission. © bpk/Museum für Islamische Kunst, SMB / Georg Niedermeiser.)

minorities lack for social occasions nor, in prosperous circles, for magnificent chambers in which to hold them, to judge from the spectacular reception hall owned by a Christian merchant of Aleppo in the first years of the seventeenth century (see figure 0.2).[7] Nonelites, too, cultivated rich

---

from the nineteenth century suggests that women cultivated similar forms of conversation to men. Phillips, *Everyday Luxuries*, 111–119; Atasoy, "Hayat sahnesi," 19–22; Strauss, "La Conversation," 263–5. For the Mamluk period, see Hirschler, *Written Word*, 45–6; Ibrahim, "Residential Architecture," 52.

7. Gonnella and Kröger, *Fabulous Creatures*; Gonnella, *Wohnhaus*. For a later period, see Grehan, "Fun."

social lives; in Anatolia and the Arab lands alike, artisans and peasants met to talk, play music, or even drink in private chambers, barbershops, or orchards.[8] Although many of these occasions were no doubt enjoyable, calling on other people was not merely a pleasure, but an obligation. According to Ottoman etiquette writers, regular visits were owed by adult children to their parents; by members of Sufi orders to one another; and by all men regardless of status to their social superiors. The resulting social pressure was such that some people—our Ghazzi included—opted to withdraw from socializing altogether. Around the age of forty, Ghazzi moved into a chamber on the eastern side of the Great Mosque of Damascus, vowing a life of seclusion. And yet, even this did not free him from social obligations: he continued to host students, scholars, and state officials for learned debates and even banquets.

Although such socializing was common to all social groups, much of it occurred in parallel. In the sixteenth century, Ottoman writers began to show increasing discomfort with mixed company of all sorts, whether across the lines of gender, religion, or class. Whereas fifteenth-century elite gatherings sometimes featured female poets alongside their male counterparts, later biographers sought to explain away such practices, which were thought to compromise the honor of a lady.[9] Likewise, few sixteenth-century writers documented the kind of interreligious dialogue that had flourished in the assemblies of earlier eras (and continued in other parts of the Islamic world).[10] As for socializing across the lines of class, the defense of one Damascene scholar who was criticized for associating with men of modest means sums up the prevailing attitude: "I am poor, so I socialize with the poor."[11] In point of fact, many gatherings were more heterogeneous than writers cared to admit. That judicial courts occasionally prosecuted unrelated men and women for mixing in private is indisputable

8. Yılmaz, "Fun," 152–3; Sajdi, *Barber*, 64–6, 147.

9. Havlioğlu, *Mirî Hatun*, 44; Havlioğlu, "Margins." High-ranking women could take part in Timurid and Uzbek salons and even drink wine there. Szuppe, "Intellectual Milieu," esp. 130–3.

10. Heyberger, "Polemic Dialogues," 496; Kafadar, "Self and Others," 145. In fifteenth-century Mamluk Damascus, the scholar Ibn Tawq hosted Christians for meals in his home. Wollina, "*Taʿlīq*," 357. For interreligious dialogue in earlier eras, see Lazarus-Yafeh, *The Majlis*. For the Mughal court, where such dialogue continued to take place, see Alam and Subrahmanyam, "Frank Disputations"; Maclean, "Real Men." Strauss argues that gatherings became more religiously diverse in the second part of the seventeenth century; indeed, in the eighteenth, Greek Phanariots mingled with Muslim powerholders in palaces along the Bosphorus. Strauss, "La Conversation," 260; Greene, *Greeks*, 200–1.

11. Ibn Ayyūb, *Rawḍ*, 202a. See also Sajdi, *Barber*, 75.

evidence that such mixing occurred.[12] Architectural remains suggest that Christians and Muslims mingled privately too: the Christian owner of the Aleppo Chamber selected the inscriptions of the reception hall to avoid offending the religious sensibility of his Muslim guests.[13] Even at the gatherings of elite Muslim men, servants were omnipresent and women sometimes watched from the wings—Ghazzi himself was rarely seen without a following of enslaved Ethiopian women.[14] However, such figures played subsidiary, supporting roles. Physically and discursively, women, Christians, and nonelites remained at the margins of that most celebrated of social spaces: the salon.

The salon was the domain of Muslim gentlemen par excellence. I define salons as exclusive gatherings held for the purpose of enlightened conversation and structured around the relationship between host and guest. Participating in such gatherings was one of the defining attributes of upper-class Muslim men, since doing so allowed them to practice many of the privileges particular to their caste. This included exercising hospitality and performing acts of generosity, pursuits that were impracticable for social groups with single-room dwellings and little disposable income. It also included utilizing refined speech and displaying bookish knowledge of the sort inacessible to anyone without a higher education.[15] Contemporary descriptions of polite conversation conceptualize it as a distinctly masculine sport, drawing on the martial language of swordsmanship or even the sexualized language of penetration.[16] Nonetheless, as exclusionary as these gatherings were, they often did bring together men from different sectors of the Ottoman elite, including scholars, administrators, and military officials.

Ottoman writers had a variety of concepts to describe the gatherings I refer to as salons. One of the most common and generic of these was the Arabic *majlis*, *meclis* in Ottoman Turkish (pl. *majalis*, *mecalis*). Literally

12. Peirce, *Morality Tales*, 258–61. In 1583 men and women were caught in a drinking party (*içki meclisi*) in Üsküdar near Istanbul. *Üsküdar Kadi Sicilleri*, 9:98. Selim II liked to spend time with his former wet nurse. Necipoğlu, "Garden Culture," 42–3.

13. Heyberger, "Inschriften"; Ott, "Wer sich fürchtet." Christians appear to have been more eager to highlight such relationships than Muslims were. Dursteler, *Venetians*, 173–80.

14. Ibn Ayyūb, *Kitāb*, 16. The scholar İdris Bidlisi (d. 1520) emphasized the value of conversing with the women of one's household, if in moderation. İnalcık, *Tarab*, 223.

15. Sajdi, *Barber*, esp. 64–6; Grehan, "Words." Described for a much earlier period in Ghazi, "Un groupe social."

16. For the former, see Chamberlain, *Knowledge*, 153–4; for the latter, see Rouayheb, *Homosexuality*, esp. 21, 25–6.

meaning "sitting" or "session," with the verb "to sit" at its root, the word—just like the French *salon*—could carry both the meaning of "assembly" and of the physical space in which such assemblies were held.[17] However, unlike in the French case, the Arabic term designated an occasion long before it indicated an architectural feature, and indeed a *majlis* could be held almost anywhere: not only in a domestic interior, but also in a courtyard, garden, or even in a publicly accessible space like a madrasa or mosque.[18] Nonetheless, privately owned reception areas played an especially important role in the lives of Ottoman elites, whose sprawling compounds housed many such spaces and acted as the center of operations for the large households that underpinned early modern Ottoman society and politics.[19] That elites could gather in the privacy of the home was a fact of enormous significance since it shielded them from the long arm of the law.[20] However, the upper classes also had the luxury of utilizing a range of public spaces for their gatherings, and Ghazzi and many of his contemporaries received visitors in highly visible locations in urban mosques.[21] Thanks to the retinues of servants that trailed most Ottoman elites wherever they went, such publicly staged hospitality mimicked many aspects of the kind practiced in private.[22] Elite salon culture thus found its expression wherever a group of Ottoman gentlemen chose to sit.

17. The term *majlis* is variously rendered in English as, among other things, "entertainment," "salon," "session," "social gathering," and "symposium." Gilliot, *Education*, xxxiii; Manz, *Power*, 197; Bray, "Adab," 13–14; Kilpatrick, "Socializing," 762–763; Lewis, "Reading," 78. Because of the generic meaning of the term, it was also used to designate a whole range of gatherings quite different from those discussed here, e.g., class lessons, court sessions, or even devotional assemblies. Allen, "Night"; Makdisi, *Colleges*, 10–12; Dozy, "Majlis," 208. Other terms used in the sixteenth century included *mujalasa* and *jamʿ*. For the former, see Ghazzī, *Maṭāliʿ*, 137; ʿĀşıḳ Çelebi, *Dhayl*, 106; for the latter, Būrīnī, *Tarājim*, 2: 98. Samer Ali distinguishes between *majlis* and *mujalasa*, with the latter connoting more egalitarian interactions. Ali, *Salons*, 16–8.

18. Ertuğ, "Entertaining the Sultan," 133; Necipoğlu, "Gaze," 310. For the usage of *majlis* in Arabic to designate a space in the home, see Ghazzī, *Kawākib*, 2: 237. It seems that such usage was more common in Arabic than in Turkish, since Caʿfer Efendi, writing in early seventeenth-century Istanbul, translates the Arabic *majlis* into Turkish as *dernek yeri* (meeting place) and *oturacak yer* (sitting place), not suggesting (as he does with other terms) that its meaning is shared in the two languages. Caʿfer Efendi, *Risāle-i Miʿmāriyye*, 89 (74r).

19. Kunt, "Households," 103. Most work on Ottoman households has focused on a later period. See Bekar, "Köprülü Family," chapter 4; Nizri, *Ulema Household*; Hathaway, *Households;* Salzmann, "Ancien Regime"; Abou-el-Haj, *"Households."* For glimpses into sixteenth-century households, see Wilkins, "Masters"; Kunt, *The Sultan's Servants*, 53–4.

20. Stilt and Mottahedeh, "Public," 737–8, 740–1.

21. Mosques were sites of sociability in the central lands as well. Ṭaşköprīzāde, *Shaqāʾiq*, 177, 250.

22. Ibn Ayyūb, *Rawḍ*, 280a; Tietze, "Luxury."

Part of the attraction of Ottoman salons was their flexibility. Depending on the needs of the host or his guests, salons could be put to a variety of different social ends. One of the most important was entertainment and leisure, as existing scholarship has shown. Many contemporaries reveled in the era's celebratory banquets (Ar. *diyafa*, Tur. *ziyafet*), lavish drinking parties (Tur. *bezm*, *meclis-i ʿişret*), and elegant soirées (Ar. *mahfil*, Tur. *mehfil*).[23] These were the sorts of occasions to which a sultan would retire to hear music and watch dancing, or to which friends would flock to engage in friendly conversation (*sohbet*) or to gaze at handsome prepubescent boys.[24] Usually, a special role was reserved for poetry and literature, and contemporaries singled out the gatherings of poets or the literati (Ar. *majlis adab*, Tur. *meclis-i şuʿaraʾ*) for particular praise.[25]

Yet, the pleasurable aspects of such occasions should not overshadow the hard work of Ottoman sociability. Initially conceptualized by Georg Simmel as a form of social interaction that was devoid of meaningful content and performed purely for its own sake, sociability has since been recast as something far more serious, as "work with a purpose."[26] In Ottoman gatherings as elsewhere, many apparently superficial interactions relied on extensive training and considerable physical and mental labor. What is more, even the most humdrum of exchanges could serve the purpose of strengthening social cohesion within groups or upholding distinctions between them.[27]

But participating in Ottoman salons also constituted work in a stricter sense. For scholars, salons were key arenas for exchanging ideas and building intellectual authority. Throughout the early modern period, not only poems, but also writings of a more academic nature were regularly conceived of and received in learned salons (Ar. *majlis ʿilm*, Tur.

23. For banquets, see Ṭaşköprīzāde, *Shaqāʾiq*, 130. For *bezm*, see Ertuğ, "Entertaining the Sultan," 124; Kut, "Bezm." For *meclis-i ʿişret*, see İnalcık, "Klasik edebiyat menşei" and İnalcık, *Tarab*. For *mahfil/mehfil*, see Ibn Ayyūb, *Kitāb*, 89; Kınalı-zade, *Tezkiretü'ş-Şuʿarâ*, 670.

24. Ertuğ, "Entertaining the Sultan"; Uludağ, "Sohbet"; Ertuğ, "Meclis"; Andrews and Kalpaklı, *The Age of Beloveds*, esp. 106–12; Strauss, "La Conversation," 252–4.

25. This has been the best studied aspect of Ottoman salons. Havlioğlu, *Mihrî Hatun*, chapter 2; İnalcık, *Tarab*, chapters 5–6; Andrews et al., *Ottoman Lyric Poetry*, esp. 33–4; Çeltik, "Şairler Meclisi"; İnalcık, "Klasik Edebiyat menşei"; İpekten, *Edebî Muhitler*, esp. 227–37; Fleischer, *Bureaucrat*, 22–3.

26. Cowan, "Spaces," 252. Simmel's original German term was *Geselligkeit*. Simmel, "Sociability"; Lilti, *Salons*, 5–7. For an appeal to take Ottoman sociability seriously and a template for how to study it, see Georgeon, "Présentation."

27. Hellman, "Furniture."

meclis-i ʿilm).[28] For the unemployed, salons were key stops on the way to new patrons: job seekers began their work by paying courtesy visits to Istanbul's power holders or securing invitations to their soirées. Political decisions, too, were often made in informal contexts; for ambassadors, a visit to the Topkapı Palace was the culmination of numerous private meetings with the sultan's advisors.[29] Even judicial verdicts were often the result of negotiations that occurred outside of the Islamic court, with many formal hearings taking place only after decisions had been reached privately.[30]

Contemporaries did attempt to separate out the various functions of informal gatherings and to differentiate work from leisure. Etiquette manuals stressed that drinking parties should only be held in the evenings and discouraged the sultan from involving his boon companions (Ar. *nadim*, Tur. *nedim*) in the affairs of the state.[31] Some men of stature reserved mornings for private sessions and afternoons for more public audiences (or vice versa).[32] However, in practice these lines were often blurry. Pleas for patronage were best couched in polite banter or rhetorical flourish and, at the assemblies held in Damascus when a new judge arrived from Istanbul, a particularly clever repartee could win a man a job.[33] Scholarly discussions gave way to poetry exchanges.[34] Paperwork catalyzed disputes over grammar.[35] A meeting Ghazzi had with a leader of a Sufi religious order and the latter's brothers in the Syrian town of Hama was typical of the different modes of interaction that coexisted in a single gathering. In a magnificent chamber in the order's lodge overlooking the Orontes river, the men spoke about what they had seen and done since they had last met. They discussed scholarly topics, both religious and secular. Ghazzi inspected the Sufi shaykh's appointment deed, jotting down an approving note in response. He issued the shaykh an academic license (*ijaza*). At one

28. Pfeifer, "Encounter"; Sievert, "Salon"; Brömer, "Scientific Practice"; Hanna, *In Praise of Books*, 72–6; Öztürk, "Okunan Kitaplar." For the importance of reading sessions for nonelites, see Değirmenci, "Gözlemler"; Öztürk, "Halk Kitapları."

29. Muslu, *Ottomans*, 47, 52; Ghobrial, *The Whispers of Cities*, chapter 3.

30. Gradeva, "*Kadi* Court," 62, 66.

31. Kafadar, "Night"; İnalcık, "Klasik edebiyat menşei," 228, 230–1; Strauss, "La Conversation," 254–6. For boon companions in earlier periods, see Yıldız, "*Nadīm*"; Chejne, "Boon-Companion."

32. The North African traveler Ibn Battuta (d. 1368/9) observed this practice in Kastamonu in the fourteenth century, and the Scottish physician Alexander Russell in Aleppo in the eighteenth. Ibn Baṭṭūṭa, *Travels*, 2:462–3; Mollenhauer, "Private," 75–6.

33. Ibn Ayyūb, *Kitāb*, 84.

34. Ibn al-Ḥanbalī, *Durr*, 1: 997.

35. Ḥamawī, *Ḥādī*, 93–4; Ḥamawī, *Bawādī*, 154b–5a; Elger, *Glaube*, 100.

point, a man from the shaykh's entourage asked Ghazzi for a legal opinion, which he provided on the spot. And, when the sun disappeared over the horizon and the black dust of the night settled into the eyes of the lands, the men performed the sunset prayer together. Since it was the month of Ramadan, they broke their fast with a sumptuous buffet. Only then did Ghazzi take his leave of the gentlemen.[36] Diverse as Ottoman gatherings were, this book uses the word "salon" as an umbrella term designating the whole spectrum of elite assemblies. It is used interchangeably with the generic "gathering" and "assembly," and supplemented by more specific designations whenever possible (e.g., banquet, scholarly gathering, soirée).

The importance of salons is confirmed by their ubiquity in the Ottoman written record. They feature in travel narratives, biographical compendia, chronicles, etiquette manuals, paintings, and poems. Arabic travel accounts (*rihla*) were often more concerned with the social landscape of a given locale than with the mosques or monuments that preoccupied better-known Ottoman travelers like Evliya Çelebi or many European visitors to the empire. The descriptions of leading figures compiled in both Arabic and Turkish-language biographical anthologies (*tarajim*, *tezkire*) also often dwelled on social gatherings. To give an extreme, but not atypical, example, a four-thousand-word biography of a fifteenth-century Ottoman scholar chronicled a banquet he hosted to honor his father; a feast followed by a lesson he held for a Persian traveler; the scholar's visit, in the company of some of his students, to the home of a vizier; a learned disputation in front of the sultan; and another debate that soured when a guest refused to take his assigned seat.[37] Prescriptive sources devote no less attention to social gatherings, and Ghazzi wrote books of etiquette (*adab*) on sharing meals, joking, and interacting with fellow members of a Sufi order, to name only a few.[38] Though these prescriptive sources should not be confused with descriptions of actual fact, the substantial overlap between theory and practice suggests how seriously prescriptions were taken.[39] Finally, paintings and poems often put salons center stage. Illustrated manuscripts regularly depicted elite gatherings, their painters supplementing textual cues with first-hand observations of Ottoman

36. Ghazzī, *Maṭāliʿ*, 50–2.

37. The scholar in question is Hocazade (d. 1488). Ṭaşköprīzade, *Shaqāʾiq*, 126–39. For biographical dictionaries as reflections of particular social circles, see Niyazioğlu, *Dreams*, chapter 1; Sajdi, *Barber*, 50–2; El-Rouayheb, "al-Būrīnī," 2; Andrews and Kalpaklı, *The Age of Beloveds*.

38. Ghazzī, *Ādāb al-muʾākala*; Ghazzī, *Muzāḥ;* Ghazzī, *ʿIshra*.

39. See the cautionary remarks in Lewicka, *Food*, 392.

social life.[40] Contemporary poetry likewise dwelt on convivial themes, with much of its stock imagery—candles, goblets, blossoms—evoking the trappings of elite sociability. Indeed, however concerned poets were with literary form, they crafted their verses from the stuff of daily life, not least from the poetic séances where those verses were so often performed.[41] Poems should thus be seen less as reflections of Ottoman salons than as participants within them.

What is the wisdom of referring to this distinctly Ottoman social form using the French term *salon*? Doing so may seem at best imprecise and at worst misleading. Few institutions have been laden with more world-historical meaning. French salons have variously been credited with incubating gender equality, the Enlightenment, democratic politics, and the bourgeois public sphere, thus taking a leading role not only in French national history but in the rise of Western modernity itself.[42] And yet, recent historiography has cut French salons down to size, rejecting some of their exalted associations in favor of a more sober account rooted in distinctly early modern conceptions of etiquette and social hierarchy. Women, it seems, played more circumscribed, more gendered roles than was once believed; if salons helped to engender egalitarian thought, then they were also vehicles of royal patronage and dominated by aristocratic notions of civility; and the public sphere that developed around these and other spaces had close ties to, indeed relied upon, state networks.[43] Even the term *salon* has come to seem anachronistic, since its use to designate a polite gathering developed only in the nineteenth century when what was left of the culture it denoted was heavily cloaked in nostalgia. Before that, contemporaries spoke of a larger culture of elite hospitality built around "houses," "circles," and, above all, "societies."[44]

This reinterpretation of the French salon clears the way for a less loaded usage of the term in other historical contexts.[45] To speak of Ottoman salons is not to imply that Ottoman sociability was just like French

40. Ertuğ, "Entertaining the Sultan"; İnalcık, *Tarab*; Ertuğ, "Ceremonies"; Tanındi, "Transformation"; Kütükoğlu, "Divân-ı Hümâyûn."

41. Andrews and Kalpaklı argue forcefully for the value of Ottoman poetry in reconstructing the past. Andrews and Kalpaklı, *The Age of Beloveds*; Andrews, *Poetry's Voice, Society's Song*, esp. chapter 7.

42. Rouget, "Academies"; Goodman, *Republic*; Gordon, *Citizens without Sovereignty*; Habermas, *Strukturwandel*.

43. Lilti, "Politesse," 9–11; Lilti, *Salons*; Cowan, "Spaces," 255, 259–61; Roche, *Siècle*; Blanning, *Culture*, 13.

44. Lilti, *Salons*, 6; Rouget, "Academies"; Lilti, "Politesse," 2.

45. Cowan, "Spaces," 260–2.

sociability, real or imagined. Not only did Ottoman salon culture by and large exclude women, but its forms of association were self-consciously Islamic and developed around substantial differences in material culture and social practice.[46] The division between "polite" and "scholarly" culture, so salient in eighteenth-century France, never operated in Ottoman circles, where self-respecting gentlemen were expected to master both. And yet, Ottoman salons did have notable similarities to elite gatherings across early modern Eurasia, including the importance of poetry, the role of patronage, and the concern with physical expressions of social hierarchies.[47] Although this book emphasizes the distinctiveness of Ottoman sociability, it uses the term salon to evoke a social form that was commensurable across coeval elite cultures.

The Incorporation of Arab Lands

At no point were salons more important than after the Ottoman conquest of the Mamluk Sultanate in 1516–7. This conquest was one of the most consequential events to occur across six hundred years of Ottoman history. In the course of just six months, Ottoman armies advanced from the Orontes to the Nile, trouncing the Mamluk forces and wresting from them some of the wealthiest and most sacred sites of the Islamic world: Cairo, Damascus, Jerusalem, Mecca, and Medina. The defeat brought a large Muslim and Arabic-speaking population under the authority of the ethnically diverse but linguistically Turcophone Ottoman ruling elite. It also enabled further conquest and, within just a few decades, the Ottomans would go on to claim territories in modern Iraq, Yemen, Libya, Tunisia, and Algeria as well (see figure 0.3).[48] Thus began four hundred years of Ottoman control over large parts of the Arab world.

Spectacular though the 1516–7 conquest was, it has often been overshadowed in historical memory by the 1453 capture of Constantinople. To be sure, historians routinely state that the events of 1516–7 helped to make the empire more Islamic as it became the warden of the holy lands and its population skewed more Muslim. However, this transformation has more often been asserted than examined. Indeed, modern scholarship on Ottoman Arab lands has often focused on the later centuries, when local actors

46. Pfeifer, "Gulper." In the nineteenth century, European observers often took issue with the exclusion of women from Ottoman salons. Strauss, "La Conversation," 262–3.

47. For the former two, see Rouget, "Academies"; Tarte, *Places*. For the latter, see Sternberg, *Status Interaction*, esp. 1–2.

48. Hathaway, *Arab Lands*, chapter 2; Rafeq, *ʿArab*, 58–80.

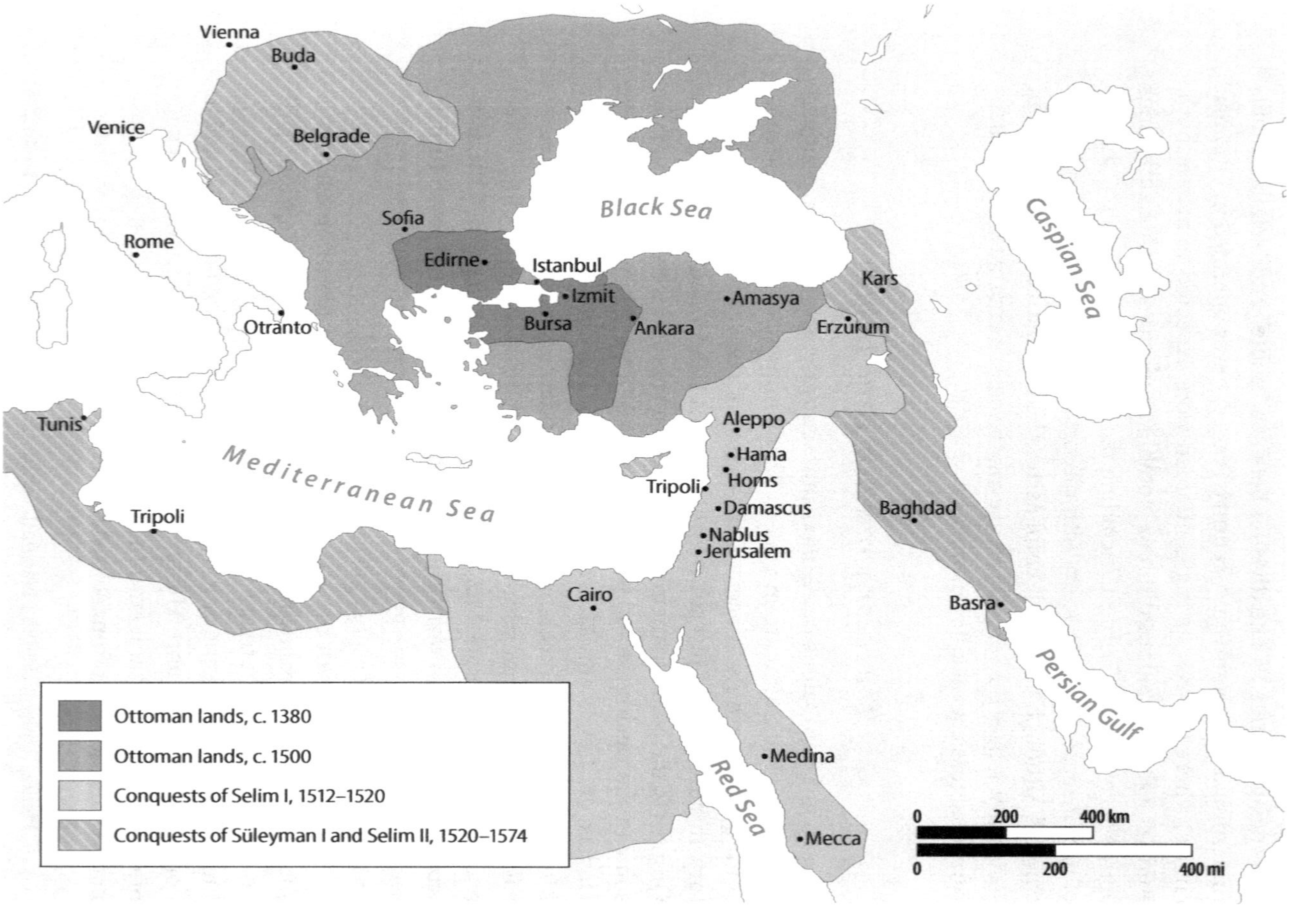

FIGURE 0.3. The expansion of the Ottoman Empire through the third quarter of the sixteenth century.

gained more visibility.[49] Those who have studied the first century of interactions have usually foregrounded legal, institutional, and administrative aspects.[50] Integration is not just an administrative affair, however.[51] This book examines the incorporation of Arab lands into the Ottoman Empire as a social and cultural process. It argues that the first decades after the conquest constitute a distinct period in Ottoman-Arab relations, one in which economic prosperity and a still emergent imperial culture afforded Arabs a prominent place in the social and intellectual landscape of the empire.[52]

When Turkish speakers and Arabic speakers met in the wake of the conquest, they did not begin with a blank slate. Theirs was a long history of encounter stretching back to the Arab expansion of the seventh and eighth centuries. What is more, since 1250, Syria and Egypt had been ruled by Turkish speakers, namely the elite slaves known as *mamluks* that were imported from Central Asia and the Caucasus and gave the sultanate its modern name. This continuous history of interaction between the two groups gave rise to a variety of ready-made stereotypes about each, for whom the same ethnonyms existed in Arabic and in Turkish: Arabs (Ar., Tur. *ʿarab*) were generous and eloquent, while Turks (Ar. *atrak*, Tur. *etrak*) were courageous and warlike.[53] However, actual relationships varied

49. Abouseif, *Egypt's Adjustment*, 16. There are too many such works to mention, but see for example Baldwin, *Islamic Law*; Mikhail, *Nature*; Grehan, *Everyday Life*; Reilly, *Small Town*; Raymond, *Arab Cities*; Raymond, *Artisans*; Van Leeuwen, *Waqfs*; Hanna, *Big Money*; Hathaway, *Households*; Khoury, *Provincial Society*; Doumani, *Rediscovering Palestine*; Marcus, *Middle East*; Abu Husayn, *Provincial Leaderships*; Rafeq, *Province of Damascus*. The literature on the nineteenth century is even more expansive.

50. For monographs focusing on Greater Syria, see Winter, *Shiites of Lebanon*; Singer, *Ottoman Beneficence*; Singer, *Palestinian Peasants*; Bakhit, *Ottoman Province*. For Egypt, see Lellouch and Michel, *Conquète ottomane*; Abouseif, *Egypt's Adjustment*. For studies treating both, see Mutawalli, *Fatḥ*; Stripling, *Ottoman Turks*. For legal aspects, see Ayoub, *Law*; Burak, *Islamic Law*; Meshal, "Antagonistic Sharīʿas"; Fitzgerald, "Methods of Conquest"; Peirce, *Morality Tales*. A handful of studies straddle the late Mamluk and early Ottoman periods: Conermann and Şen, *The Mamluk-Ottoman Transition*; Fitzgerald, "Methods of Conquest."

51. More recently, scholars have begun to focus more on cultural aspects of provincial integration, including Taner, *Caught in a Whirlwind*; Emre, *Ibrahim-i Gulshani*; Lellouch, *Les Ottomans en Égypte*; Winter, *Society and Religion*. See also some of the contributions in Conermann and Şen, *The Mamluk-Ottoman Transition*.

52. Most studies of the two groups' mutual perceptions have examined a later period, when a sharper ethnic consciousness began to develop. Tamari, "National Consciousness"; Rafeq, "al-Nabulsi"; Winter, "Polemical Treatise"; Baer, "Egyptian Attitudes."

53. Karmī, *Masbūk al-Dhahab*, 40; Haarman, "Ideology"; Şeşen, "Eski Arablar'a Göre Türkler," esp. 14–5.

much more than such conventions let on, not only depending on political circumstance, but also due to the enormous diversity within each group.

Indeed, few contemporaries understood the sixteenth-century encounter as one between "Turks" and "Arabs." For one, contemporaries rarely used the word "Turk" to refer to those who resided in Anatolia and the Balkans, the region where Ottoman control had been concentrated before the 1516–7 conquest. Rather, both residents themselves and their Arabic-speaking neighbors preferred the word "Rumi" (*rumi*, pl. *arwam*).[54] The name literally meant "Roman," referring to the inhabitants of the Eastern Roman Empire—called *Rum*—whose lands Turkish speakers had by and by taken until the Ottomans delivered the final deathblow in 1453. The term suited the Ottomans just fine, since they took pride in this imperial heritage and associated "Rumi" with an urbanized population distinct from the more pastoral "Turk."[55] The label also accommodated the ethnic diversity of the Ottoman elite. Though Rumis were speakers of Turkish, one could become a Rumi if one was born into a Greek, Serbo-Croatian, or German family, as long as one went on to embrace a Turkish, Muslim habitus.[56] As such, the category was as much an ethnic as a sociocultural one.[57]

The word "Arab" was indeed employed by contemporaries, but in ways that fail to map neatly onto modern usages. *ʿArab*, not unlike *atrak*, had a tribal tinge, and was often used to refer to the nomadic Bedouin who inhabited deserts from North Africa to the Arabian Peninsula. Instead of "Arabs," contemporaries often used the term "the sons of the Arabs" (Ar., *awlad al-ʿarab*, Tur. *evlad-i ʿarab*) to refer to the settled, Arabic-speaking population of the region.[58] However, even this was not a purely ethnic category. As Jane Hathaway has shown, in some usages it could include people of Persian and Central Asian origin, and thus have a more generic

54. This should be distinguished from the noun *Rum*, which was used to designate Christian Orthodox populations, though there was slippage between the two terms. Although *Rumi* predominates in my sources, Arab commentators used others as well, including *ʿajam* (non-Arab) or, rarely, *ʿuthmāniyya* (Ottoman). Lellouch, "Turc"; Masters, *Arabs*, 13–4; Kafadar, "Rome"; Özbaran, *Bir Osmanlı Kimliği*; Behrens-Abouseif, *Egypt's Adjustment*, 134.

55. Kafadar, "Rome," 11; Fleischer, *Bureaucrat*, chapter 10.

56. Arabic sources sometimes referred to Turkish as the "Rumi language" (*al-lugha al-Rumiyya*). Ghazzī, *Lutf*, 358.

57. Kafadar, "Rome," 13.

58. This term was used already in the late Mamluk period. Blecher, *Prophet*, 85. For examples from the sixteenth century, see Ibn Ṭūlūn, *Quḍāt*, 311; Ibn Ayyūb, *Kitāb*, 43, 50; Ḥamawī, *Ḥādī*, 70; Emre, *Ibrahim-i Gulshani*, 218, 312; *3 Numaralı Mühimme Defteri*, 418; *7 Numaralı Mühimme Defteri* 3:120.

meaning akin to "Easterner."[59] Be that as it may, authors writing in both Turkish and Arabic often referred to "Arabs" as a collective, especially when paired with other groupings. Ghazzi was representative when he praised Istanbul as the meeting place of learned men from amongst the "Arabs, Persians, and Rumis."[60] As such, this book is framed as one about encounters between "Rumis" and "Arabs."

These were messy categories whose nuances and inconsistencies deserve greater scholarly attention. They were further complicated by contemporaries' keen class consciousness. Most educated, well-to-do Arabs would have believed themselves to have more in common with Rumi elites than with the Arabic-speaking cobblers who mended their shoes. Nevertheless, even within the elite, ethnic affiliation corresponded to concrete and sometimes intensely felt differences. In the Arab provinces, Rumis were identifiable not only by their language and distinctive clothing, but also by their monopoly on leading political offices. Such patterns inevitably saturated old concepts with new meaning. They also meant that, however internally variable Rumis or Arabs may have been, identification with them was a fact not only of significance, but also of consequence.

This book begins in the decades preceding the conquest, when Syria and Egypt were under the rule of the Turkish-speaking Mamluks and Ottoman power was concentrated in Southeastern Europe and Anatolia (see figure 1.1). Despite this political division, the two empires harbored a similar salon culture, as Chapter One shows. The travels of ʿAbd al-Rahim al-ʿAbbasi (d. 1555), a Cairene scholar and Ghazzi family friend, and Müʾeyyedzade ʿAbdurrahman (d. 1516), an influential Ottoman official, show how salons furthered social and intellectual exchanges between the two neighboring polities. Yet differences remained. Though scholars working in Mamluk lands perceived themselves to be at the center of global Sunni Islamic learning, many of their Ottoman contemporaries felt a greater affinity to the Persian world. Likewise, while gentlemanly conversation in Mamluk lands revolved mostly around Arabic, in Ottoman elite circles Turkish and Persian played far more important roles. As such, salon culture in the two regions had marked differences on the eve of the conquest.

If salons had always been important in spreading ideas across the region, they acquired new political functions in the wake of the conquest, as Chapter 2 explains. The new rulers knew they lacked the fine-grained

59. Hathaway, "*Evlâd-i ʿArab*"; Hathaway, *Arab Lands*, 74. See also Chapter 6 of this book.

60. Ghazzī, *Maṭāliʿ*, 122. For such pairings in a Turkish-language work, see ʿĀşıḳ Çelebi, *Meşâʿirü's-Şuʿarâ*, 610, 792.

knowledge of the new provinces required to successfully incorporate them. Whom to trust? Whom to appoint? These questions became a matter of state security in the early 1520s, when rebellious holdovers from the former Mamluk administration tried to seize power and restore the old order. Informal encounters between Rumi and Arab elites played an important part in addressing these concerns and in helping the Ottoman system take root. Much of this impetus came from locals themselves. Badr al-Din al-Ghazzi and his father Radi al-Din lost no time in reaching out to the Ottoman elites now passing through Damascus with greater frequency, including leading members of the provincial administration like governors and judges. The informality of salons allowed them to act as sites for the exchange of unlike things: locals supplied information and legitimacy in return for appointments and patronage. What is more, the relationships established within salons often lasted decades, long after salongoers had parted ways.

However, by no means were salons places of trust and collaboration alone; competition was one of the cornerstones of elite sociability. One of the most pressing concerns of sixteenth-century Ottoman high society was to clarify social hierarchies. The conquests had introduced a new group of elites into the imperial system, elites that had to be accounted for, their specific position within the social order ascertained. Salons acted as theaters for this process because they materialized status in highly visible ways. Seating arrangements were especially charged, since where someone sat in a gentlemanly circle was a function of his social standing. In Damascus, Ottoman officials took the head at many a polite assembly, presiding over local magnates by virtue of their office. And yet, as Chapter 3 shows, what made the transactional world of the salon so complex was that it recognized many different, and often competing, social currencies. As a gathering in the residence of the Damascene chief judge Hasan Bey (d. 1576) reveals, different claims to high social status—office, age, wealth, learning, lineage—had to be weighed against one another. As salongoers negotiated their particular place in the salon, they also negotiated their place in the Ottoman social order.

Yet external factors alone did not determine status in the salon. Chapter 4 demonstrates that gentlemanly gatherings helped to shape social hierarchies by virtue of the pursuit that Ottoman gentlemen valued most: polite conversation. In both Turkish-language circles at the Ottoman center and Arabic assemblies in the provinces, it was expected that participants would be not only paragons of gallantry and social comity, but also wellsprings of learning and masters of improvised verse. However, when Turkish-speaking Ottoman elites entered Arabic-language circles, with little choice but to speak Arabic and to draw from the Arabic literary canon, they did not always perform at levels they were accustomed to in Turkish-language gatherings and that reflected their intellectual stature. The imperfect performances that sometimes resulted would have been easier to brush off were it not for the scholarly and religious cachet Arabic enjoyed in Islamic societies the world over. For the local Arab literati, though, this represented an opportunity; they were able to use their skills to acquire considerable respect and authority.

Chapter 5 explains how salons allowed Arab scholars to pass their cultural and intellectual authority to their Rumi colleagues. Informal gatherings were important vehicles for the transmission of knowledge. By aiding the circulation of books and ideas across the Ottoman imperial domain, salons accelerated Rumis' engagement with Arabic-language intellectual traditions. Some of Ghazzi's closest Rumi contacts in Damascus were its chief judges *(qadi al-qudat)*. These men, who were appointed from Istanbul, represented some of the most powerful figures of the provincial administration. Most of them were also active scholars. As such, many of them took advantage of their time in Damascus to benefit from its intellectual riches; not only did they avidly collect books, many of them even studied with Ghazzi, showing special interest in his knowledge of hadiths (Ar. *hadith*, Tur. *hadis*), as the narrations about the life, deeds, and words of the Prophet Muhammad were called. Rumi interest in local scholarly traditions culminated in the figure of Kınalızade ʿAli (d. 1572), a chief judge and extraordinary scholar with whom Ghazzi had especially intense exchanges.

Cumulatively, the interactions salons permitted bore considerable results. By the 1570s, Ghazzi's student Muhibb al-Din al-Hamawi (d. 1608) could depict the empire as unified by a shared elite culture. As Chapter 6 shows, the Ottoman policy of rotating officials, coupled with Arab efforts to seek support in Istanbul, had created a truly empire-wide network of patronage. Still, just as these relationships were solidifying, other aspects of the relationship between Arabs and Rumis shifted. As the economy slowed and competition for positions skyrocketed, Arabs, like other provincial scholars, found their access to the imperial elite to be increasingly restricted. Younger scholars no longer enjoyed the same independence and admiration that Ghazzi did. Whereas Ghazzi taught Çivizade Mehmed (d. 1587), an Ottoman official from an esteemed Istanbul family, Ghazzi's student Hamawi joined the official's household as a scribe. Broader cultural shifts also led Arabs to lose some of their influence. Ottoman Turkish had gained in importance over the century, as had poetic and literary traditions in that language. Learned Arabs with only a basic knowledge of Turkish increasingly found themselves excluded from the salons in which those traditions were performed. Coupled with the increasing mastery of Arabic letters by Rumi elites, the visibility that Arabs in Ghazzi's generation had enjoyed began to fade.

Badr al-Din al-Ghazzi's life and writings act as the central archive from which I reconstruct the world of Ottoman salons. However, he is not always center stage. Much more, the book proceeds by following Ghazzi's network: his family members, his friends, his students, and his acquaintances. Many of the key narrative sources for sixteenth-century Damascus were written by members of his inner circle: the chronicler Ibn Tulun (d. 1546) attended his banquets; the travel writer Muhibb al-Din al-Hamawi took his classes; the biographer Hasan al-Burini (d. 1615) spent four years as his apprentice; and Najm al-Din al-Ghazzi (d. 1651), one of the city's most important historians and author of the oft-cited biographical compilation of sixteenth-century notables, was his son. The price of this kind of proximity is that most of these accounts were far from impartial. Ghazzi's son was borderline hagiographic, but even those authors with less panegyric tendencies tended to exaggerate Ghazzi's influence, whether out of a sense of duty or local pride.[61] I have sought to counteract such tendencies by triangulating Damascene accounts with Turkish-language sources from the imperial center; indeed, one of the book's fundamental premises is that central and provincial sources can be fruitfully combined. Nevertheless, the narrative of this book no doubt reflects a distinctly Arab perspective, and as such occasionally a challenge to the view from Istanbul.

Ghazzi was not representative of all provincial notables, not to speak of his less privileged contemporaries. His influence came from having been born into a distinguished family and to a father who cleverly navigated the political transition to Ottoman rule; while the Ghazzis survived the conquest or even improved their standing as a result of it, other notable families would experience those years as the beginning of a nosedive into irrelevance. In important ways, Ghazzi's experience was also very Damascene. Not only did the city enjoy a less traumatic transition into the new

61. Some of these authors, like Burini and Najm al-Din, wrote decades after Ghazzi's death. As such, discursively they—Najm al-Din in particular—belong to a different era. However, both relied on sources from Ghazzi's lifetime. Najm al-Din consulted the register of students Ghazzi himself kept (now lost), and Burini built on his four-year apprenticeship with Ghazzi. Both also made use of oral traditions.

order than did Cairo, which had to lay down its imperial crown, it was also host to more frequent exchanges between Rumis and Arabs, since the Rumi community was smaller and better integrated into local social life.[62] Finally, Ghazzi did not take part in the full breadth of salon culture that existed in the Ottoman Empire. He appears not to have attended the parties at which men drank wine and admired the beauty of young boys—indeed, he lambasted those who did.[63]

Nevertheless, the salons described here do illuminate important aspects of the relations between Arabs and Rumis. Cultural exchange between the two groups is often assumed to have begun in earnest in the eighteenth century, when Arab elites, no longer attached to Istanbul through a strong centralized state, were drawn in instead by a soft cultural "Ottomanization."[64] Salons show that such exchange began much earlier, gaining steam immediately after the conquest of 1516–7 and intensifying in the decades to follow. However, the Ottomanization of the sixteenth century did not primarily entail provincial elites emulating the culture of the imperial center; this book shows the myriad ways in which central elites learned from their colleagues in the provinces. Indeed, salons allow us to complicate the seemingly straightforward hierarchy placing conqueror over the conquered. To be sure, serving the Ottoman sultan and dispensing favors on his behalf conferred an immediate and formidable sort of power on Rumi officials, one keenly felt in the Ottoman salon. However, learned Arabs wielded forms of cultural capital that afforded them influence in these settings as well. In a society that ascribed great value to eloquence and erudition, political power constituted only one form of authority. The peculiar demands of elite sociability did much to determine the nature of the interaction between these two groups in the decades after the 1516–7 conquest.

Salons also suggest the role that Islam played in configuring the relationship between Rumis and Arabs. Much of the recent research on early modern cross-cultural encounters has focused on exchanges across religious divides, especially across the fraught Christian-Muslim boundary.[65] Interactions within the Muslim community have more rarely been

62. Winter, "Syria," 47–8.

63. Burini, *Tarājim*, 1: 251–2.

64. Khoury, "Ottoman Centre," 155; Fahmy, *All the Pasha's Men*; Khoury, *Provincial Society*.

65. To name only a few: Bevilacqua, *Arabic Letters*; Graf, *The Sultan's Renegades*; Rothman, *Brokering Empire*; Davis, *Trickster Travels*; Dursteler, *Venetians in Constantinople*; Greene, *A Shared World*.

subjected to the same kind of analysis, in part because of an underlying belief that a shared religion made them less complicated. This book suggests that, in part, it did; relations between Rumis and Arabs were greatly simplified by the fact that the two groups privileged the same sacred texts and shared a basic epistemological framework. And yet, in other ways this affinity also made the encounter more complicated. Historically, there had been a great diversity in the ways in which Sunni Muslims practiced their faith and in the peculiar textual emphases they set; the legal schools (*madhhab*s) that set apart the Hanafi Ottomans from the majority Shafiʿi and Maliki Arabs were only the very tip of the iceberg.[66] As legitimate as this diversity was to contemporaries, it did not stop them from making normative judgments about the ways in which Muslims from other regions behaved. In the wake of the 1516–7 conquest, Arab scholars regularly judged Ottomans on their interpretation of Islamic law or adherence to Muhammad's example. Many of the tensions of the postconquest encounter between Arabs and Rumis thus emerged not in spite of, but rather because of, their shared religion.

While this book focuses on salons in Damascus and Istanbul, it also offers insight into the role informal gatherings had in shaping Ottoman society, culture, and governance more broadly. More research must be done on salons in different parts of the empire, not least in the European provinces where the predominance of Christian populations made for very different social dynamics. Nonetheless, it seems that all across Ottoman lands, salons played certain key roles.[67] First, salons were crucial sites for defining and policing the boundaries of the Ottoman elite. The astronomically high standards of gentlemanly conversation were unachievable for men lacking a madrasa education, thus barring the vast majority of the population from participation. In times of economic prosperity—such as the decades immediately after the conquest—elite circles were permeable to well-educated men with less distinguished family pedigrees. Yet, as soon as there was a perceived social imperative to exclude, access to salons was restricted, hindering newcomers from benefiting from the favors distributed within them.

66. Burak, *Islamic Law*; Terzioğlu, "Sunnitization"; Bauer, *Die Kultur der Ambiguität*; Meshal, "Antagonistic Sharīʿas."

67. Ottoman territories formerly under Byzantine control were inheritors to the *theatron*, an institution similar to the Islamic salon. Marciniak, "Byzantine *Theatron*." Samer Ali argues that the origins of Islamic salons lay in, among other things, Greek symposia, gatherings associated with wine-drinking, music, eating, and poetry. Ali, *Salons*, 13–32. For Ottoman-era salons in Southeastern Europe, see İpekten, *Edebî Muhitler*, 221–223.

Second, salons facilitated the circulation of culture across the empire. Informal gatherings of elites offered valuable opportunities for showcasing objects, ideas, and values. One of the key ways in which this occurred was through the presentation of gifts, physical or verbal, an act whose impact was heightened by the audiences that often bore witness to the spectacle. But more subtle forms of influence were at work as well, as salongoers spotted books they had never read or made note of the other guests' sartorial choices. Transfers in these contexts were especially successful because they were mediated through human relationships—the affection of a friend or the authority of an esteemed scholar. Rather than circulating in an impersonal marketplace, objects and ideas traveled saturated with additional, more personal layers of meaning.

Finally, the intense and repeated interactions that took place in Ottoman salons played an important role in imperial governance. Traditionally, modern scholars have looked to the formal bureaucracy to understand the way in which the empire was governed in the sixteenth century, and rightly so, given how well oiled and functional that bureaucracy was. However, as Christine Philliou has suggested, to focus instead on a broader notion of governance is to recognize the range of relationships that helped to uphold a political order; such relationships were limited not only to the state apparatus but also comprised networks, customs, and beliefs.[68] In the sixteenth century as in later centuries, formal mechanisms of rule were inextricably intertwined with, and indeed relied upon, a more informal substrate of Ottoman salons. Recent studies of the seventeenth and eighteenth centuries have suggested just how important informal structures could be in promoting imperial cohesion at a time when central power was more limited.[69] This book shows that even in the sixteenth century, when centralized power was at its height, the Ottoman imperial machinery ran in part on informal relationships and on a sense of common culture. The secret to Ottoman state success lay in part in the development of a sense of community that encouraged cooperation and identification with the imperial project. The sociability that salons enabled was a key ingredient of the glue that held the Ottoman Empire together.

68. Philliou, *Biography of an Empire*, xxiii.

69. Philliou, *Biography of an Empire*; Khoury, "Ottoman Centre"; Hathaway, *Households*.

CHAPTER ONE

A World Divided

WHEN THE ARAB SCHOLAR ʿAbd al-Rahim al-ʿAbbasi first arrived in Istanbul around the turn of the sixteenth century, the city was well on its way to becoming *Islambol*, or "full of Islam," as the Turkish pun went. The rubble from the 1453 Ottoman siege of the Byzantine capital had long been cleared, and out of its ashes had risen madrasas and minarets. Even more than ʿAbbasi's hometown of Cairo, Istanbul was a city of immigrants, with newcomers—forced and voluntary—bringing their languages, breads, and books into rapidly expanding neighborhoods. As stonemasons and blacksmiths shaped the built environment, storytellers and wordsmiths forged its mystique. Sometimes, they compared the city to that great Islamic capital of their time, first timidly, and then with increasing confidence:

> City of Istanbul, where the beauties of the world reside.
> It is the second Cairo according to the wise.
> Its homes are the gardens of paradise, its mosques the pillars,
> to the level of Mani's painting does every last one rise.[1]

The inhabitants of the Ottoman and Mamluk empires were no strangers before the 1516–7 conquest that brought them under a single imperial rule. As peripheral as the Ottoman principality in Anatolia may have been to the wider Islamic world when it was founded around 1299, it was always already connected to it. As recent scholarship has emphasized, Islam served as force of global connection long before European forms of globalization took hold. As a result, whatever local diversity Muslims

1. Sirozlu Saʿdi in Çelebi, *Dîvân Şiirinde Istanbul*, 49. Translation modified from Kim, *Age*, 30. See also Çelebi, *Dîvân Şiirinde Istanbul*, 25, 45–6.

found traveling through Islamic lands, they also met with shared cultural elements that helped to make unfamiliar territories recognizable.[2]

This chapter shows that the gentlemanly salon was one such recognizable element. On the eve of the 1516–7 conquest, when ʿAbbasi left home, the Ottoman and Mamluk empires harbored similar cultures of sociability. In both domains, exclusive assemblies called *meclis* in Turkish, *majlis* in Arabic, allowed elite men to cultivate their literary interests on the one hand and discuss scholarly subjects on the other. Though courtly gatherings were much remarked upon, they were only the most visible of a vast pyramid of male social gatherings that encompassed the entirety of the two polities.

One thing all of these assemblies had in common was their openness to visitors. For a Muslim man of a certain station, no sooner had he alighted in a city or town than he would be summoned to the reception halls of local magnates. This chapter is built around the stories of two such men. The first is ʿAbd al-Rahim al-ʿAbbasi (d. 1555), our traveler and a close friend of the Syrian Ghazzi family whose networks are at the heart of this book. Born in Cairo in 1463, ʿAbbasi visited Istanbul as a refugee from the political tumult of the Mamluk Empire in its last decades before it capitulated to the Ottomans in 1517. The second is Müʾeyyedzade ʿAbdurrahman (d. 1516). Müʾeyyedzade, a Turkish speaker who never met the Ghazzis—though his younger brother later would—was born in Ottoman Amasya in 1456, he, too, the son of a chancery official. When he also was forced into exile in his early twenties, Müʾeyyedzade traveled first to Mamluk Aleppo, and then to Shiraz in Persia. As the two men moved between empires, they brought their ideas and etiquette with them, thus helping conversational cultures across the wider region to converge. As the first half of this chapter suggests, while salons fed on shared understandings, they also helped to generate them, contributing measurably to the informal network of like-minded individuals that has been referred to as an Islamic "Republic of Letters."[3]

And yet, however gleefully ideas may have romped across the Middle Eastern expanse, they did not do so freely. The Mamluk and Ottoman empires were kin, but in a family of unequals, as the second half of this chapter shows. In the late medieval period, the Mamluk Sultanate had established itself as one of the centers of Sunni Islamic culture worldwide,

2. Touati, *Islam and Travel*; Bennison, "Muslim Universalism."

3. Binbaş, *Intellectual Networks*; Peacock and Yıldız, *Islamic Literature*, esp. 20–3; Musawi, *Letters*.

if not perhaps its leading center. Ottoman scholars were quickly establishing a learned tradition of their own, and yet, culturally speaking, they lacked the kind of gravitational pull exerted by their Arab neighbors to the south. As a result, people and ideas did not diffuse evenly across the region: throughout the fourteenth and fifteenth centuries, Ottoman elites showed more interest in Mamluk Arab lands than most Arab elites did in the Ottoman world.

Be that as it may, for the Ottomans, the Arab world was only one place to look for inspiration, and one that often took a back seat to the Turco-Persian lands to the east. Those intellectually vibrant regions had long since served as a touchstone for the Anatolian elite. Indeed, across the fifteenth century, it was Persian gentlemanly culture that provided the most salient model for Ottoman salons. This meant that, although Ottoman and Mamluk gatherings resembled one another in their basic form, in their particular manifestations, significant differences remained. Istanbul as a whole may have been a second Cairo, but its edifices looked to Mani, that legendary Persian painter.[4] On the eve of the 1516–7 conquest what would prove to be the enduring influence of Arab culture in the Ottoman Empire was by no means assured.

A Shared World

ʿAbbasi and Müʾeyyedzade were socialized hundreds of miles apart, but in their experiences and interests they were remarkably close. Their parallel lives are emblematic of the remarkable similarities within the Islamic ecumene around the turn of the sixteenth century. Their interlocking trajectories are reflective of the extensive networks that united it. Although next to nothing is known about the two men's eventual encounter in Istanbul, it left a lasting mark, and formed part of the broader movement of culture and ideas between the two polities in the fourteenth and fifteenth centuries. To see this we must look not only to madrasas and to mosques—those widely praised pillars of Islam—but also to homes, those verdant gardens of paradise.

Underpinning the commonalities in Ottoman and Mamluk salons was a set of common cultural orientations, chief amongst them religious. The Mamluk Empire was a bulwark of late medieval Islam. The Empire, which stretched across Greater Syria, Egypt, Southeastern Anatolia, and

4. Mani b. Fatik (d. 270s), the founder of Manichaeism, was memorialized in the Persian tradition as a great artist. Akın-Kıvanç in Muṣṭafā ʿĀlī, *Epic Deeds*, 8n9.

the Arabian Peninsula (see figure 1.1), had been founded in 1250 by elite military slaves—hence the designation *mamluk*, which means slave in Arabic. These Mamluks were Turkish speaking and imported from Central Asia and the Caucasus, and thus had little in common with the native Arab population over which they ruled. Nor did the Mamluks have any natural claim to authority within the Muslim community, since they were born into Christian and pagan populations before their forced conversion to Islam. However, they did successfully defend key Muslim territories from the Mongols and give shelter to the caliph, the spiritual successor to Muhammad and religious figurehead whose ancestor had fled the Mongol invasion of Baghdad in 1258. What is more, the Mamluks invested heavily in Arabic literature and learning, helping to confirm cities like Cairo and Damascus as some of the most sparkling centers of Islamic culture worldwide.[5] Add to that Mamluk protection of Mecca and Medina, holy sites visited for the annual hajj pilgrimage, and it comes as no surprise that the empire enjoyed great visibility in the post-Mongol Islamic world.[6]

Though the Ottoman state began as a more modest venture on the outskirts of the Islamic world, it shared with the Mamluks a basic religious and political repertoire. Founded by Turcoman Muslims who had settled in northwestern Anatolia in the wake of the Mongol invasions, it thrived on exchanges with its Byzantine neighbors and conquered large parts of Christian-dominated lands of Southeastern Europe. Still, from its earliest days, the Ottoman principality relied on the legal system, literary genres, and institutions that were staples of Islamic societies; the Ottomans set up their first pious foundation (*waqf*) in 1324 and their first madrasa in 1331.[7] Although the early Ottoman court and that of its rival Turkish principalities could hardly compete with Mamluk Cairo in matters of patronage, by the middle of the fifteenth century Ottoman lands were becoming an increasingly attractive destination for scholars and intellectuals from abroad.

Within their ruling cadres, both empires also shared a common Turco-Persian cultural orientation. The period starting in the mid-eleventh century has been seen as inaugurating a "Turkish age" in the Islamic world, since its largest political formations were all ruled by dynasties of Turkic descent.[8] By the second half of the fifteenth century, the leaders of

5. Berkey, "Culture and Society," 376–7.
6. Dekkiche, "New Source."
7. Kafadar, *Two Worlds*, 61; Baltacı, *Osmanlı Medreseleri*, 72.
8. Bosworth, *Turks*, xlv.

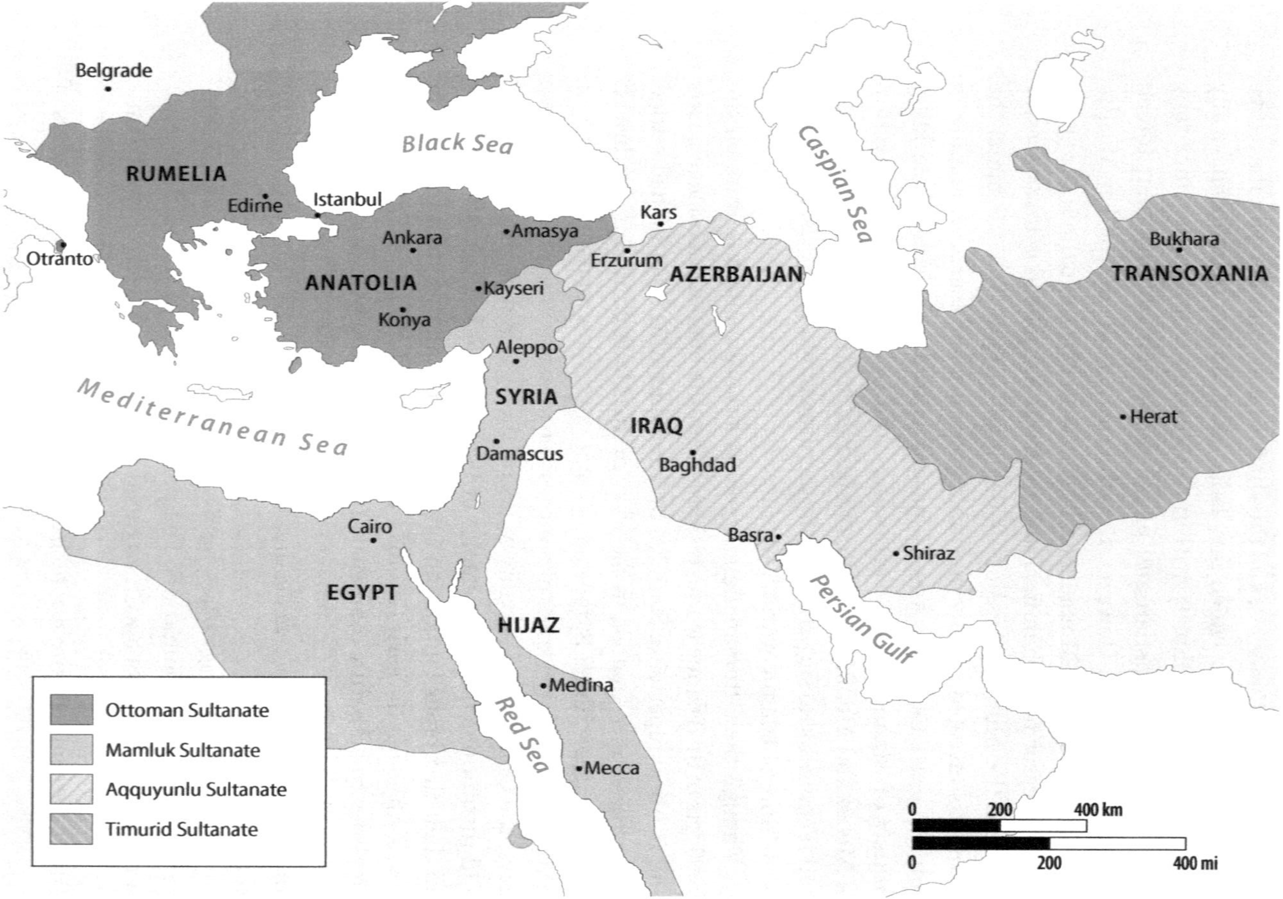

FIGURE 1.1. Ottoman, Mamluk, Aqquyunlu, and Timurid territories in the second half of the fifteenth century.

the most prominent of these polities—the Ottomans, the Mamluks, the Aqquyunlu in western Iran, and the Timurids in eastern Iran and central Asia—shared not only the Turkish language, but kindred legal traditions and cognate political claims.[9] Thus, although most Mamluk residents were ethnically Arab and used Arabic in writing and in speech, the military class that governed the sultanate set itself apart from locals with its interest in Turkish and its embrace of Persian culture. In Ottoman territories, Turkish was even more widespread: unlike in Mamluk lands, where Arab administrators showed little interest in the language, here Turkish was the lingua franca for communication within the multiethnic bureaucratic elite.

It is against this shared religious and cultural backdrop that the serpentine trajectories of ʿAbbasi and Müʾeyyedzade can best be understood. Both partook of a larger culture that placed great emphasis on lineage, and indeed both descended from distinguished families with pious ancestors. ʿAbd al-Rahim ibn ʿAbd al-Rahman al-ʿAbbasi was born in Cairo as the scion of a prominent Syrian family that traced its origin to the Prophet Muhammad's uncle and the progenitor of the Abbasid ruling house, al-ʿAbbas ibn ʿAbd al-Muttalib (d. c. 653).[10] Because of this association, ʿAbbasi was considered a *sayyid*, or descendant of the Prophet Muhammad, an illustrious status that conferred privileges on those who possessed it across all Islamic societies.[11] Müʾeyyedzade ʿAbdurrahman was born into an equally influential family in Amasya, a prosperous provincial capital in today's northern Turkey.[12] He too, had religious roots, if not quite as deep and hallowed as ʿAbbasi's. Müʾeyyedzade came from a line of shaykhs of a leading Sufi lodge in the city, and some historians claimed that he hailed from a famous eleventh-century Sufi proselytizer from Iran.[13]

Both families matched this blessed past with an equally respectable present in government service. Both had benefited from a regional

9. Markiewicz, *Kingship*, chapter 5; Moin, *The Millenial Sovereign*; Burak, *Islamic Law*; Hodgson, *Venture of Islam*, 2: 17.

10. For biographies of ʿAbbasi, see Sakhāwī, *Ḍawʾ*, 4: 178–9; Ṭaşköprīzāde, *Shaqāʾiq*, 411–2; Ghazzī, *Kawākib*, 2:161–5. For modern works, see Heinrichs, "al-ʿAbbāsī"; Öznurhan, "Abbâsî."

11. Heinrichs, "al-ʿAbbāsī," 13.

12. For biographies of Müʾeyyedzade, see Sehī Bey, *Heşt Bihişt*, 125–7; ʿĀşıḳ Çelebi, *Meşâʿirü's-Şuʿarâ*, 1495–503; Kınalı-zade, *Tezkiretü'ş-Şuʿarâ*, 1: 318–25; Kurnaz, "Aile"; Aksoy, "Müeyyedzâde Abdurrahman Efendi," 485–6; Menzel, "Muʾayyad-Zāde," 272.

13. This was Abu Ishaq Kazeruni (d. 1035). ʿĀşıḳ Çelebi, *Meşâʿirü's-Şuʿarâ*, 1495; Kınalı-zade, *Tezkiretü'ş-Şuʿarâ*, 1: 318; Aksoy, "Müeyyedzâde Abdurrahman Efendi," 485.

political shift that gave new importance to the chancery.[14] ʿAbbasi's father served as chief chancery secretary (*katib al-sirr*) in Damascus, an influential and sensitive position since it required him to handle state papers and correspondence with the Mamluk sultan in the empire's second city.[15] Likewise, Müʾeyyedzade's father acted as chancery secretary (*nişancı*) to the Ottoman Prince Bayezid in Amasya, which was an important cultural center and a favorite residence of sultans-in-waiting.[16]

As youths, ʿAbbasi and Müʾeyyedzade enjoyed a similar intellectual formation. Both would have begun their formal studies with a focus on the Arabic linguistic disciplines, especially grammar, syntax, and rhetoric.[17] They probably would have even used many of the same textbooks, since by 1300, these disciplines were taught through a common literary canon shared from Bukhara to Cairo (ʿAbbasi memorized some of these textbooks in full).[18] This linguistic training, together with instruction in logic, was a prerequisite for the more advanced study of Islam's foundational texts, the Qurʾan and the hadiths (Ar. *hadith*, Tur. *hadis*), as the accounts of the words and deeds of the Prophet Muhammad were called. From this fertile soil grew the formidable scholarly tradition on which Muslim students focused at more advanced stages, especially the fields of jurisprudence and Qurʾanic exegesis. However, neither ʿAbbasi nor Müʾeyyedzade limited himself to the disciplines he studied formally. With great élan, both pursued literary arts like poetry and rhymed prose, which were generally honed outside of the madrasa context.[19]

14. Markiewicz, *Kingship*, esp. 50, 177.

15. ʿAbbasi's father Muwaffaq al-Din al-ʿAbbasi was appointed army inspector (*nazir al-jaysh*) in 1473–5 and *katib al-sirr* in 1485. Sakhāwī, *Ḍawʾ*, 4: 49, 7: 283; Heinrichs, "al-ʿAbbāsī," 13. For the *katib al-sirr* in Cairo, see Muslu, *Ottomans*, 33–4.

16. For Amasya's intellectual environment, see Karataş, "City"; İpekten, *Edebî Muhitler*, 170–81; Kappert, *Osmanischen Prinzen*, 19–67.

17. For ʿAbbasi's education, see Sakhāwī, *Ḍawʾ*, 4: 179; Ghazzī, *Kawākib*, 2: 161–2; ʿĀşıḳ Çelebi, *Dhayl*, 107–9; Heinrichs, "al-ʿAbbāsī," 14. Little is known about Müʾeyyedzade's education in Ottoman lands, and much of what we know about contemporary curricula comes from sixteenth-century sources. The rest of the paragraph is based on: Ṭaşköprīzāde, *Shaqāʾiq*, 290–4; Uzunçarşılı, *İlmiye Teşkilatı*, 19–31, 39–43; İhsanoğlu, "Institutions," 377.

18. This core formed around *The Key to the Disciplines* (*Miftah al-ʿulum*) written by the Khwarazm-born scholar Yusuf Sakkaki (d. 1229). Bauer, "Adab"; Smyth, "Controversy," 590. This cluster of works was so important that it gave its name to a whole category of Ottoman madrasas (*miftah medreses*). İhsanoğlu, "Institutions," 2: 377; Uzunçarşılı, *İlmiye Teşkilatı*, 19, 21, 39. ʿAbbasi memorized *The Epitome of The Key* (*Talkhis al-miftah*), Muhammad al-Qazwini's (d. 1338) summary of Sakkaki's work. ʿAbbasi, *Maʿahid al-tansis*, 1b; Heinrichs, "al-ʿAbbāsī," 14.

19. For the importance of *adab* for Mamluk scholars, see Bauer, "Literarische Anthologien der Mamlūkenzeit," 78–85; Bauer, "Adab."

The existence across the region of such similar interests, curricular and extracurricular, allowed those who pursued them to move easily across political divides. Madrasa students had long been one of the most restless of social groups in Islamic societies, consistently venturing to the distant corners of the earth in search of knowledge. Well into the fifteenth century Anatolian students were especially mobile. Despite the fact that the Seljuks, the dominant political force in Anatolia from the late eleventh to the late thirteenth century, had founded dozens of madrasas in cities like Konya and Kayseri, many local scholars also spent some time abroad in more established centers of learning.[20] Mamluk lands were an especially beloved destination. Some Anatolians who studied in the great Arab capitals eventually settled there permanently, as did two of ʿAbbasi's most important teachers: Muhyi al-Din al-Kafiyaji (d. 1474) and Amin al-Din al-Aqsaraʾi (d. 1475). Both became leading Hanafi muftis in Mamluk Cairo and enjoyed great respect amongst sultans and scholars alike.[21] Others of Anatolian origin returned home after a few years, gaining employment in the rapidly expanding Ottoman bureaucratic and educational system. One of the most famous of these was Şemseddin Fenari (d. 1431), who studied in Cairo in the 1370s and went on to found an Ottoman scholarly dynasty.[22] But there were many others: of those Ottoman scholars known to have pursued their studies outside Ottoman territory in the fourteenth and fifteenth centuries, about a third went to Syria and Egypt.[23]

In the late 1470s, Müʾeyyedzade followed suit in leaving the Ottoman realms for his education, if unwittingly. Probably thanks to his father's connections, the young Müʾeyyedzade had become close friends with

20. The Seljuks built fifty-six madrasas in Anatolia in the thirteenth century alone. Atçıl, "Mobility," 318. For travel for study, see Peacock and Yıldız, *Islamic Literature*; Ökten, "Scholars and Mobility"; İhsanoğlu, "Institutions," 371–2; Lekesiz, "Değişme," 26–31.

21. Kafiyaji was born in a small town near Bergama on the Aegean coast in the late 1380s. He settled in Cairo in the late 1420s, after a long ambulatory period studying with scholars in Anatolia, Persia, and Syria. For biographies of Kafiyaji, see Sakhāwī, *Ḍawʾ*, 7: 259–61; Ṭaşköprīzāde, *Shaqāʾiq*, 64–6; Gökbulut, "Al-Kafiyeci"; Rosenthal, "al-Kāfiyad̲jī." Aqsaraʾi instead went to Cairo when he was very young and completed most of his education in Mamluk lands. Sakhāwī, *Ḍawʾ*, 10: 240–3; Burak, *Islamic Law*, 32n27, 33. Carl Petry has estimated that in the fifteenth century, no more than three percent of the civilian elite of Cairo not native to the city came from the lands of Rum. Petry, *Civilian Elite*, 68.

22. Repp, *The Müfti of Istanbul*, 73–98; Ṭaşköprīzāde, *Shaqāʾiq*, 22–3.

23. To be precise: 32% in Egypt and Syria, 49% in Transoxania and Iran, and 19% in Anatolia. This is from a group of sixty-three scholars mentioned in Taşköprīzade's biographical dictionary of Ottoman scholars as having studied outside Ottoman domains (of about 250 in this period total). Lekesiz, "Değişme," 166; İhsanoğlu, "Institutions," 372. Ertuğrul Ökten, also using Taşköprīzade, arrives at a similar conclusion. Ökten, "Scholars and Mobility," 62. For a close study of one such Rumi learned traveler, see Yıldız, "From Cairo to Ayasuluk."

the Ottoman Prince Bayezid—too close, it seems, since he was accused of belonging to a cabal tempting the young dynast into a life of opiates and lechery (though many later biographers claimed this was a lie disseminated by jealous rivals). When Bayezid's father, the ruling Sultan Mehmed II (r. 1444–6, 1451–81), got wind of this state of affairs, he ordered those who were misleading his son to be executed. Tipped off about the decree ahead of time, Müʾeyyedzade shaved his beard, disguised himself as a dervish, and fled to Aleppo, then under Mamluk control.[24] Once in Aleppo, Müʾeyyedzade, who was in his early twenties, made the most of a bad situation and began studying a popular book of Arabic grammar.[25] He also made friends with a wealthy gentleman, who, recognizing the young man's talent, sponsored his journey to Shiraz in today's Iran, where Müʾeyyedzade settled down to study for several years.[26]

Müʾeyyedzade's experience abroad served him well after he returned to Anatolia; he eventually advanced to the highest echelons of the Ottoman bureaucracy. His exile came to an end in 1483, after Mehmed II died and Bayezid ascended the throne.[27] First appointed professor in Istanbul, then chief judge in Edirne, in 1501 Müʾeyyedzade was named military judge (*kadıasker*) of Anatolia, an influential post that gave him a seat on the imperial council and a say in judicial and teaching appointments.[28] Though Müʾeyyedzade's friendship with the ruling sultan surely contributed to this series of promotions, his experience abroad no doubt helped as well.[29]

In the meantime, in Mamluk lands, ʿAbbasi was making a similar shift from the academic sphere into government service. Sometime during his early to mid-twenties around the time that Müʾeyyedzade returned from Persia—ʿAbbasi moved from his natal Cairo to Damascus. He continued studying there, eventually coming into the orb of one Muhammad Radi al-Din al-Ghazzi (d. 1529). Radi al-Din, who would later father our Badr

24. Sehī Bey, *Heşt Bihişt*, 126; Ṭaşköprīzāde, *Shaqāʾiq*, 291; ʿĀşıḳ Çelebi, *Meşâʿirü's-Şuʿarâ*, 1495–6; İpekten, *Edebî Muhitler*, 172–3. Taşköprīzade says 1476, but other sources suggest it was later, perhaps 1479. Pfeiffer, "Teaching the Learned," 286n5.

25. Namely Abu'l Qasim al-Zamakhshari's (d. 1144) *Kitab al-mufassal fi'l-nahw*. Ṭaşköprīzāde, *Shaqāʾiq*, 292; Tamīmī, *Ṭabaqāt*, 4: 292.

26. Kınalı-zade, *Tezkiretü'ş-Şuʿarâ*, 320.

27. Kınalı-zade, *Tezkiretü'ş-Şuʿarâ*, 320; Aksoy, "Müeyyedzâde Abdurrahman Efendi," 485.

28. His professorship was at the Kalenderhane Madrasa. Aksoy, "Müeyyedzâde Abdurrahman Efendi," 485.

29. According to Taşköprīzade, Müʾeyyedzade had to actively earn his standing upon his return by demonstrating his learning to leading scholars. Ṭaşköprīzāde, *Shaqāʾiq*, 292.

al-Din, was an influential member of the Damascene community and a prominent Sufi leader. In the late 1470s, just a few years before ʿAbbasi's arrival in the city, Radi al-Din had been appointed deputy judge (*naʾib*) of the influential Shafiʿi school of law.[30] Although Radi al-Din was only five years older than ʿAbbasi, he seems to have become something of a mentor to the younger man; Radi al-Din taught ʿAbbasi and guided him in spiritual matters.[31] During one period of seclusion spent in the same house, as ʿAbbasi later recalled, the disciple would wake up in the middle of the night to the voice of Radi al-Din commanding him to rise and pray, despite the fact that three locked doors separated the two and there was no way he could have heard him.[32] In 1480, ʿAbbasi began his own teaching career, taking up a lectureship at the Nasiriyya Madrasa in Damascus; appointments at other key institutions of higher education in the city followed.[33] In 1488, at the age of twenty-five, ʿAbbasi followed in his father's footsteps in accepting an appointment as the city's confidential secretary.[34] Though ʿAbbasi never ceased to be a serious scholar, this move launched him into the messy politics of the late Mamluk period.

In their youth as in their maturity, a fair portion of ʿAbbasi's and Müʾeyyedzade's lives unfolded in informal social gatherings. Both Mamluk and Ottoman lands boasted a vibrant salon culture. In Cairo, the Mamluk Sultan Qansawh al-Ghawri (r. 1501–16) held regular soirées in which courtiers and learned guests recited poetry, told jokes, debated religious issues, and discussed politics.[35] Beyond the royal citadel, in Cairo and Damascus alike, a variety of other urban elites—both of Mamluk slave descent and of Arab origin—held similar sorts of gatherings for edification or amusement.[36] Some of these occasions were very serious, featuring

30. Ghazzī, *Kawākib*, 2: 4–5. For biographies of Radi al-Din, see Ḥaṣkafī and Ibn Ṭūlūn, *Mutʿat al-adhhān*, 2: 771; Ibn Ayyūb, *Rawḍ*, 229a; Ghazzī, *Kawākib*, 2: 2–6.

31. Najm al-Din al-Ghazzi uses the verb *lāzama*, which refers to the close mentoring relationship developed between teachers and their advanced students. Ghazzī, *Kawākib*, 2: 162. Radi al-Din taught many students in the field of Sufism. Ghazzī, *Kawākib*, 2: 194–5.

32. Ghazzī, *Kawākib*, 2: 162; Ghazzī, *Maṭāliʿ*, 142.

33. He also taught at the Zahiriyya madrasa, among others, and stayed in Damascus until 1492. Sakhāwī, *Ḍawʾ*, 4: 179; Ibn Ṭūlūn, *Mufākaha*, 1: 16.

34. Sakhāwī, *Ḍawʾ*, 4: 49, 179; Ibn al-Ḥimṣī, *Ḥawādith*, 213.

35. These discussions were recorded by Ghawri's courtiers. Two of these have been published in ʿAzzām, *Majālis*. Mauder, "Being Persian"; Mauder and Markiewicz, "New Source"; Irwin, "Political Thinking"; Flemming, "Šerif"; Flemming, "Nachtgesprächen." For a gathering in the garden of the earlier Sultan al-Muʾayyad (r. 1412–21), see Blecher, "Commentary," 274–82; Blecher, *Prophet*, chapter 5.

36. For the soirées of the prince Nasir al-Din Muhammad ibn Jaqmaq (d. 1444), see Flemming, "Literary Activities," 250; Irwin, "Mamluk Literature," 27–8. Earlier, the

academic debates in which men found their intellectual authority and sometimes their employment to be at stake.[37] Others clearly built on more profane pleasures, including wine drinking, musical performances, and the aesthetic appreciation of prepubescent boys (earning the disapproval of pious-minded contemporaries).[38] As a leading scholar who worked in the service of the Turcophone ruling elite, ʿAbbasi would have taken part in the whole range of gatherings. His formal education and intellectual prowess allowed him to contribute easily to learned discourse. At the same time, he was also adept at the sort of literary flourishes that characterized much salon banter. One of his earliest and to this day most famous works—a commentary on a style manual he had memorized as a child—also functioned as a repository for the kinds of anecdotes, poems, and literary critiques that came in handy in a literary soirée.[39] These were just the sorts of topics ʿAbbasi would have discussed with his friend and mentor Radi al-Din al-Ghazzi, alongside the spiritual matters that also concerned them.[40]

Müʾeyyedzade partook of a similar sociable culture in Anatolia. In Ottoman lands, too, the royal court took a leading role in nurturing literary and learned debate. The feast and the fight—*bezm ü rezm*—were the well-known pillars of successful political rule, and Ottoman sultans cultivated the first as enthusiastically as they did the second.[41] Bayezid's grandfather Murad II (r. 1421–51) was known to have composed

---

amir Yusuf ibn Yaghmur (d. 1265) cultivated a literary salon dominated by North African immigrants, while the military commander and man of letters Sanjar al-Dawadari (d. 1299/1300) had a well-known *majlis* visited by dignitaries, scholars, and poets. See, respectively, Irwin, "Mamluk Literature," 10; Haarmann, "Arabic," 97–8. For the gatherings of the local Arab population, see Musawi, *Letters*. For Mamluk-era writings celebrating salon culture, see Ali, *Salons*, 16–7; Irwin, "Mamluk Literature," 9, 13–4, 17, 19; van Gelder, "Muslim Encomium."

37. Blecher, "Shade," 67–98; Blecher, "Commentary," 274–82.

38. Bauer, "al-Nawājī," 326–9; van Gelder, "Muslim Encomium." For popular pleasure spots in Damascus, see Hafteh, "Garden Culture."

39. This was his *Frequented Places for Clarification: Commentary on the Poetic Proof-texts of The Epitome* (*Maʿahid al-tansis fi sharh shawahid al-talkhis*), a commentary on Qazwini's *Talkhis al-miftah*. This would become his most famous work in the central Ottoman lands, with eighteen copies preserved today in the Süleymaniye Library; I have used MS Yeni Cami 1035. For an indicative translation, see Heinrichs, "al-ʿAbbāsī," 15–8. Bauer calls this sort of writing a "commentarial anthology" (*Kommentaranthologie*) and emphasizes its role in providing fodder for polite conversation. Bauer, "Literarische Anthologien der Mamlūkenzeit," 72, 74, 77.

40. Traces of these conversations can be gleaned from Radi al-Din's poems as ʿAbbasi later cited them to Radi al-Din's son Badr al-Din. Ghazzī, *Maṭāliʿ*, 187–92.

41. İnalcık, "Klasik edebiyat menşei," 268–9.

impromptu poetry in the company of his courtiers; Bayezid's father Mehmed II was an enthusiastic host of learned disputations, allowing some to carry on for several days.[42] Bayezid himself, like most other princes before and after him, became inured to cultured conversation during his time as provincial governor.[43] It was in this context that he befriended Müʾeyyedzade, who according to later historians became his *musahib*, or trusted companion and giver of advice.[44] The day jobs of the other members of this circle were diverse—the group featured two treasurers, a chancery secretary, a calligrapher, and, unusually, a woman—but they all spent their evenings pursuing more rarefied pleasures, including poetry and wine.[45] As a later biographer explained, "like the Pleiades they came together every night" for friendly conversation, and "like a halo around a moon, they took the wine cup in their midst, never letting the crimson glass drop from their hands as if it were a red coral rosary."[46] Müʾeyyedzade's own poetry gestures at a similar set of activities. One of his verses ran:

> Let us drink, let us drink, let us drink wine.
> How much longer must we drink water like a cow?
> In the afterlife there might be a reckoning about wine,
> But let's drink it without reckoning for now.[47]

Although Ottoman poets, like Muslim poets the world over, routinely invoked wine as a metaphor for the intoxicating effects of God's love, there is no doubt that many viewed salons as a chance to enjoy the beverage's physical manifestations as well.[48] Indeed, as we have seen, according to

42. For the first, see Sehī Bey, *Heşt Bihişt*, 94–5; for the second, Ṭaşköprīzāde, *Shaqāʾiq* 124–5.

43. Many members of Bayezid's Amasya circle followed him to Istanbul, where they continued to enjoy his patronage. Havlioğlu, *Mihrî Hatun*, chapter 3. See also Kafadar, "Between Amasya and Istanbul."

44. ʿĀşıḳ Çelebi, *Meşâʿirü's-Şuʿarâ*, 1495. For the *musahib* in Persian and Ottoman traditions, see Dikici, "Perfect Companions"; İnalcık, "Klasik edebiyat menşei."

45. Sehī Bey, *Heşt Bihişt*, 126. The circle included Beyazid's chancery secretary Kutbi Pasha Çelebi (d. 1520/1), his finance ministers Taci Bey (d. 1485) and Cezeri Kasım Pasha (d. before 1532/3), and the calligrapher Shaykh Hamdullah (d. 1520). The woman was Mihri Hatun; though female participation in Ottoman salons was rare in the fifteenth and sixteenth centuries, Amasya was, relatively speaking, a hotbed of female literary activity. İpekten, *Edebî Muhitler*, 172–3; Havlioğlu, *Mihrî Hatun*, esp. chapter 3.

46. Kınalı-zade, *Tezkiretü'ş-Şuʿarâ*, 1: 318.

47. Sehī Bey, *Teẕkire-i Sehī*, 28.

48. Matthee, "Alcohol"; İnalcık, *Tarab*, 222; Andrews, "Gardens," 106; Tolasa, *Araştırma*, 133–6. In one salon, the vizier Mahmud Pasha (d. 1474) shared the story of how

Müʾeyyedzade's detractors, alcohol was only one of a vast set of sordid and degenerate pleasures in which some of the prince's companions indulged.

As in Mamluk lands though, this pleasure-seeking drive did not come at the expense of serious intellectual content. Over the course of a single evening, a participant could be expected to speak cogently not just about poetry, but also about philosophy, law, and history, as the chief judge of Istanbul and Müʾeyyedzade's father-in-law Molla Kestelli (d. 1496) was known to do effortlessly when he entertained guests—a feat all the more impressive considering the amount of hashish he would all the while consume.[49] But even for those who preferred more sober events there was excitement to be had. Ottoman salons were favored arenas for that most beloved of fifteenth-century spectator sports: learned debate. The sixteenth-century historian Ahmed Taşköprizade (d. 1561), who compiled the biographies of Ottoman scholars from the reign of Osman to his own day in his book *The Crimson Peonies Concerning the Scholars of the Ottoman State* (*al-Shaqaʾiq al-nuʿmaniyya fi ʿulamaʾ al-dawla al-ʿuthmaniyya*), affords us a sense of the lasting importance of these debates; he narrated many of them in great detail despite the fact that they had taken place many years before his birth.[50]

As intimate as many gentlemanly circles may have been, they were not just opportunities to meet with close friends; they also served to build relations with wanderers and newcomers.[51] This was especially true in courtly circles, where rulers competed with one another to attract international celebrities.[52] Sultan Ghawri's court in Cairo brought together scholars of Arab, Turkish, and Persian origin.[53] In Ottoman lands, sultans valued foreign-born expertise as well, and Mehmed II in particular

---

he had been a heavy drinker in his youth, until a good friend persuaded him to drop the habit. Ṭaşköprīzāde, *Shaqāʾiq*, 156–7, see also 217–8.

49. Also called Molla Qastalani. Ṭaşköprīzāde, *Shaqāʾiq*, 144–5; Aksoy, "Müeyyedzâde Abdurrahman Efendi," 485. His drug habit was also mentioned in Ghazzī, *Kawākib*, 1: 307.

50. Ṭaşköprīzāde, *Shaqāʾiq*, 79–80, 117, 124–5, 126–37, 141; Brown, "Formalism," 400–1. For contextualizations of Taşköprizade's book, see Burak, *Islamic Law*, 94–8; Anooshahr, "Writing."

51. For earlier examples of this, see Yıldız, "*Nadīm*"; Kedar, "Multilateral Disputation," 162–83; Stroumsa, "*Sūʾ*," 70.

52. Ibn Battuta was invited to the regional courts of almost every Turkish principality in fourteenth-century Anatolia. Yıldız, "Court Literature," 200–1.

53. Flemming, "Šerīf," 81–93; Irwin, "Political Thinking." For Persians, see Mauder, "Being Persian." The Anatolian-born scholar ʿAlaʾeddin al-Rumi witnessed scholarly debates in Timur's court in Samarkand and attended courtly hadith sessions in the citadel of Cairo. Suyūṭī, *Bughya*, 208–9; Mecdī, *Tercüme-i Şaḳāʾiḳ*, 69; Ṭaşköprīzāde, *Shaqāʾiq*, 47. For other examples, see Markiewicz, *Kingship*, 107–8; Musawi, *Letters*, chapter 1.

was remembered as a sultan who attracted bright men from abroad.[54] Even when visitors passed through the capital only briefly, Mehmed would invite them to debate his own courtiers, as did one North African scholar particularly versed in the occult sciences (*al-ʿulum al-ghariba*). When Mehmed found that the members of his inner circle were totally ignorant of the matters on which the Maghrebi scholar discoursed, he demanded a native scholar be brought who was more learned. Thereupon the Ottoman scholar Hızır Bey (d. 1459) came to court, and was able to answer questions on sixteen different sciences, leaving the North African dumbfounded.[55]

Outside of royal courts, the salons of the elite were permeable to newcomers as well. When the aforementioned Ottoman scholar Şemseddin Fenari, who had returned home after studying in Cairo in the 1370s, visited his Egyptian alma mater in 1419, "the outstanding men of the age met with him, discussing and debating with him and acknowledging his excellence."[56] In the 1430s, when a bright young east Anatolian scholar called Ahmed Gürani (d. 1488) burst onto the Cairene intellectual scene, he quickly rose into the ranks of the distinguished people and "attended the important gatherings [*al-majālis al-kibār*]."[57] He traveled in similarly high-powered circles after controversy forced him to relocate to Ottoman lands; when, in the last months of his life, the aging statesman retreated to a garden outside of Istanbul, the viziers visited him there once a week.[58] Ambassadors and their retinues, too, spent a fair amount of their missions in the homes of imperial officials, where weeks or even months of preparatory meetings paved the way for their eventual reception in the court.[59]

As part of this larger pattern, then, ʿAbbasi entered the social circles of Istanbul during his own period of exile. His story was not unlike Müʾeyyedzade's. The last decades of the Mamluk Sultanate were tumultuous and characterized by entrenched—often violent—factional wars, from which it was difficult for high-ranking government officials like ʿAbbasi to

54. Sehī Bey, *Heşt Bihişt*, 97; Laṭīfī, *Tezkire-i Laṭīfī*, 62.

55. Ṭaşköprīzāde, *Shaqāʾiq*, 91–2.

56. Ibn Ḥajar, *Inbāʾ al-ghumr*, 3: 465; Ṭaşköprīzāde, *Shaqāʾiq*, 23. The Mamluk Sultan invited Fenari to a gathering in his court, hoping to learn about the situation in Ottoman lands. Ibn Ḥajar, *Inbāʾ al-ghumr*, 3: 216. See also Repp, *The Müfti of Istanbul*, 86–91.

57. Sakhāwī, *Ḍawʾ* 1: 241. He became one of the boon companions (*nadim*) of the Mamluk Sultan Çakmak (r. 1438–53), and had a close relationship with the chancery secretary Kamal al-Din al-Barizi. For the former, see al-Biqāʿī, *ʿUnwān*, 6b. For the latter, Ibn Taghrībirdī, *Nujūm*, 3: 344; Maqrīzī, *Durar*, 1: 259.

58. Ṭaşköprīzāde, *Shaqāʾiq*, 89.

59. Muslu, *Ottomans*, 47, 52. For examples of an ambassadorial visit that lasted five months, see Muhanna, "The Sultan's New Clothes," 191.

stay aloof. When, in the winter of 1497, a challenger to the Mamluk throne invaded Damascus, he recruited ʿAbbasi to his cause in hopes of using the sayyid's lineage to bolster his own claims to rule.[60] Probably as a result of this alliance, ʿAbbasi was forced to leave the city when the coup failed, though he himself was vague on this point: "the people I knew turned their backs on me, their affection vanished for me, and my city shunned me. So I departed from it fearful and vigilant [Q 28:21], drowning in waves of discontent."[61] ʿAbbasi had faced trouble once before for a debt he owed, leading him to go into internal exile in Mecca.[62] This time, he went even farther afield. "Bewildered, in my extreme distress, I knew not whether to turn east or west." Finally, God sent him a vision of the Ottoman Sultan Bayezid II (r. 1481–1512), and ʿAbbasi knew where he had to go.[63]

Having arrived safely in Ottoman lands, ʿAbbasi seems to have been drawn into the orb of Müʾeyyedzade, whose residence had developed into a popular gathering place for poets and scholars.[64] Since Müʾeyyedzade was known to be especially welcoming to those from abroad, it comes as little surprise that he hosted ʿAbbasi, who according to the historian Taşköprizade "visited him and honored him greatly."[65] Though nothing more is known about their encounter, given their similar educational backgrounds and overlapping literary interests, there is every reason to believe they would have had plenty to talk about. Since Müʾeyyedzade had spent time studying in Aleppo, he was probably more comfortable than many of his Ottoman colleagues conversing in Arabic. Also unlike many of his Ottoman contemporaries, Müʾeyyedzade was known to compose poetry in that language, and could thus not only appreciate the lines of verse ʿAbbasi often cited in conversation, but perhaps even match them.[66] Müʾeyyedzade and ʿAbbasi might have even had common acquaintances dating back to Müʾeyyedzade's Aleppine adventure.

60. Ibn al-Ḥimṣī, *Ḥawādith*, 310–7. For this rebellion, see Miura, "Salihiyya Quarter," 164; Miura, *Dynamism*, 153; Lapidus, *Muslim Cities*, 88.

61. ʿAbbāsī, *Fayḍ*, 2a.

62. Sakhāwī, *Ḍawʾ*, 4: 179; Heinrichs, "al-ʿAbbāsī," 14–5.

63. ʿAbbāsī, *Fayḍ*, 2a.

64. Ṭaşköprīzāde, *Shaqāʾiq*, 411. Around that time, Müʾeyyedzade was moving from Edirne, where he had been serving as chief judge, to Istanbul, where he became military judge of Anatolia in September 1501. Aksoy, "Müeyyedzâde Abdurrahman Efendi," 485. ʿĀşıḳ Çelebi, *Meşâʿirü's-Şuʿarâ*, 1498. Though Müʾeyyedzade's role as a patron of the arts intensified after he became chief military judge, it had already begun beforehand. Markiewicz, *Kingship*, 83; İpekten, *Edebî Muhitler*, 138–40. See also the case of Basiri in this chapter, who arrived in 1495–6 and sought Müʾeyyedzade's help.

65. Ṭaşköprīzāde, *Shaqāʾiq*, 411.

66. ʿĀşıḳ Çelebi, *Meşâʿirü's-Şuʿarâ*, 1496; Kurnaz, "Aile," 655.

However, the culmination of ʿAbbasi's trip to Anatolia was no doubt his audience with the ruling sultan himself. According to Taşköprizade, ʿAbbasi entered Bayezid's court in the context of a Mamluk embassy, but this is belied by ʿAbbasi's own account, which, as mentioned previously, states in no uncertain terms that he came to Ottoman lands as a refugee.[67] It is possible that Müʾeyyedzade made the introductions, given his continued friendship with Bayezid and his known role in mediating talent from abroad.[68] In any case, ʿAbbasi decided to present the sultan with a work that he had just finished, a commentary on the canonical hadith collection *The Authentic Collection* (*al-Jamiʿ al-sahih*), which had been compiled in the ninth century by the revered traditionist Muhammad al-Bukhari (d. 870).[69] The ink had barely dried on ʿAbbasi's commentary when he submitted it to the sultan. Despite having worked on it for many years in Damascus, he had only managed to complete the first half while in that city; ʿAbbasi finished, signed, and dated the piece in Istanbul on March 15, 1501, dedicating it to Bayezid.[70] The sultan must have been impressed with the book, which had few contemporary equivalents in Ottoman lands, for he not only presented ʿAbbasi with a monetary reward, but offered him an appointment to teach hadith at the madrasa the sultan was building in Istanbul.[71]

In presenting his work to the sultan, ʿAbbasi was representative of a larger group of Mamluk-educated travelers who helped to channel Arabic scholarly and literary currents into Ottoman salons. Predating him in this

67. Ṭaşköprīzāde, *Shaqāʾiq*, 411.

68. Markiewicz, *Kingship*, 118–9.

69. The work was entitled *The Bounty of the Creator: A Commentary on Obscurities in the Sahih of Bukhari* (*Fayd al-bari bi-sharh gharib Sahih al-Bukhari*). ʿAbbāsī, *Fayḍ*. There are multiple copies of this work in the Süleymaniye Library, including MS Atıf Efendi 529; MS Hamidiye 298; MS Hamidiye 299; MS Ragıp Pasha 299. Kātib Çelebi, *Ẓunūn*, 551; Heinrichs, "al-ʿAbbāsī," 18. Apparently, ʿAbbasi wrote a second commentary on this work in Anatolia, but it was never finished and is now lost. ʿAbbāsī, *Fayḍ* MS Atıf Efendi 529, 1a; Ghazzī, *Kawākib*, 2:164; Heinrichs, "al-ʿAbbāsī," 18.

70. Although Najm al-Din al-Ghazzi claims to have read that the book was completed in Cairo, ʿAbbasi states in his colophon that he finished it in Istanbul. ʿAbbāsī, *Fayḍ*, MS Hamidiye 299, 488a; c.f., Ghazzī, *Kawākib*, 2:164; Heinrichs, "al-ʿAbbāsī," 18. The work appears in the Ottoman palace catalogue of 1502–3 as *The Penetrating Light: Commentary on the Sahih of Bukhari* (*al-Dawʾ al-sari sharh Sahih al-Bukhari*). It is still preserved in the Topkapı Palace Library with the stamp of Bayezid II. Göktaş, "Hadith Collection," 320, 324. Radi al-Din al-Ghazzi wrote an endorsement (*taqriz*) of ʿAbbasi's book, as Katib Çelebi mentions in his entry on it. ʿAbbāsī, *Fayḍ*, MS Atıf Efendi 529, 315b; ʿAbbāsī, *Fayḍ*, MS Hamidiye 299, 488b; ʿAbbāsī, *Fayḍ*, MS Ragip Pasha 299, 475b; Kātib Çelebi, *Ẓunūn*, 1:551.

71. Ṭaşköprīzāde, *Shaqāʾiq*, 411. Bayezid's mosque and madrasa complex was built between 1500–5. Goodwin, *Ottoman Architecture*, 168–75.

role was the Mamluk-trained scholar ʿAbd al-Rahman al-Bistami (d. 1454), who drifted from city to Anatolian city in the first decades of the fifteenth century, giving lessons and composing Arabic-language odes for the scholars and officials he met along the way.[72] Molla Gürani was another such influential migrant, contributing his expertise in Arabic verse and Mamluk politics to conversations in the Ottoman court.[73] Such travelers left their mark not only on the study of prophetic traditions, ʿAbbasi's discipline of choice, but also on jurisprudence and medicine as those fields took shape in Ottoman lands.[74] Those with experience in Mamluk lands also helped to feed a growing interest among Ottoman elite circles in Arabic-language poetry, as exhibited not just by Müʾeyyedzade's intellectual commitments, but also those of his father-in-law (and lover of cannabis) Molla Kestelli, who was known to ponder Arabic odes at his soirées.[75] An incident involving Mehmed II is indicative of this intensifying concern for Arabic poetry. When the sultan asked his chief military judge about a particular Arabic verse one day, catching the judge at a loss, the sultan immediately had him removed from his position and sent to teach at a madrasa, saying the judge still had much to learn.[76] Thanks to this sort of atmosphere, by the first years of the sixteenth century, the Topkapı Palace library boasted over one hundred and fifty volumes of Arabic-language poetry.[77]

The similarities in sociability across the early modern Middle East made Muslim gentlemen highly mobile. Well-trained scholars like Müʾeyyedzade and ʿAbbasi easily found a foothold in the places they went,

72. Ṭaşköprīzāde, *Shaqāʾiq*, 46–7; Atçıl, "Formation," 65; Fleischer, "Ancient Wisdom"; Fazlıoğlu, "Osmanlı İlim," 234–5, 237–9.

73. Gürani presented Mehmed II with a six-hundred-line poem on the science of prosody (*ʿilm al-ʿarud*) and was present at court when Bayezid II received a Mamluk envoy in 1485. Suyūṭī, *Naẓm*, 39; ʿAzzām, *Majālis*, 166.

74. The Arab historian Muhammad al-Sakhawi (d. 1497) claimed that Ibn al-Jazari, about whom more in this chapter to follow, had helped to spread the study of hadith in Anatolia. Pfeifer, "Hadith Culture," 45n74. In the arena of jurisprudence, Fenari and the scholar and poet Ahmedi (d. 1412) helped to popularize the work of the Cairo-based jurist Akmal al-Din al-Babarti (d. 1384). Atçıl, "Formation," 53, 58. For medicine, see Yıldız, "From Cairo to Ayasuluk." For possible origins of Turkish *mevlid* works, which began appearing in the early fifteenth century, see Hagen, "Mawlid," 369; Ṭaşköprīzāde, *Shaqāʾiq*, 216; Sehī Bey, *Heşt Bihişt*, 204.

75. Ṭaşköprīzāde, *Shaqāʾiq*, 144–5. The Seljuks of Anatolia as well as the Aydinids, rulers of an Anatolian principality, had already taken some interest in Arabic poetry. Yıldız, "*Nadīm*," 96; Yıldız, "Court Literature," 224.

76. The scholar in question was Manisazade Muhyiddin (d. after 1481). Ṭaşköprīzāde, *Shaqāʾiq*, 191. Mehmed then found a scholar who both memorized and composed Arabic poetry and was able to identify the verse. Ṭaşköprīzāde, *Shaqāʾiq*, 197.

77. Qutbuddin, "Arabic Philology," 617–22.

as did the literary and scholarly knowledge they carried with them. Comparable salon cultures did much to advance this state of affairs, offering as they did a mutually comprehensible and flexible social form through which ideas could be exchanged. The Islamic Republic of Letters was not just a virtual community bound by a common set of written texts. It was also a physical and embodied network, built and sustained one face-to-face exchange at a time.

A World Divided

As cosmopolitan as this world was, it was not free of hierarchies. A focus on mobility, so all-pervasive in recent historical scholarship, can sometimes obscure the patterns that structured the circulation of people and ideas. In fact, movement between the Mamluk and Ottoman empires was asymmetrical. Throughout the fourteenth and fifteenth centuries, Ottoman elites were far more interested in Mamluk intellectual developments than Mamluk-based gentlemen were in the Ottoman cultural scene. At the same time, many educated Ottomans looked not to their southern Arab neighbors, but rather to their eastern Persophone colleagues for literary and social models. In many of the pursuits that played a role in the salon, the Persian example reigned supreme.

Broadly speaking, Ottoman scholars had more reason to travel to Mamluk lands than Mamluk-born scholars did to Ottoman lands in the two centuries before 1516–7. According to Taşköprizade's mid-sixteenth century biographical compilation, of those scholars living in Ottoman lands in the fifteenth century, about fifteen percent had had some sort of experience in Mamluk lands.[78] In the same period, according to comparable sources from Mamluk lands, a mere one percent of the Mamluk elite ever found reason to travel to Anatolia.[79] The two groups' reasons for traveling diverged as well. Whereas Ottoman students, as we have seen, often went to Mamluk

78. This value is derived from averaging the rounded percentage of the reigns of Mehmed I (19%); Murad II (10%); Mehmed II (12%); Bayezid II (19%), that is, from the period 1413–1512. A significant number of those entered Mamluk domains en route to the hajj pilgrimage. Since hajj travel was often accompanied by friendly and scholarly encounters, I take that to be a serious opportunity for cultural exchange. See, for example, Markiewicz, *Kingship*, 106–17.

79. I have calculated this using Petry's numbers, which were based on two Mamluk biographical dictionaries of the late fifteenth century. Of the 4,631 fifteenth-century notables he studied, 60 traveled to Rum. Petry, "Travel Patterns," 56n6, 86. Sakhawi's dictionary, which Petry used, is more capacious than Taşköprīzade's, so Petry's figure includes military and political officials.

lands in search of teachers, Mamluk travelers rarely entered Ottoman territory to study.[80] Instead, most came after they had completed their education, a substantial number, like ʿAbbasi, under duress.[81]

A similar pattern emerges in the written tradition. Ottoman scholars engaged eagerly with works written in Egypt and Syria throughout the fifteenth century, using trips to the region to buy books and translating many of them into Turkish when they returned home.[82] By one calculation, of thirty-three basic textbooks taught in Ottoman madrasas between the fourteenth and sixteenth centuries, only one was written by an author based in Anatolia, in contrast to ten from today's Egypt.[83] On the whole, Mamluk-based scholars did not return the favor. Writings from Anatolia were equally poorly represented among the foundational works studied by men like ʿAbbasi in Damascus and Cairo.[84] Ruling circles did evince interest in Ottoman Turkish literature. Sultan Ghawri not only welcomed Anatolian scholars to his court, but also commissioned an anthology of Turkish-language verse that included the compositions of Ottoman poets alongside those of Mamluk provenance.[85] Still, such interests echoed only

80. Petry does not examine travel to Anatolia for study in either of his two articles discussing the mobility of Mamluk notables. My own examination of Sakhawi's dictionary, while not exhaustive, found that most of the individuals who traveled to Ottoman lands from the Mamluk Sultanate did so for other reasons. Of a random sample of forty scholars who traveled to Ottoman territory, two are stated to have gone there to study. Petry, "Reconsidered," 167–8; Sakhāwī, *Ḍawʾ*, 4: 198–9 and 11: 26–7. Molla ʿArab (d. 1496), who began his studies in Aleppo before continuing his education in Anatolia with Molla Gürani, is a notable exception. Ṭaşköprīzāde, *Shaqaʾiq*, 150.

81. Ibn al-Jazari, who was at the court of Bayezid I (r. 1389–1403) from 1395–6 until 1402, went to Istanbul after a dispute with the Mamluk regime. Ṭaşköprīzāde, *Shaqāʾiq*, 36–38; Binbaş, "Eyewitness," 157–9; Muslu, *Ottomans*, 35. Molla Gürani was sent into exile around 1440 for having insulted the founder of the Hanafi legal school. Ibn Taghrībirdī, *Nujūm*, 15: 344; Maqrīzī, *Durar*, 1: 259–60; al-Biqāʿī, *ʿUnwān*, 6b; Sakhāwī, *Ḍawʾ*, 1: 241. For others that went to Ottoman lands fleeing misfortune, see Sakhāwī, *Ḍawʾ*, 1: 369; 3: 59, 156, 221; 4: 33.

82. Erünsal, *Ottoman Libraries*, 10–1.

83. This calculation is based on later sources, making it difficult to know the extent to which it reflects fifteenth-century reading habits. Many of the Syrian and Egyptian works in question predated the Mamluks. Lekesiz, "Değişme," 39–47, 164.

84. One notable exception, memorized by ʿAbbasi in his youth, was a work on logic written by Siraj al-Din al-Urmawi (d. 1283). Urmawi was born in today's Iran and educated in Iraq, but worked for many years in Konya under Seljuk patronage. He also spent time in Damascus and Cairo and enjoyed great esteem there. Sakhāwī, *Ḍawʾ*, 4: 179; Heinrichs, "al-ʿAbbāsī," 13; Çağrıcı, "Sirâceddin el-Urmevî."

85. Ghawri's divan featured poems by Ghawri himself, a Mamluk vizier, and the Ottoman poets Ahmed Pasha (d. 1496/7) and Ahmedi. Conermann, "Ibn Ağās," 161; Atıl, "Mamluk Painting," 169. Both Ghawri and Ashraf Qaytbay (r. 1468–96) composed Turkish-language poetry. Irwin, "Mamluk Literature," 3–4, 6; Haarmann, "Arabic" 85; Flemming,

dimly outside of Mamluk royal circles, where mainstream literary culture remained mostly Arabophone.[86] Within the scholarly class, the net movement of knowledge was very much from Mamluk to Ottoman lands.

This imbalance resulted in part from differences in the maturity and self-perception of the scholarly community in the two empires. Syria and Egypt had long been home to a venerable learned tradition. The cultivation of Islamic learning had begun in earnest under the Fatimids (909–1171), who, from their eventual seat in Cairo, supported a variety of scholarly institutions, of which al-Azhar is only the most famous.[87] The Mongol conquests of the thirteenth century further bolstered the Mamluks' cultural role, as the center of gravity in the Islamic world moved westwards, first to Damascus and then to Cairo.[88] Continuous Mamluk patronage of learning strengthened the trend and, by the early sixteenth century, there were, by a conservative estimate, more than 280 madrasas in operation in Cairo and Damascus alone.[89] Even the most ordinary of these boasted a collection of over two thousand books, a mammoth number by the global standards of the day.[90]

The situation in Ottoman lands was quite different. To be sure, in Anatolia the patronage of Islamic learning dated back to the eleventh century, and, by the middle of the fifteenth century, there were close to seventy madrasas scattered across Ottoman territory.[91] Still, throughout the first century and a half of Ottoman rule, the Islamic intellectual landscape in the region—especially in Ottoman lands, much of which had previously been under Christian rule—was still comparatively inchoate.[92] Though madrasas were endowed with books and librarians, they usually started out with modest resources. Even those founded by sultans—that is, the wealthiest of institutions—might begin with a few dozen books at

---

"Literary Activities," 253; Flemming, "Nachtgesprächen," 22–3; Eckmann, "Kiptschakische Literatur," 299. See also ʿAzzām, *Majālis*, 74; Frenkel, "Mamluks," 65–70.

86. Of course, there were many practicing scholars who were of Mamluk slave origin as well as marriage ties between Arab scholarly and Mamluk military families. However, the reception of Turkish-language literature in the scholarly mainstream was circumscribed. Berkey, "Silver Threads"; Haarmann, "Arabic"; Flemming, "Literary Activities."

87. Walker, "Fatimid Institutions of Learning."

88. Humphreys, "Egypt," 451; Berkey, *The Formation of Islam*, 187; Gökçe, "Hadis Çalışmaları," 41.

89. Miura, "Salihiyya Quarter," 269; Petry, "Paradox," 190.

90. Hirschler, *Medieval Damascus*, 3.

91. Atçıl, *Scholars*, 29.

92. This distinguished the Ottoman principality from many of its neighbors, which were founded in regions that had long been under Muslim control.

the beginning of the fifteenth century, growing to a few hundred by the century's end.[93] Until the early fifteenth century, sultans had no choice but to rely on foreign scholars to train students and to staff their bureaucratic and judicial systems.[94] Even as the Ottoman educational system became more independent in the course of the fifteenth century, migrant scholars continued to be viewed as valuable assets.

As a result, Mamluk-trained scholars were consistently welcomed in Ottoman lands. Many Ottoman students educated in Syria or Egypt returned home to teach the next generation, as Fenari did.[95] Others educated abroad became tutors to Ottoman princes. Ibn al-Jazari (d. 1429), a Syrian scholar educated in Cairo and Damascus, was appointed tutor to the sons of Bayezid I, while Gürani taught Bayezid II's son Mehmed (later Sultan Mehmed II).[96] For much of the fifteenth century, these migrants would fulfil important governmental roles, drafting foreign correspondence for Ottoman sultans or occupying top posts like military judge and chief mufti (*şeyhülislam*).[97] As the Ottoman poet Mesihi (d. 1512) mused:

> O Mesihi, there is no place for you, even if you descend from the skies.
> Go away and then come back from Iran or the Arab lands.[98]

Thus, when ʿAbbasi was invited to teach at an imperial madrasa at the turn of the sixteenth century, he was exemplary of a longstanding trend.

The Ottoman veneration of imported talent stands in stark contrast to the way that Syrian and Egyptian scholars could treat those born elsewhere. To be sure, many members of the Mamluk ruling elite welcomed such foreign-born scholars, as we have seen. However, matters were different when it came to the scholarly classes of Damascus and Cairo. These were self-assured about what they took to be their international preeminence. One fourteenth-century scholar declared that Cairo "benefited

93. The madrasa Murad I established in 1430 had 71 books; Mehmed II's in 1470 had about 300. Erünsal, *Ottoman Libraries*, 12, 15, 20–2.

94. Atçıl, *Scholars*, esp. 32.

95. Atçıl, *Scholars*, 35; Atçıl, "Mobility," 325–6. Molla Fenari later became chief mufti. Repp, *The Müfti of Istanbul*, 73–98.

96. For Jazari, see Binbaş, "Eyewitness," 169–170; for Gürani, Ṭaşköprīzāde, *Shaqāʾiq*, 84–5.

97. Gürani did all of these things. Walsh, "Gūrānī"; Repp, *The Müfti of Istanbul*, 166–74. Ibn al-Jazari, his son, and Ibn ʿArabshah (d. 1450) also received positions in the Ottoman chancery, drafting letters to foreign dignitaries. Muslu, *Ottomans*, 35; Muslu, "Ottoman-Mamluk Relations," 65–6.

98. Translation from Kuru, "The Literature of Rum," 559.

from the most honorable of writers as no other kingdom did" and "had the kind of notables and men of letters that no other country had."[99] Leading learned men in Cairo saw themselves as net exporters of ideas, as the claims of one of ʿAbbasi's teachers, Jalal al-Din al-Suyuti (d. 1505), suggest. Suyuti boasted that his works had "traveled to all countries, and have reached Syria, Rūm, Persia, the Hijaz, the Yemen, India, Ethiopia, North Africa, and Takrūr, and have spread from Takrūr to the ocean."[100] Though such braggadocio could be found elsewhere as well, Suyuti was indeed revered all across the Islamic world, as the circulation of his books and fatwas as well as his role in the Islamization of North Africa attest.[101]

This kind of confidence could translate into a dismissive attitude toward scholars educated outside Mamluk lands. Mamluk scholarship had been forged in dialogue with works written in medieval Persia and Central Asia.[102] Nonetheless, in the fifteenth century, foreign-educated scholars were sometimes treated with suspicion. The fate of one Persian-born hadith scholar in early fifteenth-century Cairo was particularly grave. The city's scholars were aghast by what they took to be his general ineptitude, the more so when he was appointed to the influential position of chief Shafiʿi judge of the city. Not only was he unable to speak Arabic correctly—"typical for the non-Arabs [*aʿājim*]," according to the Cairo-based historian Ibn Taghribirdi (d. 1470)—but, in front of an audience that included the Mamluk Sultan, the Persian scholar was shown to be unable to answer questions on the technicalities of interpreting hadith.[103] Corruption charges led to a prison sentence and in the end the beleaguered scholar only avoided execution by the skin of his teeth. Though this was an extreme case, the general skepticism vis-à-vis foreign-educated scholars was not unusual; Ibn Taghribirdi, who was himself of Rumi origin, explained that the Persian scholar suffered "because of the disgust of the Arabs [*awlād al-ʿarab*] towards him, as was often evident between the Arabs and non-Arabs."[104] Though migrants could gain great

99. Ahmad al-Qalqashandi (d. 1418) as cited in Musawi, *Letters*, 6.

100. As quoted in Saleh, "Al-Suyūṭī," 77. For another exporter of knowledge, see Petry, "Travel Patterns," 76.

101. Saleh, "Al-Suyūṭī," 78; Geoffroy, "al-Suyūṭī"; Blecher, "'Usefulness Without Toil,'" 182–3. Mehmed II was said to have made such claims as well. Ṭaşköprīzāde, *Shaqāʾiq*, 161.

102. Such influence continued in the later Mamluk period, though newer books from the region were sometimes hard to come by in Syria and Egypt. Saleh, "Gloss," esp. 238.

103. Ibn Taghribirdi as cited in Blecher, *Prophet*, 85, and ff. The scholar in question was Shams al-Din al-Harawi (d. 1426).

104. Ibn Taghribirdi as cited in Blecher, *Prophet*, 85.

scholarly visibility in Mamluk lands, this was often a function of having assimilated into local scholarly culture, as ʿAbbasi's teachers Kafiyaji and Aqsaraʾi had.[105]

Whatever conceit scholars in Mamluk lands may have cultivated about their international preeminence, for the Ottomans, the Mamluk Empire was not the only intellectual point of reference. Another geographical region competed with the Eastern Mediterranean for cultural vitality in the period: the Turco-Persian cultural sphere comprising western Afghanistan, Azerbaijan, Iran, Iraq, and Transoxania, referred to collectively by Ottomans as *ʿacem* (Ar. *ʿajam*). In the thirteenth and fourteenth centuries, cities like Samarkand, Shiraz, and Tabriz rivaled their Mamluk counterparts in intellectual dynamism, bringing forth generations of scholars who would shape Islamic scholarship for centuries, most notably Saʿd al-Din al-Taftazani (d. 1390) and al-Sayyid al-Sharif al-Jurjani (d. 1413).[106] At the beginning of the fifteenth century, the Timurid Sultan Shah Rukh (r. 1409–47), who governed from Herat, proclaimed himself "the renewer" of the religion and "the sultan of Islam" (*mujaddid, padshah-i Islam*), investing new energy into the patronage of scholarship that would defend Sunni orthodoxy.[107] He was followed by the likes of Sultan Husayn Bayqara (r. 1469–1506), who helped to make Timurid Herat one of the most beguiling cultural and intellectual centers of its era.[108]

Understandably, this environment proved attractive to Ottoman intellectuals. Anatolia had a long history of relations with Persia and Central Asia. The region had been exporting dynasts, mystics, merchants, and seminomads to Anatolia since the eleventh century; the house of Osman was not alone in tracing its origins to these regions, as Müʾeyyedzade's own family lore suggested.[109] The cultural influence of the Turco-Persian Seljuks long outlasted their political control of Anatolia, and the Turkish principalities that succeeded them starting in the late thirteenth century continued to look to that tradition for models of

105. Molla Fenari also received respect in Mamluk lands, though he, too, had been educated in part in Cairo. Ṭaşköprīzāde, *Shaqāʾiq*, 22–3. There were of course exceptions, such as ʿAlaʾ al-Din al-Hisni (d. 1483), who finished his education in Eastern Anatolia before receiving a madrasa appointment in Mamluk lands. Petry, "Travel Patterns," 75.

106. Pfeiffer, *Politics*, 1–11.

107. Pfeiffer, *Politics*, 4–5; Subtleny, "Curriculum," 211–2. This has been referred to as the "Timurid Renaissance." For the larger context for such claims, see Markiewicz, *Kingship*.

108. Atçıl, "Mobility," 320; Subtelny, "Art and Politics."

109. For the Ottoman encounter with the Persianate world, see Kartal, *Şiraz'dan İstanbul'a*.

refinement and sociability.[110] A shared preference for the Hanafi legal school facilitated scholarly exchanges.[111] This Persian orientation is reflected in Mü'eyyedzade's intellectual biography. Having fled initially to Aleppo, Mü'eyyedzade remained there only for a few months. The reason is telling: having completed his study of Arabic grammar, he "hoped to study other disciplines, but could not find anyone who could teach them to him."[112] Mü'eyyedzade's interests probably lay in the rational sciences (*al-ʿulum al-ʿaqliyya*), especially astronomy and geography, widely cultivated in Persian lands at the time.[113] So he took the first chance he got to attach himself to a caravan that would take him to Shiraz, the home of the polymath Jalal al-Din al-Dawani (d. 1502). Dawani would become Mü'eyyedzade's most important teacher, and in the three or four years Mü'eyyedzade spent under his supervision, he studied not only astronomy and mathematics, but also Arabic, Qur'anic exegesis, and hadith.[114]

In the second half of the fifteenth century, the longstanding relationship between Anatolia and Persia conspired with contemporary political developments to the east to cause an influx of Persian intellectuals into Ottoman lands. The period saw protracted political instability in both Timurid and Turcoman polities, driving many local intellectuals to search for safer and more stable working conditions. Anatolia was an increasingly attractive destination for them.[115] Mü'eyyedzade himself played a key role in bringing about this state of affairs, helping refugees from the east find protection and positions in Ottoman lands.[116]

Because of this migration, the Persian influence came to outpace the Arab role in many cultural spheres. Although Ottoman elites continued to seek inspiration from their Arab neighbors, this influence was displaced by the interests of the now sizeable Persian community who had joined their ranks. The percentage of the Ottoman scholarly class with some experience in Arab lands dropped steadily over the course of the first two centuries of Ottoman rule, from an average of twenty-four percent across

110. İnalcık, "Klasik edebiyat menşei"; Yıldız, "*Nadīm*."

111. Atçil, "Formation," 39–42; Subtelny and Khalidov, "Curriculum," 223.

112. He stayed in Aleppo for less than a year. Ṭaşköprīzāde, *Shaqāʾiq*, 292; Sehī Bey, *Heşt Bihişt*, 126.

113. Pfeiffer, "Teaching the Learned," 309–11; Lekesiz, "Değişme," 28.

114. Ṭaşköprīzāde, *Shaqāʾiq*, 292; Pfeiffer, "Teaching the Learned"; İpekten, *Edebî Muhitler*, 173; Anay, "Devvani," 257.

115. Markiewicz, *Kingship*; Atçıl, "Mobility," 319–24; Sohrweide, "Dichter."

116. Pfeiffer, "Teaching the Learned," 290–1; Atçıl, "Mobility," 322.

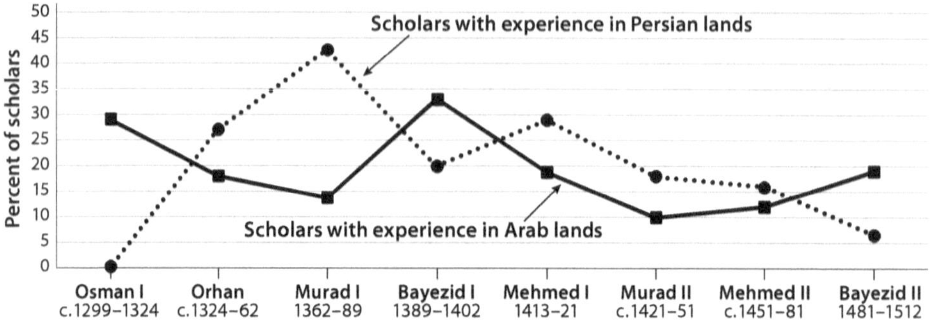

FIGURE 1.2. The percentage of scholars working in Ottoman lands with experience abroad, 1299–1512. During the reigns of all but three sultans, the percentage of Ottoman scholars with experience in Persian lands exceeded that of scholars with experience in Arab lands. Calculations based on Taşköprizade, *al-Shaqaʾiq al-nuʿmaniyya.*

the fourteenth century to an average of fifteen percent in the fifteenth.[117] The overall percentage of Persian scholars declined as well, but less so, averaging twenty-three percent in the fourteenth century and eighteen percent in the fifteenth (see figure 1.2).[118]

Interactions with Persian lands left an indelible mark on Ottoman salon culture. Persia and Central Asia, too, were home to a flourishing culture of salons (often referred to there, too, as *majalis*) for enlightened conversation, poetic discussion, musical entertainment, and wine-drinking.[119] Anatolian scholars traveling to Persian lands often joined these meetings. The Ottoman scholar ʿAlaʾeddin ʿAli Fenari (d. 1497/8), a descendant of the famous Şemseddin who had studied in Egypt, told awed students in Istanbul that his extensive knowledge of poetry stemmed from

117. These are averages derived from Taşköprīzade's biographical dictionary, taken from the reigns of Osman to Bayezid II, that is, from the period 1299–1512. By sultanic reign, the percentage of scholars who had spent time in Arab lands was: Osman (29%); Orhan (18%); Murad I (14%); Bayezid I (33%); Mehmed I (19%); Murad II (10%); Mehmed II (12%); and Bayezid II (19%). The sudden increase in Bayezid II's reign resulted from an increase of Ottoman scholars going on the hajj. This accounts for nine of twenty scholars with experience in Mamluk lands. Only two scholars from Bayezid's reign came from Arab lands; five were Persians who had spent time in Mamluk lands before traveling to Rum. Calculations include individuals known to have traveled to these locations even if Taşköprīzade omits that information, but excludes people with names like "al-ʿAjami" about whom nothing more is known. The sample sizes from the early period are very small making these indicative rather than actual numbers.

118. For scholars who had spent time in Persia, the percentages were: Osman (0%); Orhan (27%); Murad I (43%); Bayezid I (20%); Mehmed I (29%); Murad II (18%); Mehmed II (16%); and Bayezid II (7%).

119. Brookshaw, *Hafiz*, esp. chapter 1; İnalcık, *Tarab*, 3–38, 159–83; Subtelny, "Scenes."

his time studying in Persia, where it was common to spend afternoons reciting verse.[120] Mü'eyyedzade, too, seems to have spent time with his teacher outside of formal class lessons, with the latter proclaiming of his student, "I was taken with his conversational brilliance and was comforted by his exalted presence . . . so that I was loath to be apart from him for an instant or abandon him for a single moment."[121]

In Ottoman lands, Persian émigrés seeking refuge were welcome additions to elite gatherings. Mü'eyyedzade's house in Istanbul was a special hub for the Persian literati.[122] It was one of the first stops of the refugee poet Basiri (d. 1534/5), who had been part of courtly circles in Timurid Herat and a companion of the Aqquyunlu Sultan before settling in Istanbul around 1495–6.[123] Basiri quickly made his way to the heart of Istanbul high society; he became the "intimate friend and boon companion" (*hemdem ve nedīm*) of İskender Çelebi (d. 1535), Süleyman's finance minister (*defterdar*). In general, it was said of Basiri that "his wit was well-received by the men of state. He gave flavor to every salon and his words mixed like milk and honey."[124] Basiri was only one of many Persian migrants whose refinement was appreciated in polite circles; another was said to be "talented in [telling] anecdotes and in evening conversation as well as in histories, tales, and recorded events. He was the king of story-telling in the salons of the important men."[125] Persians were so well respected that one well-traveled Ottoman poet passed himself off as one in the Ottoman court, a ruse that won him "great respect and esteem."[126]

The Persian influence deeply affected the literary and intellectual culture that found an audience in elite gatherings. Persian-language literary traditions received intensified attention in Ottoman learned circles.

120. Ṭaşköprīzāde, *Shaqā'iq*, 183–4. A Persian poet active in the late Timurid period described the arrival of an Anatolian visitor in Herat who challenged locals to solve his *mu'ammas*, a form of riddle popular across the Islamic world. Subtelny, "Scenes," 140–2, 144. See also Bencheneb, "Lughz"; Çavuşoğlu, "Notlar," 24.

121. Dawani as quoted in Pfeiffer, "Teaching the Learned," 320 (translation mine).

122. 'Āşıḳ Çelebi, *Meşâ'irü's-Şu'arâ*, 1498; Markiewicz, *Kingship*, 82–4; Kurnaz, "Aile," 658–60.

123. Basiri had arrived as an ambassador from the Aqquyunlu court but stayed when the winds of politics changed there. 'Āşıḳ Çelebi, *Meşâ'irü's-Şu'arâ*, 421; Sehī Bey, *Heşt Bihişt*, 279–80; Laṭīfī, *Tezkire-i Laṭīfī*, 101–3; Çavuşoğlu, "Basîrî," 105–6.

124. 'Āşıḳ Çelebi, *Meşâ'irü's-Şu'arâ*, 421.

125. This referred to Derviş Şemseddin (d. after 1513), who also came to Anatolia from the Persian lands. 'Āşıḳ Çelebi, *Meşâ'irü's-Şu'arâ*, 1435; Aksoy, "Derviş Şemseddin," 197–8. Another scholar for whom Mü'eyyedzade acted as an important patron was İdris Bidlisi. Markiewicz, *Kingship*, 120–1.

126. Sehī Bey, *Heşt Bihişt*, 208; Laṭīfī, *Tezkire-i Laṭīfī*, 289–90.

Alongside their longstanding interest in Persian poetry, Ottoman scholars began to write histories in Persian as well.[127] Müʾeyyedzade did his part to buoy the trend, bringing with him from Shiraz volumes that had previously been unavailable in Ottoman lands and himself composing Persian verse.[128] The cumulative effect on the Ottoman literary tradition was significant; at the beginning of the sixteenth century the palace library boasted over three hundred volumes of Persian-language poetry, compared to fewer than fifteen in Turkish.[129]

Persian models also inspired the burgeoning Turkish-language literary tradition. Historically speaking, Turkish was something of a newcomer to the elite cultural scene—only in the first half of the fifteenth century did poetry and literary prose in that language make an earnest debut in Ottoman lands.[130] To prove that Turkish was a language suited to literary pursuits, Ottoman poets began not only to translate Persian classics into it, but also to compose their own Turkish-language works using classical Persian genres.[131] In the 1490s, a poet who had spent some time in Herat became the first in Ottoman lands to adapt the Persian "quintet" genre (*khamsa*) into Turkish.[132] For years to come, Persian poetry would serve as the measure of literary excellence, the standard against which Ottoman poets were evaluated, and the example to be emulated and, ideally, exceeded.[133]

Persian models inspired not just literary forms but also the social practices in which those forms took shape. Verse, love, candles, wine: in both regions, these were not only literary tropes, but the physical realities of the salon. It was said of one contemporary Ottoman poet, "his poetic expressions [*maʿānī*] stemmed from the exigencies of the salon [*meclis*]; like [the poet] Hafiz of Shiraz, his poetry included the trappings of the drinking party. He discussed beautiful boys, candles, and drink and drew on the wine-pourer, the harp, and the lute [*rebāb*]."[134] Salon etiquette drew on

127. Markiewicz, *Kingship;* Yıldız, "Historical Writing"; Melville, "Historiography"; Hagen, "Translations"; Fleischer, *Bureaucrat*, 236; Sohrweide, "Dichter."

128. Ṭaşköprīzāde, *Shaqāʾiq*, 294; Pfeiffer, "Teaching the Learned," 288–9; Aksoy, "Müeyyedzâde Abdurrahman Efendi," 485.

129. Kim, "Persian Verse," 642. The Persian impact was likewise felt in the field of political thought. Sariyannis, *Political Thought*, chapters 1–2; Yılmaz, *Caliphate Redefined*.

130. Kuru, "The Literature of Rum," 551. This was true in Timurid Herat as well. Subtelny, "Scenes," 148.

131. For translations, see Sehī Bey, *Heşt Bihişt*, 141, 143, 165, 173. For response poetry, Sehī Bey, *Heşt Bihişt*, 115; Kim, *Age*, chapter 3.

132. This was Bihişti (d. c. 1511). Kim, "Persian Verse," 637.

133. This is particularly evident in the biographical compilation of Sehi Bey, discussed in Chapter 4. See also Kim, *Age*, 96–103.

134. This refers to the poet Revani (d. 1524). Laṭīfī, *Teẕkire-i Laṭīfī*, 170.

Persian models as well. One of the most popular books of manners in Ottoman lands was the Persian *Book of Kabus* (*Kabusname*), which, though a work in the mirrors-for-princes genre, offered advice for drinking parties useful even to men who were not royalty. Written in the eleventh century by a displaced Iranian nobleman for his son, the work had been translated and adapted into Turkish six times by the end of the fifteenth century (at least three of these were prepared for Ottoman patrons).[135] In fact, though the preferred Turkish word for enlightened conversation, *sohbet*, stems from the Arabic *suhba*, its meaning has less in common with the Arabic usage—where it connotes companionship or being in the company of someone—than with the Persian, where it denotes intimate or cultured conversation.[136]

By and large, the Arabic-language tradition simply did not enjoy the same visibility in Ottoman gentlemanly circles. We have seen that the palace library had about half as many Arabic poetry anthologies as it did Persian ones in this period.[137] What is more, the differing natures of the two collections suggest a very different form of engagement with them. Whereas the Persian collection featured a number of contemporary or near-contemporary poets, the vast majority of the Arabic volumes originated in the Abbasid period, with only a handful of early Mamluk-era poets and none from the fifteenth century. Whereas the Persian collection included the works of a number of Ottoman poets, only one or two such local poets can be identified among the authors of the Arabic works.[138] Nor were there Arabic anthologies featuring the sorts of verse commonly performed orally (*muwashshah*, *zajal*).[139] In short, while the Persian books reflect an active and lively engagement, the Arabic books signal an interest that was more academic. Indeed, as Tahera Qutbuddin has

135. The work was written by Kayka'us ibn Iskandar (d. after 1082/3). İnalcik, "Klasik edebiyat menşei," 227–30; Doğan, "Kabus-nâme Çevirileri," 37–56. İdris Bidlisi, who moved from the Aqquyunlu to the Ottoman court at the beginning of the sixteenth century, offered advice on convivial gatherings in a work on rulership that he presented to Sultan Selim I. İnalcık, *Tarab*, 221–5.

136. Strauss, "La Conversation," 253. For *sohbet* in the Ottoman context, see Andrews and Kalpaklı, *The Age of Beloveds*, 106–12.

137. Kim, "Persian Verse," 642. C.f., Qutbuddin, "Arabic Philology," 617–22. The following is based on a comparison between Kim and Qutbuddin's articles and the lists appended to their texts.

138. Qutbuddin, "Arabic Philology," 611, 621–2. Kuru notes that compiling Persian poetry anthologies was rare in Ottoman lands, and for the most part Persian poems were appended to the end of divans dominated by Turkish verse. Kuru, "The Literature of Rum," 560.

139. Qutbuddin, "Arabic Philology," 614.

argued, the Arabic collection of the palace functioned above all as a teaching collection.[140]

As a result of the influence of Persian literary and sociable culture, in certain key ways, Ottoman salons diverged from Mamluk ones. Turkish and Persian did have a prominent role to play in the salons of the Mamluk ruling class. However, outside of Turcophone ruling circles, the situation was different. There, Arabic continued to be the language of literary production and polite discussion. Anthologies collecting the sorts of poems and anecdotes that gentlemen were expected to recite in polite assemblies focused on Arabic, and Arabic continued to be the ultimate measure of scholarly expertise.[141] So too did models of polite etiquette differ from those widespread in Ottoman lands. *The Book of Kabus*, for instance, was not widely known in Syria and Egypt. Although a Mamluk official ordered a copy of the Turkish translation in 1459, the Persian original was not translated into Arabic until the twentieth century.[142] To be sure, etiquette manuals popular in Mamluk lands shared with *The Book of Kabus* a common basis in the broader Islamic normative tradition, especially in the hadith.[143] However, in Arab lands these accounts were subject to differing interpretative traditions, and, what is more, they coexisted with expectations of gentility and refinement inspired by the courts of Abbasid Baghdad or Muslim Spain.[144]

One more factor moderated the influence of Mamluk literature and scholarship on Ottoman intellectual culture as the conquest of 1516–7 neared. Over the course of the fifteenth century, the Ottoman educational sphere had developed apace, with an explosion of new madrasas joining older Anatolian centers of learning that by and by came under Ottoman control. The result was an educational and bureaucratic system that no

140. Qutbuddin, "Arabic Philology," 607.

141. Bauer, "Literarische Anthologien der Mamlūkenzeit," esp. 104–6; Haarmann, "Arabic," 81–5; Blecher, *Prophet*. Arabic literary forms in the Mamluk period did contain increasing allusions to and translations from Persian poety. Musawi, *Letters*, 36.

142. Doğan, "Kabus-nâme Çevirileri," 42–3; Najmabadi and Knauth in Kaykāʾūs, *Das Qābusnāme*, 15.

143. Najmabadi and Knauth in Kaykāʾūs, *Das Qābusnāme*, 19. See also Marlow, "Advice."

144. Irwin, "Mamluk Literature," 9–10. In the first years of the sixteenth century, the palace library did not contain most standard works of Arabic literary prose. Qutbuddin, "Arabic Philology," 614. Hüseyin Yılmaz has emphasized that the Ottoman tradition of advice literature as it pertained to political theory had influences quite separate from those widespread in Mamluk lands. Yılmaz, *Caliphate Redefined*, esp. chapter 1.

longer relied on foreign-trained scholars, as the general downward trend in figure 1.2 attests. Although, as we have seen, men like ʿAbbasi could still receive a warm welcome in the Ottoman elite, the state could now easily fill academic and government positions without relying on outside expertise. Over the course of the fifteenth century, an ever smaller percentage of scholars chose to leave Ottoman lands for their higher education—Müʾeyyedzade himself, after all, had not left home by choice.[145] By the beginning of the sixteenth century, a gifted foreign-born scholar could complain of being undervalued at the Ottoman court.[146]

From the Arab perspective, this was just as well. Given the choice, most members of the civilian and scholarly elite preferred to stay within the confines of the Mamluk Sultanate.[147] This held true for ʿAbbasi, too. In the end, he declined Bayezid's invitation to teach at the imperial madrasa. Instead, he explained, he "longed to return to his hometown [*waṭan*]."[148] By 1502 or 1503, ʿAbbasi was back in Cairo, meeting with the aging luminary Jalal al-Din al-Suyuti in the latter's residence.[149]

Conclusion

Elites of the Mamluk and Ottoman polities sustained significant and ongoing cultural exchange before the conquest of 1516–7. Both groups belonged to the larger Islamic community that extended from North Africa to Southeast Asia. Since the very founding of the Ottoman state at the dawn of the fourteenth century, scholarly study, diplomacy, and, on occasion, personal necessity acted as catalysts for face-to-face exchanges between inhabitants of the two neighboring polities. These exchanges were especially impactful because of the remarkable openness of Ottoman institutions to foreign input straight through the fifteenth century.

As a result of these exchanges, elite inhabitants of the Mamluk and Ottoman empires developed a comparable salon culture. This culture manifested most spectacularly in royal and princely courts, but in both polities, courtly assemblies existed on a spectrum of gatherings that

145. Atçıl, "Mobility," 327.

146. Markiewicz, *Kingship*, esp. 93–8.

147. Petry, "Travel Patterns." One notable exception was Ibrahim al-Halabi (d. 1549), who likely settled in Istanbul before the Ottoman conquest of his hometown of Aleppo. Has, "Ibrāhīm al-Ḥalabī," 7n1.

148. Ṭaşköprīzāde, *Shaqāʾiq*, 411; also quoted by Ghazzī, *Kawākib*, 2: 164.

149. ʿĀşıḳ Çelebi, *Dhayl*, 109.

differed in degree of power and resources, not in kind. In both regions, topics of conversation were broadly similar since participants had been socialized into the same scholarly tradition and viewed poetry as an important communicative tool. In both regions, such cultured conversation could be accompanied by music and wine. This shared cosmopolitan culture lends credence to the notion of an Islamic Republic of Letters whose participants paid little heed to political or geographical boundaries.

Yet a focus on cosmopolitanism and mobility alone elides the hierarchies that inflected this republic.[150] The Ottoman and Mamluk empires enjoyed different statures within the international Muslim community; when the Ottomans were founding their first madrasa in Iznik in 1331, the Mamluks had already established themselves as the leading cultural force of Sunni Islam. Although the Ottomans went on to build up their own cultural world with remarkable speed and creativity, exchanges between Ottoman and Mamluk elites remained asymmetrical. Members of the Mamluk ruling cadre did show an increasing interest in Ottoman culture, especially courtly culture; however, outside of ruling circles, culture mainly traveled out of Mamluk lands and into the Ottoman Empire. Whether measured in books, translations, instruction, or scholarly travel, through the fifteenth century, Ottoman elites showed more interest in Mamluk intellectual products than the other way around.

Still, from an Ottoman perspective, Mamluk lands were only one source of cultural and intellectual inspiration—and by virtually all measures, not the most important. Over the course of the fifteenth century, an ever-smaller percentage of Ottoman scholars gained any direct experience in the lands of their great neighbor to the south. In the decades leading up to the conquest, a variety of factors conspired to make Arabic literary and intellectual traditions less immediately visible in Ottoman lands than their Persian counterparts. In matters of scholarship, etiquette, and literature, the Ottomans eagerly imported and increasingly appropriated Persianate cultural traditions. As a result, Ottoman salons were ever more infused with a Persian flair.

Thus, although Ottoman and Mamluk lands shared the broad outlines of salon culture, on the eve of the 1516–7 conquest, fundamental differences in language, literature, and etiquette persisted. However smooth exchanges across the Islamic world might be, the distribution of culture and contacts between various regions within it remained "lumpy." A close

150. Markiewicz makes a similar point. Markiewicz, *Kingship*, 15.

look at the culture of the salon suggests the limits of interconnection, the areas where culture cannot go.[151]

Historians can be forgiven for understating those limits, not simply because recent trends in historiography have encouraged the perception of mobility, but also because Ottoman sources themselves do. Sixteenth-century Ottoman intellectuals, aware that they might be considered parvenus, were eager to emphasize the excellence of local academic traditions and their longstanding links to older centers of Islamic learning. This latter goal makes Taşköprizade's biographies of Ottoman scholars such a rich source for tracking the sorts of influences highlighted here. Yet his need to emphasize the vintage of Ottoman scholarship also makes him a problematic one. It was presumably Taşköprizade's unwillingness to recognize some of the asymmetries between the Ottoman and Mamluk scholarly spheres that led him to write that ʿAbbasi had come with the Mamluk embassy, although ʿAbbasi himself stated openly that he had fled misfortune. It seems that, in the sixteenth century, Taşköprizade found the suggestion that ʿAbbasi arrived in Istanbul under duress embarrassing. We could take this omission as a mere oversight, were it not for a similar editorial decision in the case of Molla Gürani.[152] The fact that ʿAbbasi was more open about his motivations for traveling in the work he presented to the sultan suggests that such discomfort took time to develop.

Indeed, the world was changing rapidly. The military and political weakness of the Mamluk Empire compared to its northern, increasingly more self-assured, neighbor was becoming ever more apparent. To the east, a messianic Turcoman movement was quickly gathering steam, culminating in 1501 with the proclamation of the Shiite Safavid Empire based in Tabriz. Within just two decades, these two developments would converge to effect the successful Ottoman conquest of the Mamluk Empire in 1516–7, forever transforming the relationship between Arab and Rumi lands. ʿAbbasi would come to be thankful for the Anatolian roots he had sown.

But ʿAbbasi had no knowledge of all of this when he returned to Mamluk lands in late 1501 or 1502. He was probably just gratified to be back with family and friends—and, moreover, new life awaited: his old teacher Radi al-Din had fathered a son while he was away. Badr al-Din al-Ghazzi

151. To modify Frederick Cooper's phrase. Cooper, "Globalization," 189. See also Rodgers, "Introduction," 10–6.

152. Ṭaşköprīzāde, *Shaqāʾiq*, 84. In the case of Jazari he does mention the difficulties that brought him from Cairo. Ṭāşköprīzāde, *Shaqāʾiq*, 37.

was born in Damascus around dinnertime on June 23, 1499.[153] His father lost no time introducing the boy to the learned world. Before Badr al-Din turned two, his father had taken him to a Sufi shaykh, who gave the toddler a Sufi robe (*khirqa*) and licensed him to transmit all of his scholarly works and all of the prophetic traditions he knew.[154] By the time Badr al-Din was ten, he had memorized not only the Qurʾan, but also two works of jurisprudence written by leading scholars of the early Mamluk era.[155] And when he turned twelve, his father took Badr al-Din to what he took to be the best place for the education of an aspiring young scholar: not Istanbul but Cairo.

153. 14 Dhu'l Qaʿda 904, according to the Muslim calendar.

154. The shaykh in question was one Muhammad al-Iskandari. Ibn Ayyūb, *Rawḍ*, 240b; Ghazzī, *Kawākib*, 3: 3–4.

155. Ibn Ayyūb, *Rawḍ*, 240b.

CHAPTER TWO

An Empire Connecting

EVERYTHING SEEMED POISED to fall into place for Badr al-Din al-Ghazzi when he returned from Cairo to his hometown of Damascus at the age of sixteen. He had spent the last few years with his father in the Mamluk capital, studying with some of the leading luminaries of his era. While in Egypt, young Badr al-Din had begun to compose poetry and issue judicial rulings; he had even started to teach. Home again in the late summer of 1515, he was ready to launch his scholarly career.[1]

One year later, Syria fell to the Ottomans. Egypt—and with it, the Mamluk Sultanate as a whole—followed suit in the spring of 1517. In a matter of months, the political edifice on which Ghazzi's future had been built crumbled. A new bureaucratic system was introduced, the legal structure adjusted. The old Mamluk establishment gave way to a new class of administrators trained in Istanbul. How did the young Ghazzi navigate this potentially traumatic transition? What roles were open to provincial elites within the new order? This chapter examines how Arab notables were integrated into the Ottoman imperial system in the first two decades after the conquest.

Scholars have long been fascinated by the ease with which the Ottoman Empire was able to incorporate new populations. As Halil İnalcık argued in a landmark article of 1954, much of this success hinged on peculiarly Ottoman instruments of rule and the gradual process by which they were introduced in conquered regions.[2] Though İnalcık focused on early

1. Badr al-Din and his father returned from Cairo in August–September 1515 (Rajab 921), after a five-year stay. Būrīnī, *Tarājim*, 2: 98; Ghazzī, *Kawākib*, 3: 4–5. Ghazzi's precociousness was not entirely unusual; Mustafa ʿAli began teaching at similar age. Fleischer, *Bureaucrat*, 24.

2. İnalcık, "Ottoman Methods of Conquest."

Ottoman expansion in Anatolia and the Balkans, historians have found similar patterns in the Arab provinces as well.[3] Even so, understanding imperial integration requires looking beyond the state apparatus. Ottoman rule was sustained not only by formal institutions but also by networks, customs, and beliefs.[4] Studying gentlemanly salons allows us to fix our attention on such informal means and appreciate the role they played in implanting the new order.

As we saw in Chapter 1, there was a long history of relations between the Arab lands of the eastern Mediterranean and the Rumi lands in Anatolia and the Balkans. Both regions participated in a shared Islamic culture. Both nurtured similar forms of sociability. Yet, although these affinities paved the way for interactions after the conquest, they did not make those interactions frictionless. As traffic between the two regions increased and exchanges between Arabs and Rumis intensified, both sides experienced moments of uncertainty and mistrust. Even Islam could act as a source of controversy, since members of the two groups sometimes favored differing interpretations of divine law.

Salons were arenas in which tensions between conqueror and conquered became visible, but also in which they could be diffused. As in earlier decades, the flexibility of salons and their openness to travelers made them vital spaces of encounter between Rumis and Arabs. What was new was their role in governance. Salons were ideal settings for the exchange of resources that were scarce in the postconquest period. Arabs lent Ottomans knowledge and legitimacy in return for appointments and financial support. But not all exchanges were so instrumental. As Ghazzi's account of his 1531 trip to Istanbul suggests, informal gatherings offered opportunities to develop less tangible assets such as friendship and trust, assets that nonetheless contributed to imperial stability as well.

Viewing imperial integration from the perspective of the salon suggests that it was not merely a top-down affair. In informal spheres, provincial actors had an important part to play. To be sure, much of our knowledge of this process was furnished by Arabs keen to exaggerate their own importance. Ghazzi himself was at pains to stress his proximity to the imperial

3. For monographs treating the conquest and incorporation of Greater Syria, see introduction, footnote 50.

4. Philliou, *Biography of an Empire*, xxiii. A growing number of monographs have begun to focus on the social and religious dimensions of the transition. For these studies, see introduction, footnote 51. The building projects that followed the conquest have been another area of focus; for these, see footnote 13 below.

elite, his son—who wrote decades later—to bolster Arab pride. And yet, if provincial narratives tended to overstate local involvement, central accounts tended to minimize it. Taking them together, we can appreciate that the new Ottoman order came about collaboratively, through the efforts of Rumis and Arabs alike.

Early Uncertainty

Like lightening did Ottoman troops descend on the Mamluk Sultanate in the fall and winter of 1516–7. Some 130,000 of them arrived on what is now the Syrian-Turkish border in late August, decimating the Mamluk army in a single day. Before all the corpses could be buried, Aleppo, just south of the battlefield, surrendered, followed over the next few weeks by Hama, Homs, and Damascus. There was blood in today's Palestine, where the Ottomans punished local resistance by executing a thousand townspeople. But the armies would stop at nothing. In January of 1517, they were outside Cairo, which was taken after just an hour's battle at Raydaniyya. By April 13, the last Mamluk Sultan's body was hanging from Cairo's Zuwayla Gate. Four centuries of Ottoman rule in Egypt, Syria, and the Arabian Peninsula had begun.[5]

For Cairo, the Ottoman conquest was a calamitous event that caused an immediate change in the city's status and role. As we saw in Chapter 1, this centuries-old capital boasted a proud cultural identity. Yet, having refused the terms of surrender offered by Sultan Selim, Cairo was punished accordingly. "The people of Egypt did not suffer in all of their history a greater hardship, and I have never heard anything like it in ancient history," the Cairene historian and witness to the events Ibn Iyas (d. 1524) lamented.[6] For three days, Ottoman soldiers sacked salons and pillaged palaces. Hundreds of administrators, merchants, and artisans were forcibly relocated to Istanbul. Again, Ibn Iyas: "the people left their homelands as well as their children and families and were forced to emigrate from their own country to a land they had never set foot on, and to interact

5. Mikhail, *God's Shadow*, chapters 18–20; Lellouch and Michel, *Conquète ottomane*, Rogan, *The Arabs*, 16–20; 1–3; Hathaway, *Arab Lands*, chapter 1; Irwin, "Gunpowder," 135–6; Bakhit, *Ottoman Province*, chapter 1. For the global context, see Hess, "Ottoman Conquest."

6. Ibn Iyās, *Badā'i' al-zuhūr*, 5: 232. For more on this chronicle, see Havemann, "Chronicle."

with people who were foreign to them [*ghayr jinsihim*]."[7] But even for those spared such a fate, the consequences were dire; the loss of the imperial throne inevitably meant a loss in patronage and prestige. The "mother of the world" (*umm al-dunya*), the beating heart not only of the Mamluk Empire but of much of the Islamic world, was suddenly reduced to a province.[8]

For Damascus, the transition was considerably less traumatic. Since the city had surrendered without a fight, there was no large-scale destruction or confiscation of property. The city experienced no great shift in its role; it had always had close ties to Anatolia, and had long since laid down its imperial crown.[9] Administratively, Damascus seems to have even gained in importance, since it was viewed by Istanbul as the more reliable partner in governance than Cairo.[10] Economically speaking, the region benefited from new Anatolian markets for its products and, thanks to dedicated Ottoman infrastructural investment, an increased flow of traffic during the annual hajj pilgrimage to Mecca.[11]

Much of Damascene administration and daily life continued unchanged in the early Ottoman period. Many of those who staffed the Syrian bureaucracy were holdovers from the Mamluks. After a brief interim rule by a Rumi governor-general (*beylerbeyi*), in 1518 the province reverted to the control of Janbirdi al-Ghazali (d. 1521), who had served as governor under the Mamluks and remained popular with the people (Khayrbak, another Mamluk official, was given the governorship of Cairo).[12] Likewise, the chief architect of the city was allowed to stay, and for decades after the conquest, the built environment remained largely unchanged. Other than Sultan Selim's construction of a mosque

7. Ibn Iyās, *Badāʾiʿ al-zuhūr*, 5: 232.

8. Winter, "Conquest"; Hathaway, *Arab Lands*, 39–40; Behrens-Abouseif, *Egypt's Adjustment*; Winter, *Society and Religion*, 7–14.

9. For a comparison of the way the conquest affected the two cities, especially the relations between local Arabs and Rumi judges, see Winter, "Ottoman Qāḍīs," 108–9. For the provincial administration in sixteenth-century Syria, see Bakhit, *Ottoman Province* and Abu-Husayn, *Provincial Leaderships*.

10. Darling, "Fiscal Administration."

11. Phillip, "Economic Impact," 112–4; Raymond, "Ottoman Conquest." Peirce observes a similar economic upswing in the Aintab region north of Aleppo, albeit with a fifteen-year delay. Peirce, "Becoming Ottoman"; Peirce, *Morality Tales*, 30–3. The Mamluks had invested more heavily in the Egyptian than in the Syrian hajj route. Petersen, *Hajj Route*, esp. chapter 5.

12. Selim reappointed Ghazali before returning to Istanbul in February 1518. Ibn Ṭūlūn, *Iʿlām*, 238, 244; Bakhit, *Ottoman Province*, 8, 19.

by the grave of the revered Sufi Ibn ʿArabi (d. 1240), which followed a local architectural idiom, the urban fabric did not acquire an Ottoman stamp until the middle of the sixteenth century. Even then, the central domes and pencil-shaped minarets that were so characteristically Ottoman were combined with local construction techniques and decorative elements.[13] Across the region, it took several decades for a recognizably Ottoman system to prevail.[14]

Still, the Ottoman leadership employed certain tactics to ensure that the new Ottoman presence would be felt immediately. Key among these was the appropriation of urban space.[15] Before his triumphal entrance into the city, Sultan Selim held audiences outside of Damascus in a palace used by Mamluk sultans and governors; after his entrance, he moved into a house requisitioned from a local notable.[16] The Great Mosque at the city center was another important showplace for the new Ottoman presence. The first Ottoman chief judge of the city, Zeynüddin Fenari (d. 1520), convened meetings there, in one of the side rooms (called *mashhad*) that had served ceremonial, political, and judicial functions in the Mamluk period (see figure 3.4).[17] Fenari also saw to it that partisans of the Hanafi legal school—the one followed by the Ottoman dynasty—received privileged access to the prayer hall; though the majority of Syrians belonged to the Shafiʿi legal school, they now had to pray behind the Hanafi prayer leader (*imam*) and the Ottoman officials who followed that rite.[18] Such measures ensured that the new order was experienced viscerally by all.

Certain administrative changes were felt quickly as well. One of the most significant of these was in the legal sphere. In the late Mamluk period, each of the four Sunni legal schools (*madhhabs*) had its own court led by a chief judge (*qadi al-qudat*) and staffed by a number of deputies (*naʾibs*). Although the four legal schools formally enjoyed equal prestige,

13. Boqvist, "Building an Ottoman City"; Kafescioğlu, "'Image of Rūm;'" Weber, "Ottoman Damascus," 432–3; Bakhit, *Ottoman Province*, 115–8. In Aleppo, the first Ottoman mosque complex was not constructed until 1546. Watenpaugh, *Ottoman City*, 39; David, "Grande Maison," 61.

14. Ze'evi, *Ottoman Century*, esp. 4; Behrens-Abouseif, *Egypt's Adjustment*; Singer, *Palestinian Peasants*, esp. 4.

15. Wollina, "Sultan Selīm"; Meier, "God Alone."

16. Bakhit, *Ottoman Province*, 8–11.

17. Ibn Ṭūlūn, *Mufākaha*, 2: 73; Behrens-Abouseif, "Fire," 284–5.

18. Ibn Ṭūlūn, *Mufākaha*, 2: 38; Wollina, "Sultan Selīm," 228–37. For Egypt, see Meshal, "Antagonistic Sharīʿas."

because most locals were Shafiʿi, its court was the most powerful, and its chief judge enjoyed a number of responsibilities and privileges not shared by the other three. This changed with the new government. The Ottomans swiftly moved to elevate the Hanafi chief judge above the other three, who lost that title.[19] This new chief judge presided over the local judicial system, with the power to appoint and remove deputy judges from all four legal schools. But he was more than a legal official; he was also charged with implementing imperial directives and overseeing a variety of local administrative tasks like tax collection.[20]

The Ghazzis potentially had a lot to lose in this brave new world. Much of the family's stature had derived from their role within the Mamluk judicial system and from strategic alliances with Shafiʿi chief judges. Both Badr al-Din's father Radi al-Din and his father before him, had served as deputy Shafiʿi judges in the city.[21] Radi al-Din had been a close confidant of the Furfur family, which had monopolized the position of chief Shafiʿi magistrate in Damascus for the last three decades of Mamluk rule.[22] Although Radi al-Din lost his job when he fell out with Wali al-Din Ibn al-Furfur (d. 1531) in the years before the conquest, the Ottoman demotion of the Shafiʿi school of law must have dampened Radi al-Din's hope that he would regain his position.[23] Indeed, many local families who had dominated the late Mamluk political scene would see a decline in their fortunes after the transition to Ottoman rule.[24]

That locals experienced uncertainty is to be expected. What is more surprising is that Ottoman administrators, too, struggled as they sought to coax the new order into taking root. Few suffered more than the first Ottoman chief judge of the city, Zeynüddin Fenari, sometimes called Zeynelabidin. Fenari was a member of the illustrious Fenarizade family, the descendant of the Şemseddin Fenari who, as we saw in Chapter 1, had

19. Burak, *Islamic Law*; Winter, "Judiciary"; Fitzgerald, "Methods of Conquest."

20. Winter, "Ottoman Qāḍīs"; Kunt, *The Sultan's Servants*, 12; Hallaq, *Islamic Law*, 80.

21. Ibn al-Ḥimṣī, *Ḥawādith*, 86. Radi al-Din had taken on this position in his late teens or early twenties. Ibn Ṭūlūn, *Mufākaha*, 1: 31; Ghazzī, *Kawākib*, 2:4.

22. Ḥaṣkafī and Ibn Ṭūlūn, *Mutʿat al-adhhān*, 2: 771; Elger, "Ghazzi," 99–100. See also Winter, "Ottoman Qāḍīs," 89. For the Furfur family, see Miura, "Urban Society" 161–4, and Miura, "Transition," 209–14.

23. Ibn Ṭūlūn, *Mutʿat al-adhhān*, 2:771; Ibn Ayyūb, *Rawḍ*, 229a. The relationship between the Ghazzis and the Furfurs must have eventually been repaired, since Wali al-Din accompanied Badr al-Din on the first part of his trip to Damascus. Elger, "Ghazzi," 100–1.

24. Miura, "Transition."

studied in Cairo in the late fourteenth century.[25] It was perhaps this history of relations with the Arab world that led our Fenari to be appointed to the judgeship, despite the fact that he was an unremarkable member of the clan. Before taking up the judgeship in Damascus, Fenari had served as the administrator for some imperial endowments in Bursa and Amasya and as judge in Tire, a town near Izmir in Western Anatolia.[26] In light of this modest employment history, his appointment to the judgeship of a major provincial capital like Damascus represented a considerable promotion, to put it mildly, and some of Fenari's missteps were no doubt a function of his inexperience.

As the first holder of the position of chief judge under the Ottoman regime, Fenari was charged with setting up the new administrative structure. However, his efforts to do so were undermined by the fact that he was sorely lacking both in local knowledge and in the allies that could help him procure it. In part, this seems to have resulted from Fenari's unwillingness to build the kind of relations with locals that would have encouraged them to cooperate. Taking up temporary residence at the house of the outgoing chief judge Ibn al-Furfur upon his arrival in the fall of 1516, Fenari allegedly refused to accept the food and drink that his host offered him, an offense grave enough to merit inclusion in a contemporary chronicle.[27] Fenari never seems to have warmed up to local elites; other than a well-attended reception on his arrival in the city, locals noted that he preferred to spend most of his time alone.[28] It is possible that this was a deliberate strategy of the new rulers, meant to underline their power; Sultan Selim also declined to meet with a group of Damascene scholars who had hoped to receive audience with him.[29] However, Fenari was no sultan, and it seems that he paid for his aloofness.

Fenari struggled to gain the trust of locals as he sought to introduce the new provincial order. This became clear when he set out to fulfill one of his first duties, namely compiling an inventory of the city's pious endowments

25. For biographies, see Ṭaşköprīzāde, *Shaqaʾiq*, 399; Ibn al-Ḥanbalī, *Durr*, 649–50; Ghazzī, *Kawākib*, 1: 20; Mecdī, *Tercüme-i Şaḳaʾiḳ*, 400; Walsh, "Fenārī-Zāde." Ibn Ayyub includes a biography of him but much of it confuses him with his ancestor Şemseddin. Ibn Ayyūb, *Rawḍ*, 280a–b.

26. Ibn Ṭūlūn, *Quḍāt*, 309. Ibn Ayyub states that he traveled to Damascus together with Sultan Selim. Ibn Ayyūb, *Rawḍ*, 74a.

27. Ibn Ṭūlūn, *Mufākaha*, 2: 29–30.

28. Ibn Tulun as quoted in Ibn Ayyūb, *Rawḍ*, 280a.

29. Ibn Ṭūlūn, *Mufākaha* 2: 29, 32. Another early judge of the city also showed little interest in locals, much to their distress. Ibn Ṭūlūn, *Quḍāt*, 314.

(Ar. *waqf*, Tur. *vakıf*), properties set aside in perpetuity for charitable purposes or towards the income of certain families.[30] When Fenari called for local waqf administrators to present their endowment deeds to the judge's team, many resisted, fearing the effort would lead to higher taxes or to the confiscation of their properties (the more so after Fenari allegedly seized the deeds of those who did heed the call). When the judge switched tactics, deciding to instead consult a local urban geography containing information on the city's endowments, its author refused to hand over the book. Although the historian Ibn Tulun (d. 1546), who had abridged the geography, did finally provide the beleaguered judge with the information he wanted, many vociferously condemned the administration on procedural grounds and remained deeply skeptical of Fenari's motivations.[31]

In part, this resistance was a reaction to a more intrusive state power. This sense certainly accounted for much of the vehement rejection of the Ottoman marriage tax, which Fenari was tasked with introducing. Whereas in the Mamluk period, qualified jurists had been able to assist couples in drawing up marriage contracts on their own, they were now required to notify the chief judge so that the appropriate fee could be collected. Local legal scholars were beside themselves with rage at the policy that manifestly curtailed their independence (and their income, since they themselves had usually taken a fee for the service). Used to the less centralized system of the Mamluks, provincial jurists understandably felt distressed and even diminished at these new laws.[32]

But many local criticisms of the new regime stemmed from genuine religious concern. Ottoman officials were no less keen than their Arab subjects to secure Islam's triumph. They took their newfound control over Mecca, Medina, and Jerusalem—the three most venerated sites of Muslim piety globally—very seriously; no sooner had Selim's armies taken Greater Syria than the sultan went about staking his claim to the holy sanctuaries and organizing the safe passage of caravans for the hajj pilgrimage.[33] Early law codes issued by the Ottomans portrayed the conquest as a religiously sanctioned one that brought justice to the region in accordance with the Prophetic example.[34]

30. Bakhit, *Ottoman Province*, 36. Ibn Ṭūlūn, *Mufākaha*, 2: 31.

31. Ibn Ṭūlūn, *Mufākaha*, 2: 73–5; Wollina, "Sultan Selīm," 224; Miura, "Ottoman Rule," 272–6; Winter, "Ottoman Qāḍīs," 90.

32. Rafeq, "Syrian *ʿUlamā*," 10–3.

33. Veinstein, "Saints sanctuaires," 233–4; Winter, "Ottoman Qāḍīs," 88–9. In the decades to follow, this region would become a veritable "Ottoman holy land." Shafir, "Holy Land."

34. Abou-el-Haj, "Legitimation." For Egypt, see Behrens-Abouseif, *Ottoman Rule*, 138, 146–7.

All this did not stop learned Arabs from questioning the conformity of certain policies with Islamic law. The marriage tax was one such policy. Standard across Ottoman lands since at least the fifteenth century, it probably had its origins in pre-Ottoman feudal practices.[35] Indeed, Arab scholars viewed it as a heretical innovation (*bidʿa*). As the Egyptian opposition to the tax argued, the Prophet had sanctioned collecting only a far more modest fee than the one the Ottomans had introduced.[36] In Syria, a jurist who confronted Fenari about the tax was shocked to hear Fenari justify it by the revenue it generated for the state; surely no amount of income was worth the moral cost, the jurist countered.[37] Another local scholar was so distressed about the discord (*fitna*) that the innovation had unleashed within the Islamic community that he reportedly wished for his own death. He expressed his opposition in a poetic lament addressing the woe the Ottomans had brought to Damascus:

> Let this poem be heard by those who prayed
> With heartfelt prayers that Damascus be saved.
> [Instead] she was cast into darkness and despair.
> She made us cry and we cried for her.
> They prayed because of the harm they'd seen
> From oppression and from tyranny.
> They prayed it would stop, and God's wrath came down
> For what had occurred, enveloping the town.
> Damascus was punished by a terrible fate:
> The *sunna* of God, which they dared to innovate [*badaʿ*].[38]

What worse punishment for the city's scholars than to be subject to disgraceful legal innovations that contravened the Prophetic example? This same sense was echoed by another Damascene scholar, Taqi al-Din al-Qari (d. 1539/40), who argued that since the Ottomans had introduced such heretical innovations, prayers completed behind them were invalid.[39]

Some of this discontent may be put down to disputes between the locally dominant Shafiʿi school and the now ascendant Hanafis. In

35. Lewis, "ʿArūs Resmi"; Sahillioğlu, "Arûs Resmi."

36. Rafeq, "Syrian *ʿUlamā*," 12.

37. Ghazzī, *Kawākib*, 3: 222–3.

38. Ghazzī, *Kawākib*, 2: 193.

39. Ibn Ṭūlūn, *Iʿlām*, 254; Winter, "Ottoman Qāḍīs," 105. Presumably, Qari was basing this claim on a stricter interpretation of Islamic law—one propagated not by his own Shafiʿi legal school but by the more conservative Hanbalis—according to which praying behind an imam who espoused heretical doctrines invalidated the prayer. Katz, *Prayer*, 143–7. Qari studied with Badr al-Din. Ibn Ayyūb, *Rawḍ*, 241a.

November of 1516, when the Shafiʿi imam of the Great Mosque was forced to cede his pride of place to his Hanafi counterpart, Qari, who was Shafiʿi, defaced the Hanafi's new bench in the mosque with a disparaging couplet.[40] But even those who did adhere to the Hanafi legal school locally expressed doubt about their Ottoman colleagues' religious expertise. The historian Ibn Tulun claimed, for example, that Fenari had been unable to correctly determine the Day of ʿArafa, the second day of the hajj pilgrimage and the auspicious date on which Selim had hoped to inaugurate his new mosque at the tomb of Ibn ʿArabi.[41] Ibn ʿArabi himself was another source of disagreement, as many scholars in Arab lands—Hanafis included—took issue with the Sufi so revered by the Ottoman establishment.[42] According to Ibn Tulun, the entire Damascene religious elite coalesced around some of these criticisms: when an Ottoman judge fled the city with his family to avoid an outbreak of the plague in 1524—a practice condemned by many Muslim jurists—"all of the sensible Arabs [*uqalāʾ abnāʾ al-ʿarab*] denounced them in light of [the precepts laid down by] the shariʿa."[43]

Badr al-Din al-Ghazzi shared some of these reservations about the competence of the Ottomans in religious matters. Witnessing the Friday prayer in the Anatolian city of Karahisar on his way to Istanbul in June 1530, Ghazzi observed, "they pray in accordance with the example of the Prophet Muhammad, and then the preacher ascends and does lots of things inconsistent with the example of Muhammad [*mukhālafat li-l-sunna*]."[44] Ghazzi listed all the ways the preacher's sermon had failed to conform to behaviors that were commendable—though not obligatory—according to Islamic law: he left out the greeting at the beginning; he sang during the sermon; he neglected to lean against a sword; he tread loudly when

40. Ibn Ṭūlūn, *Mufākaha*, 2: 38.

41. Fenari considered it sufficient that five people see the crescent moon to determine the beginning of the month, while according to Ibn Tulun—also a Hanafi—it was at least thirty. Ibn Ṭūlūn, *Mufākaha*, 2: 75; Shafir, "Holy Land," 10–2; Shafir, "Road," 185. In Cairo, Kemalpaşazade (d. 1534), enormously venerated as a scholar in Ottoman lands, faced similar challenges; Ibn Iyas called him "more ignorant than a donkey." Markiewicz, *Kingship*, 139. The Hanafi scholar Ibrahim al-Halabi likewise had much to criticize about Ottoman religious practices. Kaplan, "Polemicist," 46–8.

42. Kaplan, "Polemicist," chapter 1; Zildzic, "Friend and Foe."

43. Ibn Ṭūlūn, *Quḍāt*, 311. Jurists had long disagreed on this issue, but starting in the early sixteenth century, consensus began to form among Ottoman scholars that fleeing plague outbreaks was permissible. This seems to have been at odds with—and indeed sometimes in direct opposition to—the interpretations of scholars native to Syria. Varlık, *Plague*, 240–6.

44. Ghazzī, *Maṭāliʿ*, MS OR 3621, 23b. The printed version reads "and then the preacher ascends and does lots of things, some of which are inconsistent with the *sunna*." Ghazzī, *Maṭāliʿ*, 106.

climbing up and down the pulpit; and he turned his body right and left both while speaking and while sitting down between sermons.[45] According to Ghazzi, things were even worse in Izmit, close to Istanbul. The preacher of that city's main Friday mosque confused Arabic letters while reading from the Qur'an, endorsed prophetic traditions that were invalid, and spouted nonsense (*turraha*) so outlandish that it was beyond words.[46]

The question is less who was right or wrong in these debates—the Islamic tradition had always been open to differing interpretations. The point is that provincial scholars had no time for such cultural relativism. In their view, the Ottomans were flawed in their application of the fundamental and indisputable tenets of divine law. Learned Arabs weaponized the Islamic religious tradition to put pressure on their new Ottoman overlords. That the Ottomans were not impervious to such pressure is suggested by their choice in Fenari's successor. When he was transferred to Aleppo in 1518, Fenari was replaced by the longtime local judge Ibn al-Furfur, who had switched to the Hanafi legal school in the mean time.[47] Istanbul must have realized just how much local expertise was needed.

Never did the obstacles the Ottomans faced in establishing themselves in Syria become more apparent than during the rebellion of Janbirdi al-Ghazali (d. 1521). Ghazali had acted as governor of Damascus late in the Mamluk period, and had been reappointed to that position at the beginning of 1518. At the news of the death of Sultan Selim in October 1520, Ghazali seized upon a moment of apparent weakness to drive the Ottomans from the citadel, take Hama and Homs, and proclaim himself sultan. One of Ghazali's first moves was to revoke the new taxes the Ottomans had imposed. Although the revolt appears to have generated only a moderate level of enthusiasm within the local establishment and was defeated within three months, the incident was not to be shrugged off; other former Mamluk officials led similar rebellions in 1522–3 in Egypt.[48]

45. For obligatory and commendable acts during the sermon, see Wensinck, "Khuṭba."

46. Ghazzī, *Maṭāli'*, 216.

47. Ibn Ṭūlūn, *Quḍāt*, 390; Ibn al-Ḥanbalī, *Durr*, 1: 649–50; Ghazzī, *Kawākib*, 1: 20, 2:22; Miura, "Transition," 209–11; Winter, "Ottoman Qāḍīs," 88–93.

48. It is difficult to assess how much elite support there was for the revolt in Damascus. It is clear that popular and military classes were enthusiastic, but the sources are reticent on merchants and men of learning. Bakhit takes this to mean that they remained aloof, though the Ottomans (as well as Venetian observers) seem to have believed otherwise; in their punitive pillaging of the city, they did not spare the houses of elites (including Ibn Tulun). Turan, "The Sultan's Favorite," 37–52; Ayalon, "Mamlūk Sultanate," 136–43; Bakhit, *Ottoman Province*, 27–34.

The Ottomans moved swiftly to quell Ghazali's rebellion. Two armies, one from the north and one from the south, converged upon Damascus and routed Ghazali's army in a single day. More than three thousand people were killed on the battlefield, and many more executed later; Ghazali's head and one thousand rebel ears were sent to Istanbul.[49] Changes in formal policy were one response to the crisis. From then on, the governor of Damascus would come from the center, his jurisdiction would be reduced, and the Ottoman garrison expanded.[50] But these formal changes also seem to have been accompanied by a more informal effort by the Ottomans to win the confidence and cooperation of the urban elite. Local men like Radi al-Din, who only stood to gain from such alliances, were most obliging.

Local Support

The Ottoman Empire was a remarkably bureaucratized state, and by the early sixteenth century it possessed specialized institutions and formal occasions for managing many aspects of political life. In Istanbul, the imperial council (*divan-i hümayun*) oversaw appointments, heard petitions and high-level court cases, and deliberated in matters of foreign relations and war. Outside the imperial center, provincial councils (*divans*) followed the same model, likewise combining consultative and juridical functions.[51] Finally, there were the judicial courts where legal disputes could be resolved. All of these occasions were, at least in principle, governed by strict protocol and, in the case of the imperial council, a tight schedule that left little time for pleasantries.[52]

However, this level of institutionalization did not imply a strict separation between the professional and the personal of the sort envisioned by modern observers of the bureaucratic state. For one, even many formalized sessions took place in private residences. Like the imperial council, which was held in the sultan's residence in the Topkapı Palace, provincial councils were held in the homes of governors.[53] For the better part of

49. Ibn Ṭulūn, *I'lām*, 252–3; Bakhit, *Ottoman Province*, 31–3.

50. Ibn Ṭulūn, *I'lām*, 253; Ibn al-Ḥimṣī, *Ḥawādith*, 553; Bakhit, *Ottoman Province*, 96.

51. Baldwin, *Islamic Law*.

52. İpşirli, "State Organization," 228–9; Kunt, *The Sultan's Servants*, esp. 26–9; Bakhit, *Ottoman Province*, 92. For Ottoman Cairo in the seventeenth century, see Baldwin, *Islamic Law*, esp. 37–9.

53. Baldwin, *Islamic Law*, 39. In the 1520s, Sultan Süleyman received diplomats in a garden palace near the Black Sea, and miniatures from the later sixteenth century show him as well as Murad III sitting in gardens attending to issues of state. Necipoğlu, "Garden Culture," 38, 43, 68.

the sixteenth century, the sessions of the chief Islamic court in Damascus were held in the chief judge's residence.[54] The home was also a space for a variety of rather more ambiguous meetings hard to pinpoint as characterized either by business or by leisure. It has been shown that much of the arbitration of disputes associated with the Islamic courts (and even registered with them) in fact occurred outside of the courtroom.[55] Conversely, in Damascus, even the seat of the Islamic court seems to have functioned as a more general meeting place alongside a place for practicing law, at least until one Ottoman judge instituted a formal protocol in the middle of the sixteenth century; elites used to drop in at their leisure until it was mandated they first seek the judge's permission to enter.[56] To be sure, the reception halls where such official meetings took place were often located in stand-alone structures or in separate wings of the house, thus enabling a separation from family life.[57] All the same, it meant that when a man hosted, he appeared in a dual role as head of state and head of house.

In the early days of Ottoman rule in Syria, the all-purpose nature of many of these gatherings proved useful in helping the new order to take hold. Salons afforded the kind of unstructured, meandering conversation that helped people to identify common interests and build up trust, of crucial importance for both sides in the wake of the conquest. At the same time, these gatherings formed a pillar of Ottoman governance, offering a venue in which information could be exchanged and the virtues of the new regime advertised.

Radi al-Din immediately went about cultivating good relations with the growing number of Ottomans who now had occasion to visit Damascus. Some of these were travelers who passed through for a couple of weeks

54. Ibn Ayyub states (beginning with a citation of Ibn Tulun): "'on the 12th of Shawwal of that year [1530] the new judge arrived in Damascus. He stayed at the house of Shihabi Ibn al-Muzalliq beneath the skull-cap [makers] on the western side.' This remains the residence of the judge until today. The deputy and the Arab judges used to pass verdicts in the hall [*qāʿa*] in the smaller eastern *iwan* and the Efendi [the chief judge] in the larger southern *iwan*, but in the days of the judge Hasan, he moved the deputies outside the hall and built for them the *iwan* where they sit today." Ibn Ayyūb, *Rawḍ*, 75a–b. Najm al-Din al-Ghazzi also says that Hasan "was the one who built the seat of the court [*majlis al-ḥukm*] at the residence of the judge [*bāb al-qāḍī*]. Previously, the deputies of this court had been in the *iwan* of the eastern reception chamber [*qāʿa*]; he built this [new] place outside the chamber." Ghazzī, *Kawākib*, 3: 141. Across the empire, judges often held court in their own homes. Imber, *Ottoman Empire*, 233; Peirce, *Morality Tales*, 98.

55. Gradeva, "*Kadi* Court," 62, 66.

56. Ibn Ayyūb, *Kitāb*, 50. For more on the judge Hasan Bey who instituted this practice, see Chapter 3.

57. Mollenhauer, "Private in Public," 71.

or months. Such was the case with Hacı Çelebi (d. 1538), also known as Müʾeyyedzade ʿAbdurrahim Çelebi, who spent time in Damascus together with his nephew sometime before 1529 while completing the hajj.[58] Hacı Çelebi was the brother of Müʾeyyedzade ʿAbdurrahman, the royal boon-companion who had received Radi al-Din's friend and former student ʿAbd al-Rahim al-ʿAbbasi in Istanbul in 1502. Müʾeyyedzade had died in the meantime (in 1514), but Hacı Çelebi probably arrived at the Ghazzis' doorstep with a recommendation from ʿAbbasi, since the latter knew both brothers personally and had intended Hacı Çelebi to convey a letter to Radi al-Din.[59]

The relationship between Radi al-Din and Hacı Çelebi was affectionate. According to Badr al-Din's later account, the visitor treated Radi al-Din "as a brother and as a friend."[60] Underpinning their bond was a shared interest in Sufism, a more experiential form of Islamic devotion that had spread across the Muslim world in the medieval period.[61] Radi al-Din was a member of the Qadiri Sufi order and a prized teacher of esoteric knowledge; he wrote a manual on the proper conduct of Sufi novices, and put this work into practice instructing youngsters in Egypt and Syria.[62] Hacı shared this orientation, having first joined, and then become the leader of, one of the most important Sufi lodges (*zaviye*) in Istanbul, one with an affinity to the Qadiri order.[63] This commonality allowed for instant recognition between the two men: "each saw that the other was a friend of God [*wālī Allāh*]," Badr al-Din explained, employing the term used in Sufi contexts for exceptionally pious individuals.[64]

58. Ghazzī, *Maṭāliʿ*, 129, 266. For biographies of Hacı Çelebi, see Ghazzī, *Maṭāliʿ*, 263–4; Ṭaşköprīzāde, *Shaqāʾiq*, 431–2; Ghazzī, *Kawākib*, 2: 165–7; Mecdī, *Tercüme-i Şaḳaʾiḳ*, 426; Ibn al-ʿImād, *Shadharāt*, 10: 364–5; Süreyya, *Sicill*, 3: 328. For Hacı Çelebi's nephew ʿAbdülhayy, see Ṭaşköprīzāde, *Shaqaʾiq*, 517.

59. Ghazzī, *Maṭāliʿ*, 151.

60. Ghazzī, *Maṭāliʿ*, 129; Ghazzī, *Kawākib*, 2: 166.

61. For Sufism in the Arab provinces in the early period of Ottoman rule, see Emre, *Ibrahim-i Gulshani*; Winter, "Sufism"; Geoffroy, *Soufisme*, chapter 5; Winter, *Society and Religion*.

62. His manual was entitled *The Precious Pearl on the Etiquette of Sufis and Novices* (*al-Jawhar al-farid fi adab al-Sufi wa-l-murid*). Ghazzī, *Jawhar*, 2a–44b. Ghazzī, *Kawākib*, 2: 194–5.

63. This was the lodge of Yavsi, an influential shaykh of the Bayramiyye-Şemsiyye order. Kurnaz, "Aile," 663–4. In the fifteenth century, the Anatolian mystic Eşrefoğlu Rumi (d. 1469/70) had been sent by his master to the Qadiri base in Hama for spiritual training. Dikmen, "Eşrefoğlu Rumi." I thank Sara Nur Yıldız for drawing my attention to this. Sufis need not have been affiliated with the same order to derive knowledge and benefit from one another. Markiewicz, *Kingship*, 116–7.

64. Ghazzī, *Maṭāliʿ*, 129; Ghazzī, *Kawākib*, 2: 166.

Alongside these more fleeting encounters, Radi al-Din also built more long-term relationships with the men who formed the backbone of the new imperial order. He made friends with an early Rumi supervisor of the new mosque complex for Ibn ʿArabi, for example, even allowing the supervisor to live at his house for some time.[65] Here, too, Sufism was decisive, since the supervisor became his disciple and student.[66] But more remarkably, Radi al-Din became close to no less than the most powerful man in the province, namely Ayas Pasha, the province's governor-general. Ayas Pasha (d. 1539) had been born into an Albanian peasant family and had entered palace service under a customary agreement that allowed Muslim Bosniaks and Albanians to be recruited into the janissary corps.[67] Eventually promoted to janissary commander, Ayas Pasha played a leading role in the Syrian and Egyptian campaigns of 1516–7. In early 1521, he was sent back to the region, this time to put down Ghazali's revolt; meeting with success, he was awarded the defeated rebel's post. As provincial governor, Ayas Pasha had a fabulously large income and a considerable amount of power. He was at the head of the provincial hierarchy, charged with keeping law and order, ensuring that taxes were collected, and implementing orders from Istanbul. The position also made him the highest military official in the province.[68] True to type, Ayas Pasha spent a portion of his tenure subduing fractious Bedouin tribes.[69]

Still, there was always time for other pursuits, and unlike Fenari, Ayas Pasha seems to have taken seriously the need to win over leading locals. He was known among Damascenes to "traffic with the scholars and build good relations with the upright."[70] He had an especially close relationship with Radi al-Din, whom he visited at his home. According to Badr al-Din, Ayas Pasha once insisted, gesturing toward Badr al-Din, "I have no friend in Damascus but this man and his father!"[71] Hyperbolic as this may have been, a considerable bond must have linked them for Ayas Pasha left the Ghazzis some of the enslaved women of his household when he departed

65. The supervisor in question was Takiyüddin Bakir (d. 1520). Ghazzī, *Kawākib*, 1: 165; Meier, "Perceptions," 428.

66. Ghazzī, *Kawākib*, 1: 165.

67. Ayas Pasha served as governor in Damascus from March to December 1521. For biographies, see Ibn al-Ḥimsī, *Ḥawādith*, 549–52; Ibn Ṭūlūn, *Iʿlām*, 253–4; Ghazzī, *Kawākib*, 2: 125–6; Kütükoğlu, "Ayas Paşa," 202–3; Parry, "Ayās Pas͟ha." See also Filipovic, "Sinan Pasha."

68. İpşirli, "Ottoman State Organization," 228–9, 232; Kunt, *The Sultan's Servants*, esp. 26–9; Bakhit, *Ottoman Province*, 92.

69. Ibn Ṭūlūn, *Iʿlām*, 353.

70. Ghazzī, *Kawākib*, 2: 125.

71. Ghazzī, *Maṭāliʿ*, 133.

for Istanbul at the end of 1521. Gifting enslaved persons was common practice in the Ottoman Empire, and served to strengthen the bonds between households as slaves brought their knowledge and experience from one owner to the next—and sometimes back again. When one of the women bore Ayas Pasha's child a few months after joining the Ghazzi household, Radi al-Din named the baby Fatima and returned her with her mother to be with Ayas.[72]

However sincere friendships between Ottoman officials and local notables may have been, they were also functional. Radi al-Din's contact with the governor must have won him clout among Damascenes, which would explain his son Badr al-Din and his grandson Najm al-Din's continual efforts to highlight their bond. It may have also won Radi al-Din something very tangible: reinstatement to his position as deputy Shafi'i judge. This occurred sometime after the conquest, at the behest, it seems, of Ayas Pasha.[73] The fact that Radi al-Din had been dismissed before the conquest may well have worked in his favor; it allowed him to present himself as an informed but untainted partner. But so, too, must have the intimate domestic exchanges with Ayas Pasha, which likely helped to convince the latter that Radi al-Din was suitable for the job.

Locals were not the only ones to benefit from such relationships; Ottoman officials did as well. Consider Badr al-Din's surprising characterization of his father's relationship with Ayas Pasha:

> [Ayas Pasha] was one of the men whose love and trust was strong, in the sayyid my father the scholar of Islam. As governor of Damascus did [Ayas] to my father come. Humbly he requested his prayers and benefaction, desirous of his help and supportive action, eager for companionship and friendly interaction.[74]

This is a stark reversal of the relationship one might expect: the pasha—the most powerful man in the province—is depicted as a supplicant, the provincial scholar as advisor and host. In part, this reflects the perspective of a boastful son eager to emphasize the respect his father commanded. In part, it reflects a discrepancy in age. Radi al-Din was in his early sixties

72. Ghazzī, *Kawākib*, 2: 125. In Istanbul, Ayas Pasha would gain a reputation for lustfulness. Andrews and Kalpaklı, *The Age of Beloveds*, 326.

73. Ibn al-Ḥimṣī, *Hawādith*, 548, 552; Ghazzī, *Kawākib*, 2: 4–5. Appointments were often made by consultation between the governor and the chief judge. Ḥamawī, *Ḥādī*, 64, 65.

74. Ghazzī, *Maṭāliʿ*, 130.

and Ayas Pasha not yet forty when the two met.[75] But it also reflects that in this early period, Ottoman functionaries sought the informal support of local elites.

Some of the attractions of such support were spiritual. The Ottoman governing class had long cultivated close ties to Sufi visionaries. At the same time that Sultan Selim refused to receive a group of local notables, he also set out to visit the home of a prominent Sufi who had been an early supporter of the Ottoman conquest.[76] Ayas Pasha had similar commitments. He welcomed impromptu visits from local Sufi leaders and accompanied them to sacred sites around town.[77] This devotional fervor also underpinned his regard for Radi al-Din; Najm al-Din called Ayas "one of the most important Sufi affiliates [*akbar al-muḥibbīn*]" of his grandfather, using to a term that described those who sympathized with an order without being fully initiated into it.[78] Indeed, men like Ayas Pasha had much to gain from Radi al-Din's esoteric knowledge. ʿAbbasi recounted that once when he was visiting Radi al-Din, one of the latter's followers arrived saying that he had had a dream that he could not remember; Radi al-Din recounted the dream, in which the Prophet Muhammad foretold the man's death. The disciple's face paled and he nodded gravely—that had indeed been it. Not a month passed and the man died.[79] A governor who carried the weight of so many decisions on his shoulders would no doubt benefit from the marvelous deeds and epiphanies (*karamat wa mukashafat*) for which Radi al-Din was known.[80]

Yet Ayas Pasha also may have been after a more mundane form of support from Radi al-Din. The Ghazzi family commanded significant respect in Damascene circles; Radi al-Din's father had been one of the city's notables (*aʿyan*), and Radi al-Din was a trusted figure in the community whose life was reported on in local chronicles.[81] The latter married well—at least

75. Ayas Pasha's birth date is uncertain but according to one source was 1482. Parry, "Ayās Pasha."

76. This was Husayn al-Jabawi (d. 1519). Bakhit, *Ottoman Province*, 9, 181–2. Selim also visited the Sufi shaykh Muhammad Badakhshi, about whom see below in this chapter. For another example of a sultan visiting a Sufi shaykh, see Ṭaşköprīzāde, *Shaqaʾiq*, 55.

77. Ghazzī, *Kawākib*, 2: 125.

78. Najm al-Din continued, "he visited him in his house, trusting in him and seeking his blessings." Ghazzī, *Kawākib*, 2: 125.

79. Ghazzī, *Maṭāliʿ*, 142–3.

80. Ghazzī, *Maṭāliʿ*, 142; Ghazzī, *Kawākib*, 2: 6.

81. Ibn al-Ḥimṣī, *Ḥawādith*, 86; Ibn Ṭūlūn, *Mufākaha*, 1: 12, 21.

twice—and was a regular guest at the wedding festivities of other prominent local families.[82] It was thus no trifle when he threw his weight behind the new ruling elite.

One of the main ways Radi al-Din expressed his support for the new order was through poetic compositions. While some other scholars were using poetry to lampoon Ottoman leaders or to decry their disregard for religious tenets, Radi al-Din was using it to praise them for upholding these very tenets. His first poetic target was none other than the hapless chief judge Fenari. For him Radi al-Din composed an epigram of the sort that had been so popular in the Mamluk period.[83] The appeal of these poems derived from their personalized quality, with the final word of the final line—and therefore the poem's rhyme—reserved for the individual to whom it was dedicated. Radi al-Din's poem read:

> I like the Rumi gentlemen [*al-sāda al-arwām*]
> For upholding Islamic law and accepting it as their creed.
> If you ask which of them is the most pious [*al-ʿabbād*],
> It is the judge of Damascus Zeynelabidin.[84]

Ending on the judge's honorific title, which meant, "the ornament of the pious ones," the poem was a catchy and memorable endorsement of Fenari's devoutness. For Ayas Pasha, Radi al-Din composed a longer, more elaborate poem which ended:

> He who pleases [God], whose love for His Truth is sincere,
> I am pleased with whatever he asks from me and to it I do adhere.
> I trust in God in my heart and remain in good cheer,
> I quake not if enemies attack and feel no fear,
> For God acts with kindness and helps the poor man persevere.
> So it is with Ayas Pasha, the king's greatest vizier.[85]

Like Radi al-Din's poem for Fenari, this one too emphasized the Ottoman official's piety and divine sanction. Written on the occasion of the pasha's promotion to vizier shortly after he returned from Damascus to Istanbul, the poem probably aimed to advance Radi al-Din's interests first

82. Ibn Ṭūlūn, *Mufākaha*, 1: 12, 21, and 1:3, respectively. See also Shoshan, "Marital Regime," 10.

83. Talib, *Epigram*; Bauer, "Mutanabbī," 10–4.

84. Ghazzī, *Kawākib*, 1: 20.

85. Ghazzī, *Kawākib*, 2: 125.

and foremost, since such lines of verse were often repaid with tangible rewards.[86]

The new government stood to gain from such poetic dedications as well. Poetry served as an important and very visible form of publicity in the early modern Ottoman Empire. As one Egyptian historian reported in order to underline the popularity of a Rumi chief judge, "the poets of the lands of Syria, Egypt, and Rum praised him with poems that became famous, extolling him and expressing their gratitude toward him at great length."[87] In the highly literate circles of the Ottoman elite, poems circulated rapidly in writing, and indeed both of Radi al-Din's verses have come to us through biographical dictionaries.[88] Poems perhaps traveled even more quickly orally. Epigrams like those that Radi al-Din composed for Fenari were especially suited to this purpose, since they were short and unobtrusive when recited in conversation. They were also easy to memorize, acting as pithy jingles by which to remember great men. Even much longer poems, of the sort Radi al-Din wrote for Ayas Pasha, were often performed live. Authors of such poems often read them aloud to their dedicatees in private assemblies.[89] Friends or acolytes of the recipient might do so as well, even in his absence. Just how purposeful such efforts were can be seen from the statement of a later scholar who informed a leading official in a letter: "[I] always enhance the salons by mentioning you, and contribute nothing to discussions except that which has to do with you."[90]

Poems like those that Radi al-Din composed for Fenari and Ayas Pasha helped to buttress the legitimacy of the new government. Both of the poems advertised the virtues of the officials to whom they were dedicated, particularly their religious devotion, assuaging the doubts some had raised about the early occupiers. Notably, both poems were also highly personalized endorsements, since in both, Radi al-Din referred to himself in the first person singular. However the verses might have circulated, they

86. This had a long history. Gruendler, "Qaṣīda"; Gruendler, "Motif vs. Genre," esp. 76–83. Bauer observes that during the Mamluk period, praise poetry ceased to be directed at rulers alone and instead "became a medium for middle-class self-expression." Bauer, "Mutanabbī," 7.

87. This was with reference to Hasan Bey, about whom see Chapter 3. Tamīmī, *Ṭabaqāt*, 1: 381.

88. Adam Talib argues that the reception of shorter poetic forms occurred primarily in the context of silent reading. Talib, *Epigram*, 205.

89. For two cases in which provincial scholars recited odes for Ottoman judges in Damascus, see Ibn Ayyūb, *Rawḍ*, 251b; Būrīnī, *Tarājim*, 1: 68–71.

90. Ḥamawī, *Majmūʿa*, 30a. See also Ḥamawī, *Ḥādī*, 55. Kadiri Çelebi was said to be "mentioned in every salon and circle." ʿĀşıḳ Çelebi, *Meşâʿirü's-Şuʿarâ*, 1311.

signaled that at least one influential local figure welcomed the new order. Especially in the 1520s, when the Ottoman presence in the region was new and the memory of Ghazali's rebellion still fresh, such personal expressions of support must have had a stabilizing effect.

Praise was not the only way in which locals like Radi al-Din offered their assistance to the new government; many also used informal channels to give the Ottoman ruling elite counsel in matters of local governance. Even the sultan was not indifferent to the advice of respected locals, according to historians both in Istanbul and in Damascus. In Ramadan 1516, Sultan Selim sought out a Sufi shaykh at the Damascene Kallasa Mosque, sitting with him for over an hour. When Selim offered him financial support, the shaykh declined and advised the sultan to care for the people instead. That night, the sultan distributed the money intended for the shaykh to pious ascetics and to those who congregated outside the mosque door.[91] Though the account, written by a Damascene, may well have exaggerated the Sufi's influence, central sources highlighted Selim's reverence for the shaykh as well.[92] Ottoman functionaries knew that it was wise to heed the advice of locals—and to be seen as heeding their advice.

Governor Ayas Pasha was amenable to local input as well. When he arrested Taqi al-Din al-Qari, one of the scholars who claimed that Rumis had introduced heretical innovations, and stripped him of all his offices, another man interceded on the slanderer's behalf. In response to this pressure, Ayas Pasha reinstalled Qari in at least some of his positions.[93] Likewise, when Ayas Pasha announced that he would be collecting eight thousand dinars after the Ottoman conquest of Belgrade in the summer of 1521, another shaykh was said to have intervened. Having dreamed that the Prophet Muhammad had counseled against such a move, the shaykh rushed to the governor to beg him to reconsider. Recognizing his error, the pasha immediately agreed. As a show of gratitude, all the scholars and Sufis of Damascus held a celebratory reading of the Qurʾan at the Great Mosque in the governor's honor.[94]

In the years to follow, Damascene learned men would repeatedly intervene to stop Ottoman functionaries from what they saw as grave missteps,

91. The shaykh in question was Muhammad Badakhshi (also Muhammad al-Bilkhashi). Ibn Ṭūlūn, *Mufākaha*, 2: 36. See also Ṭaşköprīzāde, *Shaqāʾiq*, 357; Ghazzī, *Kawākib*, 1: 89–90; Bakhit, *Ottoman Province*, 10.

92. Ṭaşköprīzāde, *Shaqāʾiq*, 357.

93. Ibn Ṭūlūn, *Iʿlām*, 253–4.

94. Ibn Ṭūlūn, *Iʿlām*, 253–4. 10,000 dinars in Ibn al-Himsi's recounting. Ibn al-Ḥimṣī, *Ḥawādith*, 551.

often of a religious nature. In 1531, Qari, ever the agitator, banded together with a group of notables to stop an Ottoman governor from building a water basin (*birka*) in the city's Great Mosque in an unlawful manner.[95] A few decades later, a group that included Badr al-Din's son protested when an Ottoman military commander had a stone from the Kaʿba in Mecca installed in the wall of the mosque the latter was building in Damascus.[96] As irritating as such lobbying efforts may have been to Ottoman administrators, in the long run they helped to buttress the new political order by keeping officials informed of local sentiment and steering them away from actions that might have led to more unmanageable opposition.

Much of this influence occurred as locals cleverly exploited the ambiguities of the informal sphere. This can be seen in an incident that took place after Fenari was transferred to Aleppo. There, Fenari was again in the unenviable position of having to enforce the new marriage tax. When he got wind that one local jurist was brazenly ignoring the law, Fenari was outraged.[97] He sent a messenger to summon the man to his residence. "You dog! You fool! I'll have your hand cut off," Fenari roared when the scholar arrived. The scholar replied calmly, "I do nothing but seek to protect these lands through learning, and if that means having my hand cut off, then so be it"—a response that only incensed Fenari further. Fenari, to believe local accounts, would surely have made good on his threat had it not been for the rebel scholar's stratagem. Having anticipated such a scene when the judge's messenger first summoned him, the scholar had instructed another local notable to pay Fenari a visit so as to be at the judge's house when the scholar showed up. In the presence of this esteemed member of the community, so the scholar hoped, Fenari would not dare punish him too harshly. The trick worked. Fenari was forced to defer his punishment, instead temporarily detaining the scholar at the house of the court summons officer. After the rebellious scholar had been led away, the notable asked Fenari, "my Lord, do you really want to do something that would bring the whole community to your door in protest? That seems like a very bad idea!" When Fenari remained obstinate, the notable fetched another grandee with close relations to the judge. Together, the two were finally able to convince Fenari to pardon the shaykh.[98] This anecdote both

95. Ghazzī, *Kawākib*, 2: 13.

96. This was Ghazzī's son Ahmad (d. 1576). Ibn Ayyūb, *Kitāb*, 15–6.

97. The scholar in question was called Ibn al-Suyufi (d. 1519). The following is from Ibn al-Ḥanbalī, *Durr*, 1: 649–50.

98. Najm al-Din al-Ghazzi claims that the jurist "died broken-hearted" as a result of this incident, but Ibn al-Hanbali, who was the jurist's contemporary and whose uncle was

reveals the power of Ottoman administrators and also indicates the way in which locals could exploit the more informal aspects of imperial governance to protect one another and to voice their concerns.

In the early decades of the Ottoman presence in Damascus, informal relationships between imperial officials and provincial elites played a significant role in entrenching Ottoman rule. Moving away from a focus on formal bureaucratic structures affords a more capacious understanding of the mechanisms by which new provinces were incorporated. For Ottomans, these relationships provided legitimacy, information, and insight into the local perspective. For locals, they could yield appointments, lower tax burdens, or, in some cases, the preservation of a limb. As repeated references to local influence in Syrian biographies and chronicles suggest, such relationships also constituted a source of pride, allowing provincial elites to buy into Ottoman governance.

Encounters in Istanbul

In 1529, Radi al-Din died. Badr al-Din, now thirty, joined a crowd of mourners at the Great Mosque of Damascus to mark his father's passing.[99] But there was little time to grieve. Misery loves company, and new trials awaited the living. According to Ghazzi, it was a time when "springs ran dry, supporters bid goodbye, the trusted became traitors, the honest became haters, the just became few, the compassionate disappeared from view, helpers were untrue, brothers turned away, and friends went astray."[100] He was too discreet to divulge the details, but at issue was almost certainly some sort of professional setback—possibly a teaching position snatched away from him by an old friend.[101] Ghazzi had no choice but to seek redress in the city that was now his capital. He took leave of his friends and weeping children and set out for Istanbul.

Badr al-Din recorded his journey in his 1534 travelogue *Full Moon Rising: Waystations to Rum (Al-Matali*ʿ *al-badriyya fi al-manazil*

involved in the affair, mentions only that he died shortly thereafter. Ghazzī, *Kawākib*, 1: 183; Ibn al-Ḥanbalī, *Durr*, 1: 650.

99. Ghazzī, *Kawākib*, 2: 6.

100. Ghazzī, *Maṭāli*ʿ, 22.

101. Ghazzī, *Maṭāli*ʿ, 134–5. Elger speculates that the reason for Ghazzi's departure was his dispute with Muhammad al-Iji (d. 1577), who wrested from Ghazzi his position at al-Shamiyya al-Kubra Madrasa in Damascus. Elger, *Glaube*, 23–4; Ibn al-Ḥanbalī, *Durr*, 2: 438; Ghazzī, *Kawākib*, 3: 37.

al-rumiyya).[102] However, contrary to what we might expect from reading the accounts of European travelers, Ghazzi only rarely turned his attention to architecture or ethnography. He did visit and describe the Hagia Sophia, that patient spectator of human vanity. He groped to capture the building in words, marveling that its structure was too large for the eye to behold, the pillars more numerous than those of Iram, the mythical city mentioned in the Qurʾan. And yet, the pillars that ultimately interested Ghazzi were not those of the church-turned-mosque, or, for that matter, any other of the buildings erected almost daily on Istanbul's streets. What interested Ghazzi were the human monuments of the Ottoman capital.[103]

The groundwork for Ghazzi's trip had been laid by his father, who bequeathed to his son the social network that he had worked so hard to build. When Badr al-Din was in his early teens, Radi al-Din had brought him along on visits to Sufi shaykhs in Cairo, and it stands to reason that these sorts of joint visits continued in Damascus.[104] Indeed, in both Arab and Turcophone lands, male children were often present at the gatherings of their fathers. One Mamluk-era etiquette manual caricatured the obnoxious guest who turned up at a private assembly only to make fun of the host's sons.[105] Such impropriety notwithstanding, the point of the practice was to impart trusted contacts to the next generation.

One of the most important of these contacts that Ghazzi inherited from his father was ʿAbd al-Rahim al-ʿAbbasi. While the Ghazzis were

102. There are a number of extant versions of Ghazzi's travel account. The original autograph copy is at the British Library (Or. 3621). Istanbul's Süleymaniye Library has another version copied in 1632/3 (1042) by ʿAbd al-Latif al-Shafiʿi (MS Fazıl Ahmed Paşa 1390). A fragment of the account is at Princeton University (Garrett MS 610Y). Another version, copied by Khalil al-Ikhnaʿi and dated 1656 (1066) exists in Moscow at the Russian Academy of Sciences (MS B799). I was not able to consult the latter, and have mostly relied on the critical edition prepared by al-Mahdi ʿId al-Rawadiyya. Ghazzi's account is discussed at length in Elger, *Glaube*, chapter 1.

103. This was standard in the Ottoman travel literature of the period. Bray, "New Worlds"; Blackburn in Nahrawālī, *Journey*, xvii–xxi. An illustrated travel account from the early seventeenth century depicts meetings with local officials as well. Taner, *Caught in a Whirlwind*, esp. 64–6.

104. Ghazzī, *Maṭāliʿ*, 62; Ghazzī, *Kawākib*, 3: 4. A marginal note in *The Sweet-Smelling Garden* claims that the ancestor of the annotator studied with Radi al-Din in the presence of Badr al-Din, although it is not clear how old the latter was at the time. Ibn Ayyūb, *Rawḍ*, 241a.

105. The said passage is from the etiquette manual of Yahya al-Jazzar (d. 1270 or 1281) and is quoted in the later anthology of Shihab al-Din al-Ibshihi (d. 1446). Lewicka, *Food*, 413. For multigenerational gatherings in Arab lands, see Gharaibeh, "Brokerage," esp. 238–51; Akkach, *Nabulusi*, 25–7. For Anatolia, see Ṭaşköprīzāde, *Shaqāʾiq*, 95, 126; İpekten, *Edebî muhitler*, 233; Fleischer, *Bureaucrat*, 22–3.

adjusting their lives to the new order in Damascus, the Cairo-born scholar and one-time devotee of Radi al-Din was busy making Istanbul his home. Having sought refuge at the court of Bayezid II in the late 1490s, ʿAbbasi had returned to Cairo as soon as he could, as we saw in Chapter 1. When the Mamluks fell, ʿAbbasi lost no time in making good on his ties to Ottoman royal circles in order to return to the capital for good. No one seemed to hold a grudge for the fact that he had refused the professorship Bayezid had offered him. According to one account, ʿAbbasi traveled from Cairo to Istanbul with the entourage of Bayezid's son Selim, sporting Ottoman garb.[106] He was on such intimate terms with Selim, so ʿAbbasi claimed, that he had a premonition of the sultan's death before it was announced publicly in 1520.[107] ʿAbbasi's salary was more concrete evidence of his continued favor with the dynasty, since at more than 200 akçes per day, it was about three times the amount awarded to the best-paid professors of the period.[108] ʿAbbasi's ties to the House of Osman continued under Selim's successor Süleyman (r. 1520–66), whom he accompanied on his military expedition to Rhodes in 1522 and at various imperial festivities.

Arriving in Istanbul, ʿAbbasi immediately put his Arabic literary skills to work in service of the imperial household. He wrote a victory announcement (*fathname*) in honor of the Rhodes conquest.[109] In 1530, when Süleyman's sons were circumcised with great pomp, ʿAbbasi commemorated the event with an account both of the religious significance of circumcision—based in large part on prophetic hadiths—and of the entertainments and feasts that accompanied it. The account was prepared for the imperial library and illuminated in a style resembling works prepared in the Mamluk court, perhaps by artisans relocated from Cairo (see figure 2.1).[110] Nine years later, when Süleyman's daughter Mihrimah was married to the the vizier Rüstem Pasha, ʿAbbasi was again present, noting details from the menu that he would put to paper as well.[111]

106. Ibn Ṭūlūn, *Mufākaha*, 2: 74.

107. Ghazzī, *Kawākib*, 2: 163.

108. Ṭaşköprīzāde, *Shaqāʾiq*, 411.

109. Ghazzī, *Kawākib*, 2: 163; Heinrichs, "al-ʿAbbāsī," 19. He also seems to have written a history of Selim's reign, but that is no longer extant. Markiewicz, *Kingship*, 144.

110. ʿAbbāsī entitled the work *Clusters of Pearls: A History of the Virtue of Circumcision* (*Kitab shamarikh al-juman fi tarikh sharif al-khitan*). The work was completed on July 16, 1530 (23 Dhu'l Qaʿda 936). ʿAbbāsī, *Kitāb*, 33a. Compare with the *İskendername* of Ahmedi prepared in Cairo in 1467–8. Atıl, "Mamluk Painting," 162. For the circumcision festival, see Şahin, "Staging an Empire."

111. Khafājī, *Rayḥāna*, 242. ʿAbbasi's *The Intimacy of Souls at the Wedding of Joys* (*Uns al-arwah bi-ʿurs al-afrah*) celebrated the 1539 marriage. ʿAbbasi, "Uns." The work has great

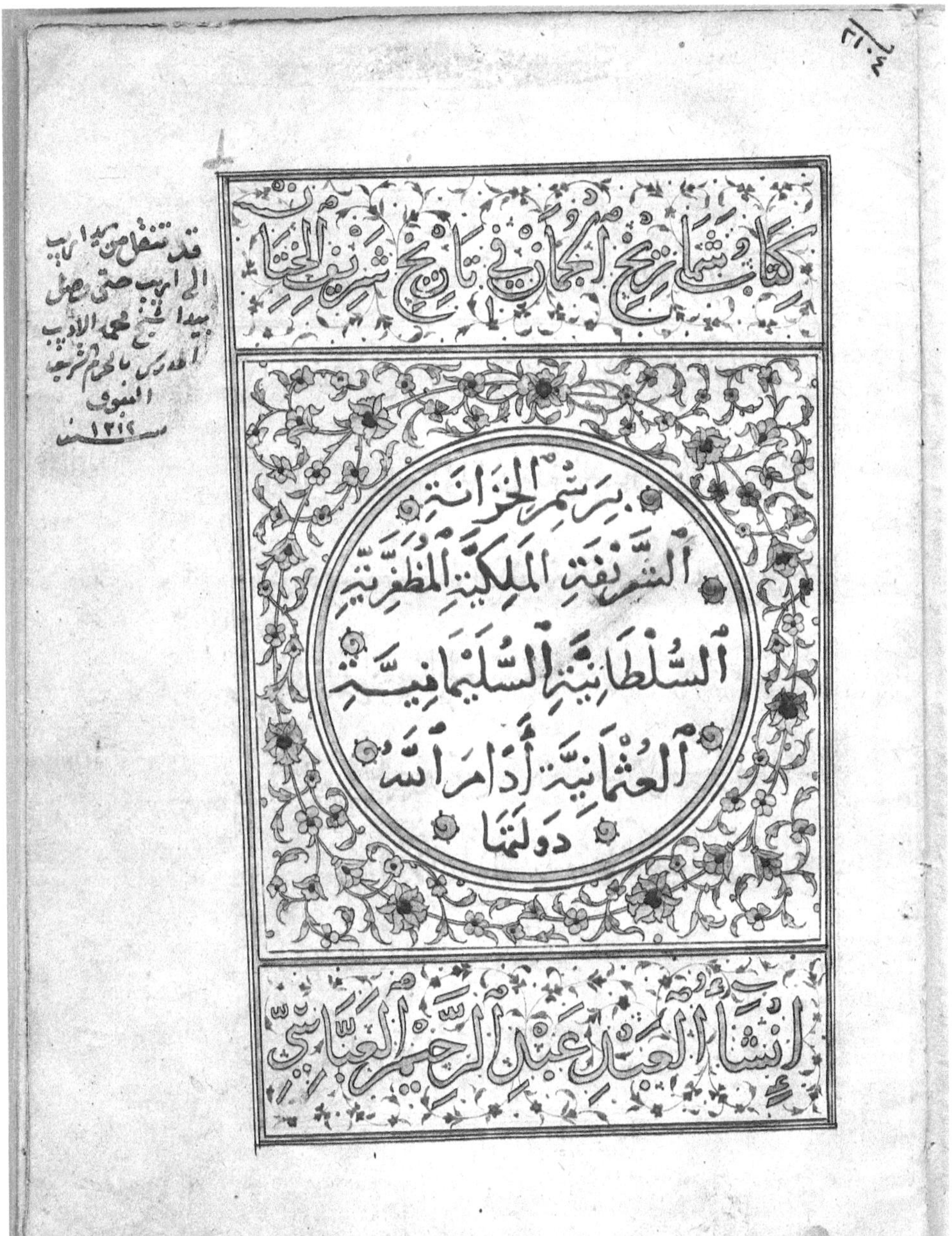

FIGURE 2.1. The illuminated heading of ʿAbd al-Rahim al-ʿAbbasi's *Clusters of Pearls: A History of the Virtue of Circumcision* (*Kitab shamarikh al-juman fi tarikh sharif al-khitan*) (1530). The text reads, "written for the honorable and victorious royal library of the Ottoman Sultan Süleyman, may God perpetuate his rule." (Reproduced by permission from the Directorate of the Turkish Institution for Manuscripts, Süleymaniye Library Istanbul, MS Yazma Bağışlar 3801, 1a.)

Not just sultans, but also the wider imperial elite received ʿAbbasi warmly. "The learned men [of Anatolia] honored him for the rare qualities they found in him," an otherwise choleric Cairene historian later reported.[112] ʿAbbasi enjoyed literary exchanges with the great scholar Ebu's-Suʿud Efendi (d. 1574), who would go on to serve Süleyman as chief jurisconsult (*şeyhülislam*).[113] He formed a friendship with the poet Baki (d. 1600), favored companion of the same sultan (see figure 0.1).[114] Like Radi al-Din, ʿAbbasi used Arabic verse to strengthen these budding relationships; he composed praise poems for Saʿdi Çelebi (d. 1539), who served as the chief judge of Istanbul for nearly a decade from late 1523.[115] Contemporaries in Istanbul valued ʿAbbasi not only for his writings but also for his conversational skills, describing him as "pleasant in conversation, beautiful in speech, unusual in his anecdotes, humble and modest, well-bred and sharp-minded."[116]

In settling in the Ottoman capital, ʿAbbasi was exceptional among the newly incorporated Arab population. Although it has been claimed that Arab bureaucrats flooded the Ottoman capital in the wake of the conquest, irreversibly changing Ottoman administration, there is little evidence to that effect.[117] Selim did, as we have seen, relocate a large group of administrators and artisans to Istanbul, but they were later allowed to return home.[118] Taşköprizade's mid-century biographical dictionary of scholars affiliated with the Ottoman dynasty records only one scholar of Arab origin under Süleyman's reign, Ibrahim al-Halabi (d. 1549), a luminary from Aleppo.[119] Arabs did indeed begin to flock to the Ottoman capital. Many if not most members of Ghazzi's social circle in Damascus went at one time or another, including—to name just a few—Ibn al-Furfur, the Shafiʿi judge and family friend; ʿAlaʾ al-Din al-Shafiʿi (d. 1563), Ghazzi's student and later opponent; and Abu al-Fath al-Maliki (d. 1567/8), a fellow

overlap with his *Nathr al-durr al-thamin fi ʿurs mawlana Jaʿfar al-Amin*. ʿAbbasi, *Nathr*. Copies of both are preserved in the Süleymaniye Library.

112. Khafājī, *Rayḥāna*, 242.

113. Heinrichs, "al-ʿAbbāsī," 20; Kātib Çelebi, *Ẓunūn*, 2: 1919.

114. Khafājī, *Rayḥāna*, 242. He also gave literary inspiration to the scholar İdris Bidlisi. Markiewicz, *Kingship*, 144.

115. Ghazzī, *Kawākib*, 2: 237. Saʿdi Çelebi occupied the position from late 1523 to c. 1533. Repp, *The Müfti of Istanbul*, 241. For other biographies, see Ghazzī, *Maṭāliʿ*, 267; Ṭaşköprīzāde, *Shaqāʾiq*, 443–5; ʿĀşık Çelebi, *Meşâʿirü's-Şuʿara'*, 983–7.

116. Ṭaşköprīzāde, *Shaqāʾiq*, 412.

117. Shaw, *History*, 85; Lowry, *Ottoman Realities*, 175.

118. Şahin, *Empire*, 45.

119. Ökten, "Scholars and Mobility," 60. For Ibrahim al-Halabi, see Ṭaşköprīzāde, *Shaqāʾiq*, 499–500; Kaplan, "Polemicist."

Damascene scholar and litterateur.[120] However, these trips usually lasted a few months or at most a year, and aimed at securing a future not at the Ottoman center but rather in the Arab provinces.

Part of the reason many Arabs did not settle in Istanbul permanently is that they were not usually offered jobs there. In the previous century, as we saw in Chapter 1, scholars trained outside of Anatolia had been invited to occupy powerful positions like chief mufti or princely tutor. However, as we also saw, as early as the mid fifteenth century, the Ottoman scholarly and administrative establishment began to become more insular, with those trained within the Ottoman system increasingly given preference over those from the outside. ʿAbbasi's own experience fits squarely into this development; having been offered a teaching post on his first trip to Istanbul at the turn of the sixteenth century, he now received a sinecure without any official appointment.

Despite not occupying an official position, ʿAbbasi had an important role to play. As a well-connected Arab who had the ear of Ottoman officialdom, he served as an intermediary for the growing number of Arab visitors hoping to achieve something in the capital. Ghazzi was one such visitor. Though ʿAbbasi's initial allegiance was to Ghazzi's father, no doubt he had had the chance to meet Badr al-Din as well, whether during the five years the family spent in Cairo, or, more recently, on his way to Istanbul, when ʿAbbasi stayed at the Ghazzi residence while Selim wintered in Damascus.[121] Now it was time for ʿAbbasi to return the favor. No sooner had Ghazzi arrived in Üsküdar, the town across from Istanbul on the Asian side of the Bosphorus, than he received a note from ʿAbbasi, with an apology that he could not welcome him personally due to a severe fever.[122] When Ghazzi crossed the Bosphorus and stepped onto the dock in Istanbul, he was greeted by the dockman, whom ʿAbbasi had informed of his arrival.[123] Ghazzi would go on to spend several months in an apartment in ʿAbbasi's residence. The fact that he stayed with an old family friend from Damascus did not mean that the young traveler isolated himself from Istanbul society, though. To the contrary, the relationships that ʿAbbasi had built in the years since his arrival in Istanbul were an important resource for the young Ghazzi. Rising star that Ghazzi may have been

120. See, respectively, Ibn Ṭūlūn, *Quḍāt*, 309; Ghazzī, *Kawākib*, 3: 184; and Ibn Ayyūb, *Kitāb*, 80–1. For other examples, see Chapter 6 of this book as well as Ibn Ayyūb, *Kitāb*, 62–3; Ghazzī, *Kawākib*, 2: 136; 3:180–1; Winter, *Society and Religion*, 1, 20, 22.

121. Ibn Ṭūlūn, *Mufākaha*, 2: 74.

122. Ghazzī, *Maṭāliʿ*, 118.

123. Ghazzī, *Maṭāliʿ*, 120–1.

in the Syrian lands, to most men in the capital, he was not a known entity. As his son later commented, ʿAbbasi "made [Ghazzi's] standing in the sciences known to the most important scholars and vouched for him."[124]

Thanks in large part to the collective efforts of ʿAbbasi and Radi al-Din, Ghazzi was quickly catapulted into the upper echelons of the Ottoman imperial elite. One of the first people Ghazzi visited was Hacı Çelebi Müʾeyyedzade, who had met with Radi al-Din in Damascus on his way to the hajj.[125] Ghazzi called on him on his first full day in the city.[126] By this time, Hacı Çelebi was an elderly man, frail and with difficulties walking. Nonetheless, he welcomed Ghazzi affectionately and embraced him like an old friend. He began with warm words for Ghazzi's deceased father, but there was more to talk about as the men "roamed and roved in the gardens of companionship." Ghazzi praised his host's conviviality: "I had no better reunion and no finer communion, no clearer conversation and no nicer disputation."[127] Sufism continued to act as a binding element, and Ghazzi may well have participated in Hacı's devotional sessions for the remembrance of God (*dhikr*). Ghazzi mentioned the "special prayers and ritual remembrances [*awrād wa adhkār*] with which he [Hacı] attracts people to his gatherings, and spiritual states and esoteric knowledge that he bestows on those gathering."[128]

Through Hacı, Ghazzi was introduced to a number of other influential figures. Hacı helped him reconnect with the former's nephew, who had accompanied him to the Ghazzis in Damascus, and introduced him to several of Hacı's own sons.[129] Also in Hacı's presence, Ghazzi made the acquaintance of one Şemseddin Mehmed Şemsi Çelebi, a professor at one of the prestigious eight madrasas in the mosque complex of Mehmed II (*sahn-ı seman*).[130] Finally, it may well have been through Hacı Çelebi that Ghazzi was introduced to the legendary scholar Ebu's-Suʿud. Ebu's-Suʿud was Hacı Çelebi's brother-in-law and, at the time of Ghazzi's visit, not yet the all-powerful chief mufti that he would later become; he was still teaching at one of the eight madrasas. Ghazzi and Ebu's-Suʿud, both of whom took a keen interest in Qurʾanic exegesis, had a discussion on the meaning of a Qurʾanic verse. "Between us there was affection and a

124. Ghazzī, *Kawākib*, 2: 163.

125. Ghazzī, *Maṭāliʿ*, 129. ʿAbbasi had relations with the family as well, as was seen in Chapter 1.

126. Ghazzī, *Maṭāliʿ*, 128.

127. Ghazzī, *Maṭāliʿ*, 129.

128. Ghazzī, *Maṭāliʿ*, 128.

129. Ghazzī, *Maṭāliʿ*, 265–6.

130. Ghazzī, *Maṭāliʿ*, 268.

friendly connection. He treated me with great civility and venerated me immensely," Ghazzi explained.[131]

Ghazzi's socializing in the Ottoman capital did not end there. Likely through ʿAbbasi, Ghazzi was introduced to Saʿdi Çelebi, the influential chief judge of Istanbul (see figure 2.2).[132] Saʿdi was ʿAbbasi's close friend and supporter; not only did ʿAbbasi write a number of praise poems for him, as we saw, he also dedicated to him one of his most popular works.[133] Saʿdi was known to have a special interest in Arab scholars. Even before the Ottoman conquest, he had studied with some eminent Cairene professors; after it, Saʿdi cultivated a close relationship with Halabi, the Aleppine migrant, whom he was said to consult on legal matters.[134] ʿAbbasi acknowledged Saʿdi's openness when he referred to his home as "the focal point [*qibla*] of aspirants, the stopping place of travelers, the meeting place of the literati, the platform of poetic illuminati."[135] This hospitality extended to Ghazzi as well, whose encounter with Saʿdi left him full of admiration for his piety and learning. "No scholar in Rum," said Ghazzi, "could be compared with him without being overshadowed by him."[136] Ghazzi summed up his account of meeting the judge with a fourteenth-century Arabic poem:

> He met me a happy and radiant creature,
> The sincerity of his joy caused his contented nature.[137]

Ghazzi's socializing continued when he was forced to flee to nearby Izmit following an outbreak of the plague in Istanbul. There, he was welcomed in person by the chief judge of the city, who later sent him fruits and meats along with some legal riddles (*alghaz fiqhiyya*) that he had been unable to solve (Ghazzi promptly solved them and sent them

131. Ghazzī, *Maṭāliʿ*, 268. Ebu's-Suʿud taught at one of Mehmed II's eight madrasas from 1527/8 to 1533. Repp, *The Müfti of Istanbul*, 276–7.

132. Ghazzī, *Maṭāliʿ*, 267; Ghazzī, *Kawākib*, 2: 237.

133. Namely, *The Frequented Places for Clarification*, first finished in Cairo. ʿAbbāsī, *Maʿāhid*, 2a–3a; Ghazzī, *Kawākib*, 2: 237. For this work, see Chapter 1, note 39. ʿAbbasi also presented to Saʿdi a book in the *maqama* genre, which presented fictional narratives in ornate rhymed prose. ʿAbbasi, *Maqāmāt*. For the genre, see Allen, *Arabic Literature*, 162–7.

134. Ghazzī, *Kawākib*, 2: 77. Saʿdi had been licensed to transmit hadith from leading scholars of the late Mamluk period. Pfeifer, "Hadith Culture," 45. It has been argued that Halabi influenced Saʿdi's criticisms of Ibn ʿArabi. Kaplan, "Polemicist," esp. 75–81.

135. ʿAbbāsī, *Maʿāhid*, 2b.

136. Ghazzī, *Maṭāliʿ*, 267.

137. Ghazzī, *Maṭāliʿ*, 267. The same poem had previously been cited in the travel account of the Andalusian traveler Khalid al-Balawi (d. after 1354), from which Ghazzi often took citations. Rawāḍiyya, *Maṭāliʿ*, 13–4; Elger, *Glaube*, 52–64.

FIGURE 2.2. Sa'di Çelebi (center right) meets with another scholar in a room lined with books. From 'Aşık Çelebi, *Meşa'irü's-şu'ara'* (c. 1600). (Reproduced by permission from the Directorate of the Turkish Institution for Manuscripts, Millet Library Istanbul, MS Ali Emiri Tarih 772, 210a.)

back).[138] Ghazzi was put up in a spacious room at the residence of Kassabzade Mehmed, a young scholar at the beginning of his career who took advantage of the presence of such a learned guest in his home to study several works with him (later, when Ghazzi was back in Istanbul and

138. Ghazzī, *Maṭāli'*, 270. For legal riddles, see Saba, *Harmonizing Similarities*, chapter 4.

Kassabzade chanced to visit the capital city, the two met again).[139] The days passed quickly with receptions and promenades as locals lined up to catch a glimpse of the visitor: "the notables of the city rushed to see me, greeting me, praying for me and requesting my prayers, reassuring me, extolling me, venerating me, and honoring me. I lived blissfully and free of sorrow and worry."[140]

Throughout his time in and around the capital, Ghazzi, like his father and ʿAbbasi before him, used poetry to curry favor with some of the empire's most powerful players. The capital's chief judge Saʿdi Çelebi was one of the recipients of Ghazzi's poetic gifts. Ghazzi composed the following epigram for him, ending, as was usual, with a play on Saʿdi's name:

The traits of Saʿdi are like the noon sun,
    From near and far they shine visibly.
If I made a poem to praise him,
    I would do so happily [*fī saʿdī*].[141]

It is unclear whether this poem was first presented to the judge orally or in writing. Nonetheless, its afterlife suggests how meaningful it must have been to its recipient: allegedly, Saʿdi had it inscribed on the wall of his reception hall.[142] Decorating reception areas with text was not uncommon in Ottoman lands, as can be seen in the Aleppo chamber dating to the first years of the seventeenth century (see figure 2.3).[143] Royal garden pavilions, favored settings for outdoor gatherings, could likewise contain poetic inscriptions.[144] Saʿdi's decision to record Ghazzi's poem in this way was no small honor, and contemporaries viewed it as such. Not only did a Damascene scholar who traveled to Istanbul return home with news of the inscription, but Ghazzi's son Najm al-Din mentioned its final destination in his biographical compendium.[145] Ghazzi had left his mark on his new capital.

139. Ghazzī, *Maṭāliʿ*, 271.

140. Ghazzī, *Maṭāliʿ*, 218.

141. Ghazzī, *Kawākib*, 2: 237.

142. Ghazzī, *Kawākib*, 2: 237. Najm al-Din states that the poem was "written" on the wall (*maktūban fī jidār majlis al-mawlā Saʿdī*), so it is also possible that it had the character of graffiti, perhaps inscribed by Ghazzi himself. Presumably, this, too, could only have been done with Saʿdi's permission.

143. Heyberger, "Inschriften"; Ott, "Wer sich fürchtet." See also Abou-Khatwa, "An Ode to Remember," 46.

144. Necipoğlu, "Garden Culture," 227.

145. Ghazzī, *Kawākib*, 2: 237.

FIGURE 2.3. Wall paneling in the Aleppo Chamber (c. 1600–1). The wood paneling of this reception hall once owned by a Christian merchant features dozens of inscriptions. Though many of them are of a religious character, they preserve a strategic ambiguity such that both Christians and Muslims would have felt at ease in the space. Museum für Islamische Kunst, Berlin. (Reproduced by permission. Azoor Photo/Alamy Stock Photo.)

For most of Ghazzi's encounters in Istanbul, Ghazzi is our sole source, with the occasional supplement from his ever-proud son. It is thus difficult, if not downright impossible, to verify the exact nature of his interactions. Were his meetings with Rumi elites hampered by divergences in literary taste or, worse still, breaches of etiquette? Misunderstandings were common in salons, as subsequent chapters will show. What is significant, then, is Ghazzi's reluctance to record such misunderstandings. *Full Moon Rising* was emphatically not about diversity—Ghazzi made next to no mention of any cultural differences between him and his hosts, and remarkably, no suggestion that they otherwise would have conversed in Turkish. Put one way, Ghazzi was fundamentally Arabocentric, willfully obscuring divergences from what he saw as the cultural norm. Put another, he worked hard to emphasize the commensurability of Arab and Rumi social worlds. Salons, Ghazzi implicitly argued, transcended ethnic differences and allowed all educated Muslim men to meet on common ground.

Ghazzi Gets a Job

As enjoyable as Ghazzi's interactions with scholars in the capital were, he had gone to Istanbul to secure a teaching appointment, and lost no time in arranging the kinds of meetings that would help him achieve his goal. On his first Friday in the city, just a few days after he arrived, Ghazzi went to visit his father's old friend Ayas Pasha. In many ways, his meetings with Ayas Pasha resembled those he had with countless others, filled with pleasantries and intellectual exchanges. Yet the stakes were different. Ayas Pasha was a vizier.[146] When Ghazzi's father met Ayas Pasha, he had done so as a host, a local, and an elder; Ghazzi junior now met the giant as a young visitor in need of a job.

The two families had exchanged letters during the eight years since Ayas Pasha's time in Damascus. Though this meant the pasha may have already known of Ghazzi's visit, Hacı Çelebi had also sent a courier to notify him that the young man had arrived.[147] The vizier responded by inviting Ghazzi to his orchard in the bucolic region of Fındıklı on the outskirts of Galata. [148] As a sign of respect, Ayas Pasha met his guest in front of his villa rather than simply waiting inside, greeting Ghazzi with "happiness and joy." "Each of us," recounted Ghazzi, "hastened toward the other as in a race, shaking hands and touching and clutching one another in an embrace, greeting one another with the sweetest salutations and showing affection for one another with the friendliest affirmations."[149] Ayas Pasha probably ushered Ghazzi to a poolside pavilion of the sort common in the summer houses of the rich.[150] Settling down to talk, Ayas Pasha steered the conversation, as was proper for a host and a man of his station. He offered his condolences for the death of Ghazzi's father and inquired about the people of Damascus. He asked where Ghazzi was staying, and, hearing that ʿAbbasi had prepared some living quarters for him, protested that Ghazzi should have stayed with him instead. Finally, Ayas Pasha asked whether there was anything else he could do for him, and it was probably then that Ghazzi explained what he hoped to achieve in the city. All the while, Ghazzi wrote, the vizier "exuded a humility and

146. Ghazzī, *Maṭāliʿ*, 129.

147. Ghazzī, *Maṭāliʿ*, 129.

148. Ghazzī, *Maṭāliʿ*, 129; for Ayas Pasha's garden, see Orhunlu, "Fındıklı," 115–6; Necipoğlu, "Garden Culture," 50n50.

149. The following is from Ghazzī, *Maṭāliʿ*, 129–31; quotation at 131.

150. Necipoğlu, "Garden Culture," 39–40, 44, 50n50.

friendliness for which there are no words and with which he did not treat anyone else."[151]

Not long after this first meeting, Ayas Pasha received Ghazzi again, this time in his residence inside the city walls. Again, the pasha "went to great lengths in his hospitality and sincerity, and showed immense joy and gaiety," as Ghazzi recorded in his travel account.[152] This time, Ghazzi brought several gifts with him: a fine crystal rosary, a magnificent Qur᾽an penned by the famous calligrapher Ibn al-Bawwab (d. 1022), and a copy of "The Mantle Ode" (*Qasidat al-burda*), a praise poem to the Prophet Muhammad written by the thirteenth-century Egyptian poet Muhammad al-Busiri (d. mid-1290s).[153] Ayas Pasha accepted the gifts enthusiastically, and rightly so, since the praise poem was immensely popular in Ottoman lands and the Qur᾽an extraordinarily precious.[154]

Ayas Pasha read some lines from the Qur᾽an, and then perused the ode, with which he must have been familiar.[155] Here and there, he read a few passages, asking Ghazzi about their meaning. Finally, he asked him whether the last two chapters of the Qur᾽an (*al-mu*ʿ*awwidhatan*) were really part of the holy text. Ghazzi answered that they were, explaining that although one of the earliest authorities on the Qur᾽an—Ibn Masʿud (d. 652/3)—had excluded the two verses, other scholars had firmly placed them within the revelation to Muhammad, including the Abbasid-era linguist Ibn Qutayba (d. 889) and the famous late Mamluk Qur᾽an commentator Ibn Hajar (d. 1449).[156]

Ayas Pasha apparently enjoyed these explanations, for he asked Ghazzi to write them down. Within a short time, Ghazzi finished a commentary on the last two chapters of the Qur᾽an, as well as two other new works—a treatise on the Throne Verse of the Qur᾽an (*Tafsir ayat al-kursi*) and a commentary on "The Mantle Ode."[157] The commentary on the ode

151. Ghazzī, *Maṭāli*ʿ, 131. Ayas Pasha also seems to have cultivated good relations with the Meccan Nahrawali family, since Qutb al-Din al-Nahrawali visited him in Istanbul in 1536–7 and brought news of his father as well. Nahrawālī, *Kitāb*, 306.

152. The following is from Ghazzī, *Maṭāli*ʿ, 131–2; quotation at 131.

153. For more on Busiri's "Mantle Ode," see Stetkevych, *The Mantle Odes*. Stetkyevych relies heavily on Ghazzi's commentary for her own understanding of the *Burda*.

154. The work of Ibn al-Bawwab began fetching high prices as early as the thirteenth century. Rice, *Ibn al-Bawwāb*, 81–2.

155. Already in the late fifteenth century there were several copies of "The Mantle Ode" in the Topkapı Palace library, and according to a late sixteenth-century treasury book, it ranked amongst the works studied by palace trainees. Qutbuddin, "Arabic Philology," 609; Fetvaci, *History*, 31.

156. Ghazzī, *Maṭāli*ʿ, 131–2. For these verses, see Bearman et al., "al-Muʿawwidhatāni."

157. For the Throne Verse, Q2:255. Ghazzī, *Maṭāli*ʿ, 132.

was heavily indebted to a work by the great Cairene scholar Zakariyya al-Ansari (d. 1520), one of Ghazzi's teachers, and Ghazzi drew many of his explanations from his teacher word-for-word. Breaking the ode into short passages, Ghazzi explained how difficult words should be vocalized and glossed the meaning of each line.[158] He dedicated the book to the pasha, writing in the opening lines, "when he kindly took me under his wing, and secured me all that I had been desiring, I was revived and life again became sweet, and my homesickness and uncertainty began to retreat."[159]

Ayas Pasha went about fulfilling his end of the bargain with equal speed. He spoke on Ghazzi's behalf to Kadiri Çelebi (d. c. 1551), the military judge of Anatolia (see figure 2.4).[160] There were two military judges (*kadıasker*), one for Anatolia, and one for Rumelia, and they were some of the most powerful men in the empire. Both were permanent members of the imperial council and charged with making appointments to all judgeships and many teaching positions in the lands under their jurisdiction—which in Kadiri's case included the Arab provinces.[161] Kadiri's support would thus be crucial when Ghazzi's case was reviewed by the council. Following Ayas Pasha's endorsement, Ghazzi went to introduce himself personally to Kadiri. Again, according to the traveler, "companionship, friendship, and love" developed between the two men, and the judge promised he would devote himself to Ghazzi's cause.[162]

As an extra precaution, Ghazzi then met with the chief military judge of Rumelia, Fenarizade Muhyiddin Çelebi (d. 1548). Here, too, Ghazzi's

158. There are several extant manuscripts of *The Essence of Commentary on* "The Mantle Ode" (*al-Zubda fi sharh al-Burda*), including (but not limited to): Süleymaniye Library, MS Laleli 3656, 201a–244b; Manisa İl Halk Kütüphanesi, MS 5256, 1b–7a; Princeton University Library, Garrett MS 1148H, 142a–171b; and the private manuscript of ʿUmar Musa Basha, used in preparation for his published edition. The work was known and copied well into the seventeenth century. Ibn al-Ḥanbalī, *Durr*, 2: 437–8; Kātib Çelebi, *Ẓunūn*, 2: 1336. Ghazzi himself described the treatise as one which "explains [the poem's] its expressions, facilitates memorization, reveals its mysteries, and clarifies that which is puzzling." Ghazzī, "Zubda," 201b; Ghazzī, *Zubda*, 39.

159. Ghazzī, "Zubda," 201b; Ghazzī, *Zubda*, 39. Ayas would go on to gain a reputation for stinginess toward the literati, since he ceased the more regular payments that had previously been the norm. ʿĀşıḳ Çelebi, *Meşâʿirü's-Şuʿarâ*, 377–8; Andrews and Kalpaklı, *The Age of Beloveds*, 325–6.

160. Ghazzī, *Maṭāliʿ*, 132–3. Kadiri Çelebi (a.k.a. Abdülkadir Hamidi Çelebi, a.k.a. Kadri) served as chief military judge of Anatolia from c. 1524–37, becoming chief mufti in 1542. For biographies, see Ṭaşköprīzāde, *Shaqāʾiq*, 443; ʿĀşıḳ Çelebi, *Meşâʿirü's-Şuʿarâ*, 1311–28; ʿAṭāʾī, *Ḥadāʾiḳ*, 164; İpşirli, "Abdülkadir Hamîdî Çelebi," 240; Repp, *The Müfti of Istanbul*, 256–63.

161. Atçıl, "Route," 503; İpşirli, "Kazasker"; İnalcık, "State, Sovereignty and Law," 75.

162. Ghazzī, *Maṭāliʿ*, 133.

FIGURE 2.4. The chief military judge of Anatolia, Kadiri Çelebi. Kadiri, who supported Ghazzi's case in the imperial council, sits in a central position and interacts with another scholar. From ʿAşık Çelebi, *Meşaʿirü'ş-şuʿara'* (c. 1600). (Reproduced by permission from the Directorate of the Turkish Institution for Manuscripts, Millet Library Istanbul, MS Ali Emiri Tarih 772, 297a.)

father may have been influential in forging a prior connection, since Muhyiddin was the uncle of none other than Zeynüddin Fenari, the Damascene chief judge for whom Radi al-Din had composed a short poem.[163] Muhyiddin was

163. Ghazzī, *Maṭāliʿ*, 266. For biographies of Fenarizade Muhyiddin, see Ṭaşköprīzāde, *Shaqāʾiq*, 384–5; Sehī Bey, *Tezkire-i Sehī*, 30; İpşirli, "Fenârîzâde"; Repp, *The Müfti of*

known for the garden parties he held for scholars and poets twice a week, though he, like Ghazzi, was a pious man and avoided the more risqué pursuits sometimes associated with these occasions; he used to wash his mouth out with rosewater if he got too carried away reciting poetry.[164] Contemporaries saw Muhyiddin as an unusually dignified and polite man, and Ghazzi agreed.[165] Finally, Ghazzi also met with Kasım Pasha (d. after 1541), the third vizier, again in a meeting that resulted in "friendship, love, affection, harmony, and companionship." He, too, promised to lend Ghazzi his support.[166]

Although this quick and promising succession of meetings was interrupted by the 1530 circumcision festivities and the sultan's sudden departure from the city, when the imperial council finally reconvened in late summer 1530, Ghazzi had met personally and could count on the support of four of the seven participating members of the imperial council. According to Ghazzi, Kadiri was especially influential in assuring his success.

> [He] gave my concern the greatest attention, and I received from him every honor and protection. He gave me a position in teaching, whose honor and value was far-reaching. It was always he who was leading, without my asking, begging or pleading. Despite our brief meeting I enjoyed his backing, and despite the fact that my novitiate status was lacking, and despite the fact that I did not visit him frequently—indeed it was [Ayas] Pasha's words of support for me and his encouragement about that which concerned me [that led Kadiri to help me].[167]

Ghazzi was obviously aware that he gained his appointment through informal channels: as he himself stated, aspiring young scholars were usually promoted after achieving the formal status of novice (*mülazemet*). According to this system, a young scholar would attach himself to a leading scholar and eventually become the latter's teaching assistant; having completed this training, the student entered his name on a waiting list that would make him eligible for posts whenever they opened up. By the late fifteenth and early sixteenth centuries, this system had been formalized in such a way as to allow senior Ottoman officials to more easily promote their protégés to judicial and scholarly positions.[168] However,

---

Istanbul, 263–72. Zeynüddin was the son of Shah Mehmed, Muhyiddin's older brother. Ṭaşköprīzāde, *Shaqā'iq*, 399; Walsh, "Fenārī-Zāde."

164. Sehī Bey, *Teẕkire-i Sehī*, 30; Laṭīfī, *Teẕkire-i Laṭīfī*, 307; İpekten, *Muhitler*, 230.

165. Ghazzī, *Maṭāliʿ*, 266.

166. Ghazzī, *Maṭāliʿ*, 133.

167. Ghazzī, *Maṭāliʿ*, 267.

168. Beyazit, "İstihdam," 30–120; Klein, "Mülazemet"; Repp, "Mulāzim"; Repp, *The Müfti of Istanbul*, 51.

appointments in Arab lands were largely excluded from this system, probably because the men serving in those areas had no attachments to Ottoman dignitaries and replacing them all with home-grown scholars from the central lands was impracticable to say the least.[169] Excluded from these institutionalized means of promotion and patronage, Arab scholars resorted to more informal means of gaining appointments.

Although Ghazzi's success in securing an appointment relied on the goodwill of many, it was nonetheless the product of an exchange. Ghazzi had brought Ayas Pasha gifts with both monetary and cultural value, and in dedicating his commentary on "The Mantle Ode" to him, Ghazzi allowed Ayas Pasha to connect his name to what was perhaps the most famous Arabic poem of all time.[170] Whereas Ghazzi's father Radi al-Din furnished Ayas Pasha with local knowledge, Ghazzi supplied him with scholarly and esoteric knowledge. It could even be argued that just as Ayas Pasha acted as a patron and protector of the Ghazzi family, Ghazzi offered Ayas Pasha a different sort of protection, since both "The Mantle Ode" and the two chapters of the Qur'an were believed to have powers to heal and to ward off evil. In exchange, Ghazzi received the deed of appointment he had gone to Istanbul to seek. He returned to Damascus, triumphant, in May 1531.

Conclusion

The breadth and intensity of the social network that the Ghazzis were able to establish is remarkable. Within just fifteen years of the conquest, Badr al-Din and his father had cultivated a loyal group of allies in both the provinces and at the imperial center. In Damascus they focused their energies on judges and governors, the most powerful representatives of the new ruling establishment. When Ghazzi traveled to Istanbul, he reached the very pinnacle of the imperial elite, enjoying regular exchanges with two viziers, two military judges, the chief judge of Istanbul, and the future chief mufti of the empire.

Thanks to Ghazzi's travelogue and a number of biographical accounts, we can reconstruct not just the existence of this network but the mechanisms through which it was formed. Relationships between Arabs and Rumis were based on a two-sided, mutually beneficial exchange of

169. Even after the novice system was formalized further in the early 1540s, appointments in eastern Anatolia and the Arab provinces usually went to those without a formal novitiate status. Atçıl, *Scholars*, 102–13, 142.

170. Homerin, "al-Būṣīrī."

resources. Arabs helped the new government to acquire information and to soften the blow of unpopular policies. They also bolstered the new political order by lending Ottoman officials legitimacy and verbal support: they circulated poems emphasizing the new rulers' moral rectitude and drafted treatises stressing their piety and learning. In return, Ottomans furnished provincial notables with material support, securing them stipends and positions in unstable times.

Such exchanges aided the incorporation of the Arab provinces, and must be seen as a cornerstone of Ottoman imperial governance. In the provinces, the input of men like Radi al-Din allowed Ottoman functionaries to make better-informed decisions about how to implement new policies or when and how to mete out punishments on locals. In the capital, the advice of men like ʿAbbasi helped administrators decide whom to trust or appoint. These relationships also led men on both sides to become personally invested in the affairs of the other. This effect was perhaps most pronounced on the side of provincial elites, as the ode Radi al-Din wrote on the occasion of Ayas Pasha's promotion suggests; a Damascene resident who had probably never been to Istanbul now had a stake in its political developments. Still, this sense of emotional investment was mutual, as the pasha's inquiries about the people of Damascus suggested.

Replicated many times across the empire, relationships like those formed by the Ghazzis helped to stabilize the imperial order. Obligations were honored over decades or even generations. ʿAbbasi built on relations he had formed in Istanbul before the fall of the Mamluk regime, and Ghazzi's contacts in Istanbul stemmed from those his father had made years earlier. Although the young Ghazzi had to renew his bond with Ayas Pasha and actively earn his position through his writings, the vizier no doubt took seriously the debts he had incurred toward Ghazzi's father back in Damascus. In the years to come, Ghazzi would repeatedly return to and rely on similar commitments.

Informal encounters played a crucial role in making exchanges between Rumis and Arabs possible. Their flexibility and ambiguity of purpose meant that unlike resources could be traded—ideas, poetry, precious objects, and practical knowledge were reciprocated with appointments, financial support, and even enslaved women. What is more, the kind of noninstrumental conversation that occurred in salons allowed the qualifications and moral standing of new acquaintances to be assessed. In some cases, it allowed true affection to develop. Ultimately, it was the layering of many different interpersonal axes that made the relationships formed within them so durable.

Viewing the establishment of Ottoman rule in Syria through the eyes of provincial notables helps to uncover the significant role Arab elites played in early Ottoman governance. In this period of imperial expansion and economic prosperity, there was a place for the knowledge and skills of provincial elites. With their understanding of local politics and their access to religious charisma, provincial elites could play informal advisory roles. With their poetic and scholarly expertise, they could contribute to the stature of Ottoman officials. The fact that this power was obtained through the exploitation of informal spaces would ultimately make it a precarious one, difficult to maintain later in the century. Nonetheless, in the first decades after the conquest, the influence of learned families like the Ghazzis was significant and real.

CHAPTER THREE

A Place in the Elite

THOUGH IT ENDED in fury, it all started with a laugh, or so Badr al-Din al-Ghazzi would later claim when he was asked about the feud. The young ʿAlaʾ al-Din al-Shafiʿi had long been studying with Ghazzi when, in class one day, for no apparent reason, the pupil suddenly began to laugh uncontrollably—not to snicker or giggle, mind you, but to howl. Ghazzi, who tolerated no such insolence during his lessons, scolded him, whereupon the young man stormed out, never to return.[1] Yet this was not the last the two would see of one another. For all of ʿAlaʾ al-Din's efforts to avoid Ghazzi, in the cramped social world of the Damascene elite, it was inevitable that the two would continue to cross paths. To the misfortune of the chief judge Hasan Bey, it was in his reception hall that ʿAlaʾ al-Din finally confronted his former teacher.

Informal gatherings offered occasions during which Ottoman elites could form mutually supportive relationships, as we saw in Chapter 2. However, this did not mean that salons were always harmonious or that they bred social parity. On the contrary, early modern salon culture helped to undergird steep hierarchies. In both Anatolia and the Arab lands, salons acted as stages for making claims about social status. Attending exclusive gatherings was itself an important marker of an elite, male identity. But even after a man had secured permanent membership in urbane circles, concerns about status remained. Salons forced participants to enact their rank through elaborate physical performances. What they wore, how they were greeted, and perhaps most of all, where they sat—all of this not only reflected but helped to define participants' relative positions within the elite. Ottoman salons reveal a concern with what Giora Sternberg has

1. Ghazzī, *Kawākib*, 3: 183.

called "status interactions," that is, social exchanges in which symbolic quarrels over reputation and authority were materialized.[2]

As key arenas for negotiations over status, salons helped Muslim gentlemen address one of their most pressing concerns in the decades after the 1516–7 conquests: clarifying social hierarchies across the newly expanded imperial domain. In this period of flux, salons allowed men from different regions and professions to come together to vie for power. Ottoman officials, who enjoyed influential posts and immense fortunes, were often thrust to the head of such gatherings, not just at the imperial center but also in the Arab provinces. However, office and wealth were only two of the competing forms of social capital recognized in Ottoman salons. Age, lineage, and learning were other factors that made someone deserving of a prominent seat. The great problem facing salongoers was reconciling these very different—if not incommensurate—claims into a single, absolute order. If a dispassionate observer could see value in all manner of personal attributes, such equanimity became impossible once they were mapped onto physical space. This made the salon intrinsically conflictual.

It also made salongoers acutely aware of human difference. The continual effort to sort through social hierarchies kept participants attuned to the particularities of one another's identities, both more visible ones like clothing and complexion and less immediately apparent ones like lineage. Thus, although salons helped to build bridges between various elite groups, they helped to reinscribe their differences as well.

Given the importance of salons in settling issues of social status, it comes as little surprise that the authors of biographical compendia often described assemblies with care. Sharaf al-Din Ibn Ayyub al-Ansari (d. 1592), a Damascene scholar and socialite, was one such author. His *Sweet-Smelling Garden* (*al-Rawd al-ʿatir*), which was completed in 1590 and offered portraits of leading figures in Damascus, offers vivid details about sixteenth-century Ottoman social life.[3] So too does *The Crimson Peonies*, the 1558 compendium of Ottoman scholars written by Ahmed Taşköprizade, based in Istanbul. Building on these and other biographical accounts, this chapter proceeds through the various steps contemporaries had to take in order to secure their place in elite circles. Gaining access was only the beginning; a gentleman then had to determine his rung within the Ottoman-wide hierarchy of social visits, followed by his

2. Sternberg, *Status Interaction*. See also Marsh, "Order."

3. The full title reads *al-Rawd al-ʿatir fi ma tayassara min akhbar ahl al-qarn al-sabiʿ ila khitam al-qarn al-ʿashir*. Parts of the book were edited and published by Ahmet Halil Güneş. There is only one extant manuscript copy, held at the Staatsbibliothek zu Berlin.

rank in a particular gathering. As this effortful and labyrinthine process makes clear, salons were not simply places where relationships of power were displayed, but where such relationships were actively negotiated.

Entering Elite Circles

After Ghazzi's triumphant return from Istanbul in 1531, his standing in Damascus rose rapidly. In addition to holding teaching positions at a number of madrasas, Ghazzi served as imam at the Great Mosque and as leader of its Qur'an reciters (*shaykh al-qurra'*).[4] He became one of the city's most prominent Shafi'i jurisconsults (*muftis*), issuing legal opinions (*fatwas*) so revered that one of his former students refused to draft his own as long as Ghazzi was alive (until Ghazzi insisted personally that the student could).[5] Despite these sundry commitments, Ghazzi found time for scholarship, writing over one hundred works in the course of his life.[6] When the Meccan notable Qutb al-Din al-Nahrawali (d. 1582) passed through Damascus in 1557–8, he reserved his highest praise for Ghazzi, whom he called "the showpiece of religious scholars in Damascus, indeed, in the entire world."[7] Contemporaries in Istanbul compared Ghazzi to the great fifteenth-century Egyptian scholars Suyuti and Ibn Hajar.[8] Contemporaries in Damascus likened him to the founders of the four Sunni legal schools:

> Shafi'i, Malik,
> Abu Hanifa and Ibn Hanbal,
> Had they known Muhammad al-Ghazzi
> They'd have said: "you're above us all!"[9]

Ghazzi's prominence was also reflected in the contacts he cultivated. As an elite man in the Ottoman lands, he was locked into an elaborate, empire-wide economy of social visits. At the heart of this economy were gentlemanly salons, the exclusive occasions to which men had to gain access if they desired visibility and influence. Though Ghazzi entered these

4. Najm al-Din records that Ghazzi served as the imam of the *maqsura* of the Great Mosque and taught at the following madrasas: the 'Adiliyya, Farisiyya, Shamiyya Barraniyya, Muqaddamiyya, Taqawiyya, and Shamiyya Juwwaniyya, in that order. Ghazzī, *Kawākib*, 3: 5. See also Ibn Ayyūb, *Rawḍ*, 242a; Būrīnī, *Tarājim*, 2: 99.

5. Ibn Ayyūb, *Kitāb*, 8; Būrīnī, *Tarājim*, 1: 16–7.

6. Ibn Ayyūb, *Rawḍ*, 241a.

7. Nahrawālī, *Journey*, 49. Ibn Ayyub shared this estimation. Ibn Ayyūb *Rawḍ*, 240a.

8. Kınalı-zade, *Tezkiretü'ş-Şu'arâ*, 669.

9. Ibn Ayyūb, *Rawḍ*, 240a.

circles with relative ease, others had to work harder to find their place in the elite.

In the early modern Ottoman Empire, one of the principal measures of a man's social status was the company he kept. "Don't ask about a man, ask about his companions," Ghazzi counseled, "for every man is guided by those who surround him."[10] Biographers took seriously this normative principle, often reporting in detail on the social circles in which their subjects traveled. For example, we learn that at a learned gathering Ghazzi held in 1527, "his brother-in-law, the chief of the honorable [waqf] supervisors attended and sat to [Ghazzi's] right; next to him sat Shihab al-Mayli, the Maliki mufti; and to his left sat Abu al-Fath al-Maliki and a group of learned men"; this information was deemed significant enough to have been recorded first in a contemporary chronicle and then recopied by Ibn Ayyub.[11] Ghazzi's student Hasan al-Burini (d. 1615), who gave a lengthy profile of his teacher in his *Biographies of the Notable Men of the Age* (*Tarajim al-aʿyan min abnaʾ al-zaman*), was even more thorough in documenting the guest lists of some of Ghazzi's gatherings, despite the fact that he wrote more than twenty years after they had taken place.[12]

As these same biographers often took care to note, some of Ghazzi's most important contacts were leading Ottoman functionaries. Just as his father had before him, Ghazzi won over the governors and judges who served in Damascus on one- or two-year appointments. One of the most affectionate of such friendships was with Hasan Bey, who was appointed chief judge in Damascus in 1552. Bedreddin ʿAbdülmuhsin (d. 1576), as Hasan was in the habit of signing his name, was severe and uncompromising. Rarely seen laughing or smiling, he was so revered that "nobody met with him other than the most eminent scholars, the leaders [*zuʿamāʾ*], and the governor's police chief [*subaşı*]."[13] Yet stern as Hasan was, he had a soft spot for Ghazzi. The most authentic proof of this from a contemporary perspective was the fact that Hasan paid visits to the local

10. The pre-Islamic poet ʿAdi Ibn Zayd as cited Ghazzī, *ʿIshra*, 12.

11. Ibn Tulun as cited in Ibn Ayyūb, *Rawḍ*, 28a. For another one of Ghazzi's feasts and its guests of honor, see Ibn Ayyūb, *Rawḍ*, 242b (also citing Ibn Tulun).

12. Būrīnī, *Tarājim*, 2: 11–2, 95–7. Burini wrote his biographical dictionary over many years, from 1601–15. El-Rouayheb, "al-Būrīnī." For other examples, see Ṭaşköprīzāde, *Shaqāʾiq*, 343; Ibn Ayyūb, *Rawḍ*, 255a; ʿAlī ibn Bālī, *ʿIqd*, 476.

13. Ibn Ayyūb, *Rawḍ*, 115a. Hasan's biographers give conflicting death dates. Ibn Ayyub gives 1566/7 (974); ʿAtayi, who follows Hasan's later career more closely and is therefore probably more reliable, 1576 (984). Ibn Ayyūb, *Kitāb*, 51; ʿAṭāyī, *Hadāʾiḳu'l-Haḳāʾiḳ*, 240.

scholar. Ibn Ayyub put it succinctly: Hasan "loved [Ghazzi] deeply and visited him in his chamber."[14]

Making and receiving domestic visits was one of the key social obligations of residents of the early modern Ottoman Empire. Doing so was part of any good Muslim's duties to others, whether to friends or family or to the adopted family of a Sufi order. According to Ghazzi's etiquette manual *The Rules of Conviviality and the Explication of Companionship and Brotherhood* (*Adab al-ʿishra wa-dhikr al-suhba wa-l-ukhuwwa*), which laid out guidelines for socializing among Sufi brethren—but with broader applicability—a key principle for maintaining good social relations was "checking up on one's brothers and inquiring about their well-being."[15] One of Ghazzi's Sufi-minded contemporaries in Egypt counseled, "it is proper for brothers to visit one another every couple of days."[16] The principle operated equally at the Ottoman center, where authors stressed the fundamentally social nature of human beings, and their reliance on one another for their livelihoods and well-being.[17]

Yet, binding as this duty may have been for members of all social strata, for elites it came to be wrapped up in the performance of power, important for maintaining one's status and critical for raising it. One of the things that distinguished elite sociability was its immense exclusivity. It was one of the privileges of the wealthy to meet in settings where access could be carefully controlled. Men of lesser means, who often lived with their families in single rooms, wanted for spaces to exercise hospitality and therefore often assembled in places that were publicly accessible—orchards, stackyards, and increasingly, coffeehouses.[18] By contrast, the rich had vast residences with multiple reception areas, allowing them to receive guests while safeguarding the privacy of their domestic quarters (and hence, of their wives and children) (see figure 3.1).[19] But elites could even regulate attendance when they met, as they often did, in full public view, whether in mosques or popular leisure spots outside urban centers. In such cases,

14. Ibn Ayyūb, *Kitāb*, 50. See also Ibn Ayyūb, "Dhayl," 327; Ibn Ayyūb, *Rawḍ*, 52a.

15. Ghazzī, *ʿIshra*, 60. For a discussion of this work, see Elger, "Ghazzi," 104.

16. Shaʿrānī, *Anwār*, 82.

17. İnalcık, *Tarab*, 221; Oktay, *Ahlâk-ı Alâî*, 429–37; Kafadar, "Self and Others," 141.

18. Yılmaz, "Fun"; Sajdi, *Barber*, 74–6; Marcus, "Privacy," esp. 167–74.

19. Mustafa ʿAli emphasized that a key distinction between elites and nonelites was that the former socialized in private, the latter in public spaces like coffeehouses and taverns. Muṣṭafā ʿĀlī, *Tables*, 111–3, 129–33. In wealthy residences built in the fifteenth and sixteenth centuries in Kayseri (though extensively modified in the eighteenth), private quarters and rooms designated for receiving male guests were separated into two structurally independent buildings. Faroqhi, *Men of Modest Substance*, 77–8.

FIGURE 3.1. The Janbulat house in Aleppo. By the seventeenth century, this residence had four different reception areas (shown in black). This included (a) a domed reception hall (*qaʿa*) adjacent to the southeastern end of the courtyard, dating to the Mamluk period; (b) an outdoor courtyard with two raised seating areas (*iwans*) facing one another over a large basin, the southern one dating to the 1550s; and (c) a *qaʿa* in the family quarters at the northeastern corner of the building (seventeenth century). (Reproduced with minor changes from David and Rousset, "Maison Wakil," 58. Courtesy of Jean-Claude David and Marie-Odile Rousset.)

exclusivity was ensured by the physical arrangement of participants into circles or semicircles, creating a sort of human shield against the prying gazes of passers-by.[20] Turbans acted as a further deterrent, signaling the stature of those assembled and warding off those of lesser means. In the rare recorded moments when such physical boundaries were transgressed, scholars could use language and knowledge to draw invisible ones.[21]

To be sure, in many parts of the empire, there were certain times of day when notables made themselves available to the larger community, throwing open their palace doors to field queries from men and women of all social backgrounds (itself a sign of power).[22] However, securing entry into the magnificent assemblies held for enlightened conversation was a different matter altogether. These were usually by invitation only. Ghazzi cajoled a friend into attending a 1534 banquet with a personalized poem playing on his titular name "the sun of the religion" (*Shams al-Din*):

> Could it be that the sun will shine its rays on me?
> How I hope that soon reunited we'll be,
> That he will rise over the gardens for our friends to see,
> To be welcomed by the guests and to bring them glee.[23]

Woe was the man who showed up unannounced. In *Table Manners* (*Adab al-Muʿakala*), a satirical treatise on mistakes to avoid while dining with others, Ghazzi reserved special mockery for the uninvited guest—*al-tufayli*—a word that also means parasite. Such men were so desperate that they devised all sorts of stratagems to join feasts after doormen had prohibited them from entering, like pretending they had just left the party but had grabbed the wrong shoes on the way out.[24]

Some groups would never have even dreamed of being invited to a salon; these were barred from participating in elite circles a priori. This included all women as well as men of modest substance. In the fifteenth century, well-heeled women—some of whom enjoyed an excellent education—could sometimes break into salons, as Müʾeyyedzade's love interest and renowned poet Mihri Hatun (d. after 1512) had in Amasya in the 1470s.[25] However, doing so was seen as potentially morally com-

20. Servants could play a similar role. Peirce, "Material World," 221–2.

21. See Hamawi and Fevri Efendi's encounter with the Egyptian student in Chapter 6.

22. Ibn Baṭṭūṭa, *Travels*, 2: 462–3; Mollenhauer, "Private in Public," 75–6.

23. Ibn Tulun cited in Ibn Ayyūb, *Rawḍ*, 242b.

24. Ghazzī, *Ādāb al-muʿākala*, 29. For this treatise, see Pfeifer, "Gulper"; Abu Hussein, "Social Dining"; van Gelder, "Arabic Banqueters."

25. Havlıoğlu, *Mihrî Hatun*, chapter 2.

promising, as the worried assurances of later biographers regarding her chastity suggest.[26] Discomfort with female participation in salons only increased over time, such that by the end of the sixteenth century, few such female interlopers are known to us.[27] Nonelite men were likewise barred from entering. These lacked the education that would have allowed them to partake of the proceedings—the linguistic sophistication, the bookish knowledge. They were also believed to lack the proper etiquette; Ghazzi's treatise on table manners, though not explicitly elitist, was implicitly based on a world in which people ate with members of the same social class.[28] Both women and commoners could sometimes play supporting roles in salons as servants or, in the case of women, dancers or prostitutes.[29] However, such auxiliaries were incorporated in ways that kept them physically and discursively marginalized.

Even for well-educated, well-to-do men who qualified in principle for entry into elite circles, actually succeeding was the result of a concerted effort. As we saw in Chapter 2, Ghazzi's father took care to introduce his son into his own social world by allowing him to be present during his meetings. Hasan Bey's entry into elite circles was more tumultuous, but no less typical of sixteenth-century Ottoman society. Of German origin, Hasan had been captured in battle as a young boy and sold as an enslaved person to a gentleman in Ankara.[30] As coercive as Ottoman slavery was, it did sometimes afford opportunities for social advancement: Hasan received a good education and entered the household of Kadiri Çelebi, the same military judge who had helped Ghazzi secure a professorship in 1530. Finally, Hasan passed into the hands of the longtime grand vizier Rüstem Pasha (d. 1561), under whose protection Hasan studied with the great scholar Ebu's-Su'ud before beginning his own career as a madrasa professor in the early 1540s.[31] Hasan likely witnessed his first polite assemblies as an attendant similar to the one flanking a portrait of his patron Kadiri engrossed in discussion with another gentleman (figure 2.4).[32] Just as these powerful figures secured Hasan madrasa appointments and judgeships, so too did they secure him a place in elite circles. Hasan may

26. Havlıoğlu, *Mihrî Hatun*, 50–2.
27. Havlıoğlu, *Mihrî Hatun*, 44.
28. Pfeifer, "Gulper."
29. Zecher, "The Çengî"; Sariyannis, "Prostitution," 51.
30. ʿAṭāyī, *Hadāʾiḳu'l-Haḳāʾiḳ*, 239.
31. ʿAlī ibn Bālī, *ʿIqd*, 444; ʿAṭāyī, *Hadāʾiḳu'l-Haḳāʾiḳ*, 239; Naguib, "Guiding," 11.
32. Kadiri was a known salon host in Istanbul. ʿĀşıḳ Çelebi, *Meşâʿirü's-Şuʿarâ*, 1311–2; İpekten, *Edebî Muhitler*, 152.

well have become friendly with Ghazzi through the mediation of Kadiri and Ebu's-Su'ud, since both of them had met Ghazzi personally during his visit to Istanbul. Hasan may even have been present when Ghazzi visited Kadiri at his home.

For those not born or adopted into leading households, securing access to salons was trickier. Doing so usually occurred through the intercession of a powerful patron. Such was the case of Ghazzi's student and later biographer Hasan al-Burini. Burini's father had been an upholsterer and perfumist in a small town near Nablus in today's Palestine. Burini relied upon a rich patron not only to finance his school books and wedding, but also to introduce him into the Damascene elite. This patron, who probably belonged to a family of merchants,

> kept the company of all the important men and judges, and praised [Burini] to them in his absence until they asked about him. [Then, meeting Burini, they] found him as virtuous and skillful as he had been described to them, and they were friendly to him and honored him.[33]

Ghazzi likewise supported the aspiring scholar by bringing Burini along to his gatherings. This was a standard part of the intense personal relationship between student and teacher referred to as *lāzama* in Arabic (meaning "to accompany someone constantly") and *mülazemet* in Turkish (designating the status of having a sponsor for one's academic career). Though there was an important intellectual component to this relationship—students would shadow professors during their lectures, taking notes for future use—it served equally to induct young scholars into the more diffuse set of mannerisms that characterized the scholarly habitus.[34] Burini described his four-year assistantship with Ghazzi in his biographical dictionary: "it honored me to behold his highness, and to witness his qualities' fineness. I observed him during his meetings [*jumū'*], from his arrival to when he was leaving."[35] Burini's lengthy biography of his teacher mentioned no less than three times that he had been a guest at one of Ghazzi's learned assemblies, suggesting just how proud he was of that fact.[36] The biographical dictionary itself is perhaps the best testament to his success in entering elite circles, since it was essentially a record of Burini's experiences in Damascus high society.[37]

33. The patron's name was Fakhr al-Din ibn Zurayq. Ghazzī, *Lutf*, 357.
34. Chamberlain, *Knowledge*, 118–9; Makdisi, *Colleges*, 114–5, 192–3; Repp, "Mulāzim."
35. Būrīnī, *Tarājim*, 2: 98.
36. Būrīnī, *Tarājim*, 2: 95–6, 101, 103.
37. El-Rouayheb, "al-Būrīnī," 2; Pfeifer, "Encounter," 230–1.

However, gaining access was only the beginning; having been accepted into the ranks of the gentlemen who regularly met in one another's homes, a man then had to establish his place within those ranks. This meant practicing the inexact science of who visited whom. The basic principle was that the more powerful the person, the less likely they were to visit anyone else. Acting as a host both symbolized and materialized a person's power. Not leaving the house was a marker of status, since it meant that others sought you out rather than you muddying your own boots to visit them.[38] Hosting was also viewed as a concrete opportunity to exercise power over others by providing for and presiding over them. Ignoring these social conventions could carry serious consequences. The *Book of Kabus*, a popular etiquette manual initially written for a medieval Muslim prince but widely read in the Ottoman Empire, urged being selective about whom one visited lest one's standing be damaged by frequenting the home of a social inferior.[39] For those who owed visits, the stakes were even higher; failure to fulfill such obligations was taken as a grave offense and could result in removal from office.[40]

Applied to society as a whole, this principle translated into a notional hierarchy of house calls encompassing the entirety of the Ottoman elite. A generic approximation of this hierarchy would follow imperial rank. At the pinnacle, the sultan could summon anyone he wished and only rarely appeared as a guest at the homes of others. Below him were the viziers, who let most other mortals come to them; below them, the pashas, who were obligated to visit few other than the viziers; next were the judges; and, finally, scholars and notables. One of the characteristics of this imagined scheme was that centrally trained Turcophone elites, who monopolized the highest governmental posts, generally occupied most of the upper rungs. This was true not only in Istanbul, but also in the provinces, where governors sat at the top of the hierarchy of house calls, and chief judges ranked a close second. In this sense, it was not merely a turn of phrase

38. Literally. When the fifteenth-century scholar Molla Gürani was reluctant to accept an invitation to the imperial palace because of the rain, the sultan offered to allow him to ride his horse all the way into the second court so that his boots would not get dirty. Normally, everyone other than the sultan was required to dismount at the end of the first court. Ṭaşköprīzāde, *Shaqāʾiq*, 87.

39. Kaykāʾūs, *Das Qābusnāme*, 113.

40. Ṭaşköprīzāde, *Shaqāʾiq*, 179–80. One informant told Molla Gürani that a certain shaykh was visiting Molla Hüsrev but not Gürani, expecting him to be angry. Ṭaşköprīzāde, *Shaqāʾiq*, 88.

when one Egyptian biographer referred to Hasan Bey as "the refuge of all seekers and the destination of all travelers."[41]

In practice, things were more complicated. For one thing, men of the very highest rank, including sultans, did routinely accept invitations from men below them in the social order—though when they did so it was usually an act that bestowed honor on the host, thus preserving the fundamental power relationship between them.[42] A bigger complication was the fact that the hierarchy itself was upended by the many men whose authority derived not from their office but from another source, especially a more sacred one. Sultans often paid visits to Sufi visionaries or to unusually learned men, as scholars, especially Taşköprizade, were keen to point out. The world of salons was tricky terrain, laid on a steep incline and riddled with land mines. Ultimately, a man's path through them had to be negotiated in practice.

Finding One's Place

Ghazzi's burgeoning friendship with Hasan Bey was cut short when Hasan was suddenly removed from the Damascene judgeship in 1553. Rüstem Pasha, Hasan's benefactor and the grand vizier since 1544, had been dismissed from his post for his alleged involvement in the murder of the Ottoman prince Mustafa. Rüstem's client in Damascus was treated accordingly. Hasan returned to Istanbul to wait things out, a strategy that seems to have worked; when, in 1555, Rüstem Pasha was reinstated as grand vizier, Hasan was granted a second term as chief judge in Damascus.[43] Hasan celebrated his return to the city with a grand welcoming reception (*majlis salam*).[44]

It was tradition in Damascus for chief judges to organize celebratory receptions when they arrived to take up a new post. Since judges were rotated every couple of years and were usually new to the locations in which they worked, these occasions allowed them to become acquainted

41. Tamīmī, *Ṭabaqāt*, 1: 381.

42. Selim II paid frequent visits to his boon companion Şemsi Ahmed Pasha (d. 1580) in Üsküdar, sometimes staying with him for two or three days at a time. Necipoğlu, *Sinan*, 493–4.

43. ʿAṭāyī, *Hadāʾiḳuʾl-Haḳāʾiḳ*, 239–40.

44. This incident is recounted twice in Ibn Ayyub's biographical dictionary. Ibn Ayyūb, *Rawḍ*, 52a, 115a–b. The second of these has also been published in the partial edition of the text: Ibn Ayyūb, *Kitāb*, 51. Ghazzi's son also recorded the incident, relying on Ibn Ayyub's account. Ghazzī, *Kawākib*, 3: 141. The following is based on those accounts. For a discussion, see Elger, *Glaube*, 69.

with the local community, or, in the words of one Damascene historian, for residents to "let [the judge] know who the distinguished men were"—and, one might add, to clarify the hierarchies between them.[45] Given the power of chief judges and their unfamiliarity with the local scene, salongoers viewed these receptions as opportunities to claim a particular social status. The stakes were often very high. On one occasion, a scholar who made an especially witty joke was awarded the job of another who had not attended.[46] Though one might expect that Hasan's familiarity with Damascene society would have made this particular party less charged, Ibn Ayyub's account suggests otherwise.

One of the basic tenets of early modern Ottoman social relations, in Arab provinces as in Anatolia, was that everyone was to be treated in accordance with their identity. This was the foundational principle of the centuries-old and highly elaborated system of etiquette referred to as *adab* (or by its plural *ādāb*) in Arabic and *edeb* in Ottoman Turkish.[47] Ghazzi began with this idea in the first pages of his advice book *The Rules of Conviviality (Adab al-ʿIshra)*: shaykhs and grandees (*akabir*) were to be respected and served; social equals given counsel; and disciples and the lower classes (*asaghir*) guided to what was right.[48] Ghazzi's contemporary, the Turcophone scholar Mustafa ʿAli (d. 1600), operated on the same principle when he divided his book of manners, entitled *Tables of Delicacies Concerning the Rules of Social Gatherings* (*Mevaʾidü'n-nefaʾis fi kavaʿidi'l-mecalis*) (1599/1600), into chapters treating "Judges, Professors, Chief Magistrates, and Others," "Cooks in the Employ of Grandees," and "The Manners of Servants," among others.[49] In the salon, this attitude translated into deep attention to and continued vigilance about the identity of other guests. According to Ghazzi, a basic requirement when interacting with others was cultivating "knowledge about them, so that you can honor them in accordance with their rank [*ʿalā qadrihi*]."[50]

Although the host's status was in large part clarified by the very fact of his hosting, he had to work to retain this honor by offering a physical context commensurate with his rank (and that of his guests). Here

45. Ibn Ṭūlūn as cited in Ibn Ayyūb, *Rawḍ*, 280a. For a reception to celebrate a judge's return home, see Ḥamawī, *Ḥādī*, 71.

46. Ibn Ayyūb, *Kitāb*, 84.

47. See Chapter 4 for more discussion.

48. Ghazzī, *ʿIshra*, 15. This was also the organizing principle of Ghazzi's work of educational etiquette, which outlined the expectations of the teacher and the student. Ghazzī, *al-Durr al-naḍīd*.

49. Muṣṭafā ʿĀlī, *Tables*. See also Oktay, *Ahlâk-ı Alâî*, 390–2.

50. Ghazzī, *ʿIshra*, 28.

as elsewhere in the early modern world, building a house was an important part of constructing a social identity.[51] According to Mustafa ʿAli, it was "obvious and clear as daylight to all understanding and cultured contemporaries" that "everybody's living quarters must be consistent with his status, that his house and residence must fit his taste and rank."[52] True to form, Ottoman elites lived in huge compounds outfitted with multiple rooms for receiving visitors (see figure 3.1). Many hosts invested special energy in the designing of these rooms. In Damascus, the reception halls of wealthy families often featured imposing domes and colorful marble inlays, and that of the Ghazzis was probably no exception (see figure 3.2).[53] Further north, in Aleppo or Istanbul, reception chambers were no less ostentatious; walls were decorated with wood paneling or colorful tiles and even ceiling beams might be lacquered with geometrical or floral schemes (see figure 0.2). Built-in latticework cupboards covered with mother of pearl displayed precious items like books or porcelain.[54] All aspects of the guest's experience were to be considered; according to one Cairene scholar, even vestibules where visitors waited to be received needed to be beautiful.[55]

Outdoor reception areas for use during the hot summer months were equally well curated to impress visitors. In Damascus, many wealthy men had courtyards fitted with elevated platforms for sitting with guests while overlooking pools or fountains and often greenery (see figure 3.3).[56] In Istanbul, the rich owned special summer compounds where they could enjoy vistas of the Bosphorus from airy pavilions (*köşk*). No expense was spared in the construction of these pavilions. One built in 1571 for a grand vizier was placed in the middle of a large pool, such that it was accessible only by a stepped bridge.[57] Rumis appear to have brought this culture to Damascus, since one governor built a similar summer palace in an orchard overlooking an offshoot of the Barada River. There, as Ibn Ayyub informs

51. Phillips, *Everyday Luxuries*, 45; Klein, "Politeness," 886.

52. Mustafa ʿAli as quoted in Tietze, "Luxury," 588.

53. See, for example, the *qaʿa* of the Robert Mouawad Private Museum in Damascus (*iwan* dated 1639/40). Weber, "Walls and Ceilings," 253–5. For the reception chamber of the Ghazzi family, see Weber, "Qa'a," 294n5.

54. For Aleppo, see David and Rousset, "Maison Wakil"; Mollenhauer, "Private in Public," 71; Weber, "Walls and Ceilings," 257–60; Gonnella, *Wohnhaus*. For Istanbul, see Phillips, *Everyday Luxuries*, chapters 2–3; Yérasimos, "Dwellings," 286.

55. Khafaji as cited in Ibrahim, "Residential Architecture," 55–6.

56. David and Rousset, "Maison Wakil", 56–8.

57. Necipoğlu, "Garden Culture," 40–1. For gardens as favored settings for gatherings, see Brookshaw, "Palaces"; Kut, "Bezm," 617. For the symbolic meanings attached to gardens in such gatherings, see Andrews, "Literary Art," 360–1.

FIGURE 3.2. Domed reception hall (*qa'a*) in the 'Azm palace in Damascus (c. 1749/50). In the foreground lies the entrance area (*'ataba*) with a fountain; in the background, the raised platform for receiving guests (*tazar*) is visible under an arch. (Michel Écochard Archive, photograph Maison Bonfils, 1867. Courtesy of the Aga Khan Documentation Center, MIT Libraries.)

FIGURE 3.3. A courtyard reception area in the Zahrawi residence in Homs dating to the first half of the fifteenth century. At the bottom of the photograph, a step can be seen leading to the raised platform where guests could be seated. (Photograph Lorenz Korn, 1995. Courtesy of Lorenz Korn.)

us, the governor dined twice weekly in a room above his garden, where he had planted herbs, flowers, and trees as fragrant as they were fetching.[58] Given the importance of such spaces in the social lives of the elite, the "sweet-smelling garden" in the title of Ibn Ayyub's dictionary was not only metaphorical, but also literal.[59]

The physical environments of polite assemblies reflected on the host even when these were held outside the domestic sphere. We have already seen the symbolic charge of Ottoman efforts to occupy particular buildings immediately after the conquest, whether Sultan Selim's seizure of the royal audience hall outside Damascus or his chief judge's appropriation of a side chamber of the Great Mosque.[60] Ghazzi's stature was legible from the fact that he hosted gatherings in the central prayer hall of that same mosque, right next to the shrine of Yahya ibn Zakariyya (known to Christians as John the Baptist) (see figure 3.4).[61] Such an honor was inconceivable for less influential members of the learned establishment, let alone for the great mass of urban dwellers who might have come to pray in the sanctuary.[62]

58. Ibn Ayyūb, *Kitāb*, 53–4; Ibn Ayyūb, "Dhayl," 328. For other pleasure spots off the river, see Hafteh, "Garden Culture," 322.

59. See also Niyazioğlu, *Dreams*, chapter 2; Andrews, "Gardens."

60. See Chapter 2.

61. Accounts written in Damascus, Cairo, and Istanbul alike mention this fact. Būrīnī, *Tarājim*, 2: 95–6; Tamīmī, *Kitāb*, 239a; Kınalı-zade, *Tezkiretü'ş-Şu'arâ*, 669.

62. Other Damascene scholars had the honor of reciting the *Sahih* of Bukhari in the Great Mosque each Ramadan, with a concluding session (*majlis khatm*) attended by the learned men of the city. Ibn Ayyūb, *Kitāb*, 43.

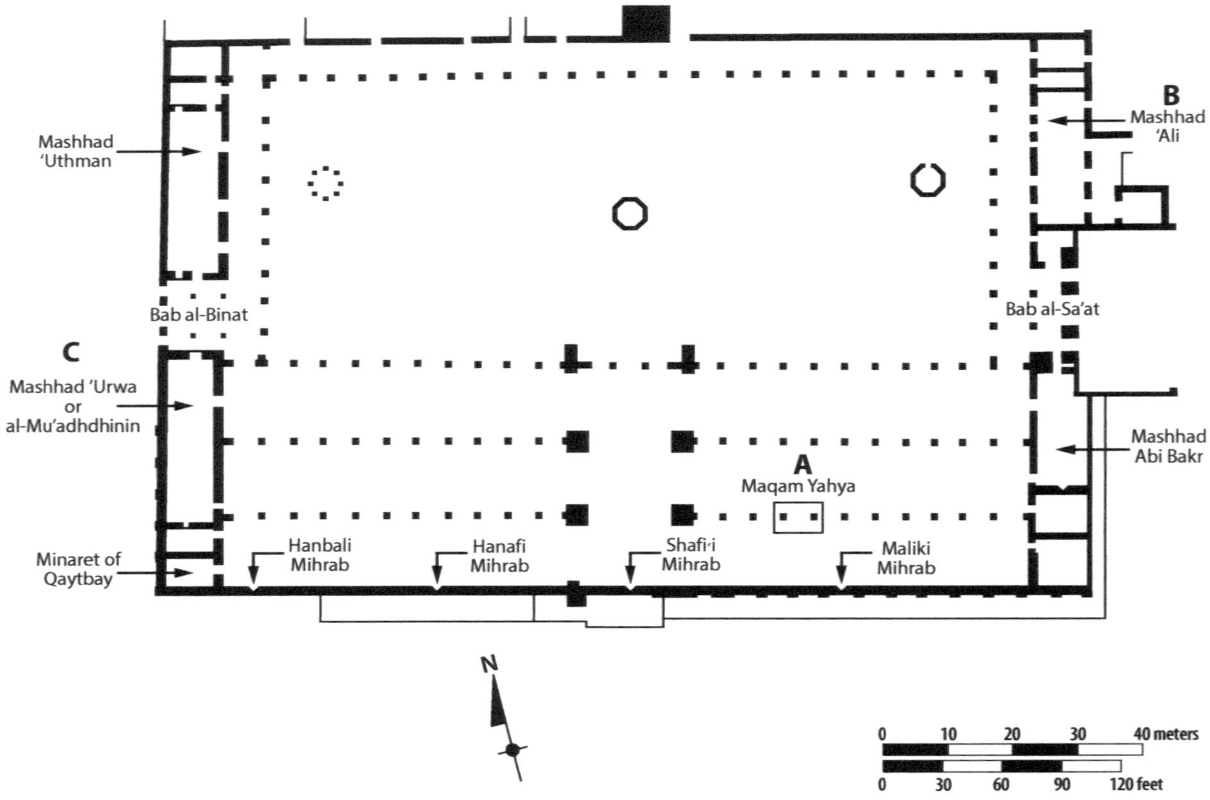

FIGURE 3.4. The Great Mosque of Damascus (the Umayyad Mosque) in the late Mamluk era. Ghazzi's celebration for his book *Qur'anic Exegesis Made Simple* was held next to the shrine of Yahya (a). Ghazzi held other gatherings in the mosque's oblong side rooms (called *mashhads*), including his celebration for his glosses on Mahalli, which took place in the *mashhad* of 'Ali (b). The first Ottoman chief judge of the city, Zeynüddin Fenari, convoked meetings in the *mashhad* of 'Urwa (c). (Reproduced with minor changes from Behrens-Abouseif, "Fire," 297. Courtesy of Doris Behrens-Abouseif.)

However conspicuous these environments may have been, it was the participants that were most on display in the assemblies of the elite. Salons were laid out in such a way as to expose all those present to considerable scrutiny. Many reception areas had a two-tiered physical structure similar to a modern theater stage. In the domed receptions halls common in Arab lands (*qaʿa*), the newly arrived guest would emerge from the doorway onto the entrance area (*ʿataba*), the lower level of the hall often fitted with a fountain.[63] There, he would be immediately visible to the guests who were already seated in one of several platforms elevated about forty to fifty centimeters above the threshold and referred to as *tazar* or *majlis* (see figure 3.2).[64] Such stage-like settings existed in Istanbul as well, as can be seen in the two-tiered layout of the gatherings of Baki and Ebu's-Suʿud (see figures 0.1, 3.5). Courtyard reception areas functioned on the same principle. There, guests would cross a spacious courtyard before climbing the step or two that led onto a raised platform framed by an arch (Ar. *iwan*, Tur. *eyvan*) (see figure 3.3).[65] Standing in the threshold or the courtyard, then, the newly arrived guest would be highly exposed and could immediately be sized up by those who had arrived before him. A person's dress came under particular scrutiny. Turbans received special attention since variations in size, shape, and color reflected a person's status or profession.[66] A period painting portrays Ebu's-Suʿud presiding over a learned gathering in Istanbul with a colossal turban on his head, no doubt a visual acknowledgement of his mammoth reputation (see figure 3.5). In Damascus, Burini recorded that Ghazzi convoked one of his gatherings wearing a "nicely shaped turban with only a small end piece hanging down, avoiding the greater length that is disapproved of [*makrūh*]."[67] As Burini's reference to the opinion of legal scholars on this practice of leaving the end of

63. Weber, "*Qa'a*," 267; Korn, "Bait," 263–80; Ibrahim, "Residential Architecture," 53. For Anatolia and the Balkans, see Yérasimos, "Dwellings," 279.

64. David and Rousset, "Maison Wakil," 56, 58; Weber, "*Qa'a*," 267; Weber, "Walls and Ceilings," 243–4. This seating area was also known as an *iwan*. Caʿfer Efendi, writing in early seventeenth-century Istanbul, glosses the Arabic *majlis* as "meeting place" or "sitting place" in Turkish (*dernek yeri, oturacak yer*). Caʿfer Efendi, *Risāle-i Miʿmāriyye*, 89 (74r).

65. David and Rousset, "Maison Wakil," 56–8. Although David and Rousset state that Syrian *iwans* did not feature raised platforms, Lorenz Korn has documented a fifteenth-century house in Homs that did. Korn, "Bait," 268. Caʿfer Efendi translates the Arabic *iwan* into Turkish as *soffa* and *çar-dak*, the latter indicating a light wooden structure similar to a trellis under which one can sit. Caʿfer Efendi, *Risāle-i Miʿmāriyye*, 86 (72v).

66. Ibn Ayyūb, *Rawḍ*, 236a; Zilfi, "Women," 396–9.

67. Būrīnī, *Tarājim*, 2: 95–6.

FIGURE 3.5. The scholar Ebu's-Su'ud presides over a scholarly gathering. Ebu's-Su'ud, seated at the top left, sports a mammoth turban and leans against an orange cushion. The other participants sit in a circle around him, with younger men—probably servants—watching from the sidelines. From Baki's *Divan* (mid-sixteenth century). (Courtesy of the Metropolitan Museum of Art, New York, www.metmuseum.org.)

the turban cloth dangling at one's shoulder suggests, dress reflected not only taste but piety.[68] Indeed, Burini noted that, on the same occasion, Ghazzi was clothed in "magnificent pistachio-colored wool," the green color usually reserved for descendants of Muhammad.[69] Another guest at the same gathering, a former student of Ghazzi, was known for sporting all sorts of furs, including those of sable, lynx, and squirrel.[70]

The impact of physical attributes was intensified by the heightened mobility of the sixteenth century. Clothing had become politicized in the wake of the 1516–7 Ottoman conquest. One of the Ottomans' first edicts banned Mamluk dress, and early chroniclers took note when this or that notable suddenly appeared in Ottoman robes (Ghazali made a point to reintroduce Mamluk attire during his 1520 revolt).[71] But long after the poisonous atmosphere of the postwar period dissipated, appearances continued to carry regional or ethnic associations. This can be seen in Damascene descriptions of Hasan Bey's appearance. On the one hand, contemporaries could not help but notice the blue eyes, fair beard, and ruddy complexion that marked him out as someone with origins in central Europe.[72] On the other hand, they noted with amazement that despite not being an Arab himself, he "liked the Arabs, so much so that he even copied them in their dress, wearing the *farajiyya* with the large, long sleeves in the manner of the Arab judges and lords [*mawālī*]."[73] That this was seen as a divergence from the norm suggests that Rumis must have been easily distinguishable from their Arab colleagues when everyone gathered for a leisurely soirée.[74]

68. A period depiction of Kemalpaşazade illustrates this dangling piece. ʿĀşıḳ Çelebi, *Meşâʿirü's-Şuʿarâ*, 296.

69. Wearing green was supposed to be a distinction reserved for true *sayyids*, but it is likely that Ghazzi took his Qurayshi descent as license to do the same thing. For Ottoman turbans, see Dankoff, "Turban and Crown."

70. This was Ismaʿil al-Nabulusi (d. 1585). Būrīnī, *Tarājim*, 2: 68. Furs and other items were regulated in Ottoman ceremonial. Zilfi, "Women," 397. Biographers often commented on the clothing of their subjects, sometimes even of those figures who lived a generation or two before them, e.g., Ṭaşköprīzāde, *Shaqāʾiq*, 108, 118, 166, 167.

71. Wollina, "Sultan Selīm," 228–9. See also Fuess, "Sultans with Horns."

72. Ibn Ayyūb, *Kitāb*, 50; Ghazzī, *Kawākib*, 3: 141.

73. Būrīnī, *Tarājim*, 1: 68 (translation taken partially from Winter). Winter mistakenly takes this description to apply to Ahmed, Hasan's son. Winter, "Ottoman Qāḍīs," 103.

74. In another biography, Ibn Ayyub notes that one Damascene scholar wore a "white linen *shadd* on his shoulders as was the habit of the Arab scholars [*ʿulamāʾ min abnāʾ al-ʿarab*]." Ibn Ayyūb, *Kitāb*, 43. Taşköprīzade also frequently commented on people's skin color, height, and facial hair, e.g., Ṭaşköprīzāde, *Shaqāʾiq*, 79, 87, 92.

In any case, under the probing eyes of the other guests, visitors standing in the threshold of the reception hall then faced the event that clarified their rank within the gathering: the greeting and the seating. This brings us to the controversy at Hasan Bey's reception. Hasan had invited leading Damascenes to his residence, including his dear friend Ghazzi.[75] Strictly speaking, Ghazzi had withdrawn from Damascene social life more than a decade earlier, having decided to forego just this sort of showy gathering for a more contemplative lifestyle. It was therefore a testament to Ghazzi's affection for Hasan that he accepted the invitation. It was probably also what threw everything into disarray.

Hasan was already sitting with other guests in the seating area of his reception hall when Ghazzi arrived. Honored by the presence of this esteemed guest, so rarely spotted in polite company, Hasan stood up to welcome him. Hasan walked to the fountain in the center of the hall to receive his friend, embracing him and kissing his hand before the assembled party.[76] This detail, original to the account of Ibn Ayyub, was not invented for literary effect. Rather, such physical interactions acted as the highly visible and tangible expressions of human relationships, as images also attest (see figure 3.6).[77] Observers of Ottoman social life carefully recorded physical gesture: was the guest embraced? How far did the host walk to meet him? Who kissed whose hand? Were tears shed? When one student accompanied his teacher into the presence of Sultan Bayezid II in the late fifteenth century, he counted how many steps the sultan took in the direction of his teacher (seven).[78] Ghazzi was attentive to such details in his travelogue as well, using them to establish a hierarchy of social relations; we have already seen with what tenderness he was met by Ayas Pasha in Istanbul.[79] Hasan, for his part, was said to have commanded so much respect that even the high-ranking men who came before him would

75. Ibn Ayyub states that Hasan held the reception in the "domed hall (*qaʿa*) that was the seat of the court," located in the judge's residence. Ibn Ayyūb, *Rawḍ*, 52a, 75a–b; Ghazzī, *Kawākib*, 3: 141.

76. Ibn Ayyūb, *Rawḍ*, 52a; Ibn Ayyūb, *Kitāb*, 51. Tasköprīzade's biographies suggests that it was normal for hosts to stand to greet esteemed guests, since he singled out those who flouted these conventions by standing up for everyone regardless of rank or for no one at all. Ṭaşköprīzāde, *Shaqāʾiq*, 251, 353.

77. In fifteenth-century Istanbul, the scholar Gürani was said to have refused to bow in front of the sultan or to kiss his hand. Ṭaşköprīzāde, *Shaqāʾiq*, 87. Painters paid close attention to gesture as well. Fetvacı, "Others," esp. 87; Değirmenci, "Osmanlı Sarayının Geçmişe Özlemi," 110; Necipoğlu, "Serial Portrait," 25–7.

78. The scholar in question was Hatibzade Muhyiddin (d. 1496). Ṭaşköprīzāde, *Shaqāʾiq*, 148.

79. Ghazzī, *Maṭāliʿ*, 50–1, 131. See Chapter 2 of this work.

FIGURE 3.6. A man kisses the hand of a Sufi shaykh. From Muhtasibzade Mehmed Haki, *Tercüme-i Şaka'ik-i nu'maniye* (c. 1618–20). (Reproduced by permission from the Directorate of National Palaces, Topkapı Palace Museum Library, MS H. 1263, 121b.)

keep their heads bowed in his presence.[80] The sight of such a personage leaping to his feet to embrace Ghazzi must have been astonishing.

It then fell to Hasan to seat his guest. This was no simple task. At first blush, one might take seating arrangements to suggest social parity among participants. Whether guests were seated on carpets spread across the floor or on a low, wide bench that sometimes ran along the perimeter of a reception chamber (*soffa*), they were usually arranged in circles or

80. Ibn Ayyūb, *Kitāb*, 50–1.

semicircles and all at eye-level with one another (see figure 3.5).[81] Yet in fact seating arrangements were profoundly hierarchical. At the head of the gathering sat the man who was, in principle, of the highest social rank: the host. Indoors, he would often sit against the back wall of the reception area with a clear view of the entire room, as Kadiri Çelebi did in the upper-floor chamber in which he is depicted in figure 2.4. Some hosts designed this back wall in such a way as to accentuate their own visibility. In one early seventeenth-century Istanbul home, the tiles above the place where the host usually sat were arranged "with the frieze curving above it, in bold relief, making a perspective, as of a throne, for the most worthy person."[82] Ghazzi used a similar strategy when he convened a gathering in one of the side chambers of the Great Mosque while sitting in the prayer niche (*mihrab*) indicating the direction of Mecca.[83]

The status of the rest of the participants was a function of their distance from the host. To the right of the host sat the guest of honor, to his left a close second.[84] From these two pillars, the hierarchy descended, and in both Arabic and Turkish, people wrote of sitting above or below, or higher or lower than others, revealing just how literally these arrangements reflected social hierarchy.[85] On rare occasions a host would go so far as to surrender his own seat to an especially esteemed guest.

81. The term *soffa* in sixteenth-century Istanbul seems to have referred either to a stone bench or, by extension, to an *iwan* or veranda featuring such a bench. Caʿfer Efendi glossed the Arabic *soffa* as "a high seat like a stone bench or porch" in Turkish and "a shady place to rest on" in Persian. Caʿfer Efendi, *Risāle-i Miʿmāriyye*, 88 (74r). Yérasimos calls the *soffa* "difficult to define in spite of its centrality to Ottoman domestic architecture." Yérasimos, "Dwellings," 279. See also Phillips, *Everyday Luxuries*, 85. Such a furnishing is mentioned by Ibn Battuta in the fourteenth century, Stephan Gerlach in the sixteenth, and Pietro della Valle in the early seventeenth century. Ibn Baṭṭūṭa, *Travels*, 2:442; Necipoğlu, "Garden Culture," 36, 41; della Valle, *Pilgrim*, 19. For sixteenth-century depictions, see Ertuğ, "Ceremonies," 263; Kütükoğlu, "Divân-ı Hümâyûn," 58–61.

82. Della Valle, *Pilgrim*, 19.

83. Būrīnī, *Tarājim*, 2: 95–6. Though the Rumi scholar Kınalızade ʿAli believed that individuals should sit according to their rank, he warned hosts against being too territorial about their own seats. Oktay, *Ahlâk-ı Alâî*, 394.

84. For the significance of the right side see also Ṭaşköprīzāde, *Shaqāʾiq*, 359. Ghazzi's gatherings followed similar hierarchies, with the Hanafi mufti sitting to his right and a leading scholar of the city to his left in one assembly. Būrīnī, *Tarājim*, 2: 96. For seating arrangements in the imperial council (which likewise reveal a preference for the right side), see Ertuğ, "Ceremonies," 260; Kütükoğlu, "Divân-ı Hümâyûn." For examples from other periods, Ibn Baṭṭūṭa, *Travels*, 2: 438–9, 441–2; Sajdi, "Dead," 126; Chamberlain, *Knowledge*, 159.

85. Laṭīfī, *Tezkire-i Laṭīfī*, 293–4; Ibn Ayyūb, *Kitāb*, 51; Oktay, *Ahlâk-ı Alâî*, 394.

If the salon demanded that a person's physical position align with his social position, the challenge was deciding how to evaluate one man's rank vis-à-vis another. As one of Ghazzi's friends, an Istanbul-based poet, put it:

If it is a salon of the learned
Everyone deliberates about his spot.
By sitting in the front, a fool
Imagines that he is on top.[86]

It was not just that many men had an exaggerated sense of their own social standing. Much worse, there were countless, often conflicting, factors that gave someone the right to a leading seat in the salon. A man's political office was no doubt the most important factor determining his seat. In Damascus, if governors or judges were not presiding as hosts themselves, they almost always occupied the seat to the host's immediate right. Just how closely particular offices were related to preferential seating is suggested by the way in which the Rumi biographer ʿAşık Çelebi (d. 1572) described Hasan's master Kadiri: "the one with the elevated seat in the gatherings of the loftiest ones and the king of the worthy men."[87]

Factors other than rank also had to be taken into consideration. First, personal relationships were honored, and hosts would often seat favored guests close to themselves as a sign of affection. When the revered Ottoman scholar Hocazade Muslihuddin Efendi (d. 1488) held a celebratory banquet when his family visited him in Istanbul, "he sat at the head of the gathering, his father was next to him, and the rest of the grandees sat according to their rank."[88] That his brothers were relegated to the place where the servants usually stood, in turn, unequivocally signaled his estimation of them. For nonkin, seating arrangements had an even more important role in clarifying relationships. When an Arab client gained the trust of an Ottoman scholar in the early 1570s, he recorded that the latter "fulfilled my hopes and gave me a closer seat [*qarraba majlisī*]."[89]

A prestigious lineage was another trait that made someone worthy of a "high" seat. As Ghazzi counseled, one of the rules of good companionship was "knowing the names of one's brethren and the names of their ancestors, so as not to infringe upon their rights."[90] The principle worked

86. Fevri (for whom see Chapter 6 of this work) as quoted in ʿĀşıḳ Çelebi, *Meşâʿirü's-Şuʿarâ*, 1228.

87. ʿĀşıḳ Çelebi, *Meşâʿirü's-Şuʿarâ*, 1311.

88. Ṭaşköprīzāde, *Shaqāʾiq*, 130.

89. Ḥamawī, *Ḥādī*, 23; or similar in Ḥamawī, *Majmūʿa*, 39a.

90. Ghazzī, *ʿIshra*, 25.

in Ghazzi's own favor, since his family traced its legacy to the Quraysh, the tribe to which the Prophet Muhammad had belonged. Both Ghazzi's father and his son composed rhymes by which to remind others of what the family was due. His father's went:

I'm nicknamed "the father of virtue" and as for my family line:
It's of the Quraysh through ʿAmir ibn Luʾayy.[91]

Being of Qurayshi descent was no doubt a badge of honor, but it did not make the Ghazzis *sayyids* or *sharifs*, direct descendants of the Prophet. This coveted status conferred a number of concrete privileges. One was exemption from certain taxes; another was occupying a distinguished seat at gatherings.[92] Though the latter was recognized in principle across the Islamic world, it was not always strictly observed. Ghazzi's friend ʿAbd al-Rahim al-ʿAbbasi, who traced his ancestry to the Prophet's uncle and was widely revered as a *sayyid*, found this out the hard way. He was furious when someone took a seat above him at an elite salon one day, comforting himself with the thought that he was not the only shining light who had to endure such slights:

So the ignorant man sits above me and does not
Heed the considerations of knowledge and pedigree!
Well, Saturn, too is higher than the sun,
But in terms of virtue the sun is always at the apogee.[93]

In the absence of a physical position that accorded with his rank, ʿAbbasi could console himself with his superiority in knowledge and virtue.

Indeed, learning, too, was valued. As revered as the fifteenth-century Rumi scholar Hocazade was, he was plagued for much of his adult life by a powerful vizier who did everything he could to undermine Hocazade's career. Still, no matter how many positions the vizier stripped him of, the scholar enjoyed such stature that the vizier himself had to acknowledge it. When Hocazade rode to the vizier's house on horseback one day, trailed by a retinue of respected professors walking on foot as if they were his servants,

91. Būrīnī, *Tarājim*, 2: 93. For Ghazzi's son's poem, see Ghazzī, *Maṭāliʿ*, MS Fazıl Ahmed Paşa 1390, 0a.

92. Kılıç, "Islamic Tradition," 132. Prophetic descent was also honored in seating arrangements in seventeeth-century Central Asia. DeWeese, "Descendants," 612–3. It also influenced the decision of Timur, the founder of the Persian Timurid Empire, to seat Jurjani above Saʿd al-Din Taftazani. Ṭaşköprīzāde, *Shaqāʾiq*, 43.

93. Ghazzī, *Maṭāliʿ*, 144. For a similar poem, see Fevri as quoted in ʿĀşıḳ Çelebi, *Meşâʿirü's-Şuʿarâ*, 1228. Prophetic descent could also influence other aspects of the way a man was treated at a salon. Aynur, "Autobiographical Elements," 19.

the vizier had no choice but to defer to his status. After coming to the door to meet the visitors, the vizier offered Hocazade his own seat (the poor professors, meanwhile, had to stand). After the scholar left, the vizier admitted that all his machinations had been ineffective in denting Hocazade's reputation: "clearly, I've been unable to diminish his standing," the vizier grumbled to himself. "I hadn't realized that he was revered for his knowledge rather than for his office [*manṣib*]!"[94] The historian Taşköprizade, from whom this story issues, was particularly adamant about the rights conferred by erudition. His biographical dictionary is full of anecdotes in which leading political figures—including the sultan himself—deferred to scholars by paying them visits or offering them an honored seat.[95]

Not all salongoers shared this value system, and scholars routinely complained that learning was being sidelined in favor of what they took to be more superficial forms of social capital. As one of Ghazzi's Rumi contemporaries lamented when a rich man sat at the front of a gathering in Istanbul:

> The low and the vile are respected in the world,
> The learned are always dropped.
> The state of the world is that of the ocean:
> The pure jewel is at the bottom, the carcass floats at the top.[96]

Even over the loudest remonstrances of the literati, wealth, too, could win some guests a desirable seat.

Many salons, especially regular gatherings of friends, likely featured seating arrangements that were habitual and therefore uncontroversial. Yet the more exceptional the makeup of an assembly was, the less likely could it invoke an agreed-upon social hierarchy upon which seating arrangements could be based. As a result, disagreements arose most often in those most exceptional of gatherings, which usually happened to be those that mattered most. Some hosts sought to forestall seating disputes by devising seating plans in advance or by instructing a trusted servant to usher guests to their designated spot.[97] But many others, loath, perhaps,

94. Ṭaşköprīzāde, *Shaqāʾiq*, 131.

95. In the illustrated version of his history, this same notion is emphasized by depicting sultans sharing carpets with revered scholars. Değirmenci, "Osmanlı Sarayının Geçmişe Özlemi," 111. See also Ṭaşköprīzāde, *Shaqāʾiq*, 43. Timur was said to have had such great respect for Taftazani that he shared his cushion with the scholar. Manz, *Power*, 197.

96. This was the poet Lamiʿi Çelebi (d. 1531/2). Laṭīfī, *Tezkire-i Laṭīfī*, 293–4.

97. In one gathering Mehmed II asked one of his guests in advance where he would like to sit. Ṭaşköprīzāde, *Shaqāʾiq*, 118–9. For an usher, see Laṭīfī, *Tezkire-i Laṭīfī*, 293.

to make the determinations that could only make enemies, left matters up to their guests.[98]

Hasan Bey seems to have taken a mixed approach. Returning to his seat on the elevated platform after having greeted Ghazzi, he invited him to sit down to his immediate right, as might be expected in light of their friendship and Ghazzi's stature. However, Hasan did not then stand to greet the next guest to arrive, Ghazzi's nemesis ʿAlaʾ al-Din Ibn ʿImad al-Din al-Shafiʿi (d. 1563). ʿAlaʾ al-Din was also a leading scholar of the city. As he made his entrance, guests might have noted his unusually small build, which he seemed to accentuate by wearing gowns that were too long for him, so that when he walked he had to hitch them up with his hands.[99] Yet ʿAla al-Din's social stature far exceeded his physical size; he was an influential jurisconsult and had the ear of the Ottoman establishment.[100] During a trip to Istanbul in 1539–40, ʿAla al-Din had earned not only great respect for his learning, but also an appointment at a madrasa in Damascus (as well as the nickname "Little ʿAlaʾ al-Din" [*Küçük ʿAlaʾeddin*]).[101] He was a cornerstone of Damascene social gatherings, and a gracious host in his own right.[102] In the Meccan traveler Nahrawali's list of all of the scholars he met while in Damascus, ʿAla al-Din's name ranked highly, and was mentioned in the same breath as Ghazzi's.[103]

Yet, as we saw, ʿAlaʾ al-Din and Ghazzi had parted on unfriendly terms. About ten years younger than Ghazzi but like him an expert in Shafiʿi law, ʿAlaʾ al-Din had studied jurisprudence (*fiqh*) with him many years earlier until his descent into uncontrollable laughter.[104] According to Ibn Ayyub, ʿAlaʾ al-Din had come to downright detest Ghazzi; he emerged as a fierce critic of one of Ghazzi's more controversial writings and "claimed that he was more learned than [Ghazzi]."[105] He even went so far as to deny ever having studied with him. Since Ghazzi had withdrawn from the Damascene social scene in the late 1530s or early 1540s, it is possible that ʿAlaʾ al-Din had managed to avoid being in close quarters with his old teacher for over a decade, and perhaps had not expected to meet him on this occasion.

98. Ṭaşköprīzāde, *Shaqāʾiq*, 134.

99. For biographies, see Ibn Ayyūb, *Rawḍ*, 200a–202a; Ibn al-Ḥanbalī, *Durr*, 94–7; Ghazzī, *Kawākib*, 3: 182–6.

100. Nahrawālī, *Journey*, 46.

101. Ibn Ayyūb, *Rawḍ*, 200b, 201a; Ghazzī, *Kawākib*, 3: 184.

102. Ibn al-Ḥanbalī, *Durr*, 1: 997; Ibn Ayyūb, *Kitāb*, 12.

103. Nahrawālī, *Journey*, 46–7.

104. Ghazzī, *Kawākib*, 3: 182–3.

105. Ibn Ayyūb, *Rawḍ*, 200b.

It is possible that ʿAlaʾ al-Din saw the occasion as a chance to make his opinion of Ghazzi public. Having reached his mid-forties, he may have felt ready to challenge Ghazzi's status as the city's leading mufti and Shafiʿi scholar.[106] Or maybe he acted in the grip of his emotions, frenzied in the unexpected presence of his rival. Either way, according to Ibn Ayyub, it was clear where ʿAlaʾ al-Din should have sat after his entry into the reception hall, namely "below" (*taḥta*) Ghazzi, that is, to his immediate right. Yet instead of removing his sandals and joining the others on the raised platform, ʿAlaʾ al-Din sat down on the edge of the platform straight across from Hasan, with his left foot tucked in beneath him and the right one on the stone ground below.[107] This was an odd move. The younger scholar had not, after all, claimed a seat that was superior to Ghazzi's—a frequent occurrence in such assemblies—but one that placed him at the physical margins of the gathering, outside of its internal hierarchy, roughly the equivalent of refusing to sit down at the table at a dinner party.[108] In the quasi-diplomatic arena of the Ottoman salon, it was a declaration of war.

Whatever ʿAlaʾ al-Din's motives, his gesture was read as a refusal to subordinate himself to Ghazzi.[109] As such, Hasan had to intervene; his duty as host was to ensure that his guests were treated with the respect they were due. Hasan called over to ʿAlaʾ al-Din: "what is preventing you from sitting below our lord the great Islamic scholar [*Shaykh al-Islām*]?" referring to Ghazzi by his honorary title. "He is older than you, and more learned." No doubt humiliated by this stinging admonition, ʿAla al-Din stood up to leave. It was Ghazzi who instead responded, adding insult to injury: "oh my lord, such are our sons—some of them treat people with honor, and others are disobedient," using a word that demeaned ʿAlaʾ al-Din as a fractious child. ʿAlaʾ al-Din left without saying a word, leaving the assembled company stunned.[110]

This incident—which Ibn Ayyub repeated twice in his compendium—is one of countless disputes over seating arrangements that Ottoman biographical dictionaries record. The ubiquity of such accounts suggests how seriously contemporaries took salons when it came to evaluating status.

106. Ibn Ayyūb, *Rawḍ*, 200b.

107. Ibn Ayyub says "he sat facing the Efendi [Hasan] in front of the chest [*ṣundūq*]." Ibn Ayyūb, *Rawḍ*, 52b, 115a–b. Ghazzi says "he sat across from the Efendi behind the chest on the side of the *iwan*." Ghazzī, *Kawākib*, 3: 141.

108. Būrīnī, *Tarājim*, 2: 96.

109. Ghazzī, *Kawākib*, 3:141.

110. Ibn Ayyūb, *Kitāb*, 51.

According to popular lore, when the fifteenth-century Persian ruler Timur sat the famed scholar Jurjani above his rival Taftazani, the latter was so devastated that he died of sorrow.[111] Closer to home, if less tragically, when Mehmed II held a banquet and announced to the leading scholar Gürani that he would be seated to his left—leaving the right-hand side for his rival—the piqued scholar responded that "his commitment to knowledge and piety would not allow him to take part in the gathering," and moved to Bursa out of protest (though he returned when the sultan invited him back).[112] Exaggerated as some of these stories may have been, they help us make sense of the shame and anger ʿAlaʾ al-Din must have felt; not only had Hasan proclaimed him less learned than his former teacher, ʿAlaʾ al-Din—unlike Ghazzi—was found at a loss for words at the moment when they might have mattered most. If ʿAlaʾ al-Din's refusal to take his seat was meant to demonstrate that he had achieved preeminence over Ghazzi, its outcome instead confirmed that he was considered the lesser man.

However powerfully this incident conveys the stakes of salons for guests, it also draws attention to the power these assemblies bestowed on hosts. It was Hasan who decided that Ghazzi deserved the seat of honor and Hasan who forced ʿAlaʾ al-Din to occupy a subordinate position. Had Hasan instead risen to greet ʿAlaʾ al-Din and invited him to sit at his right, ʿAlaʾ al-Din's experience—and perhaps even his professional fortunes—would likely have differed considerably. Because they made decisions about greetings and seating arrangements and in directing conversation, hosts wielded considerable power in helping to construct social hierarchies. As such, it mattered that Ottoman officials were thrust *ex officio* into the role of host. Not only did these officials control the formal levers of power; they were also arbiters of social status. To be sure, their judgments were not cast in stone. Locals could and did form their own opinions over who was more learned, and likely influenced Ottoman officials who came from elsewhere and possessed little advance knowledge of local society. Nonetheless, Ottoman officials could certainly put their hand on the scale.[113]

111. Ṭaşköprīzāde, *Shaqāʾiq*, 43.

112. The rival in question was Molla Hüsrev. Ṭaşköprīzāde, *Shaqāʾiq*, 118–9. For other examples, see Ṭaşköprīzāde, *Shaqāʾiq*, 43, 134; Ibn Ayyūb, *Rawḍ*, 28a (citing Ibn Tulun); Būrīnī, *Tarājim*, 2: 11–2, 95–7.

113. Ghazzi's son speculates that ʿAlaʾ al-Din was silent because he knew how much Hasan Bey respected Ghazzi, underlining the extent to which hosts shaped interactions between guests. Ghazzī, *Kawākib*, 3: 141.

Whatever privileges Ottoman functionaries may have enjoyed as hosts, even they did not escape judgment. Ibn Ayyub recounted the story of Ghazzi and ʿAlaʾ al-Din in Hasan's biography (and again in the biography of Hasan's son Ahmed), rather than in his portraits of ʿAlaʾ al-Din or Ghazzi. This suggests that he thought the anecdote conveyed above all something about the judge. Indeed, one of the most sacred responsibilities of any salon host was to ensure that no guest would suffer embarrassment. However a guest might misbehave, Ghazzi intimated, the host's honor would be besmirched if the proceedings did damage to one of the guests.[114] Even during class lessons, it was important that if an unexpected visitor appeared, a professor should always be kind and welcoming, but should "not turn towards him or look at him too often, thus making him feel like an outsider, since that would embarrass him."[115] By this light, Hasan Bey was hardly the embodiment of a sensitive and judicious host. Rather, he lost control over his own gathering, proving equally helpless in preventing ʿAlaʾ al-Din from insulting Ghazzi as he did Ghazzi from firing an insult back. On top of that, Hasan Bey suffered the premature departure of one of his guests.

What happened after ʿAlaʾ al-Din's abrupt exit that day supports the sense that Ottoman hosts, however esteemed, could not escape judgment. The next guest to arrive at Hasan Bey's salon was the preacher (*khatib*) of the city's Great Mosque.[116] Hasan Bey welcomed him and exclaimed in an expression of respect, "dear preacher, you are my father!" The preacher declined modestly, subordinating himself verbally to the judge: "Oh no not at all, my lord, so help me God. I am the father of all the judges except for you, my lord—I am your son and you are my father!" On the surface, the interaction seemed like a standard, if somewhat idiosyncratic, exchange of obsequies. But as the preacher later explained to those who had witnessed the scene, it had a subtext. "Did you hear the gentleman's words to me, 'you are my father?'" he asked. "That would imply that I am a Christian, since he is a [former] slave of Rüstem Pasha and has Christian origins and a Christian father!" To avoid this implication, the preacher continued, "I responded to him in the way you heard, that he is my father, since he is a Muslim," and since, according to Islamic law, that would have made the metaphorical son Muslim as well.

114. Ghazzī, *Ādāb al-Muʾākala*, 16.

115. Ghazzī, *al-Durr al-naḍīd*, 208.

116. The scholar in question was Abu al-Baqaʾ al-Biqaʿi (d. 1558). The following is based on Ibn Ayyūb, *Rawḍ*, 115b, with a slightly different version on 52a–b. For Biqaʿi see Nahrawali, *Journey*, 54; Ibn al-ʿImād, *Shadharāt*, 10: 502; Ghazzī, *Kawākib*, 1: 76, 3: 13, 174.

Though Ibn Ayyub's descriptions of this occasion are frustratingly brief, it seems safe to assume that Hasan had never meant to imply that the preacher was Christian. Rather, it was the preacher who turned his host's innocuous comment into a sectarian matter, taking a statement intended to establish an affinity between the two and using it instead to emphasize Hasan's alterity. Moreover, by claiming later that he had referred to Hasan Bey as "my father" only to avoid being insinuated as a Christian, the preacher intimated that his compliment for Hasan Bey had in fact been insincere. Ibn Ayyub's short gloss on the preacher's words suggests this subversive potential, preempting anyone that might think it untoward to win laughs at the expense of the chief judge. "It was just a harmless joke," he reassured readers.[117]

Be that as it may, one thing is certain: Hasan's religious background formed an important part of how the judge was received in Damascene salons. One of the peculiarities of the sixteenth-century Ottoman imperial elite was that many were born Christian. Not just Hasan Bey, but many other judges and governors had been recruited from Christian populations before being converted to Islam, a practice regularized through the devşirme levy that forced Balkan boys into palace service. Like Hasan, these recruits were subject not only to extensive religious training, but also to years of linguistic and behavioral instruction that recast them in the Ottoman imperial mold. It remains unknown to what extent the Christian origins of these converts continued to shape their self-understanding in adulthood.[118] The comments of the preacher suggest that, at least for many others, it remained a crucial part of how they were perceived.

Matters of identity were never far from the minds of sixteenth-century salongoers. For hosts as for guests, salons were stages on which status could be performed and evaluated. The shared conviction that all people were to be treated in accordance with their social status charged even the most innocuous interactions with great meaning. In salons as elsewhere, attributes of high status as defined by political office were no doubt important, giving Ottoman officials a level of influence and wealth that was overpowering. But this power was never absolute. Lineage, learning, and even religious pedigree also affected the respect men enjoyed and the privileges that accrued to them.

117. Ibn Ayyūb, *Rawḍ*, 52b.

118. It is known that they continued to be involved in their communities of origin and to make use of the connections and skills that their backgrounds afforded them. Barkey, *Empire of Difference*, 124; Dursteler, *Venetians in Constantinople*, 119–23.

Ghazzi in Retreat

If gaining access to elite circles was an achievement, there was no show of greater confidence than willfully withdrawing from them. Around the age of forty, Ghazzi retreated into a cell at the eastern corner of the Great Mosque.[119] As his son later explained, this was necessitated in part by the constant stream of visitors at his door: "generation after generation found use in his knowledge and traveled to him from far-away places, and it became necessary for him to withdraw from people in the middle of his life."[120] Ghazzi was not alone in choosing this path—a number of other scholars and mystics from the period did too.[121] Still, the decision was widely remarked upon. In Aleppo, "that which was famous about Badr al-Din in the phases [of his life] was his seclusion [*iʿtizāl*] from people in his residence, his commitment to books of learning, and the dedication of his pen to composing useful works."[122] ʿAlaʾ al-Din took to calling Ghazzi "the bat of darkness," since he was so rarely seen by the light of day.[123] On the one hand, Ghazzi's decision to retreat was infused with spiritual meaning. There had always been a tension in Sufi practice between engaging with society and withdrawing from it. That in the centuries preceding Ghazzi most Sufis had advocated for engagement only made his decision more impressive.[124]

On the other hand, however motivated by spiritual necessity, Ghazzi's renunciation was also a show of might. That withdrawal was a form of power was most obviously modeled by sultans themselves, who began to recede from public life in the later fifteenth century.[125] But the same was true on Ghazzi's more modest scale. Burini made the political implications

119. The room into which he retreated was called "the Aleppo cell" (*al-khalwa al-Ḥalabiyya*). Ibn Ayyūb, *Kitāb*, 50; Būrīnī, *Tarājim*, 2: 94; Ghazzī, *Kawākib*, 3:7. Unfortunately, I have been unable to locate this chamber, despite the efforts of many kind colleagues to help me do so. My thanks to Doris Behrens-Abouseif, Walter Denny, Issam Hajjar, Lorenz Korn, Dana Sajdi, and Stefan Weber for their advice on this question.

120. Ghazzī, *Kawākib*, 3: 5. Ghazzi must have begun his seclusion sometime between 1534, when he attended a feast hosted by Ibn Tulun, and 1552, when Hasan Bey arrived in Damascus, probably sometime in the late 1530s or early 1540s. Ibn Ayyūb, *Rawḍ*, 242b; Ibn Ayyūb, *Kitāb*, 50.

121. Other scholars in sixteenth-century Damascus chose the same path. In Ghazzi's own social circle this included his colleague and friend Shihab al-Din al-Tibi the elder and the poet Fevri Efendi. Ibn Ayyūb, *Kitāb*, 8; ʿĀşıḳ Çelebi, *Dhayl*, 113.

122. Ibn al-Ḥanbalī, *Durr*, 2: 438.

123. Būrīnī, *Tarājim*, 1: 251.

124. Landolt, "Khalwa."

125. Necipoğlu, *Architecture*, 15–22.

of Ghazzi's renunciation explicit when he wrote of his former teacher, "he did not frequent the houses of anyone, rich or poor, and he did not submit to any ruler or amir."[126] The vow was remarkable because it signaled Ghazzi's independence.

For all this, Ghazzi did not in fact retreat from the world of socializing after he took his vow. Although his visit to Hasan Bey seems to have been a rare exception when Ghazzi ventured out of his chamber into a private residence, on plenty of occasions he himself received individuals or even entire groups. To be fair, these gatherings usually had an academic purpose, mostly consisting of celebrations when he completed a book or class. But the gatherings also faded into more convivial occasions, since they were often followed by banquets that plenty of nonscholarly types, including the city's grandees, attended.[127]

In other words, Ghazzi's vow merely meant that he would not seek out the wealthy and powerful; they were still welcome to come to him. As his son Najm al-Din later explained, "he did not visit judges, rulers, or grandees; instead, they came to his noble residence seeking knowledge, blessings, and prayers."[128] Though Najm al-Din tended to exaggeration in matters concerning his father, more disinterested sources also attest to Ottoman officialdom's interest in the scholar. In the early 1560s, when the Rumi scholar Kınalızade ʿAli arrived in Damascus as chief magistrate, only two men did not rush to meet the new judge. The first was ʿAlaʾ al-Din, who was very ill. The second was Ghazzi. Instead, according to Ibn Ayyub, Kınalızade himself sought out the two men—but, tellingly, as Ibn Ayyub's account made clear, first Ghazzi, and then ʿAlaʾ al-Din, who died six days later.[129] The fact that both Ibn Ayyub and Ghazzi's son recorded these details in their biographies of Kınalızade demonstrate how important both men took them to be.

By the 1570s, when Ghazzi was nearing the end of his life, he not only could compel others to visit him, he could refuse them, even turning away a provincial governor, if we are to believe Ghazzi's son. Najm al-Din claimed that when Derviş Pasha (d. 1579) arrived in Damascus as governor in 1571, he sought an audience with Ghazzi. Initially Ghazzi refused, and only consented after a second and third request. When the governor

126. Būrīnī, *Tarājim*, 2: 94.

127. Ghazzī, *Kawākib*, 3: 5–6. See also Chapter 4 of this work. Continuing to associate with others while in seclusion was also common in the central Ottoman lands. Niyazioğlu, "Reclusion," 230.

128. Ghazzī, *Kawākib*, 3: 5.

129. Ibn Ayyūb, *Rawḍ*, 204a; Ghazzī, *Kawākib*, 3: 187.

arrived, Ghazzi nevertheless offered him a seat next to him, as a sign of his respect. According to Najm al-Din, Derviş refused the honor, insisting, as a show of his greater deference, that he sit in front of him instead. Ghazzi then admonished the governor for the insolence and treachery of his police chief (*subaşı*), upon which the governor censured the chief and promptly let the chief go.[130]

Ghazzi does not seem to have acted in this way in a deliberate show of strength. He himself felt honored by the visits of distinguished figures, as emerges from his record of the visit of another chief judge, Çivizade Mehmed Efendi (d. 1587), to one of his final class sessions: "through his presence he bestowed an honor on me, since he saw me as deserving."[131] Still, some saw Ghazzi as insolent in his unwillingness to treat others with the customary respect that visiting them conferred. Another Ottoman chief judge, Maʿlulzade Mehmed Efendi (d. 1585), who was appointed to Damascus in 1567 or 1568, was incensed that Ghazzi "did not regularly visit him in accordance with the practice of Damascenes."[132] Nor could Maʿlulzade forgive Ghazzi for spurning the funeral cortège for Maʿlulzade's daughter when she died during the family's stay in Damascus (though Ghazzi had paid his respects by leading the worshippers in prayer at her funeral service). When Maʿlulzade was appointed chief military judge in Istanbul in the spring of 1573, he took his revenge, as we shall see in the final chapter.

Maʿlulzade's actions may have simply been the expression of a surly nature, since many other chief judges were happy to attend Ghazzi's learned gatherings.[133] But it may also have been the sign of the times. Ghazzi lived through an era that witnessed the growing erosion of scholarly independence at the hands of a centralizing state, not just in Damascus but all across the Ottoman Empire. It is against this backdrop that the historian Taşköprizade, Ghazzi's colleague in Istanbul, sought to highlight stories in which this trend was reversed, in which rulers deferred to scholars rather than the other way around.[134] "He is the Ottoman Sultan, surely it is appropriate to bow to him and kiss his hand," a student protested to his teacher, a famous scholar of the fifteenth century, after the scholar seemed to spurn the sultan during a royal audience. "You're wrong," the teacher responded. "It is enough of an honor for him that a scholar like me

130. Ghazzī, *Kawākib*, 3: 5. For more on Derviş Pasha, see Ibn Ayyūb, *Rawḍ*, 125b–126b.
131. Ghazzī, "Ijāza," 232b.
132. Ghazzī, *Kawākib*, 3: 28.
133. See Chapter 5 of this work.
134. Anooshahr, "Writing."

would visit him at all—he's satisfied with that."[135] As both Taşköprizade and Ghazzi knew all too well, in the sixteenth century, this kind of behavior could come at a steep price.

Ghazzi's decision to retreat from Damascene social life was a powerful one. It was not a route open to many of his contemporaries, since for most of them it would have meant a descent into obscurity as well as exclusion from the prestige and patronage salons were so central in allocating. It is no small measure of Ghazzi's sacred and social stature that, in his case, it only acted to increase his influence.

Conclusion

Salons acted as key spaces for establishing and reproducing elite male status in sixteenth-century Ottoman lands. Simply taking part in these exclusive assemblies was a sign of privilege, since doing so required an invitation and the means to reciprocate. Yet which place a gentleman secured for himself was significant as well. A man's role within the empire-wide economy of hospitality reflected his specific position on the social ladder, as did the seat assigned to him at a given gathering. However, salons did not merely reflect status as it was decided elsewhere. As arenas where determinations of relative rank were made, salons also helped to generate social relations.

Socially homogenous as salons may have been, salon protocol made participants aware of the subtleties of human difference within the Ottoman elite. This requirement was built into the inherited concept of *adab*, which demanded that each individual be treated according to his or her particular identity and which thus required people to make continual judgments of one another as they interacted. However, salon culture was especially fraught because it turned such judgments into a zero-sum game. Seating arrangements allowed for only one single order, forcing salon-goers to weigh very different claims to elite status against one another. It was not only a question of deciding who was more learned. It was a question of judging how learning stacked up against wealth or lineage. Conflict arose from the effort to organize all these competing and often conflicting claims within an absolute hierarchy.

Such a hierarchy did not exist in the multiple and overlapping jurisdictions of the Ottoman social world. However, as hosts and guests collectively managed seating arrangements, they did important work. On the

135. The scholar in question was Hatibzade Muhyiddin. Ṭaşköprīzāde, *Shaqāʾiq*, 148.

one hand, they familiarized themselves with many different dimensions of their contemporaries' identities, including their professional careers, scholarly achievements, family histories, and personal fortunes. On the other hand, they developed their own vision of the ideal social order and the place of particular individuals within it.

Many different factors helped to determine where a person might rank within a given circle. Political office was important, as a result of which Ottoman officials often presided. Still, this was only one form of authority recognized in the salon. No matter how overwhelming the power granted by the sultan, it always coexisted—and sometimes competed—with powers that derived from God. This included the sacred charisma found in select Sufis as well as the exceptional command of religious learning found in select scholars. The first had helped to empower Ghazzi's father, the second Ghazzi himself. As a result, Ghazzi came to preside at most of the gatherings he attended during the last two decades of his life.

Ethnicity as an attribute played no direct role in these calculations—being Rumi or Arab did not in itself make someone more or less worthy of a seat at the front of the salon. Nonetheless, other attributes mapped onto these groupings in significant ways. Crucially, since Rumis dominated the upper rungs of the Ottoman government, so too did they tend to occupy a leading role in the salon. To a certain extent, this was offset by other qualities that tended to favor Arabs, especially descent from the Prophet's family or tribe, which both ʿAbbasi and Ghazzi could claim; that many Rumis fell short on this measure emerges from the preacher's joke about Hasan's father.[136] Still, lineage could soften, but rarely trump, the immense power granted to Ottoman officials. The fact that those officials so often presided in salons meant that they enjoyed a disproportionate role not only in running the formal workings of the empire, but also in determining the informal hierarchies that regulated social life.

In their concern with ceremonial and status, Ottoman salons echoed the protocols of royal courts. The likeness was not coincidental. To a certain extent, Ottoman salons did model themselves on the sultan's court, and were populated by many people who were familiar with palace ritual.[137] But these similarities are also redolent of a broader early modern culture of status interactions, found not only in royal palaces across

136. Starting in the second half of the sixteenth century, more and more Rumis began to claim sayyid status. Canbakal, "Descendents"; Canbakal, "Nobility"; Kılıç, *Osmanlıda Seyyidler ve Şerifler*, 65–6.

137. For gatherings in the Ottoman court, see Ertuğ, "Entertaining the Sultan," 129–32.

Eurasia but also at dinner tables and in church pews.[138] The dispute in Hasan Bey's salon suggests that materialized shows of status were common not only to Paris and Naples, but, in their roughest outlines at least, also to Damascus and Istanbul.

ʿAlaʾ al-Din never stopped feuding with his former teacher. He even brought the quarrel into new domans. He contrived to redirect the stream that fed the Ghazzi family fountain so that it would instead supply his own.[139] Ghazzi, however, would eventually prevail. He claimed that the very day ʿAlaʾ al-Din died, the stream miraculously returned to its former route to the Ghazzi household. At the service when ʿAlaʾ al-Din was buried, Ghazzi led the mourners in prayer. And finally, when ʿAlaʾ al-Din's widow remarried, she was betrothed to none other than Ghazzi.[140] The product of this union was Najm al-Din al-Ghazzi, the son who would go on to do most to perpetuate the Ghazzi family legacy. Inside the salon and outside of it, Ghazzi was the more powerful man.

138. Sternberg, *Status Interaction*; Marsh, "Order."

139. Ibn Ayyūb, *Rawḍ*, 242a.

140. For the service, see Ghazzī, *Kawākib*, 3: 185; for his widow, see Ibn Ayyūb, *Rawḍ*, 242a–b.

CHAPTER FOUR

The Art of Conversation

BADR AL-DIN AL-GHAZZI WAS CONGENIAL enough a conversationalist, but he was too earnest and restrained to be one whose verbal feats regularly made it into the history books. His friend and former student Abu al-Fath al-Maliki (d. 1567/8), on the other hand, was a true literary don. While Ghazzi debated legal issues in the Great Mosque of Damascus, Maliki held a court of sorts across the river at the Yalbugha Mosque, drafting satirical verses and staging poetry duels at one of the mosque's western windows in the morning and on its eastern side, overlooking the city, in the evenings. There, the literati would "meet in his presence and bring one another to judgment before him."[1] Maliki himself was a master in Arabic strophic poetry as well as the short, witty epigram. Never mind that he was often adrift in a haze of opium. Even when his head dropped on his knees, and everyone was sure he had fallen asleep, Maliki "would still understand what was said to him and what was being discussed in his salon and reply with the prettiest expression and the best interpretation."[2]

Salons were first and foremost places of conversation, and a man's verbal skills were a constant source of interest to Ottoman gentlemen. Although, as we saw in Chapter 3, office, lineage, and academic stature helped to define how a person was treated in the salon, speech acted as an independent source of authority that could contribute to—or detract from—one's standing. This was because conversation in elite circles was extraordinarily demanding. Whether in a light-hearted literary soirée or a serious scholarly discussion, such conversation required, among other

1. Ibn Ayyūb, *Kitāb*, 77. For other biographies of Maliki, see Ibn al-Ḥanbalī, *Durr*, 2: 143–5; Ghazzī, *Kawākib*, 3: 21–5. For the Yalbugha Mosque, see Rīḥāwī, "Jāmiʿ Yalbughā."

2. Ibn Ayyūb, *Kitāb*, 77. Ghazzi regretted Maliki's drug habit, and news of it reached as far as Aleppo. Ibn al-Ḥanbalī, *Durr*, 2:145.

things, eloquence, spontaneity, a capacious memory, poetic talent, and an understanding of religious and scholarly texts. Although these expectations weighed especially heavily on bookish types like Ghazzi and Maliki, ordinary Muslim gentlemen were not exempted from their burden.

Expectations of conversational excellence held as much in the imperial heartland as they did in the Arab provinces. However, as we saw in Chapter 1, salon culture in the two regions had, historically speaking, been quite different, with substantial divergences in language, literary repertoire, and intellectual concerns. These differences had significant consequences for how Rumis and Arabs interacted in the wake of the 1516–7 conquest. At least initially, the divergence did not always work in the favor of Ottoman elites trained at the imperial center, who could be left looking less eloquent and erudite than they in fact were. Such was the importance of conversation that it could reverse power relations between the conquering Ottomans and their Arab subjects.

One might wonder, though: who cared if a Muslim gentleman used the wrong vocalization of an Arabic word or recited a poem with a skewed meter in a private courtyard in Damascus? The answer is: other Muslim gentlemen, and possibly some gentlewomen. Although salons were comprised of small groups, they served as important arenas for judging intellect and character. Furthermore, their actual audiences were often much bigger than those sitting around a circle. Salons were places where reputations were made, not just locally but, with the growing mobility of people and texts, across the empire as a whole. What happened in the salon did not stay in the salon.

Speaking

Gentleman placed great value on the art of conversation in the early modern Ottoman Empire. Contemporary books on manners often included advice on conversational etiquette, and Ghazzi devoted an entire treatise to the rules of joking alone.[3] Turkish speakers were so serious about refined talk that they had a special word for it—*sohbet*, meaning conversation that was both enlightened and intimate.[4] As effortless as such conversation was supposed to appear, mastering it required years of education

3. The book could very loosely be translated as *Joking without Provoking* (*al-Murah fi al-muzah*). Ghazzī, *Murāḥ*. For Turkish works treating the same subject, see Oktay, *Ahlâk-ı Alâî*, 388–92; Kayasandık, *Konuşma Adabı*.

4. Uludağ, "Sohbet"; Andrews and Kalpakli, *The Age of Beloveds*, 106–12; Strauss, "La Conversation." The word "sohbet" has a slightly different meaning in Sufism, connoting the

and practice. The prerequisite was a command of *adab* (*edeb* in Turkish). *Adab*, which has been compared to the Latin *urbanitas* or the Greek *paideia*, connoted two distinct though interrelated things: first, proper etiquette, that is, gentility and social tact; second, literary and polite knowledge, that is, the stories, poems, and witticisms that made for a genial and enlightening soirée.[5] These expectations did as much as anything else to shape social relations within the salon.

One of the central principles of *adab* was that a person's interactions with others had to be calibrated to accord with their social station, as we saw in Chapter 3. Applied to polite conversation, this meant that who one was determined what one could say. In general, the convention acted to consolidate power at the top of the social hierarchy. Leading members of a salon could expect to receive regular encomia from their guests in the form of the panegyric odes so often recited in polite company.[6] They could also expect near-universal concurrence with their own views. In one gathering Ghazzi held in the late 1560s in the central hall of the Great Mosque of Damascus, whose participants included not only Maliki the litterateur but two leading members of the Ottoman administration, Ghazzi announced that he had discovered seven errors in the widely admired Arabic dictionary by Muhammad al-Firuzabadi (d. 1414). The meeting fell silent at the sound of this bold and improbable claim, and some of the participants exchanged concerned looks. However, no one dared to voice dissent. Ghazzi proceeded to enumerate the seven errors in detail, again without any resistance. Only after the session ended did one local scholar question his findings, not in person but in the form of a private letter (which Ghazzi duly rebutted).[7] If it was obviously unwise to challenge leading figures, some contemporaries felt that it was unseemly even to compliment them, "for educated people regard the complimenting of a superior by an inferior as an insult."[8] Status

---

transformative companionship offered by a master to his disciples. Moore, "Companionship"; Kafadar, "Self and Others."

5. Jaakko Hämeen-Anttila sums it up pithily as "suitable things to know and to act upon." Hämeen-Anttila, "Adab"; Gabrieli, "Adab"; Bonebakker, "Adab." For comparisons with *paideia*: Ali, *Salons*, 33; Khalidi, *Historical Thought*, 83; Brown, "Late Antiquity."

6. Ibn Ayyūb, *Rawḍ*, 251b; Būrīnī, *Tarājim*, 1: 68–71; İnalcık, *Şair ve Patron*, 23–35.

7. This was during Ghazzi's 1568 or 1569 gathering to mark the completion of his rhymed Qurʾan commentary. The Ottoman officials in question were Çivizade the chief judge and Fevri the chief Hanafi mufti, about which more to come in this chapter. Būrīnī, *Tarājim*, 1: 11–2, 2: 97–8.

8. Muṣṭafā ʿĀlī, *Tables*, 120. Such hierarchies were upheld in the written sphere as well, where the length and language used in biographies of scholars varied according to their social status. Niyazioğlu, *Dreams*, 57–8.

influenced not only what one could say but when one could speak, and Sultan Selim I was reported to have said that "it is appropriate for the greater man to start the conversation."[9] These kinds of conventions helped to entrench someone's status once he had achieved it.

Despite the fact that discourse usually acted to reinforce social hierarchies, it also had some power to generate, or at least influence, them. Speech was one of the main vehicles through which men could acquire authority within the salon. This was no simple matter. It required a mastery of a wide range of humanistic genres, including grammar, rhetoric, poetry, and history, as well as a familiarity with religious and scholarly writings. The hallmark of the cultivated gentleman was that he could put this knowledge into action: he was a weaver of witty anecdotes, a deft dodger of barbs, a clever poet, and a fierce debater.[10] The litterateur, called *adib* (Tur. *edib*), was especially committed to these pursuits, and both Maliki as well as the Rumi Fevri Efendi (d. 1571), the chief Hanafi mufti of Damascus, won that honorable appellation.[11] But even more sober scholars like Ghazzi or the military-minded Ayas Pasha were expected to model these characteristics.[12] Just how widespread this culture was can be seen from the range of people who appear in contemporary dictionaries of poets, one of the main genres where genteel talk was on display: from sultans, viziers, and military judges to soldiers and craftsmen.[13]

Broadly speaking, the expectations for refined conversation were shared between the Arab provinces and the central Ottoman lands. In both places, it relied upon several discrete though interrelated skills. Its foundations were correct pronunciation, proper grammar, and comfort with higher linguistic registers. This was no small feat in Arabic, then as now a highly demanding language whose colloquial and written forms

9. This was not as self-serving a statement as it may seem. Selim allegedly said this following his encounter with the shaykh Badakhshi in Damascus to explain why he stayed silent until the Sufi spoke. Ṭaşköprīzāde, *Shaqā'iq*, 357.

10. Ali, *Salons*, 13–7; Allen, *Introduction*, chapter 5, esp. 134–5; Stroumsa, "*Sū'*"; Bonebakker, "Adab." For this ideal in action, see Ḥamawī, *Ḥādī*, 54–5.

11. ʿĀşıḳ Çelebi, *Meşâʿirü's-Şuʿarâ*, 1233. For Fevri, see Laṭīfī, *Teẕkire-i Laṭīfī*, 216; ʿĀşıḳ Çelebi, *Meşâʿirü's-Şuʿarâ*, 1221–56; ʿĀşıḳ Çelebi, *Dhayl*, 111–4; Kalpaklı, "Fevrî."

12. Poetry had become increasingly important to elite communication in the Mamluk period. Bauer, "Adab"; Bauer, "Literarische Anthologien der Mamlūkenzeit."

13. Although *adab* has often been contrasted with *ʿilm*—the more specialist knowledge of religious sciences—the distinction should not be overstated in our period, both because linguistic disciplines were required to interpret religious texts and because literary knowledge had come to be ineluctable for a man of status. Bauer, "Adab"; Enderwitz, "Adab"; Bauer, "Literarische Anthologien der Mamlūkenzeit," 79–85.

differed greatly.[14] Although it is hard to imagine that the vernacular was never used in sixteenth-century Arabic-language gatherings, their literary focus and the frequent presence of non-native speakers whose training was in the written form meant that in many cases it might have been preferable to employ a formal idiom.[15] Contemporary accounts are full of explosive incidents in which men challenged others (native speakers or not) on the proper vocalization of an Arabic word.[16] Though some saw such challenges as mere pedantry, others felt the very survival of Arabic to be at stake, threatened as the language seemed to be by its growing distance from the "pure" Arabic of the Bedouins and its rapid adoption by non-native speakers.[17]

In Turkish-language gatherings, too, sophisticated speech was prized, with the learned employing ever more Persian and Arabic loan words in the course of the sixteenth century.[18] The *Book of Kabus*, the eleventh-century etiquette manual that remained popular in Turcophone circles throughout the sixteenth century, warned sophisticates not to fall into the language of the people when consuming alcohol.[19] Although sixteenth-century Ottoman Turkish had undergone less lexicographical standardization than Arabic had and thus possessed less of a normative charge, being corrected in that language was also a source of great embarrassment, even for those who did not speak it fluently. When Ebu's Suʿud Efendi corrected Maliki the litterateur's pronunciation of the Istanbul neighborhood in which he was staying (Bayezid), Maliki was so offended that he refused to ever meet with the great Rumi mufti again.[20]

14. Mamluk-era scholars were often judged on their grammatical mastery. Bauer, "Literarische Anthologien der Mamlūkenzeit," 90.

15. In learned gatherings in earlier centuries, participants often resorted to dialectal forms, since classical Arabic was considered tedious and tiresome. Szombathy, "Ridiculing the Learned," esp. 110–1. James Grehan argues (of the seventeenth and eighteenth centuries) that conversing in literary Arabic (*fusha*) was one of the distinguishing features of the educated classes. Grehan, "Words," 995.

16. Ḥamawī, *Bawādī*, 160b; Būrīnī, *Tarājim*, 2:95–6. It was said of Ibn Tulun that he never uttered or wrote a word without making a mistake. Ibn Ayyūb, *Rawḍ*, 236a.

17. Musawi, *Letters*, 85–7.

18. For this development, see Woodhead, "Ottoman Languages"; Fleischer, *Bureaucrat*, 253–4. Grehan suggests that in seventeenth- and eighteenth-century Damascus, Ottoman officials and soldiers were associated with coarser, more virile speech. Though this was true for soldiers in the sixteenth century, I've not found this association with Ottoman officials, who appeared to share similar ideals of linguistic polish. Grehan, "Words," 997–8.

19. İnalcık, "Klasik edebiyat menşei," 228.

20. Ibn Ayyūb, *Kitāb*, 80–1; Ibn Ayyūb, *Rawḍ*, 239b. For discussions of etymology and semantics in Turkish-language salons, see Aynur, "Autobiographical Elements," 23–4.

Speaking correctly was a necessary but insufficient condition for participating in polite discourse, however. Speech in the salon, whether in Arabic or Turkish, was supposed to be beautiful, that is, fluid, vivid, and even surprising. Salongoers enjoyed poems and rejoinders as much for their form as for their content. This is clear from Ghazzi's effusive description of his conversations with his Arab host ʿAbd al-Rahim al-ʿAbbasi in Istanbul in 1530–1. "In his gatherings [*mujālasa*], I feel that I am a guest of al-Qaʿqaʿ ibn Shawr," Ghazzi rhapsodized, referring to the pre-Islamic poet famous for his hospitality, continuing:

> I harvest from his banter fruits so nice, sweeter than those of paradise. I drink the water of his rushing, flowing seas, the strings of his verse are better than pearls or the planets one sees. I gather from the petals of his prose that which is superior to the wild narcissus, more fragrant than the moringa and the lotus, and more intense than the scent of the rose and the narcissus.[21]

Ghazzi's images illustrate the ideals of polite discourse, broadly shared amongst his contemporaries: fluid as poured water, orderly as a string of pearls.[22] But the passage also captures the aesthetic, even sensual, pleasure men derived from speech, a pleasure greater than stroking a flower petal or biting into ripe fruit. Turkish speakers valued the same sorts of characteristics, and maintained a rich vocabulary to characterize those who were particularly eloquent, witty, or fluent in their speech.[23]

Beauty alone was not enough, though; conversation was supposed to be fruitful, as Ghazzi's harvest metaphors suggest. Poetry, which has been called "the most important and valued form of social communication among Muslims," was the highest-yielding element of the literary repertoire of a gentleman.[24] Verse played an important role in cementing relationships between men, as we have seen. At the same time, in the sixteenth century as in the centuries before, poetry was also a source of live entertainment.[25] This was especially true at gatherings of poets (Ar. *majlis adab*, Tur. *meclis-i şuʿaraʾ*), where gentlemen gathered around wine, candles, and often prepubescent boys to traffic in lines of verse.[26] But

21. Ghazzī, *Maṭāliʿ*, 137.

22. Gelder, "Poetry for Easy Listening."

23. Kut, "Introduction," 10.

24. Ahmed, *What is Islam*, 21. See also Andrews et al., *Ottoman Lyric Poetry*, 4.

25. Ali, *Salons*; Gruendler, "Motif vs. Genre," 76–83.

26. İnalcık, *Tarab*, chapters 5–6; Andrews et al., *Ottoman Lyric Poetry*, esp. 33–4; İnalcık, "Klasik edebiyat menşei"; Hanna, *In Praise of Books*, 73; İpekten, *Edebî Muhitler*, 227–37; Fleischer, *Bureaucrat*, 22–3.

any conversation was made better by poetry. As such, people regularly committed hundreds, if not thousands, of poems to memory. The scholar Isma'il al-Nabulusi (d. 1585), a fellow traveler in Ghazzi's social circles, "memorized lots of beautiful Arabic poems, and employed them when he spoke in the salons of notables."[27] Verse also took a leading role in many of Ghazzi's conversations with 'Abbasi in Istanbul, as we know because Ghazzi's record of them crossed fifteen manuscript pages of his 1534 travel account.[28] This record also typifies the immense poetic range of many contemporaries. 'Abbasi and Ghazzi both recited many of their own compositions to one another, whether they took the form of long odes (*qasida*), shorter poems (*maqtu'*), or riddles (*uhjiyya*).[29] At the same time, the two gentlemen also invoked the compositions of earlier generations, including many women. 'Abbasi recited poems by the seventh-century Arabian female poet al-Khansa' (d. after 630), the fourteenth-century Cairene scholar Fatima bint al-Munajja al-Tanukhiyya (d. 1400), the fifteenth-century Tunisian poet Shihab al-Din Ahmad al-Tunisi (d. 1504), and Ghazzi's father Radi al-Din.[30]

Yet the arts of poetic recitation were more arduous—and more surprising—than merely delivering rehearsed lines. The true gentleman flourished in off-the-cuff conversation; he retained massive amounts of material, which he could draw on in an instant, selecting the most suitable parts and adapting them for the occasion. When the Rumi scholar Şemsi Çelebi mentioned to Ghazzi in Istanbul that although his hair had turned completely white, he was not yet fifty, Ghazzi responded by reciting the verses of a thirteenth-century Egyptian judge Ibn Daqiq al-'Id (d. 1302):

> I wished that white hair would come fast
> That the end of youth would advance at last
> so as to gain from youth its energy
> And from old age its dignity.[31]

Şemsi took satisfaction in the poem, and no wonder, since an apt citation could elevate the present by connecting it to an exalted past, transforming the banalities of everyday life into something enchanting.

27. Būrīnī, *Tarājim*, 2: 68.

28. Ghazzī, *Maṭāli'*, MS Or. 32b–47a.

29. For the *maqtu'*, see Talib, *Epigram*. For riddles, see Subtelny, "Scenes," 140–3; Bencheneb, "Lughz." Elias Saba argues that riddles were central to Islamic salon culture, serving both playful and didactic purposes: "A book of riddles prepares one for participation in a *majlis* and stimulates an actual *majlis*." Saba, *Harmonizing Similarities*, 137.

30. Ghazzī, *Maṭāli'*, 138–60.

31. Ghazzī, *Maṭāli'*, 268–9; Ebied and Young, "Ibn Daḳīḳ al-'Īd."

Indeed, skillfully deployed, poems could intensify the impact of a given moment. Many of the stock images of Ottoman poetry—wine goblets, candles, cypresses, the moon—corresponded to physical features of the salon.[32] Poems referencing these elements sharpened salongoers' attention to their immediate surroundings and allowed them to verbalize powerful sensory experiences. At one gathering in an orchard when the apple trees were in bloom, Nabulusi, the Damascene scholar, recited the lines of a Syrian poet:

We entered the gardens when they bloomed
    And were topped with pearly dew.
We saw the end of the flowering sprigs,
    When the blossoms fell from the tips of the twigs.[33]

Just as these poems invited an intense awareness of a physical environment, they simultaneously pushed listeners to transcend it. Many common literary tropes had symbolic or mystical meanings: the gardens of paradise, the intoxication of God's love, the guiding light of the shariʿa, the face of Muhammad.[34] When the sixteenth-century Rumi poet exhorted his addressees to light up their hearts with "the lamp of a wine glass," then, he helped them to take a mundane act—even an illicit one—and supercharge it with mystical meaning.[35] This ability to mediate between the physical and the transcendent made poetry a powerful actor in the salon.

The true man of letters could not only recall existing poems to match a given moment; he could craft new ones on the spot as well. When Ghazzi was invited to a banquet at a former student's house in Cairo in the winter of 1545–6, conversation turned to a new abridgement of a classic scholarly text nicknamed *The Slave* (*al-Khadim*).[36] The abridgement had been given the title *The Redaction of The Slave* (*Tahrir al-Khadim*), which had the double meaning of *The Emancipation of the Slave*. One of the guests

32. Laṭīfī, *Tezkire-i Laṭīfī*, 170; Andrews, "Gardens."

33. Būrīnī, *Tarājim*, 2: 70.

34. Ahmed, *What is Islam*, 32–46; Andrews, "Gardens," esp. 99–104; Andrews, "Literary Art," 360.

35. Laṭīfī, *Tezkire-i Laṭīfī*, 179. For another example, see Andrews, "Literary Art," 359. Scholars have debated whether Ottoman poetry—*gazels* especially—should be understood as an idealized exercise in aesthetics or rooted in concrete reality. The salon buttresses recent arguments that it was the "double nature" of this poetry that gave it its power. Havlioğlu, *Mihrî Hatun*, 59–60; Andrews and Kalpaklı, *The Age of Beloveds*, 85–6.

36. The book that had been abridged was *The Slave of Rafiʿi and the Garden* (*Khadim al-Rafiʿi wa-l-rawda*) by Muhammad al-Zarkashi.

at the banquet, one Nur al-Din, could hardly contain his enthusiasm for the ingenuity of this pun.[37] Ghazzi, who admitted that the title was good, was less convinced by the book's content. Impromptu, he composed the following poem:

Nur al-Din was truly amazed,
By the book *The Emancipation of The Slave.*
I said to him, "that's obtuse,
Since an emancipated slave has no use!
While in bondage, he served his purpose,
But when freed he became superfluous."[38]

Using the same pun that Nur al-Din so admired, Ghazzi's poem could also be understood to mean: "I said to him, 'that's obtuse / since its abridgement has no use! / In the original it served its purpose / but when abridged it became superfluous.'"[39] This was the ideal impromptu poem: tremendously witty and devastatingly sharp.

Extemporizing poetry was prized in Turcophone circles as well. A gift for impromptu verse earned the poet and mufti Fevri his pen name meaning "off-the-cuff" or "immediate." The Turkish *gazel* (Ar. *ghazal*), which usually focused on themes of love and longing, was the quintessential poetic form of the Rumi salon, since it was relatively short and easy to recite.[40] But it was only the foundation for a whole set of what Jan Schmidt calls "responsive genres," poetic forms that either built on (*tahmis, müstezad*) or vied with (*nazire*) existing lines of verse. As Schmidt points out, such playful genres "must have contributed to the jollity of poetic sessions."[41] In the right company, they could also contribute to a poet's purse. Leafing through the anthology of the Persian poet Hafiz (d. 1389/90) in the presence of Sultan Mehmed II one day, a group of Ottoman gentlemen paused upon a line of verse that the sultan found especially pleasing. When one of the courtiers modified it on the spot,

37. The guest in question was Nur al-Din al-ʿAsili (d. 1585). Ḥamawī, *Ḥādī*, 55.

38. Ghazzī, *Kawākib*, 3: 181.

39. For another instance in which Ghazzi demonstrated his improvisational skill, see Būrīnī, *Tarājim*, 2:100. See also Tamīmī, *Ṭabaqāt*, 1:382.

40. *Gazels* usually had five to seven couplets, all following the same rhyme scheme. Kuru, "The Literature of Rum," 567–8; Andrews, *Poetry's Voice, Society's Song*. Lewis emphasizes the importance of the recited *ghazal* in the medieval Persian tradition. He distinguishes "the poetical and wine *majles* in which ghazals came to be recited" from the more formal occasions for performing *qasidas*. Lewis, "Reading," 79. Arabic *ghazals* were often much longer. Bauer, "Ibn Ḥajar."

41. Schmidt, "Poets," 168. See also Havlioğlu, *Mihrî Hatun*, chapter 5.

preserving the original meter and rhyme, the sultan repaid these metaphorical gems of speech with veritable ones.[42]

However important poetry was, it was only one part of the expansive knowledge that an elite Muslim man was expected to display in conversation. Many of the poems that ʿAbbasi recited to Ghazzi in Istanbul were embedded in historical anecdotes: a horse race held for the Abbasid Caliph Harun al-Rashid (d. 809); the student outcry at their teacher Fatima bint Tanukhiyya's divorce; the death from shame of a fourteenth-century scholar at having proposed to the sultan an incorrect reading of one of the verses of al-Khansaʾ.[43] The ideal was to be able to draw on a repertoire of interesting tidbits, like the professor from Bursa who "enriched the salons; he had many histories and conversation pieces [*muḥāḍarāt*] to hand and knew countless odes, tall tales, and odd trivia [*shawārid*]."[44] Some contemporaries, recognizing how useful such knowledge was—and how difficult it was to acquire—compiled entire encyclopedias of gentlemanly knowledge; ʿAbbasi himself had composed a work that functioned as such, since it offered biographical information and commentary on well-known Arabic poems.[45]

Yet even poetic prowess was not enough to satisfy the standards of enlightened discourse. Just as often, salon conversation demanded a mastery of scholarly knowledge as well. This was especially true for learned gatherings (Ar. *majlis ʿilm*, Tur. *meclis-i ʿilm*) held explicitly for intellectual exchange. All across the Middle East, long before the institutionalization of learning in the madrasa—and long after—scholars had seen learned gatherings as opportunities to discuss books, test the skills of their rivals, and settle intellectual disagreements.[46] In some cases, debates in these gatherings occurred in the rigorous, formalized mode of the scholarly disputation (*mujadala, mudhakara*), a serious method for intellectual engagement and a popular form of entertainment in medieval Islamic courts.[47] The most spectacular and dramatic

42. Laṭīfī, *Tezkire-i Laṭīfī*, 79.

43. Ghazzī, *Maṭāliʿ*, 138–41.

44. The scholar in question was Necmi Çelebi (d. 1570). ʿĀşıḳ Çelebi, *Dhayl*, 107. See also Taşköprīzāde, *Shaqāʾiq*, 82; Būrīnī, *Tarājim*, 2:70.

45. This was ʿAbbasi's *Frequented Places for Clarification*, for which see Chapter 1, note 39. See also Bauer, "Literarische Anthologien der Mamlūkenzeit," esp. 72, 74, 92.

46. Lazarus-Yafeh, *Majlis*; Chamberlain, *Knowledge*, esp. 162–7; Makdisi, *Colleges*, 11; Dozy, *Supplément*, 1: 208.

47. Taşköprīzāde, *Shaqāʾiq*, 117, 124–5; Stroumsa, "*Sūʾ*"; Chamberlain, *Knowledge*, 164n82.

of these debates were widely remembered, such that the seventeenth-century Rumi scholar Katib Çelebi (d. 1659) included a special section on them in his bibliographical dictionary.[48] However, not all learned gatherings followed so structured a format; those that Ghazzi regularly convened also featured open-ended discussions on topics of Ghazzi's choice.

In fact, scholarly content was not restricted to scholarly gatherings. Most elite conversation combined literary and scholarly pursuits (*adab* and *ʿilm*). The light-hearted poems and anecdotes that ʿAbbasi and Ghazzi exchanged gave way to more serious devotional and legal subjects when ʿAbbasi asked Ghazzi about how to properly perform the night prayers (*witr*) and whether it was lawful to enslave those who had apostasized. Answering such questions required instant recall of the expansive Islamic intellectual tradition, surely one of the reasons why some boys began their studies by memorizing entire tomes. Ghazzi had been one such boy, and his efforts paid off.[49] He answered ʿAbbasi briefly but comprehensively, citing the opinions of different scholars—and even specific chapters from their works, when pressed—before stating his own verdict.[50] Indeed, a scholar's knowledge was on call at all times; even an innocuous personal conversation could turn into an occasion for learned discussion. When the Ottoman scholar Molla Lutfi from Tokat (d. 1495), himself a man of immense wit and learning, revealed during a soirée that he had once sweated blood until it stained his clothing, most of the guests laughed, until one piped up that there was actually nothing funny about that whatsoever, since the physician and philosopher Ibn Sina (Avicenna) (d. 1037) had mentioned the disease in a chapter of his *Canon of Medicine* (*Qanun fi al-tibb*). Soon no one was talking about poor Lutfi anymore and instead marveling at the medical erudition of this learned guest. "Have you read *The Book of Healing* (*Kitab al-shifaʾ*)," another book by the same author, the polymathic guest asked another attendee. Only those parts for which he had had immediate use, the other guest admitted. "I read it seven times in its entirety," the first responded, "and even the seventh time it was like being a student in the

48. Kātib Çelebi, *Ẓunūn*, 1: 221–3; Naguib, "Guiding," 27. Later scholars would often return to and weigh in on those debates. Taşköprīzāde, *Shaqāʾiq*, 161.

49. His father had made him memorize unabridged versions of grammar and law manuals. Ibn Ayyūb, *Rawḍ*, 240a.

50. Ghazzī, *Maṭāliʿ*, 194–5. In a fifteenth-century learned debate, the scholar Hocazade could cite even the line of a book in which a particular claim appeared. Ṭaşköprīzāde, *Shaqāʾiq*, 134.

first lesson with a new teacher."[51] Modesty aside, this was exactly the kind of range (and depth) for which contemporaries strived. Ghazzi's exchanges with ʿAbbasi exemplify the roving, exploratory character of the best kind of learned discourse: "We roamed in the squares of conversation, plunged into the seas of disputation, revealed the secrets of discourse, unearthed the treasuries of intercourse, contemplated novel thoughts, and lost ourselves in the pursuit of *adāb*."[52]

Cultured conversation brought immense pleasure to the lives of early modern gentlemen. Some of this pleasure derived from that which conversation offered by way of novelty and surprise: the witty riposte, the flash of insight, the clever wordplay. Some of it derived from what was familiar, from allusion, recognition, and recall.[53] In either case, though, it was nothing for the faint of heart. The joys of enlightened discourse were matched only by the toils required to partake in it.

Judging

Salon conversation was often harmonious and amicable. Ghazzi and ʿAbbasi seem to have felt genuine affection for one another, and their exchanges show little sign of grandstanding or unease. The bosom buddies (*hem-dems*) who shared their every breath with the Istanbul poet and scholar ʿAşık Çelebi consoled him during his darker days.[54] Friends could even carve out moments of intimacy and tenderness during large gatherings, confiding in their neighbors out of earshot of the other guests.[55] Be that as it may, salons could also be very competitive, and served as venues for judging others in front of sizable audiences.

Competition was baked into the foundations of many of the salon's standard conversational formats.[56] The most obvious of these were the formal debates mentioned previously. But there were also more casual ways of testing a rival: posing a difficult question, for example, or introducing a riddle. Even poetry could be channeled into competition through the

51. The guest with such impressive medical knowledge was Molla Kestelli, mentioned in Chapter 1. Taşköprīzāde, *Shaqāʾiq*, 145–6. For Lutfi, see Laṭīfī, *Tezkire-i Laṭīfī*, 295–7; Gökyay and Özen, "Molla Lutfi."

52. Ghazzī, *Maṭāliʿ*, 128.

53. Havlioğlu, *Mihrî Hatun*, 106–7; Andrews, "Golden Age," 356.

54. ʿĀşıḳ Çelebi, *Meşâʿirü's-Şuʿarâ*, 989, 1549.

55. Ṭaşköprīzāde, *Shaqāʾiq*, 145; Ḥamawī, *Ḥādī*, 32.

56. Chamberlain notes the importance of military metaphors in describing social competition among scholars in the Mamluk period. Chamberlain, *Knowledge*, 153–4. See also Andrews, "Power."

fashion for response poems in both Arabophone and Turcophone lands. Salons could thus elicit the apprehension of a modern academic conference. In fifteenth-century Herat, it was rumored that meeting with ʿAli Shir Navaʾi (d. 1501), one of the great literary giants of his time, "causes such consternation that, for example, if a person is called upon in the assembly, it is possible that he might not even be able to answer."[57]

The physical organization of many assemblies heightened the impact of such adjudicative discursive modes. As we saw in Chapter 3, many reception chambers placed participants on stage, literally elevating the level of discussion. The circular seating arrangement further enhanced the salon's theatrical quality. In the sixteenth and seventeenth centuries, the elevated platforms where men assembled could measure up to twenty square meters. If guests sat along the perimeter of the seating area with their backs against the three walls—as they did when sitting on the sofa—the distance separating two participants might have been up to three or four meters, requiring salongoers to deliver their words with considerable force in order to be heard.[58] As a result, in many assemblies, especially larger ones, speaking had less the character of a private confession than of a public declaration. Guests had to expect that anything uttered softly to a neighbor might be exposed to the whole assembly, as Molla Lutfi found out the hard way: he had initially confided only to his neighbor about his blood-stained clothing.

In these environments, men were regularly exposed to open scrutiny if not to outright competitive matches. Learned debates had especially high stakes, since the authority of scholars hinged on their ability to articulate and defend their ideas in person.[59] But literary discussions could be no less cutthroat; in the hands of Maliki the litterateur, for example, casual sparring turned into full-fledged tournaments. One of Damascus's best poets was Mamaya al-Rumi (d. 1580), who had his origins in the central Ottoman lands but who had come to Syria as a young boy.[60] After initially

57. As quoted in Subtelny, "Scenes," 142.

58. A single sitting area in the three-winged Aleppo Chamber, for example, measured 3.5m × 3.5m (12.25m^2), but is one of the smallest extant specimens from the period. David and Rousset, "Maison Wakil," 57, 66. See also Gonnella and Kröger, *Angels*; Gonnella, *Wohnhaus*. The outdoor seating area in the Zahrawi residence in Homs, built in the the fifteenth century, measured 4 × 5m (20m^2), as did the early seventeenth-century *qaʿa* in the Kastaflis residence in Tripoli in Greater Syria. Korn, "Bait," 266; Börner, "Wohnhausarchitektur," 97.

59. Taşköprīzāde, *Shaqāʾiq*, 132; Blecher, *Prophet*.

60. Ibn Ayyub says "he came to Damascus when he was small and grew up there." Ibn Ayyūb, *Kitāb*, 83. For Mamaya, see Masarwa, "Performing the Occasion"; Bosworth, "Janissary Poet."

embarking on a military career, he later retrained—with Maliki—as a poet, though without forsaking his fighting spirit. When another poetry virtuoso from Cairo visited Damascus in 1564, Maliki arranged for Mamaya to compete to compose the best *zajal*, a form of Arabic poetry that relied heavily on the vernacular and was often sung.[61] Their duel took place at Maliki's base in the northern porch of the Yalbugha Mosque.[62] The Cairene recited his composition first while the literati that had assembled to witness the spectacle looked on. Then it was Mamaya's turn. He rose to his feet and delivered a performance so spectacular that "the assembly swayed and the audience began to sing." The spectators decided unanimously that their own had prevailed, and drafted a scroll to celebrate "the overthrow of Cairo by Damascus."[63]

Much of the adjudicative work performed in Ottoman assemblies was live and immediate. The historian Hasan al-Burini boasted that when he read one of his odes aloud to the Damascene scholar Nabulusi, the latter trembled with joy.[64] Such visceral responses coexisted with more cerebral forms of feedback. The apple blossom poem Nabulusi recited at a spring picnic (quoted previously) provoked a discussion about whether it was superior to the poem to which it was a response.[65] The salons of Anatolia and the Balkans worked in much the same way. The poet and biographer of poets Latifi (d. 1582) reserved special praise for one contemporary of his who "was well-versed in the discipline of poetry and discussed the art of rhetoric [*beyān*] with the very best poets in parties and salons."[66] Much to Latifi's chagrin, though, this colleague—so Latifi felt—was exceptional in the deep knowledge he brought to bear on the art of literary criticism; most others who weighed in on such matters at salons, Latifi maintained, were clueless about actual quality, and it was in part to rectify what he viewed as the sorry state of connoisseurship in his day that Latifi set out to write his compendium.[67] In serious ways, then, contemporary literary taste was shaped in and by the salon.

One could be forgiven for assuming that however high the pressure may have been in salons, the stakes were quite low. After all, these literary

61. Alvarez, "Muwashshaḥ"; Alvarez, "Zajal, medieval."

62. Ibn Ayyūb, *Kitāb*, 83; Rīḥāwī, "Jāmiʿ Yalbughā fī Dimashq," 134–5.

63. Ibn Ayyūb, *Kitāb*, 83.

64. Būrīnī, *Tarājim*, 2:64. For a similar response on the part of Mehmed II, see Taşköprīzāde, *Shaqāʾiq*, 98.

65. See also the response when Najm al-Din al-Ghazzi presented his work in a literary gathering. Ghazzī, *Lutf*, 103. For an earlier period, see Gruendler, "Qaṣīda," 329.

66. Laṭīfī, *Tezkire-i Laṭīfī*, 317.

67. Laṭīfī, *Tezkire-i Laṭīfī*, 33; Andrews, "Latifi."

verdicts were usually cast in small, exclusive circles inaccessible to the overwhelming majority of Ottoman society; one of the great benefits of meeting in the domestic sphere was that it insulated guests from public scrutiny. However, salon audiences were much larger than the attendance lists or the conversation transcripts included in contemporary accounts initially suggest. This is most obvious in the case of publicly held gatherings. Worshipers at the Yalbugha Mosque could have hardly ignored the raucous poetic performances that took place in its northern courtyard under Maliki's direction, and some may have paused to watch (especially since the poems performed were partly in dialect). But even domestically held gatherings were not as private as they initially appear. Many meetings that were ostensibly one-on-one were in fact held in the presence of other members of the host's household, whether sons there to watch or attendants there to serve. A Sufi shaykh who visited a merchant's reception chamber in Bursa did so before an audience of his host's sons, servants, and slaves.[68] Contemporary miniatures regularly depict such junior members of the salon standing next to or behind the figures engrossed in conversation (see figures 2.2, 2.4, and 3.5). Some such spectators may have even been women; Ghazzi owned a number of enslaved Ethiopian women and was "rarely seen without one to three of them."[69]

Other spectators of elite gatherings were hidden, but no less of a presence. In the Arab provinces, many reception areas were flanked by upper galleries covered by lattice woodwork windows (*mashrabiyya*), visible in the courtyard of the Zahrawi house pictured in figure 3.3. Accessible from side rooms, as they often were, these galleries allowed women or servants of the house to watch and listen to the proceedings below without themselves being seen.[70] The same thing was possible not only in the Üsküdar Palace pavilion where sultans and their consorts spent their summers, but also in the most important assembly room of the empire—the imperial divan.[71] That invisible spectators formed one of the intended audiences for polite conversation is suggested by a satirical story in a late Mamluk etiquette manual that caricatured the guest who deliberately let his turban slip so that the wife of the host could admire his silky hair; for her ears, too, he countered the aging host's admission of his waning libido

68. Taşköprīzāde, *Shaqāʾiq*, 126. See also Taşköprīzāde, *Shaqāʾiq*, 131.

69. Ibn Ayyūb, *Kitāb*, 16.

70. David and Rousset, "Maison Wakil," 57; Gonnella, *Wohnhaus*, 26–9; Korn, "Bait," 278.

71. Ergin, "Ottoman Royal Women's Spaces," 96–7; Necipoğlu, "Garden Culture," 36; Necipoğlu, *Architecture*, 174–5.

with loud pronouncements of his own sexual prowess.[72] This concealed audience meant that, if a gentleman suffered embarrassment at a given gathering, he did so not only in front of his peers, but also their household.

An even larger audience for a given conversation emerged as a result of the gossip that tore like gusts of cold wind through the empire's reception chambers. Men often discussed the literary or poetic skills of their absent colleagues, and not always charitably. The historian Burini, for example, acquired a reputation for writing praise poems so desperate that they verged on outright begging, as one of his acquaintances, a local judge, teased. When Burini's odes were read aloud in the author's absence, the judge would interrupt to warn the listeners of the impending appeals for financial rewards. When these indeed followed, the judge would exclaim triumphantly, "see, it's just as I told you!"[73] In a meeting in Jerusalem, a Syrian judge, two Ottoman officials, and their local host spoke at length about the talents of one absent Damascene poet, the host defending him and the visitors exposing him as a fraud.[74] Not all such discussions were malevolent. Fathers, uncles, or teachers regaled younger generations with stories of the gatherings they had witnessed or heard about.[75] As men traveled, they took these stories with them, spreading the reputations of particular gentlemen across the empire.

Perhaps the most enduring way salon conversations contributed to a man's reputation was through the written word. Many popular literary genres featured partial transcripts of such conversations. This included travelogues, as we have already seen. Ghazzi's autograph copy of *Full Moon Rising* devotes more than thirty pages to his conversations with ʿAbbasi, and many more to his interactions with other leading scholars.[76] This makes the travel account something of a literary anthology, one that strings together the poems, riddles, anecdotes, and academic queries he encountered with the thread of his journey to and from Istanbul.[77] Another genre that opened up private salons to public inspection

72. The said passage is from the etiquette manual of Yahya al-Jazzar (d. 1270 or 1281) and quoted in the anthology of Shihab al-Din al-Ibshihi (d. 1446), suggesting it continued to be a type recognizable to contemporaries. Ibshīhī, *al-Mustaṭraf*, 1: 270–1; Lewicka, *Food*, 412–3.

73. Ghazzī, *Luṭf*, 358, 359.

74. Ḥamawī, *Ḥādī*, 33.

75. Taşköprīzade's father and teachers were some of his main sources for information about the fifteenth century, allowing for a much greater density of material than for the generation or two before that. Taşköprīzāde, *Shaqāʾiq*, 133–6, 144, 145, 147, 150, etc.

76. Ghazzī, *Maṭāliʿ*, fols. 32b–47a.

77. Bauer, "Literarische Anthologien der Mamlūkenzeit," 78.

was the biographical dictionary, which compiled profiles of the key figures of a given place or time. Although understood as a branch of historical writing, these dictionaries often profiled men who were still alive or who had passed away recently enough to have left a living memory. The title of a biographical dictionary by Ghazzi's son Najm al-Din reveals the deep connection between biographical dictionaries and salon conversation—*The Delicacies of Conversation and the Finest Fruits: Biographies of Great Men from the First Part of the Eleventh Century* (*Lutf al-samar wa qatf al-thamar min tarajim aʿyan al-tabaqat al-ula min al-qarn al-hadi ʿashar*). Reading about great men was itself a friendly conversation, the title suggested, but it also, as the text revealed repeatedly, emerged from such conversations.

These written sources often recorded anecdotes from particular gatherings or cast summary judgments on the conversational skills of their protagonists. Though Ghazzi used his travel account mostly to praise his interlocutors—chiefly ʿAbbasi—other sixteenth-century travel writers were less kind. When Ghazzi's former student and small-town judge Muhibb al-Din al-Hamawi (d. 1608) recorded his travels to Cairo and Istanbul in the 1570s, he offered praise for the literary bravura of some of the men he met but also harsh critiques of others, many identified by name.[78] Likewise, many biographical entries included vignettes from certain gatherings or a sentence or two about their subjects' verbal skills. One Turkish-language dictionary of poets described Molla Lutfi, the scholar whose bloody sweat became the subject of debate, in the following way:

> In scholarly conversations he elucidated key points; in debates he made brilliant remarks in the most beautiful language; and in parties and salons [*maḥāfil ü mecālis*] he always had the right jokes and pleasantries for the great scholars and men of rank.[79]

Generic as some of this praise may sound—and in some cases must have been—many biographers were personal acquaintances of those they profiled and described them with care.[80] Ibn Ayyub described his close friend Burini as being "witty with words, an excellent orator, and a delightful

78. For more on Hamawi's travel account, see Chapter 6.

79. Laṭīfī, *Tezkire-i Laṭīfī*, 296. See also Ṭaşköprīzāde, *Shaqāʾiq*, 102, 139, 147. Tolasa, *Araştırma*, 137–9.

80. Taşköprīzade's descriptions of the speech of men from earlier generations—whom he never met personally—vary greatly, suggesting such information might have been passed along by oral tradition. Ṭaşköprīzāde, *Shaqāʾiq*, 147, 188, 200.

companion [*laṭīf al-ʿibāra, ḥasan al-muḥāḍara, ḥelu al-muʿāshara*]."[81] Ghazzi's son Najm al-Din, another personal acquaintance, characterized Burini as "eloquent and quick-tongued, with a sound memory, a sharp mind, and witty expressions [*fasīḥ al-ʿibāra, ṭalīq al-lisān, matīn al-ḥifẓ, ḥasan al-fahm, laṭīf al-muḥāwara*]."[82] Though many of these skills could be displayed equally at lectures or class lessons, the salon was its own arena in which to excel. Najm al-Din observed that Burini "was never in a scholarly gathering [*majlis ʿilm*] without being its nightingale."[83]

Written evaluations of Ghazzi's conversational skills were more equivocal. To be sure, his biographers praised the scholar's well-attended gatherings and his poetic quips. However, most of them—that is, all but his son Najm al-Din—never failed to mention Ghazzi's stutter. Burini explained that he was a good teacher despite his "difficulty speaking" (*thaqīl al-nuṭuq*).[84] Ibn al-Hanbali (d. 1563), writing from Aleppo, commented that Ghazzi was a respected scholar "in spite of his difficulty expressing himself [*ʿiyy*] and his speech irregularity [*ʿadam al-iṭṭirād*]."[85] Some contemporaries cast this impediment as a sign of God's favor—ʿAşık Çelebi, Ghazzi's Istanbul contemporary who also had a stutter, saw it as a mark of distinction bestowed on some of those who descended from the Prophet. Yet it was also widely recognized that it represented a significant setback.[86] Authors expressed their gratitude that Ghazzi's stutter was suspended when he read the Qurʾan, and Ibn al-Hanbali ended his biography: "Praise God for protecting His Book from the ugliness of such a stutter, which cannot be resisted or removed by those whom it afflicts and whose possibilities it limits."[87]

Thanks to these kinds of writings, the speech of men traveled far beyond the walls of a given reception hall. Indeed, it could even echo in other assemblies: the works that contained these summary judgments were read not only silently by individuals, but often were performed live

81. Ibn Ayyūb, *Kitāb*, 49.

82. Ghazzī, *Lutf*, 357.

83. Ghazzī, *Lutf*, 359. Burini likewise wrote of Nabulusi, "he beautified the salons with his conversation and delighted the participants with his pleasant deliberations." Būrīnī, *Tarājim*, 2: 70.

84. Būrīnī, *Tarājim*, 2: 98.

85. Ibn al-Ḥanbalī, *Durr*, 2: 438–9. For *ʿiyy*, see Montgomery, "Al-Jāḥiẓ on Misarticulation." The use of the word *ʿiyy* for stutter is somewhat unusual (rather than *tamtam*, *faʾfaʾ*), since earlier scholars had associated the term with linguistic ineptitude rather than a speech disorder. Nuwayrī, *Nihāya*, 3: 349–52; Nasser, "Arabic Qurʾān," 28–9; Montgomery, "*Kitāb*," 117–8.

86. ʿĀşıḳ Çelebi, *Meşâʿirü's-Şuʿarâ*, 1121.

87. Ibn al-Ḥanbalī, *Durr*, 2: 438–9.

as entertainment as well. The judge Hamawi read portions of his travel account to friends at a salon in Damascus.[88] At other gatherings in the same city, gentlemen listened to excerpts of biographical dictionaries.[89]

Exclusive, elite gatherings held in the domestic sphere were not quite as private as they may at first seem. The way a man spoke, his ability to compose poetry, his conversations, assertions, and gaffes were not only judged by those live and present; they were reported upon in other assemblies or even recorded in writing. This gave salons a disproportionate role in making reputations and disseminating them across neighborhoods, cities, and regions. Lurid stories passed by word-of-mouth undermined competitors. Written descriptions of these gatherings served as snapshots that insiders could save and as tabloids through which outsiders could peer into a glamorous world. Participants must have known full well that on any given evening, other salongoers might be gathering tales for a history or a travel account they planned to write, and they acted accordingly.

Meeting

How did the lofty expectations and sometimes harsh realities of salon conversation affect relations between Rumis and Arabs? On the whole, conversational forms were shared across the expanded Ottoman lands, giving the two groups a good basis for exchange. The problem was that there were also significant differences in substance.

The most basic difference, from which most others followed, was language. In the Arab provinces, the linguistic foundation of polite gatherings was Arabic. To be sure, as interactions with Turcophone Ottomans intensified in the sixteenth century, more and more Arabs began learning Turkish (and even Persian); though Ghazzi himself never seems to have learned the language, both Burini and Nabulusi, Damascenes of a later generation, did.[90] However, Turkish did not become a serious language of poetry or conversation in Arab learned circles, as Burini acknowledged when he stated that Nabulusi "knew Turkish and Persian," but (as we have seen) "memorized lots of beautiful Arabic poems and employed them when he

88. Ḥamawī, *Bawādī*, 190a–193b; Elger, *Glaube*, 76.

89. Muṣṭafā ʿĀlī, *Künhü'l-Ahbâr*, 470b. I thank Evren Sünnetçioğlu for drawing my attention to this reference. Other historical works, such as chronicles, were written with oral performances in mind as well. Sajdi, *Barber*, 158–62.

90. For Nabulusi, see Būrīnī, *Tarājim*, 2:68. Najm al-Din al-Ghazzi noted that Burini knew Persian like a native speaker, and began learning Turkish later in life. Ghazzī, *Lutf*, 357. Nahrawali, born about a decade after Ghazzi in 1511–2, learned Turkish. Blackburn in Nahrawālī, *Journey*, xi.

spoke in the salons of the notables."[91] In the polite circles of the Turcophone ruling elite, Turkish was the language of choice. Although Ottoman elites were often polyglot from birth and usually learned Arabic and often Persian as well, Ottoman Turkish was the lingua franca for spoken encounters within the ruling class.

One might expect that Ottoman power holders, arriving in Arab lands, would not want to engage with the language of the subject population. Indeed, whereas in earlier centuries sultans had used a variety of different languages for their correspondence with other rulers, in the sixteenth century Süleyman switched to employing only Turkish—except with those rulers who spoke Arabic.[92] Indeed, Arabic was not simply the language of a subject population; it was what Sheldon Pollock has called a cosmopolitan language, one of universal relevance to all Muslims (and many non-Muslims) across the Islamic world. What is more, it was a sacred language, since the Qurʾan was in Arabic and was (and is) believed by Muslims to be the word of God.[93] This in turn made Arabic the basis for most scholarly and legal activities as the Qurʾan, along with hadiths, were the main sources of Islamic law. In Ottoman lands as in other Muslim polities of the early modern period, Arabic was the premiere academic language.

The status of Turkish was quite different. If Arabic had enjoyed universal credentials for centuries, Turkish was only just shedding its reputation as an "ethnic language" that served more particularist interests.[94] Although Turkish had begun gaining in prestige since the fifteenth century, it only slowly caught up to Arabic in its academic, religious, and literary importance. Into the early sixteenth century, the suitability of Turkish for the kind of literary connoisseurship cultivated in elite circles could still be debated, and authors who wrote in the language felt compelled to offer apologias for their choice.[95] All this meant that while Arab scholars could not be expected to master Turkish, learned Rumis very much could be expected to master Arabic. This was especially true of scholars, but even (albeit to a lesser extent) of military or political types who cultivated Arabic for devotional purposes.

Ottoman elites, especially scholars, devoted enormous energy to learning Arabic. Children who attended primary schools (*mektebs*) did not

91. Būrīnī, *Tarājim*, 2: 68.

92. Veinstein, "Interprètes," 66.

93. Pollock, *Language*, 2–30. Hagen distinguishes between Arabic as a "transnational language" and Ottoman Turkish as an "ethnic language." Hagen, "Ottoman Empire," 502.

94. Hagen, "Ottoman Empire," 502; Yavuz, "Yazılış Sebepleri."

95. Yıldız, "Law Manual"; Yavuz, "Yazılış Sebepleri."

receive systematic training in Arabic, but their main pursuit was inextricably linked to that language, namely, reading and memorizing the Qur'an.[96] So too did those educated in the imperial palace receive Arabic-language instruction. Anyone who went on to undertake higher-level studies had to undergo rigorous foundational training in Arabic grammar, syntax, and style. Many Turcophone scholars went above and beyond these formal requirements, as the historian Taşköprizade noted in his biographical dictionary. This included many of those men with whom early Arab travelers to Anatolia like ʿAbbasi and Ghazzi had extensive contact, including the Müʾeyyedzade brothers, Saʿdi Çelebi, and Kadiri Çelebi. These types could not only read in Arabic comfortably, but also draft entire treatises in the language.

However, a mainstream Anatolian education did not prepare men for the fast-paced verbal acrobatics that won them acclaim in the gentlemanly salon. In the early fifteenth century, it could not even be taken for granted that Rumi scholars could comfortably read in Arabic. One jurist explained that he had decided to translate a Hanafi law manual into Turkish because many of his contemporaries had difficulty understanding Arabic, preferring not only to speak and teach in Turkish but also to read in it.[97] Another fifteenth-century Ottoman scholar based in a madrasa in Jerusalem had enough difficulty sight-reading the language that when community members submitted a request for a legal ruling (Ar. *fatwa*, Tur. *fetva*) written in Arabic, he had to ask someone else to explain its meaning.[98] Even if many preeminent Turcophone scholars of the fifteenth and sixteenth centuries did manage Arabic effortlessly in its written forms, this did not necessarily correspond to spoken fluency. In most educational institutions, the emphasis was on mastery of the written language, and even in lessons where Arabic works were being discussed, the language of instruction was usually Turkish.[99] As a result, spoken Arabic discourse was a challenge for many Rumis.

Nor did Arabic enjoy wide popularity as a poetic language in the central Ottoman lands. As we saw in Chapter 1, the Arabic tradition of belles lettres had a much weaker hold historically on the Ottoman elite. To be sure, many Rumi gentlemen could recite or even compose verse in Arabic,

96. Hagen, "Ottoman Empire," 503.

97. The scholar in question was Devletoğlu Yusuf, though his work was far more than a straightforward translation; it adapted the original in the light of local concerns. Kuru, "The Literature of Rum," 558; Yıldız, "Hanafi Law Manual."

98. ʿUlaymī, *Uns*, 2: 350–1. For this, see Burak, "Dynasty," 117.

99. Hagen, "Ottoman Empire," 503.

as even those biographers focused on Turkish-language literature were quick to point out.[100] However, generally, Arabic took a back seat to Persian in literary matters; unlike the latter, Arabic only rarely served as an example to be emulated and superseded.[101]

Even in the realm of scholarship, where writing in Arabic was standard the Islamic world over, learned Rumi men did not always have the same interests as their Arab counterparts. Of course, as members of the same religious community and academic tradition, they shared a set of canonical texts and epistemological assumptions, a common tradition solidified over centuries of exchanges. However, substantial differences remained. The discipline of hadith studies was one such area of difference, with fifteenth-century Anatolian scholars a good deal less engaged in the project that Arab scholars pursued with such élan.[102] Jurisprudence was another, as Guy Burak has shown; the Hanafi predilection of most Rumi scholars left Arabs feeling increasingly marginalized.[103] Finally, there were significant divergences in political thought, as Hüseyin Yılmaz has argued: intellectuals writing in the service of the Ottoman dynasty tended to look to the Persianate tradition rather than to so-called classical Arabic models.[104]

Given these differences in linguistic, literary, and scholarly preferences, it comes as little surprise that mixed-company gatherings bringing Rumis and Arabs together could sometimes be strained. Anatolian learned men knew what value their Arab colleagues placed on proper Arabic on the eve of the Ottoman conquest. When the Sufi shaykh İbrahim-i Gülşeni (d. 1534), born in Diyarbakir, made plans to resettle in Cairo around the turn of the sixteenth century, his patron in Southeastern Anatolia tried to dissuade him with tales of the mockery he would face for his broken Arabic (a warning that, in the event, proved well-founded).[105] Perhaps to avoid such ridicule, in the early months of the Ottoman occupation of Syria, some Rumi scholars avoided discoursing in Arabic altogether. When the Damascene scholar Ibn Tulun turned up at Sultan Selim's camp in

100. Sehī Bey, *Heşt Bihişt*, 147, 155, 160, 178, 192, 194, 204, etc.

101. Sehi Bey highlighted Rumis' response verses to Persian poets and their translations from Persian into Turkish. Sehī Bey, *Heşt Bihişt*, 115, 141, 143, 165, 173. See also Kuru, "The Literature of Rum," 560.

102. Pfeifer, "Hadith Culture."

103. Burak, *Islamic Law*.

104. Yılmaz, *Caliphate Redefined*. See also Sariyannis, *Political Thought*, chapters 1–2.

105. Emre, "İbrahim-i Gülşeni," 77; Emre, *Ibrahim-i Gulshani*, 98–9. Ibn Battuta describes an encounter with an Ottoman jurist who had purported to know Arabic until the arrival of the Arab traveler revealed otherwise. Ibn Baṭṭūṭa, *Travels*, 454–5.

the fall of 1516 in hopes of meeting with scholars traveling in the royal entourage, his ambition was thwarted when he found he was unable to converse with them—thirty-six in all—"because of [my] lack of knowledge of their language."[106] Whether due to their insufficient knowledge of Arabic or their misgivings about speaking it, no one seems to have suggested it as an alternative.

Those Rumis who did venture to converse with Syrian scholars in Arabic had to endure humiliating criticisms of any mistakes they made. Learned Arabs did not suspend judgment about the Arabic skills of their Rumi colleagues simply because it was not their mother tongue (and in fact often their third or fourth language). With searing sarcasm did Ghazzi praise the efforts of the mosque preacher in Izmit near Istanbul (whom he also criticized on religious grounds) in 1530: "He was one-of-a-kind in his incorrect Arabic, his confusion of letters and words was absolutely fantastic."[107] Hamawi, Ghazzi's student and fellow travel writer, was especially attuned to these sorts of gaffes and loved to recount them. One such story was so good that Hamawi's great-grandson included it in his seventeenth-century biography of his ancestor. A group of Damascenes had gathered to say goodbye to a departing Ottoman magistrate who had been transferred to Aleppo. The judge declared gallantly, "if there is something you need from the Aleppo [*al-Ḥalab*]"—using the definite article for the city that does not usually take one—"then feel free to let me know so that I can send it to a Damascus [*ilā Shām*]," leaving out the definite article for the city that usually does. Hamawi supposedly replied, "we have no need of anything at all except the definite article [*al-alif wa-l-lām*] that left Damascus: do us a favor and send it!"[108]

That the definite article was tricky for some Turcophone scholars is understandable enough as there is no equivalent in Turkish. Yet Hamawi had little patience for the issue. On business one day in the reception hall of an accountant (*muhasebeci*), he happened to encounter the Ottoman judge of the Hawran region in Southern Syria, a certain Muhyi Efendi. When discussion turned to a document that Hamawi had signed as "the judge of al-Qadmus," Muhyi insisted (wrongly and, one might say, outrageously) that this Syrian town where Hamawi worked did not in fact

106. Ibn Ṭūlūn, *Mufākaha*, 2:31. He had more luck with one "Idris the Rumi," with whom he met several times when Idris was in Damascus in 1517. Idris had met with Ibn Tulun's uncle on a pilgrimage to Mecca. Ibn Ṭūlūn, *Mufākaha*, 2: 59; Wollina, "Sultan Selīm," 224.

107. Ghazzī, *Maṭāliʿ*, 216.

108. Muḥibbī, *Khulāṣa*, 3: 329–30.

take an article. Hamawi corrected him, briefly summarizing the consensus of grammarians. However, the judge did not believe him, insisting that Hamawi was in the wrong and consulting others on the question. When even their support of Hamawi's claims did not convince the obstinate judge, Hamawi was left with no choice but to draft a treatise settling the matter once and for all (excerpts of which he included in the travel account).[109]

Yet language was just the beginning. Given the differences in the intellectual traditions of Anatolia and the Arab lands, at times Ottoman scholars had trouble earning the academic recognition they craved (and deserved). Take one of the earliest Ottoman chief judges of Damascus, a man called Yusuf who arrived to administer the province in the summer of 1521. Yusuf arrived at a difficult time for the Ottomans in Damascus, having taken over only a couple years after Zeynüddin Fenari's rocky start in that position (and the subsequent reappointment of a long-time local judge). Yusuf can thus be credited doubly for having the courage to give a lecture—presumably in Arabic—in the Great Mosque of Damascus. However, he may well have come to regret the decision, for the lecture was a fiasco. For starters, the turnout was meager, a major blow since attendance was a measure of approval and locals had much to gain from the judge's favor; only three local scholars and some Rumis (*khalq min al-arwam*) attended.[110] The judge had arranged to present his thoughts on a gloss (*hashiya*) of the seminal Qur'an commentary *The Revealer of the Truth of the Revelations* (*al-Kashshaf ʿan haqaʾiq al-tanzil*) by the medieval scholar Abu al-Qasim al-Zamakhshari (d. 1144). The gloss Yusuf chose to lecture on was a well-known one written by the Timurid scholar Jurjani, and audience members had brought their own copies of it along. Yet, when the judge began his lecture, listeners found that their manuscript copies differed from Yusuf's. Unruffled, Yusuf carried on with the lecture using his own version, leaving his listeners lost. This was unfortunate, but forgivable. What local scholars could not excuse was the fact that the only other exegetical authority Yusuf mentioned in his lecture was Jurjani's contemporary and Persian rival Taftazani; Yusuf failed to recognize the work of other authorities such as the Iraqi scholar Sharaf al-Din al-Tibi (d. 1342).

Here was a moment when the intellectual differences between the two locales came clearly to the fore. Though scholars in both regions generally

109. This incident took place in the winter of 1573–4. Ḥamawī, *Ḥādī*, 93–4; *Bawādī*, 154b–155a; Elger, *Glaube*, 100.

110. The following account is from Ibn Ṭūlūn, *Quḍāt*, 310–1. Ibn Ayyub copied it into his history as well. Ibn Ayyūb, *Rawḍ*, 74a–b.

relied heavily on Zamakhshari's commentary, their preferences diverged when it came to the many glosses that had come to shape its reception.[111] In part, this difference was down to practicalities. Persian thinkers had a pride of place in the Ottoman scholarly tradition; refugees from the east and Ottoman scholars who had chosen to study there had turned Jurjani and Taftazani into the intellectual touchstones of a generation or more of Ottoman scholars.[112] In contrast, in Arab lands, books from the east were often hard to come by; the Cairene scholar Suyuti, writing in 1497, was aware of but unable to secure a full copy of the work by Jurjani that Yusuf discussed in his lecture.[113] Though Syrians seem to have had readier access to it, the divergences between their respective manuscript copies hints at similar discrepancies within the textual tradition. Alongside these practicalities, though, there appears to have been a deeper intellectual disagreement. Taftazani's work was better known than Jurjani's in Arab lands—Suyuti read it in full—but it seems to have found less appreciation than it did in the Ottoman heartland, if Suyuti is any indication. He judged it to be unoriginal, derivative of none other than the gloss of Sharaf al-Din al-Tibi, whom Syrians had so missed in Yusuf's lecture and whom Suyuti considered to be the best of all commentators on Zamakhshari.[114] Nevermind that Yusuf might have afforded them new reflections on a gloss that locals may have had few chances to study previously; there seems to have been a robust sense of what was (or was not) intellectually worthwhile. In any case, the general estimation of Yusuf was low, and local scholars remained aloof. As Ibn Tulun explained, "none of the Arab professors [*mudarrisīn awlād al-ʿarab*] visited him other than the superintendent of the two holy sanctuaries Taqi al-Din al-Qari." The slight was not lost on Yusuf, who "resented the Arabs [*abnāʾ al-ʿarab*] for not visiting him."[115]

İshak Çelebi (d. 1542), who arrived to take up the same post as chief judge in 1536, seems to have had similar difficulty integrating into the local social scene. When he arrived in Damascus at the age of seventy, he had spent time in the company of sultans and was widely recognized for his poetry and scholarship.[116] A year or so after İshak's death, Sehi Bey wrote in his biography of the judge,

111. Saleh, "Gloss."

112. They were immensely popular subjects of debate in the fifteenth-century Ottoman salons, as the biographical dictionary of Taşköprīzade shows.

113. Saleh, "Gloss," 236.

114. Saleh, "Gloss," 236.

115. Ibn Ṭūlūn, *Quḍāt*, 310–1.

116. Eke, "Klâsik Sanatlar"; Savaş, "İshak Çelebi, Kılıççı-zâde."

> he was distinguished amongst the paragons of the time and the virtuous of the age, and was respected amongst the people of learning for all sorts of virtues. He gave so much care and attention to fluidity of language, firmness of speech, [*selāset-i suhanda ve metānet-i elfāẓda*] and matters of rhetoric [*maʿānā*] that it is impossible to describe.[117]

What is more, everywhere he traveled, İshak left behind a reputation for flirtation and revelry.[118] Yet İshak's reception in Damascus was lukewarm. He had been to the Arab lands once before, but seems to have had little contact with the locals on that occasion, having been called to entertain the war-weary Sultan Selim (he may have been one of the scholars in the camp of the same sultan who declined to converse with Ibn Tulun).[119] The second time around, İshak had only marginally more contact with his Damascene colleagues. Although Ibn Tulun mentioned that the judge was skilled in composing Persian poetry, this probably found only limited resonance among Arab locals. That the historian made no mention of Arabic suggests that composing verse in this language was not one of İshak's strengths. Otherwise, his evaluation was as follows:

> His greatest interest was in reading the *Hidāya* [*al-Hidaya fi al-furuʿ*, the compendium of Hanafi law by Burhan al-Din al-Marghinani] with his students, but that did not come to pass. He was involved in scholarship but restricted himself to practicing law, and for that reason he mostly preferred keeping to himself in his house [*al-taḥajjub fī'l-bayt*].[120]

This is hardly a resounding endorsement of the judge, especially when contrasted with Sehi's emphatic praise. The implication seems to be that, as a practitioner rather than an intellectual, İshak did not engage with the local scholarly scene. This was quite a divergence from İshak's earlier life of socializing and intellectualizing; though this might be put down to his advanced age, the judge did continue to seek the company of young boys, if only, claimed Ibn Tulun, to look at them and speak with them.[121] It seems

117. Sehī Bey, *Heşt Behişt*, 158.

118. Laṭīfī, *Tezkire-i Laṭīfī*, 90; ʿĀşıḳ Çelebi, *Meşâʿirü's-Şuʿarâ*, 328–41; Kınalı-zade, *Tezkiretü'ş-Şuʿarâ*, 161.

119. ʿĀşıḳ Çelebi, *Meşâʿirü's-Şuʿarâ*, 328; Kınalı-zade, *Tezkiretü'ş-Şuʿarâ*, 162–3.

120. Ibn Ṭūlūn, *Quḍāt*, 319. ʿAşık Çelebi narrates İshak's interaction with a local Arab woman, but in the context of his legal practice. ʿĀşıḳ Çelebi, *Meşâʿirü's-Şuʿarâ*, 335.

121. In other words, he did not have the sort of physical contact with them that jurists deemed unlawful. Ibn Ṭūlūn, *Quḍāt*, 319.

that İshak had less interest—or more difficulty—in socializing with the more mature inhabitants of the city.

Other arrivals from the Ottoman center likewise appear to have been less active in Damascene salons than they would have been back home. At one of Ghazzi's assemblies in the mid-1570s, a debate erupted when Ghazzi discussed a prophetic account according to which it was permissible to buy and sell concubines, known by the Arabic word *surriyya*. Sitting to Ghazzi's immediate left was Isma'il al-Nabulusi, reciter of poems about apple blossoms. Although thirty years younger than Ghazzi, Nabulusi nonetheless interrupted Ghazzi to correct him: the plural of *surriyya* was pronounced *sarārīy*, not *sarārīyy* with the stress on the final syllable. Ghazzi ignored the remark and carried on with the same final stress as before. Thereupon Nabulusi repeated his suggestion, which Ghazzi again ignored. At the third correction, Ghazzi lost his patience, slammed his fist against the ground, and hissed, "Is this what you stay up worrying about at night? Ibn 'Abd al-Birr said in chapter so-and-so of his commentary on Tirmidhi's *Compilation* that it is pronounced with the emphasis" (Ghazzi knew the precise chapter, but the historian who recorded this anecdote omitted it). When Nabulusi fell silent, a student who was present courageously jumped in to mediate, saying, "My lord, so-and-so stated that both of them are acceptable." And the conversation moved on to other things. All of this transpired in the presence of the chief Hanafi mufti of Damascus, the Rumi scholar who sat to Ghazzi's immediate right.[122] Yet, despite the fact that he occupied the seat of honor and was probably older than most of the participants, the mufti appears not to have uttered a word. The same thing had been true at the assembly in which Ghazzi claimed to have found seven errors in the Arabic dictionary of Firuzabadi. The chief judge of Damascus, Çivizade Mehmed Efendi, and the chief Hanafi mufti of the city, Fevri Efendi, both sitting to Ghazzi's right, again seem to have followed along as silent spectators.[123] We might take this as evidence that Arab scholars were simply unwilling to acknowledge the talents of scholars from the Ottoman center were it not for the alacrity with which they praised the contributions of a select few.[124] It thus stands

122. This was the Rumi scholar Mehmed Mu'idzade. Būrīnī, *Tarājim*, 2: 96. For Mu'idzade, see Ghazzī, *Kawākib*, 3: 85; Murādī, *'Arf*, 34–5.

123. Of course, Burini did not provide exhaustive transcripts of these conversations, meaning that we cannot be sure they did not contribute; still, noteworthy contributions were usually recorded.

124. Especially Kınalızade 'Ali, e.g., Ibn Ayyūb, *Rawḍ*, 203b, 204ab; Tamīmī, *Tabaqāt*, 239a. For more on Kınalızade, see Chapter 5.

to reason that Rumis simply did not take a leading role in shaping these debates.

Those scholars who did participate actively in Arabic-language gatherings did not always receive the recognition for their multilingualism that that they may have deserved. This seems to have been the case for Muhyiddin Mehmed Çelebi (d. 1564), the son of the chief mufti Ebu's-Suʿud Efendi who served as chief judge of Damascus in the last years of the 1550s. In elite circles in the central lands, Mehmed was recognized as a man of some literary skill: ʿAşık Çelebi praised him as one who "achieved perfection in the Arabic sciences and excelled in the literary arts."[125] Indeed, Mehmed's spoken Arabic was good enough to allow him to poke fun at the lisp of his friend and constant companion in Damascus, a local Arab scholar.[126] Yet these talents did not suffice in the view of Nahrawali, the Meccan traveler who had showered praise on Ghazzi on a stopover in Damascus. When Mehmed expressed only lackluster appreciation of an ode Nahrawali presented to him during their meeting, the Arab scholar declared that this was "because of his inadequate sophistication in literature and lack of experience with diction among eloquent Arabs."[127] No doubt Nahrawali's bruised ego lurked behind this assessment. However, the fact that he thought that the criticism might stick suggests the kind of currency that such dismissive tropes about Ottoman scholars had.

Indeed, occasionally we detect a lingering trace of the dismissive attitude that had reigned vis-à-vis Ottoman scholarship on the eve of the conquest. The Rumi scholars Çivizade and Fevri, who had been present when Ghazzi attacked the dictionary of Firuzabadi, received a rude reception during a trip to Jerusalem with their colleague Hamawi—collector of Arabic grammatical mistakes—in Ramadan of 1571. The three men spent much of their time with a scholar from a local learned family.[128] They "spent most of our evenings in our lord the shaykh's company, perfectly content thanks to his cheeriness and amiability," as Hamawi explained in his travel account.[129] Çivizade, who was himself from an illustrious learned family in Istanbul and had taught at the capital's best madrasas,

125. ʿAşıḳ Çelebi, *Dhayl*, 72.

126. Ibn Ayyūb, *Kitāb*, 44.

127. Nahrawālī, *Journey*, 37–40.

128. This was ʿAbd al-Nabi Ibn Jamaʿa, who did not feature in the biographical dictionaries of his day; Najm al-Din al-Ghazzi gives him a mere mention in the biography of Ibn Jamaʿa's father, who is referred to as "one of the distinguished ones of Jerusalem." Ibn Jamaʿa does appear with suitably flattering titles in a court record of 1555. Ghazzī, *Kawākib*, 3: 65; Bakhīt in Ḥamawī, *Ḥādī*, 101.

129. Ḥamawī, *Ḥādī*, 32.

enjoyed especially animated conversations with their host. These often turned to scholarly matters. However, despite Çivizade's stature, which dwarfed the Jerusalemite's,

> If the shaykh our lord [the host] was asked a question, he answered revealing remarkable acumen. [But] when he spoke of the basics he did so as if giving a lesson, believing that they were new to the one he was addressing.[130]

Their host's tendency to present basic information as if it was revelatory no doubt spoke to his own intellectual limitations. But it also spoke to his low estimation of his guests' capacities.

So too did the host's response to the work of Fevri Efendi, a man of even greater stature than Çivizade. An immensely esteemed poet and scholar who had had close relations with Sultans Selim and Süleyman, Fevri was so respected that Çivizade let him sit in his own litter for most of the trip to Jerusalem. As such, when Fevri presented his gloss on parts of ʿAbdallah Baydawi's (d. 1286) famous Qurʾan commentary over the course of several evenings in Jerusalem, he naturally expected that his host would "express the plaudits that are for a man of his stature reserved, and praise him with the praise that he most certainly deserved, and describe his virtues—extensive as they were—with fitting words."[131] Yet Fevri received no such praise. What awaited him was only the backhanded compliment of his host, who said, "By God, clearly I was remiss, thinking that *you* would never compose a tract like this! There was nothing you wrote that was not true, you offered—my dear Mufti—insight all the way through."[132] Though there is no indication what about Fevri's identity made it hard to believe that he could have produced such a tract, the evaluation surely stung the proud and revered mufti. There is no doubt that Hamawi narrated these incidents in an effort to lampoon the Jerusalemite rather than his fellow travelers, one of whom was his patron. Their host's poor manners and his lack of respect for his Rumi guests betokened his own parochialism, since he could not recognize a great scholar when he saw one. Still, the encounter also suggests the difficulty even very high-ranking Rumi officials could experience in earning the respect of Arab scholars.

Instances of outright disrespect in live gatherings must have been exceedingly rare. As we have seen, and as Fevri's expectations for praise

130. Ḥamawī, *Ḥādī*, 31–2.

131. Ḥamawī, *Ḥādī*, 32.

132. Emphasis mine. Ḥamawī, *Ḥādī*, 32–3. Fevri's work had received a far more favorable reception in Damascus, as we shall see in Chapter 5.

confirm, salon conversation usually deferred to power relationships. We can assume that in most live encounters, as in most written descriptions, the overwhelming tendency was to laud the skill and intellect of the Rumi scholars that held the reigns of power (and could easily punish Arabs for any insubordination, actual or perceived). Still, the silence about the talents of these men in early Arabic-language writings—in marked contrast to the active and witty personae that Turkish accounts record—suggests that, at least in the first decades after the conquest, many Rumis were not particularly memorable participants in Arabic-language salons. As flattering as Ghazzi's descriptions of others in his travel account always were, he recorded no poems and few insights from his Rumi interlocutors, in sharp contrast to the many pages he set aside for the words of ʿAbbasi, his Egyptian-born friend who settled in Istanbul.[133] To be fair, Ghazzi's account generally functioned as a showcase for his own ability to enlighten and teach others, and he was similarly reluctant to credit the intellectual contributions of his conversation partners in Aleppo or Hama.[134] At the same time, his slight of these provincial scholars is of an entirely different order than his neglect of the chief judge of Istanbul or the military judge of Anatolia, two of the most powerful and learned men in all the empire.

One can imagine what Arab scholars may have thought or said off the record. They had inherited from previous generations the conviction that perfection in Arabic—not simply proficiency but an ability to appreciate its finer points—was the distinctive trait of an Islamic scholar, what separated him from not only the masses but also from the middling sorts.[135] Those who dabbled in Arabic poetry without having fully mastered it had long been the object of jest. The Anatolian-born poet Mamaya al-Rumi, king of *zajal*, tore up all of his previous poetry after his formal training in literature and grammar in Damascus later in life. Not only was Arabic linguistic knowledge crucial, it subtended the other Islamic disciplines. One fourteenth-century scholar devoted an entire section of his literary anthology to the grave misunderstandings that could arise if a scholar insufficiently versed in linguistic sciences tried to interpret prophetic hadiths.[136]

133. The two exceptions were Hacı Celebi's wisdom that repeating "our God" five times ensured one's wish be fulfilled, and Ebu's-Suʿud's explication of a Qurʾanic verse. Ghazzī, *Maṭāliʿ*, 264, 268.

134. He did mention one scholar's thoughts on the fair treatment of animals, another's on partaking in a funeral without being ritually pure, and the poem of a third. Ghazzī, *Maṭāliʿ*, 63–5.

135. Bauer, "Literarische Anthologien der Mamlūkenzeit," 90, 104–6; Haarman, "Arabic," 81–5.

136. Bauer, "Literarische Anthologien der Mamlūkenzeit," 85–7.

None of this is to say that the scholarship of the central lands was inferior to that of the Arab provinces. Being able to engage with a written tradition at an advanced level is a skill altogether distinct from making witty remarks or composing verse. However, given the valence of the Arabic language and its centrality to scholarly practice, it was just a short step from pointing out someone's grammatical mistake to questioning their scholarly expertise.

That Rumi scholars valued the opinions of their Arab colleagues is suggested by the experience of one of the few who won them over, Kınalızade ʿAli. Kınalızade spent several years serving as chief judge in Damascus and Cairo in the 1560s, attracting enthusiastic accolades from local scholars (and not least from Ghazzi himself). The biography of Kınalızade by his son Hasan Çelebi Kınalızade (d. 1604) shows that this kind of recognition mattered at the imperial center. Hasan Çelebi went to great lengths in his Turkish-language biography to demonstrate the respect his father earned during his conversations with Arab scholars, many of whom he mentioned by name. He claimed that his father was so knowledgeable and eloquent that he left some of his interlocutors stuttering, and others at a complete loss for words. Summarizing his father's time in Cairo, Hasan explained, "in gatherings and parties [*mecālis-ü meḥāfilde*] the grandees and people of rank recited most solemn assurances of praise and encomium, each of them testifying [here he switched to Arabic], 'indeed he is an example of the wonders of God.'"[137] There is no doubt ample hyperbole in Hasan's phrasing, but the fact that he included such anecdotes in the biography of his father suggests it was the kind of thing his Turkish-speaking audience might know to appreciate.

As accomplished as Rumi scholars were in the sixteenth century, their training did not always prepare them for preeminence in Arabic-dominated salons. Arab elites appear to have had little appreciation for the fact that these scholars may have excelled in literary or scholarly arenas different from their own. Instead, they often leaned on cultural stereotypes according to which Ottoman scholars were seen as less learned. In the cultural politics of sixteenth-century Arab lands, failing to master Arabic in all of its literary and scholarly forms was a failure of learning in general. Although centrally trained scholars found plenty of other ways to buttress their own power in and outside of salons, the importance of language and learning was such that, at times, it could cause a reversal of the power differential between conquerors and conquered.

137. Kınalı-zade, *Tezkiretü'ş-Şuʿarâ*, 670.

Conclusion

Ottoman salons offered aesthetic and literary pleasures of the highest order. They also presented formidable challenges. The ideal of refined discourse across early modern Ottoman lands could be attained only after years of preparation. It relied on advanced linguistic training, dogged memorization, and a grounding in the scholarly tradition. Although this ideal only rarely may have been achieved fully, biographical dictionaries suggest it was taken seriously by all. Speakers strove to achieve more sophisticated and learned speech, and listeners evaluated others by those rubrics as well.

The expectations for cultured conversation did much to shape interactions between Rumis and Arabs in the wake of the conquest. On the one hand, *adab* as etiquette required conversation to follow social hierarchies. This sheltered Rumi officeholders from open criticism or even ridicule. On the other hand, *adab* as literary culture meant that Rumis were often at a disadvantage in Arabic-language conversations; no less learned than their Arab counterparts, they nevertheless sometimes appeared to be so on account of their different education. Because of the universal nature of the Arabic language and its special meaning for Muslims, Rumis could not easily discount this tradition nor claim indifference toward it. Some mastery of Arabic and its attendant literary tradition was an ineluctable part of a Muslim gentleman's cultural repertoire, in the same way that Latin was in early modern European culture.

With its very particular conventions and expectations, the salon posed a challenge to many Rumi scholars in the decades after the conquest. Many could not use their language and learning to acquire the authority and visibility that befitted their status. Some responded with silence, others by withdrawing from learned circles altogether. To be sure, the power of Ottoman officials over Arab scholars ensured that open criticism remained rare, but it does not take much imagination to picture the dread that many Ottoman scholars must have felt when faced with the most learned men of Damascus.

This unease was compounded by the salon's multiple audiences. Not only might wives and servants be watching from the sidelines, the mockery withheld today could be released to peals of laughter to another audience tomorrow. In addition, impressions gained from salons, or even incidents that unfolded within them, often entered the written record. At best, salons, then, were semiprivate. To be sure, they were exclusive and accessible only by a select few, but much of what happened within them was viewed as being in the public domain, at least insofar as it was acceptable to report on them in writing.

The dilemmas that Rumi scholars faced in the salon help us to better grasp the role—still poorly understood—of language in early modern Ottoman society. Historians would do well to pay more attention to spoken forms of language alongside written ones.[138] Much scholarly, and indeed personal, authority was derived from verbal utterances in live contexts. This had considerable consequences for Rumi scholars. Although there is no doubt that many—if not most—scholars could easily participate in written forms of Arabic, speech presented greater difficulties. Conversational structures were not just empty forms filled with content as men encountered one another; rather, they shaped the possibilities for interactions and the power relations within them.

Salon encounters also reveal the immense power that language had to distinguish and to discipline in Ottoman lands. It has sometimes been suggested that, unlike in the modern era when language has been coopted by powerful or even repressive states and used to draw sharp divisions, in the early modern period—especially in the Mediterranean—language played a gentler, if not even democratizing, role.[139] To be sure, the Ottoman state did not seek to weaponize language in the way that modern states often have, including Turkey. Yet educated elites were intensely normative about language and used it as an important tool of exclusion. Language constituted one of the main ways they distinguished themselves from the vast majority of the population. It also helped them gain and enforce authority within the elite. In the early decades after the conquest, this sometimes worked in the favor of educated Arabs.

138. Grehan, "Words."
139. Dursteler, "Speaking in Tongues."

CHAPTER FIVE

The Transmission of Knowledge

NEVER WERE THE gardens of Ottoman culture more verdant than in the sixteenth century.[1] Teeming but well tended, they bore fruit in everything from history-writing to poetry and jurisprudence. Modern scholars agree that this creative outpouring had a number of different causes, from the general wealth that rained down on the empire in the period, to the willingness of patrons to channel new ideas, to the carefully structured system of madrasas that descended like stepped terraces across the imperial realm. Scholars also recognize that this fervor resulted from the openness of Ottoman intellectuals, their willingness to take the best of any cultural tradition—Islamic or Christian—and graft it onto their own.

Rarely, however, have historians linked this intellectual vitality to the incorporation of Arab lands. This chapter argues that the 1516–7 conquest was an event of crucial significance for the history of Ottoman thought. Turcophone elites in Anatolia and the Balkans had always been in dialogue with the Arabic-language literary and scholarly tradition, but the conquest spurred new interest in it and afforded new levels of access to it. What is more, this interest did not result from a unilateral shift among Rumi scholars, often viewed as the main motors of cultural change. Rather, new intellectual priorities at the Ottoman center emerged in response to, or even under the guidance of, scholars in the newly acquired provinces.

It is little wonder that few have connected sixteenth-century Ottoman intellectual achievements to Arab influence. Indeed, one could be

1. Parts of this chapter have been published previously as Pfeifer, "Encounter"; Pfeifer, "Hadith Culture."

forgiven for thinking that Arab scholars were excluded from the Ottoman intelligentsia altogether. Their names were omitted from centrally produced biographical compilations of the empire's learned class. Their colleges were never fully incorporated into the Ottoman educational hierarchy. With some exceptions, Rumis were appointed to the influential teaching positions in Anatolia and the Balkans, and Arab scholars taught at madrasas in the Arab lands. Likewise with exceptions, for most of the sixteenth century, students from these respective regions pursued their studies locally. Under such circumstances, could anything like meaningful exchanges have really taken place?

This chapter suggests that they did. We miss this when we focus on madrasas as the main sites for the production and transmission of knowledge. The Mamluk lands had harbored a system of higher education less formalized than the Ottoman one, one in which madrasas were only one component of a mixed economy of learning spaces.[2] But even in Ottoman lands, where higher education had been subject to government oversight since the middle of the fifteenth century, informal gatherings held outside the madrasa offered valuable opportunities for instruction and debate. Precisely because of their flexibility, salons became prime sites for intellectual encounters between Arab and Rumi scholars in the wake of the 1516–7 conquest. Salons shaped tastes in reading, helped circulate ideas, and even accommodated formal instruction.

As a result of these encounters, intellectual traditions previously popular primarily in Arab lands spread rapidly across the empire. Chief judges, who were some of the most learned and powerful Ottoman officials in Syria, were also some of the most receptive to new ideas. They took a special interest in hadiths, the words and deeds of the Prophet Muhammad. These accounts, which had been passed down orally after the Prophet's death, were not only an important source of Islamic law, they also conferred spiritual blessings and helped to cement scholarly genealogies.[3] As Rumi scholars came into contact with men like Ghazzi, they were able to access new ways of sealing their belonging within the Islamic intellectual and devotional community.

2. Berkey, *Transmission*; Chamberlain, *Knowledge*. Recently, Paula Manstetten has softened this distinction somewhat, arguing that starting already in the eleventh century, higher education in Damascus became increasingly institutionalized. Manstetten, "Institutionalisation."

3. For an enlightening treatment of the postclassical hadith tradition, without which this chapter could not have been written, see Davidson, *Tradition*. See also the classic Brown, *Hadith*.

If early Rumi travelers had sometimes lacked the cultural reference points current in Arabic salons, those same salons contributed to the process by which that disadvantage was overcome. There is no better emblem of this than Kınalızade ʿAli (d. 1572). Kınalızade was a prodigious scholar who was educated in the central lands and spent nearly four years as chief judge of Damascus in the 1560s. A dear friend of Ghazzi and his sometime student, Kınalızade also became Ghazzi's challenger in the scholarly ring.

Reading

One of the most important, yet often underappreciated, effects of the Ottoman conquest of Syria, Egypt, and the Arabian Peninsula is that it immediately made Arabic-language books more accessible to the Rumi elite. The victors seized some manuscript collections as spoils of war, not only in Aleppo and Cairo but also in Damascus, where a historian complained that an early chief judge toured the city's libraries confiscating books illegally and reserving many of them for Rumis alone.[4] However, Ottoman learned men did not acquire local knowledge traditions primarily through plunder. More often they came upon books in a less spectacular fashion, alongside locals rather than in spite of them.

Reading in the premodern period in general, and in Islamic societies in particular, was a social, and often performative, activity, and Ottoman lands were no exception.[5] Books were read aloud not only to edify illiterate audiences, but also to entertain the highly educated participants of the gentlemanly salon. Salongoers frequently drew on the written tradition from memory, as we saw in Chapter 4. However, they often conjured physical copies of books in gatherings as well. Sometimes, books might provide the backdrop to salons, visible in the niches in which they were arrayed (see figures 2.2, 5.1). Other times, they moved to center stage. Gentlemen viewed domestic visits as opportunities to conduct book inspections, as Ghazzi's student the historian Hasan al-Burini made clear in his early seventeenth-century biographical dictionary. Burini obviously had a chance to examine the volumes of the Ottoman chief judge Ahmed Efendi (d. 1587), who served in Damascus from 1586, since he noted their beautiful calligraphy.[6] That

4. Ibn Ṭūlūn, *Quḍāt*, 315; Hirschler, *Medieval Damascus*, 52; Erünsal, "Vakıf Kütüphaneleri." For Aleppo and Cairo, see Erünsal, *Ottoman Libraries*, 30.

5. Değirmenci, "Kişi"; Öztürk, "Halk Kitapları"; Öztürk, "Okunan Kitaplar."

6. Būrīnī, *Tarājim*, 1: 67. The Venetian ambassador Francesco Contarini likewise had a chance to survey the books of an Ottoman official who invited him to his home. Dursteler, *Venetians in Constantinople*, 178.

books featured prominently in learned conversation is also clear from the illustrated version of ʿAşık Çelebi's biographical dictionary *Senses of Poets* (*Meşaʿirü's-Şuʿaraʾ*), which frequently depicts its subjects holding codices as they talked (see figures 0.1, 2.2, 2.4, and 5.1).[7]

Salons played a role in almost every phase of a book's life, from its conception to its publication. The very idea to write a book on a particular subject often arose in a salon. Ottoman authors so often claimed that a social gathering had inspired their work that modern scholars have sometimes been tempted to dismiss these claims as merely a trope. Even if we allow that on occasion such statements did act as a generic form of legitimization, plenty of other evidence suggests that books were often written in response to live debates.[8] Sometimes ideas came about in response to the request of a powerful patron, as we saw in the case of Ayas Pasha's commissions for Ghazzi in Istanbul. Other times new ideas were the result of animated discussion. Ghazzi's travel account, for example, was inspired by his conversations with his friend ʿAbd al-Rahim al-ʿAbbasi, whom he credited not only with the idea for the work, but with its title too.[9]

Once authors had an idea for a book, they did not retreat into their studies to think and write in solitude. Rather, many writers used salons to seek feedback on works in progress. The Rumi scholar Mustafa ʿAli, who spent several years in Damascus in the household of the provincial governor when Kınalızade was chief judge, explained that he would frequently meet with the magistrate to discuss their works in progress.[10] There the friends subjected one another's writings to intense scrutiny, and it was from Kınalızade that ʿAli claimed to have learned that "true friendship means to look on a friend's work with the eye of an enemy."[11] Such practices may explain the loose-leaf paper occasionally shown in visual depictions of scholarly meetings, such as the portrait of Saʿdi Çelebi in figure 2.2.

But it was upon the completion of a book that its social life truly began. Given that the Ottoman Empire remained a manuscript culture into the eighteenth century, presenting a book at a salon represented a form of publication in the sense of releasing it for public use. Though Mustafa ʿAli complained about men who wasted precious time in learned assemblies

7. The same is true for other contemporary depictions of salons. See Taner, *Caught in a Whirlwind*, 90–2, 94.

8. Ṭaşköprīzāde, *Shaqāʾiq*, 148; Niyazioğlu, *Dreams*, chapter 1.

9. Ghazzī, *Kawākib*, 2: 163.

10. Fleischer, *Bureaucrat*, 43.

11. Mustafa ʿAli as quoted in Fleischer, *Bureaucrat*, 43.

FIGURE 5.1. ʿAli, the father of the biographer ʿAşık Çelebi, receives another scholar next to shelves containing books. From ʿAşık Çelebi, *Meşaʿirüʾs-şuʿara*ʾ (c. 1600). (Reproduced by permission from the Directorate of the Turkish Institution for Manuscripts, Millet Library Istanbul, MS Ali Emiri Tarih 772, 245a.)

reading aloud from their already established works, most salongoers seem to have been more tolerant of such practices, which could both amuse and enlighten.[12] Indeed, the nightly programming at an Ottoman soirée could include works with high entertainment value like travel accounts as well as more strenuous reads like Qurʾan commentaries.

Back in Syria, Badr al-Din al-Ghazzi promoted his works especially avidly in live gatherings. Long after he had formally withdrawn from society, Ghazzi continued to convoke assemblies known as "concluding sessions" (*majlis khatm*). He held two kinds of concluding sessions: one when he finished writing a book, when it served as a book launch; the second when he finished teaching a book—usually one of his own—in which case it functioned as a graduation celebration of sorts.[13] The gatherings were designed to give maximum exposure. Leading scholars of the city were invited for an afternoon of learned discussion, usually in the central prayer hall of the Great Mosque. Afterwards, other members of the community joined them for a grand banquet in Ghazzi's chamber. Though conversation could touch on many different topics, including ones unrelated to the book being celebrated, contemporary historians remembered these assemblies by the titles they were held to honor.

It paid off to promote one's books in this way, since attendees often followed up by seeking to secure their own copies. In the months Ghazzi spent with ʿAbbasi in Istanbul, the younger scholar made copies of "countless works" written by his host, surely prompted by what ʿAbbasi had told him about them.[14] In some cases, the link between live gathering and written record was even more immediate. Ghazzi explained that he copied down some of the long odes ʿAbbasi recited to him; Ghazzi, in turn, "recited to him many other things, many of which [ʿAbbasi] recorded by his own hand."[15]

As gatherings increasingly united men of Arab and Rumi descent, they helped to set books into motion across the empire. Structures of patronage drew books written in the Arab lands northwards to Anatolia and the Balkans; the writings Ghazzi prepared for Ayas Pasha during his 1530–1

12. Muṣṭafā ʿĀlī, *Tables*, 170.

13. "If he finished teaching or writing a book, he held a banquet and made its completion festive. He invited the important people and the poor [*fuqarāʾ*]. He entertained them and was equally hospitable to the poor as to the military officials." Ghazzī, *Kawākib*, 3: 5–6. Other members of the community also held celebratory final sessions at the conclusion of a course, including Ghazzi's nemesis ʿAlaʾ al-Din al-Shafiʿi. Ibn Ayyūb, *Kitāb*, 35–6. This practice continued into the eighteenth century. Reichmuth, "az-Zabīdī," 78.

14. Ghazzī, *Maṭāliʿ*, 138.

15. Ghazzī, *Maṭāliʿ*, 148, 181, respectively.

trip are a representative example. The culture of gift-giving tended in the same direction. During their stay at the home of a Jerusalemite scholar in the 1570s, the chief judge Çivizade and the Hanafi mufti Fevri Efendi received a tour of their host's private library.[16] While examining the books, Fevri noticed one in particular, *The Perfection* (*al-Itqan*), a work probably written by either Jalal al-Din al-Suyuti or Ibn Hajar, since both academic celebrities of the late Mamluk period wrote a book by that name. Fevri asked his host if he could borrow the book. Reading it in the days that followed, Fevri decided he liked it so much that he wanted to keep it, occasionally dropping hints to this effect until his host grudgingly agreed.[17] Such situations meant that books often traveled against the gradient of power.

Salons allowed books of local repute to win fame across the Ottoman Empire—or in the case of one of Ghazzi's works, infamy. Ghazzi nearly became the victim of his own success at promoting his written oeuvre. A book he had repeatedly celebrated with concluding sessions was his versified Qurʾan commentary, which he had completed in the early 1550s.[18] The commentary's verse form was unusual, as Ghazzi himself acknowledged, calling it a book "that no one had attempted besides me and that forged a path no one had traveled before me."[19] He had written it in rhyme in the hope that students might more easily understand and memorize it, and for that reason gave it a title which can be loosely translated as *Qurʾanic Exegesis Made Simple* (*al-Taysir fi al-Tafsir*). As well-meaning as Ghazzi's intentions may have been, the commentary became something of a liability. Although the Qurʾan was widely appreciated for its linguistic beauty and contained some elements of poetic style, including rhyme, it was distinct from poetry, and understood as such by contemporaries.[20] Moreover, both the Qurʾanic text and the Prophet Muhammad expressed reservations about rhymed verse, whose grip some attributed to demonic

16. See Chapter 6 for more information on this journey.

17. Ḥamawī, *Ḥādī*, 34 (see also Bakhit's appendix nr. 17). Ghazzi also brought copies of his own books to Istanbul and presented two of them as a token of thanks to his host ʿAbbasi. ʿAbbasi immediately read them both cover to cover. Ghazzī, *Maṭāliʿ*, 192.

18. Also called *Taysir al-bayan fi tafsir al-Qurʾan* or *al-Tafsir al-manzum*. Tamīmī, *Ṭabaqāt*, 239a; Kātib Çelebi, *Ẓunūn*, 2: 730–1. According to Ghazzi, the commentary was written in the years from 1552–54/5 (959–62). Ghazzī, *Taysīr*, MS Ayasofya 99, 331b. There are three copies of the versified commentary in the Süleymaniye Library (one of which is incomplete): MSS Ayasofya 98 and 99; MS Fatih 632; MSS Yeni Cami 39, 40, 41. Çollak and Akpınar, "Gazzi, Bedreddin," 537.

19. Ghazzī, "Ijāza," 239b.

20. Bauer, "Relevance," 704–6.

powers.[21] Critics charged that by placing excerpts of the Qurʾan into his rhyme scheme, Ghazzi had turned the word of God into poetry. In discussing the Qurʾanic verse "Guide us on the straight path" (*ihdinā al-ṣirāṭ al-mustaqīm*) (Q1:6), for example, Ghazzi wrote:

The support one might request from God hath
Been outlined in the words "Guide us on the straight path."[22]

In this example, Ghazzi incorporated the Qurʾanic verse into his meter and rhyme scheme (see figure 5.2). Other accusations were more severe. Some claimed that by adding the letter *alif* to the end of some Qurʾanic verses, as one often did in Arabic poetry for the sake of the rhyme, Ghazzi had committed the far more serious offense of altering parts of the Qurʾan.[23]

The book polarized learned audiences. In Damascus, one of its most hostile critics was Ghazzi's longtime rival ʿAlaʾ al-Din al-Shafiʿi, whom we encountered in Chapter 4 when he snubbed Ghazzi by refusing to sit next to him. But thanks to the networks that spread news like wildfire, the book soon became a topic of discussion further afield. According to Ghazzi's student Burini, all the leading scholars of the period debated the book, with responses that ranged from outright rejection to glowing praise.[24] The traveler Qutb al-Din al-Nahrawali, who arrived in Damascus in 1557 from the Arabian Peninsula, mentioned both the book and the objection to it in his short profile of Ghazzi.[25] Visitors from Anatolia engaged with it as well. Burini was present when one Rumi judge asked Ghazzi about it; in response, Ghazzi insisted angrily, "I did not versify the Qurʾan and I did not change any of its words!"[26]

Eventually, the controversy reached the apex of the imperial learned hierarchy. A nineteenth-century Yemeni historian claimed that discussions of Ghazzi's commentary were so vehement that the sultan convoked a meeting of scholars to deliberate on it.[27] A period source corroborates

21. ʿĀşıḳ Çelebi, *Meşâʿirü's-Şuʿarâ*, 134–68; Reynolds, *The Emergence of Islam*, 95–6; Goodman, *Islamic Humanism*, 34–43.

22. In the original, Ghazzi rhymed the word *mustaqīm*, meaning straight, with the word *karīm*, meaning generous. Ghazzī, *Taysīr*, MS Ayasofya 98, 5b.

23. For various critiques, see Būrīnī, *Tarājim*, 2: 94–5, 104; Ghazzī, *Maṭāliʿ*, MS Fazıl Ahmed Paşa 1390, 0a; Kātib Çelebi, *Ẓunūn*, 1: 454.

24. Būrīnī, *Tarājim*, 2: 94.

25. Nahrawali, *Journey*, 48.

26. Būrīnī, *Tarājim*, 2: 104. The memory of this controversy lasted into the seventeenth century, when the bibliographer Katib Çelebi mentioned it. One of his sources for the controversy was Nahrawali's travel account. Kātib Çelebi, *Ẓunūn*, 1: 454.

27. The historian in question was Muhammad al-Shawkani (d. 1834). Shawkānī, *Badr*, 252.

FIGURE 5.2. An excerpt from Badr al-Din al-Ghazzi's versified Qur'an commentary *Qur'anic Commentary Made Simple* (*al-Taysir fi'l-tafsir*). The Qur'anic verse that Ghazzi discusses in this passage is introduced in red ink at the top left (*ihdinā al-ṣirāṭ al-mustaqīm*), and is repeated, again in red, in the versified portion one line below. (Reproduced by permission from the Directorate of the Turkish Institution for Manuscripts, Süleymaniye Library Istanbul, MS Ayasofya 98, 5b.)

that the work was reviewed by the powerful chief mufti of the empire, Ebu's-Suʿud.[28] Ghazzi as we have seen was no stranger to the mufti: the two had met in Istanbul in 1530, when Ebu's-Suʿud was an instructor at one of the eight madrasas founded by Mehmed II. At first, upon hearing of the book's premise, Ebu's-Suʿud cautiously condemned the book.[29] Yet when he reviewed the work, he found nothing wrong with it, and even, according to our later source, rewarded its author with money and honor. Though the later account may well be exaggerated, Burini does report that Ebu's-Suʿud eventually accepted the book as licit.[30] In any case, Ghazzi remained undeterred; he continued to champion the book as one of his greatest achievements and to hold celebratory gatherings whenever he finished teaching it.[31]

Though many Rumis kept their distance from this particular work, in general learned gatherings in the provinces stimulated an appetite for Arabic-language books among scholars from the Ottoman center. Chief judges were especially eager. Some of the books in which these judges took an interest dated to the pre-Ottoman period. Kınalızade commissioned

28. Būrīnī, *Tarājim*, 2: 104.

29. Būrīnī, *Tarājim*, 2: 94, 104.

30. Būrīnī, *Tarājim*, 2: 104; Shawkānī, *Badr*, 2: 252.

31. The Süleymaniye Library has an incomplete copy of the prose version, entitled *Taysir al-bayan fi tafsir al-Qur'an*. The book was completed in 1555 (962). Ghazzī, *Taysīr*, Süleymaniye Library, MSS H. Hüsnü Paşa 11-M2, 11-M3, 11-2, 11-3, 11-M4, 11-7, 11-10, 11-11. Another incomplete copy is in Birmingham, MS Islamic Arabic 1374. Ghazzi held another celebratory gathering for the work in 1569/70. Būrīnī, *Tarājim*, 1: 11–2; Būrīnī, *Tarājim*, 2: 97.

a copy of the classic Arabic-language biographical dictionary of Ibn Khallikan (d. 1282), a one-time chief judge in Syria.[32] A few years later Çivizade ordered a history by a fourteenth-century Syrian scholar.[33] These same collectors pursued the work of their Syrian contemporaries as well. Kınalızade copied in his own hand a pilgrimage manual by the esteemed local scholar Shihab al-Din al-Tibi the Elder (d. 1571/2), as well as a portion of one of Tibi's poems.[34] Bostanzade Mehmed (d. 1598), chief judge in Damascus in the mid-1570s, asked Ghazzi's son Najm al-Din for copies of some of his works.[35] Ahmed Efendi, whose library Burini had visited, commissioned copies of the poetry anthologies (*diwan*) of local poets, including that of the legendary local Janissary poet Mamaya al-Rumi.[36]

As a result of such acquisitions, the numbers of Arabic-language books in the private libraries of Rumi scholars swelled. Ahmed Efendi, Burini reported, "had books that I never saw in the possession of other high-ranking Rumi lords," including a work by the legendary Damascene scholar Abu Zakariyya al-Nawawi (d. 1277), and, above all, a fantastic array of poetry anthologies.[37] Kınalızade's collection was even more impressive; contemporaries estimated that he returned to Istanbul after his time as chief judge with close to five thousand volumes acquired in Syria and Egypt.[38] This pattern was not limited to scholars. Sixteenth-century inheritance registers reveal that viziers and governors who served in some capacity in Arab lands on average owned a greater number of Arabic books than ones who did not.[39]

Silent and individualized reading of the sort we consider standard today was only one of the many ways in which books were consumed in the Ottoman Empire. Informal gatherings were important to the conceptualization, reception, and dissemination of the written word. As such,

32. This was *Kitab wafayyat al-aʿyan*, copied for Kınalızade by the historian Ibn Ayyub. Ibn Ayyūb, *Rawḍ*, 204b.

33. This was the history of Ibn Habib (d. 1377). Ḥamawī, *Majmūʿa*, 32b–33a.

34. Ibn Ayyūb, *Rawḍ*, 204b; Ghazzī, *Kawākib*, 3: 187.

35. Ghazzī, *Luṭf*, 104. Bostanzade had good things to say about the Ghazzi family in general. Winter, "Ottoman Qāḍīs," 102.

36. Ahmed had copies made of the poetry anthologies of Ibn Hijja al-Hamawi (d. 1434) and ʿAli Ibn Mulayk al-Hamawi (d. 1512). Ibn Ayyūb, *Rawḍ*, 52b.

37. Būrīnī, *Tarājim*, 1: 67. Tamīmī also remarked on Ahmed's Arabic and on his personal library. Tamīmī, *Ṭabaqāt*, 1: 382. It is possible that some of these books had belonged to Ahmed's father Hasan Bey, since he was an avid collector of books. Būrīnī, *Tarājim*, 1: 72; ʿAṭāʾī, *Ḥadāʾiḳ*, 240.

38. Ibn Ayyūb, *Rawḍ*, 205a.

39. This included Hadım Hasan Pasha (d. 1598) and Üveys Pasha (d. 1590), both of whom served as governor in Egypt. Fetvacı, *History*, 49–53.

they played a key role in transmitting Syrian tastes to the Ottoman center. The thousands of Arabic books that made their way to Anatolia in the wake of the conquest certainly reflected the priorities of acquisitive conquerors. However, they also followed the intellectual proclivities of Arab scholars, which they conveyed to Rumis in homes and gardens across the Ottoman Empire.

Teaching

It is well known that in the second half of the sixteenth century, more and more Arab scholars spent time in Istanbul studying with Rumis trained and employed at the imperial center.[40] It is less well known that, at the same time, many Rumis—even ones at the height of their career—spent some time studying with Arabs. Again, informal gatherings held outside of the madrasa context had a part to play. Sixteenth-century salons frequently acted as sites for the transmission of knowledge from teacher to student. These helped Arabic learning to gain greater prominence among Rumis.

Advanced coursework in the Ottoman Empire was intensely formalized; classes met regularly and followed a set of widely accepted rules. Ghazzi himself obviously valued such rules, since he discussed them at length in his 1526 book on educational etiquette, *The Well-Ordered Pearls on the Etiquette of Teaching and Learning* (*Al-Durr al-nadid fi adab al-mufid wa-l-mustafid*). His manual stressed that the behaviors permissible in informal gatherings were different from those allowable in a classroom setting. The teacher, for example, should never cross his legs or rest on his elbow while teaching, though he was free to do so when speaking with students in other contexts.[41] Ghazzi advised students that regular attendance of classes was so important that not even minor illness exempted them from it.[42] However, he and his contemporaries recognized that class was not the only place where learning could take place. One Rumi scholar, reminiscing about his student days in Istanbul, recalled that one of his professors used to have his students over for dinner on days when there was no class. "During those discussions," he recalled, "we resolved complex issues that we had been unable to resolve during the lesson."[43] Contemporaries had a rich vocabulary that they could apply to informal instances

40. See Chapter 6 for this development.

41. Ghazzī, *al-Durr al-naḍīd*, 195. For this book and the larger tradition of which the book was a part, see Melchert, "Etiquette"; Gacek, "Technical Practices"; Sharkas, "Manual."

42. Ghazzī, *al-Durr al-naḍīd*, 121.

43. Ṭaşköprīzāde, *Shaqāʾiq*, 285.

of knowledge transmission, such as "learning [literally 'taking'] from" (*ya'khidhu 'an*) or "benefiting intellectually from" (*yastafīdu min*).

Ghazzi had ample chance to use such verbs when he traveled to the Ottoman capital in 1530–1. While still in Syria, he transmitted prophetic traditions to two local scholars and taught portions of scholarly texts—including one of his own—to a third.[44] Such activities intensified when he arrived in Istanbul. Ghazzi found his greatest intellectual admirer in Hacı Çelebi, the old friend of his father Radi al-Din, who welcomed Ghazzi into his home in Istanbul. Hacı Çelebi had already studied with Ghazzi's father on a stopover in Damascus during his pilgrimage to Mecca.[45] Although Hacı was decades older than Badr al-Din al-Ghazzi, he was nonetheless now determined to study with him as well. Ghazzi described the relationship as reciprocal. "I benefited intellectually from him and he from me, and I learned from him and he from me [*istafadtu minhu wa istafāda minnī wa akhadhtu 'anhu wa akhadha 'annī*]."[46] However, Ghazzi's account of what he himself learned from Hacı was in fact very limited: that whoever addressed God in his prayers uttering "*rabbanā*" five times would be granted his wish.[47] What Ghazzi taught Hacı was vast in comparison: two of the commentaries he had completed in Istanbul, one on "The Mantle Ode" and the other on the "Throne Verse" of the Qur'an; a discussion of the internal word of God (*al-kalam al-nafsi*); an ode Ghazzi wrote in which each line ended with the letter "*qaf*"; another ode in which each line ended with the letter "*kha'*"; and some apotropaic passages that warded off the plague when carried on the body.[48]

When Ghazzi left the city for a stay in nearby Izmit, his host there, a young man called Kassabzade Mehmed, took advantage of his guest's learning too. Kassabzade studied portions of Ghazzi's commentaries on "The Mantle Ode" (as Hacı had) as well as on *The Thousand-Line Poem* (*al-Alfiyya*) on Arabic grammar by Ibn Malik (d. 1274). He also took interest in Ghazzi's immense trove of prophetic accounts, and asked Ghazzi to

44. Ghazzi taught an Aleppine scholar parts of his commentary on *The Thousand-Line Poem* (*al-Alfiyya*) by Ibn Malik, as well as parts of *The Path* (*al-Minhaj*), presumably Nawawi's *Path for Seekers* (*Minhaj al-talibin*), a work of Shafi'i jurisprudence. See Ghazzī, *Maṭāli'*, 50–2, 61, 68.

45. Ghazzī, *Kawākib*, 2: 166.

46. Ghazzī, *Maṭāli'*, 263.

47. As proof, Hacı cited a series of Qur'anic verses in which Abraham addressed God in this way (Q14:37–41). Although Ghazzi had never heard of this convention, he immediately conjured up another set of verses in which this was the case (Q3: 191–195), much to the satisfaction of Hacı Celebi. Ghazzī, *Maṭāli'*, 264.

48. Ghazzī, *Maṭāli'*, 263–4.

issue him an academic license (*ijaza*) permitting him to transmit those accounts to others.[49] The license Ghazzi issued Kassabzade took a particularly generous form; it permitted him to transmit everything that Ghazzi had been licensed to transmit by his teachers.[50]

This kind of knowledge transmission was so important to Rumis that they involved multiple generations at once. Kassabzade asked Ghazzi to issue academic licenses to his three sons.[51] Hacı brought his three sons in front of Ghazzi as well, and at least one of them was present when Ghazzi presented his scholarly works to the boy's father.[52] One of Hacı's nephews—the son of the deceased ʿAbdurrahman Müʾeyyedzade, who had helped Ghazzi's friend ʿAbbasi when he had fled Mamluk lands for Istanbul—also came to study with Ghazzi in Istanbul.[53]

Scholars trained in the Ottoman center continued to study with Ghazzi after he returned to Damascus. Some of these were boys or young men in the midst of their scholarly studies. Take for instance Ahmed, the son of Ghazzi's close friend Hasan Bey, the chief judge of Damascus at whose party Ghazzi was challenged by a former student.[54] According to the historian Burini, Hasan "worked hard to ensure that his son [Ahmed] would memorize the sayings and poems of the Arabs [*kalām al-ʿarab*]."[55] He saw to it that "some of the greatest scholars taught [his son Ahmed] when he entered Syria and Damascus," in the words of another historian, who offered a long list of Ahmed's teachers that culminated with Ghazzi.[56]

Mature Rumis who traveled through the Arab provinces long after they had finished their studies also sought to profit from Ghazzi's learning. The list Ghazzi kept of all of his students featured some of the most ambitious and high-profile scholars to have passed through Damascus in the sixteenth century, including the chief judges Kınalızade ʿAli, Çivizade Mehmed Efendi, and Bostanzade Mehmed as well as its chief Hanafi muftis Fevri Efendi and Mehmed Muʿidzade (d. 1576).[57] Some of these

49. Ghazzī, *Maṭāliʿ*, 270–1. For *ijazas* in the postclassical period, see Davidson, *Tradition*, chapter 3.

50. This was known as an *ijaza mutlaqa*. Davidson, *Tradition*, 129–35. See also the *ijaza* Ghazzi issued to Çivizade, mentioned in this chapter.

51. Ghazzī, *Maṭāliʿ*, 271.

52. Ghazzī, *Maṭāliʿ*, 265.

53. Ghazzī, *Maṭāliʿ*, 266.

54. See Chapter 3 for Ghazzi's relationship with Hasan.

55. Būrīnī, *Tarājim*, 1: 68.

56. Tamīmī, *Ṭabaqāt*, 1: 382.

57. Ghazzī, *Kawākib*, 3: 6. Najm al-Din relied on this list in his own account of Ghazzi's students. The printed edition of Najm al-Din's text refers to "the two muftis Fawzi Efendi and Ibn al-ʿAbd," but this is probably a later error. Fevri is often mistaken as Fawzi in

studied several disciplines with Ghazzi. Çivizade, for example, is known to have covered Islamic jurisprudence (*fiqh*) with him as well as the Qur'an commentaries of Zamakhshari and Baydawi.[58] Kınalızade studied Qur'anic commentary and recitation with Ghazzi.[59]

But by far the most popular and significant of intellectual pursuits for which Rumi scholars approached Ghazzi concerned hadith. Accounts relaying the words and actions of the Prophet were part of a shared tradition across the Islamic world, and Ottoman scholars, like their contemporaries the world over, had studied the prophetic traditions for many generations to support their legal and exegetical work. However, in Mamluk lands, in addition to studying hadiths, scholars had also invested great energy in transmitting them. These scholars prided themselves on the fact that each account had been passed down orally from one generation to the next in an unbroken chain (called an *isnad*) leading back to the Prophet himself. This practice served to establish a connection to the Prophet, who was seeming more distant with every passing generation.[60] People went to great lengths to gather accounts with the fewest possible intermediaries between contemporaries and the Prophet, seeking written licenses (*ijazat al-riwaya*) that would permit them in turn to pass that account along. Collecting hadith accounts in this way was understood as an act of piety and a way of securing blessings from God.[61] It was also a sign of status, since gaining access to particular transmitters required entry to particular social circles or the resources to travel.[62]

Prophetic accounts were also popular subjects of polite and scholarly conversation in Arab lands. Arab scholars often turned their favorite hadiths into verse and recited them to others for enjoyment—both Ghazzi and his father did so.[63] They discussed various interpretations of particular

---

Arabic sources, and another manuscript of *Kawakib* speaks of Ibn al-Muʿid instead, which I take to be more likely since he was indeed one of the Hanafi muftis of the city and is mentioned elsewhere as having attended one of Ghazzi's concluding sessions. Būrīnī, *Tarājim*, 2: 95–6; ʿAlī ibn Bālī, *ʿIqd*, 483; Ghazzī, *Kawākib*, 3: 85. Najm al-Din's later biography of Bostanzade does not mention explicitly that he studied with Ghazzi, though he does say that he benefited from him intellectually (*ḥamala ʿanhu min fawāʾidihi*). Ghazzī, *Lutf*, 102–6.

58. Ibn Ayyūb, *Rawḍ*, 241a, 260a; Ghazzī, *Kawākib*, 3: 27.

59. He also studied linguistic disciplines (*al-maʿana wa al-bayan*) with Ghazzi's colleague Shihab al-Din al-Tibi. Ibn Ayyūb, *Rawḍ*, 204b.

60. Davidson, *Tradition*. Not only scholars engaged in hadith transmission, but it was seen as one of the special duties of scholars.

61. Stefan Reichmuth has called this "*isnad* piety." Reichmuth, "az-Zabīdī," 72.

62. Davidson, *Tradition*; Brown, *Hadith*, 46–9.

63. Būrīnī, *Tarājim*, 2: 101; Ghazzī, *Maṭāliʿ*, 187.

accounts or disagreed over a given narration's reliability. On a stopover in Aleppo on the way to Istanbul, Ghazzi was asked by a local mufti whether the hadith was authentic according to which Muhammad had stated, "if the fear and the hope of the believer were weighed, they would be equal."[64] The question of which of the two emotions should dominate in a pious Muslim had a long history in the written tradition.[65] Ghazzi answered by citing two different scholarly opinions: although the Cairene scholar Muhammad al-Zarkashi (d. 1392) had argued that the tradition was well known but without solid basis, a variant of it narrated by the Iraqi ascetic Thabit al-Bunani (d. ca 744/5) had been included in one of the collections of the great traditionist Ibn Hanbal (d. 855). All of this, Ghazzi explained, had been laid out by the late Mamluk scholar Jalal al-Din al-Suyuti. For good measure, Ghazzi then recited two poems by the medieval poet Abu Nuwas (d. 815), one about hope and the other about fear (his interlocutor, the mufti of Aleppo, wrote the poems down).[66] Recalling and condensing such debates on the spot was no doubt a mark of Ghazzi's virtuosity, but his was but a superlative version of the standard conversations about hadith in contemporary Arab learned circles.

Little is known about Ottoman hadith culture, but it seems that, prior to the 1516–7 conquest, scholars in Anatolia and the Balkans did not transmit or discuss prophetic accounts with the same enthusiasm and intensity as their colleagues in Arab lands did. Rumis of that period rarely seem to have engaged in hadith transmission. The biographer Taşköprizade recorded few early Ottoman scholars who had been licensed to transmit particularly short hadith chains (*isnad ʿali*), and the exception proves the rule: none other than Ghazzi's old friend ʿAbd al-Rahim al-ʿAbbasi, trained in Damascus and Cairo in the last decades of Mamluk rule.[67] Nor does hadith seem to have been as popular a topic of gentlemanly or learned discussion in the Ottoman heartland. As late as the seventeenth century, the Rumi traveler Evliya Çelebi noted that Arab scholars placed a greater emphasis than their Rumi counterparts on prophetic traditions, and expressed his astonishment that some had memorized twenty or thirty thousand of them.[68]

With proliferating opportunities to converse with Arabs after the conquest, Rumis were increasingly exposed to a learned culture that stressed

64. Ghazzī, *Maṭāliʿ*, 67.

65. Melchert, *Hadith*, 214.

66. Ghazzī, *Maṭāliʿ*, 67–8.

67. For a more detailed discussion see Pfeifer, "Hadith Culture." For ʿAbbasi, see Ṭaşköprīzāde, *Shaqāʾiq*, 411.

68. Ayaz, "Dârulhadisleri," 63.

both the transmission and the discussion of hadiths. A scholar's hadith licenses were an important part of his credentials and a matter of public knowledge; in sessions where traditionists offered live hadith commentary, common in the fifteenth century, proceedings began by listing the transmitters from whom they had been licensed.[69] Informal learned conversation would likewise have directed the attention of Ottoman scholars towards hadith. The Rumi mufti Muʿidzade was present—albeit conspicuously silent—when Ghazzi discussed a prophetic account discussing whether it was permissible to sell enslaved concubines.[70] The poem Kınalızade copied by one of his teachers in Damascus was inspired by another account enjoining Muslims to take care of one another.[71]

Given the blessings believed to accrue from transmitting hadith and the piety that doing so signaled, some Rumis must have felt humbled when faced with their hadith-oriented Arab counterparts. After all, they were missing out on the blessings that such transmission could afford them. It is clear that Rumis were eager to gain from their Arab colleagues' expertise in this area. The case of the chief judge Çivizade Mehmed is particularly well documented. Çivizade had been a frequent visitor to Ghazzi's cell while serving as chief judge in Damascus in 1569–70, attending a few of Ghazzi's lectures as well as a concluding session for the versified Qurʾan commentary.[72] When Çivizade returned to the capital in October 1570, after a brief stint in Cairo, he attended another of Ghazzi's concluding sessions, this time for two glosses (*hashiyas*) Ghazzi had written on a commentary on a famous work of Shafiʿi law by the Syrian jurist Nawawi.[73] After the gathering was over, Çivizade approached Ghazzi to ask him for an academic license. This Ghazzi granted on the spot in a chamber in the Great Mosque (see figure 3.4).

The transfer of knowledge and authority that resulted was immense: an extant copy of the *ijaza* spans over eighteen pages.[74] In it, Ghazzi grants Çivizade permission "to recite on my authority all of my writings, all that was licensed to me, and all my [hadith] accounts [*muṣannafātī wa mustajāzātī*

69. Blecher, *Prophet*, 85.

70. Būrīnī, *Tarājim*, 2: 95–6.

71. The teacher in question was Shihab al-Din al-Tibi. Ibn Ayyūb, *Rawḍ*, 204b.

72. Ghazzī, "Ijāza," 232a; Ibn Ayyūb, *Rawḍ*, 260a; Būrīnī, *Tarājim*, 2: 97; Ghazzī, *Kawākib*, 3: 27.

73. These were two glosses on Jalal al-Din al-Mahalli's (d. 1459) *The Commentary on The Path* (*Sharh al-minhaj*), which discussed Nawawi's *Path for Seekers* (*Minhaj al-talibin*).

74. Ghazzī, "Ijāza."

wa marwiyātī]."[75] The great bulk of the document is concerned with listing the genealogies by which Ghazzi licensed Çivizade to henceforth transmit the prophetic traditions. This included a number of chains of transmission that were especially short, and hence, especially prestigious.[76] Other chains he transmitted were prestigious by virtue of the men who formed the links within them. One, for example, had been passed down only by the most elevated scholars (*al-ʿulāʾ al-aʿlām*).[77] In being authorized to transmit the account, Çivizade joined a line of luminaries that included Ibn Hajar—by far the most important hadith scholar of the fifteenth century—a number of chief judges of Cairo in the Mamluk period, and a famous Persian theologian whose teaching in Mecca and Medina was so influential that he won the honorary title "Imam of the Two Holy Cities."[78]

Ghazzi's license also afforded Çivizade access to other new intellectual genealogies. For one, the *ijaza* permitted Çivizade to transmit all of Ghazzi's own works.[79] Ghazzi enumerated what he viewed as the most important of these, including the rhymed Qurʾan commentary as well as the two legal glosses that Çivizade knew from the concluding session he had attended. Ghazzi may also have chosen to mention those works he thought would be particularly interesting to Çivizade and his colleagues from the Ottoman center: he listed his travel account to Istanbul as well as his commentaries on "The Mantle Ode" and on *The Thousand-Line Poem*, works that Rumis had studied with him in the Ottoman capital.[80] Yet perhaps more importantly, Ghazzi's license also authorized Çivizade to transmit all the texts that Ghazzi's teachers had licensed him to teach, not just works of hadith but also of jurisprudence, Qurʾanic commentary, rhetoric, and any and all other fields to which Ghazzi's teachers had turned their attention. Ghazzi again listed the names of his teachers, noting that they were some of the most revered scholars of late Mamluk Egypt and Cairo, including Jalal al-Din al-Suyuti and Zakariyya al-Ansari (d. 1520).[81] Although some of these had licensed Ghazzi to teach only a single book, Suyuti had licensed Ghazzi to teach all of his works, which numbered more than five hundred in all. For Çivizade, then, the implications of Ghazzi's license were immense. In one fell swoop, Çivizade gained a

75. Ghazzī, "Ijāza," 232b.
76. Ghazzī, "Ijāza," 234a.
77. Ghazzī, "Ijāza," 237b–238a.
78. The Persian theologian was Abu al-Maʿali al-Juwayni (d. 1085).
79. Ibn Ayyūb, *Rawḍ*, 241a.
80. Ghazzī, "Ijāza," 239b–240a.
81. Ghazzī, "Ijāza," 239a–b.

concrete and verifiable claim of authority over a vast and prestigious scholarly inheritance.

Çivizade was not the sole beneficiary of a remarkable transfer of this sort. Each of the five high-profile Rumi scholars mentioned previously are known to have been licensed to transmit hadith by Ghazzi as well.[82] Of the five, Kınalızade seems to have devoted himself to hadith with the greatest seriousness; he not only heard hadith accounts from Ghazzi, as Çivizade did, but also studied the science of hadith (*ʿilm al-hadith*) with him, that is, the principles of hadith transmission or the history of its transmitters.[83]

Nor was Ghazzi the only Arab scholar who transmitted hadith accounts to Rumi colleagues. His old friend ʿAbd al-Rahim al-ʿAbbasi was another. As another extant license suggests, ʿAbbasi was approached in his home for permission to transmit hadith by the poet and biographer ʿAşık Çelebi. ʿAbbasi agreed, issuing ʿAşık Çelebi an *ijaza* to transmit one particularly celebrated hadith compilation (Bukhari's *Authentic Collection*) on ʿAbbasi's authority, and everything else that ʿAbbasi had been licensed to transmit by his teachers.[84] The biographer Taşköprizade, a native of Bursa, sought out foreign expertise in hadith as well, transmitting prophetic accounts on the authority of a Tunisian scholar who in turn had studied with one of the students of the great hadith scholar Ibn Hajar; Taşköprizade, too, was granted permission to transmit everything that had been licensed to that scholar.[85]

This pattern suggests the important role Arab scholars played in helping to pass on the Islamic scholarly tradition as it had developed in late medieval Syria and Egypt. At informal gatherings that took place outside of the madrasa, Ghazzi and others quite literally authorized Rumi scholars to assimilate the late Mamluk intellectual tradition. Yet at heart, what was being transferred was even more universal and significant: Ottoman scholars were being given the authority to protect and pass on the very heart of Sunni Islam, the legacy of Muhammad himself. This is particularly striking when one considers the names of those who had transmitted particular hadiths in the license Ghazzi issued to Çivizade; until that moment, the carriers of the tradition had lived almost exclusively in

82. Ghazzī, *Kawākib*, 3: 6.

83. Ibn Ayyūb, *Rawḍ*, 203b. Tibi the Elder also granted Kinalizade an *ijaza* licensing him in the fields of hadith, Qurʾanic exegesis, Qurʾanic recitation, and rhetoric. Ibn Ayyūb, *Rawḍ*, 204b.

84. ʿĀşıḳ Çelebi, *Dhayl*, 107–8. By this time, it had become common to license others to transmit not only individual hadith accounts but also entire collections.

85. Ayaz, "Dârulhadisleri," 48. The scholar in question was Muhammad al-Maghushi (d. 1540). Ṭaşköprīzāde, *Shaqāʾiq*, 451–3, 555; Mecdī, *Tercüme-i Şaḳāʾiḳ*, 524–5; Blackburn in Nahrawālī, *Journey*, 44n118.

Arab and Persian lands.[86] With Ghazzi's permission, the line of transmission entered into new territory.

Excelling

The exchanges between Arab and Rumi scholars quickly added up. As more and more Turcophone scholars gained first-hand experiences in Arab lands—or were taught by men who had—the number that could boast proficiency in the academic and literary pursuits of those lands swelled. Unlike earlier Rumis, who had sometimes struggled to assert themselves in gatherings with Arab scholars, members of this new generation could prove themselves as well in person as on paper.

The shift is perhaps clearest in the case of Ahmed Efendi, who had been encouraged by his father (and friend of Ghazzi) Hasan Bey to study with scholars in Egypt and Syria. Hasan himself had probably not been an especially talented Arabist, since none of his biographers commented on his Arabic. However, Hasan's efforts to groom his son for excellence in this arena paid off; when Ahmed followed in his father's footsteps as Damascene chief judge in 1585–6, some thirty years after his father, his reputation already preceded him. Burini wrote, "I heard about him close to ten years before his arrival as chief judge in Damascus, and that he was an expert in all aspects of the Arabic language and memorized the eloquent odes."[87] It was said that Ahmed knew by heart more than twenty thousand lines of Arabic poetry, both ancient and modern. Nor did he have trouble extemporizing Arabic poetry. Faced with a spirited but unsightly musician during one leisurely soirée, he remarked to the other guests,

> Ours is a singer in whose melody passion reigns,
> His face is ugly but in both aspects he entertains.[88]

Although Ahmed was too old and weak to display his literary and linguistic talents by the time he arrived in Damascus—he died after a year of service—Burini, who visited the judge, did "see some traces of his knowledge of Arabic."[89]

Such Arabophilia among Rumis probably took on its most exceptional form in Kınalızade ʿAli, who fit as seamlessly into Arab learned circles as

86. ʿAbbasi's chain of transmission included Amin al-Din al-Aqsaraʾi, an Anatolian-born scholar, but he lived and worked in Mamluk lands for his adult life.

87. Būrīnī, *Tarājim*, 1: 67.

88. Tamīmī, *Ṭabaqāt*, 1: 382–3.

89. Būrīnī, *Tarājim*, 1: 67.

any homegrown scholar. Kınalızade arrived to take up his position as chief judge in Damascus in 1563/4 as an already imposing intellectual figure from an esteemed learned family. According to his son Hasan Çelebi Kınalızade, the magistrate mastered Arabic flawlessly, and not just in its written form. Meeting one prominent Arab scholar in Egypt, Kınalızade senior "spoke in such a beautiful and eloquent way that Bekrizade [the Egyptian] was forced to respond and started to stutter."[90] In Damascus, his son continued, "when conversing and expounding with the aforementioned city's scholars and honorable people, because [Kınalızade] was so knowledgeable in Arabic, the Arab scholars were baffled and impressed by his expertise."[91] Although Hasan was as prone to exaggeration as any other proud son when it came to his father's virtues, Kınalızade's Rumi biographers singled him out for his language skills as well.[92] Arab historians did not remark on Kınalızade's verbal fluency, but they did call his Arabic poetry outstanding.[93] In fact, his erudition and intellect were such that he could—by some accounts—outwit even that most awe-inspiring of local minds, Badr al-Din al-Ghazzi.

Kınalızade cultivated close ties with many local scholars during his time in Damascus. The historian Ibn Ayyub "visited him often" and the jurist Isma'il al-Nabulusi would long recall the pleasures of "those nights we snatched from the hands of time."[94] And, of course, there was no way around Ghazzi. The two men's relationship began immediately after Kınalızade's arrival: when Ghazzi declined to go out to welcome the arriving judge as did all of the other notable men of the city, Kınalizade went to meet him instead.[95] This awkward beginning did not stop the two men from becoming close friends during Kınalızade's nearly four-year tenure as chief judge in the city. When Ghazzi visited the judge one day, Kınalızade recited to him a poem that compared his facial features to the letters of the Arabic alphabet *dal* [د] and *dhal* [ذ], differentiated by a single dot:

I see in your curved temple the letter *dal* [د],
Yet it's been dotted with your mole.
Dotted, the *dal* became a *dhal* [ذ],
Now my soul will surely perish from dole.[96]

90. Kınalı-zade, *Tezkiretü'ş-Şu'arâ*, 2: 671. See also Ṭaşköprīzāde, *Shaqā'iq*, 90.
91. Kınalı-zade, *Tezkiretü'ş-Şu'arâ*, 2: 668.
92. This included 'Ata'i, Mustafa 'Ali, and 'Aşık Çelebi. Kınalı-zade, *Tezkiretü'ş-Şu'arâ*, 658, 668, 671; 'Aṭā'ī, *Ḥadā'iḳ*, 239; Oktay, *Ahlâk-ı Alâî*, 60; Fleischer, *Bureaucrat*, 43.
93. Ibn Ayyūb, *Rawḍ*, 204a–b.
94. For the former, Ibn Ayyūb, "Dhayl," 329; for the latter, see Ḥamawī, *Majmū'a*, 30a.
95. Ibn Ayyūb, *Rawḍ*, 204a; Ghazzī, *Kawākib*, 3: 187.
96. Ghazzī, *Maṭāli'*, MS Fazıl Ahmed Paşa 1390, 0a; Ghazzī, *Kawākib*, 3: 187.

Kınalızade demanded a response poem to his expression of adoration, which Ghazzi delivered on the spot.[97]

Friendship did not keep the two scholars from becoming intellectual competitors. As an Egyptian historian explained, "they had interesting discussions and extraordinary expressions that enriched the people, set an example, were memorialized in stories, and stored in histories."[98] This aspect of their relationship, too, began immediately. Not long after Kınalızade arrived in Damascus, in 1563 or 1564, Ghazzi invited him to one of his concluding sessions, once more in honor of the versified Qur᾽an commentary.[99] As usual, the gathering was held in a highly visible location, the shrine of Yahya in the main prayer hall of the Great Mosque (see figure 3.4). Conversation turned to the influential Qur᾽an commentary of the Cairo-based scholar Abu Hayyan al-Gharnati (d. 1344) and the later parsings (*iʿrab*) of that commentary by Abu Hayyan's students, especially al-Samin al-Halabi (d. 1355).[100] Kınalızade proposed and Ghazzi agreed that the Egyptian exegete Suyuti was mistaken when he claimed that the comments of a second student of Abu Hayyan were derivative of Halabi's—it was clear that both students had responded directly to the master.[101] However, when the discussion turned to some of Halabi's criticisms of his teacher, Kınalızade and Ghazzi disagreed. Kınalızade sided with the student, insisting the criticisms were legitimate; Ghazzi favored the teacher. When the gathering disbanded, the matter remained unresolved.

Unsatisfied, Kınalızade went home and consulted some of the books in his library only to find that the fifteenth-century Egyptian scholar Ibn Hajar, too, had found Halabi's critiques to be well-founded.[102] Kınalızade made a copy of the relevant passage of Ibn Hajar's work, appended some verses to it, and sent it to Ghazzi.[103] Ghazzi replied, also in verse, again

97. Ghazzī, *Maṭāliʿ*, MS Fazıl Ahmed Paşa 1390, 0b; Ghazzī, *Kawākib*, 3: 187.

98. Tamīmī, *Ṭabaqāt*, 239a.

99. The following is based on Tamīmī, *Ṭabaqāt*, 239a–240a; Ghazzī, *Kawākib*, 3: 187–90.

100. This was Abu Hayyan's *al-Bahr al-muhit* and Halabi's *al-Durr al-masun*. Saleh, "Gloss," 246; Gilliot, "Kontinuität," 63–4.

101. This second student was Ibrahim al-Safaqisi (d. 1342). Tamīmī, *Ṭabaqāt*, 239a; Saleh, "Gloss," 246–7; Gilliot, "Kontinuität," 63–4.

102. Tamīmī, *Kitāb*, 239a; Kınalı-zade, *Tezkiretü'ş-Şuʿarâ*, 669; Ghazzī, *Kawākib*, 3: 188. For the passage of Ibn Hajar to which Kınalızade referred, see the former's biographical dictionary, Ibn Ḥajar, *Durar*, 1: 339–40.

103. Tamīmī, *Ṭabaqāt*, 239b; Ghazzī, *Kawākib*, 3: 188.

eliciting a response from Kınalızade. Unable to convince the other, each eventually penned a treatise outlining ten points in defense of his position.[104] The debate remained public as the scholars of Damascus reviewed each treatise and weighed in on who they thought had made the better case. While Ghazzi's son Najm al-Din is tellingly silent on this point, according to both Kınalızade's son and the Egyptian historian—a third-party observer who drew on multiple local informants—the majority of Damascene scholars sided with Kınalızade.[105]

Kınalızade was a singular scholar, and his brilliance cannot be reduced to his historical context. Nonetheless, comparing his performance with that of Yusuf, an earlier chief judge in Damascus, suggests the changes that the Ottoman intellectual world had undergone in the intervening decades. In 1521, as we have seen, Yusuf had given a lecture in the Great Mosque on a gloss on the medieval scholar Zamakhshari's Qur'an commentary *The Revealer* written by the Persian scholar Jurjani. To the dismay of local scholars, though, Yusuf had slighted the gloss of the fourteenth-century scholar Sharaf al-Din al-Tibi—viewed as the authoritative study of *The Revealer* in Arab intellectual circles—and mentioned only the gloss of Jurjani's fellow Timurid thinker Taftazani.[106] Some four decades later, Kınalızade still viewed Taftazani's gloss as one of the very best in existence. However, he also recognized that Tibi was the originator of the tradition of glossing in which Taftazani stood, one followed by a host of scholars working primarily in Iran and Central Asia. What is more, Kınalızade contextualized this Persian strand alongside a second strand of Qur'anic commentary grounded in medieval Egypt—the strand of Abu Hayyan and his students over which he had debated Ghazzi, and, according to many contemporaries, prevailed.[107] As Walid Saleh has noted, Kınalızade was representative of "a remarkable display of universality, the only place where the achievements of Arabic Cairo and the *'ajam* Persian sphere were fully united."[108] Decades of exchanges had made for a truly integrated intellectual tradition.

104. Tamīmī, *Ṭabaqāt*, 240a; Ghazzī, *Kawākib*, 3: 189.

105. Tamimi the Egyptian historian's account was not wholly impartial, since it drew on Kınalızade's own description of the event. Tamīmī, *Ṭabaqāt*, 239a; Kınalı-zade, *Tezkiretü'ş-Şu'arâ*, 669–70; Kātib Çelebi, *Ẓunūn*, 730–1.

106. Ibn Ṭūlūn, *Quḍāt*, 310–1; Ibn Ayyūb, *Rawḍ*, 74a–b. See Chapter 4 for this episode.

107. Saleh, "Gloss," 238–47.

108. Saleh, "Gloss," 250.

That a Rumi scholar prevailed over the pride of Damascus was an upset of historical dimensions. Kınalızade's son Hasan Çelebi, ever the promoter of his father, wrote in his Turkish-language biography of the debate:

> Because the Arab scholars did not have these sorts of particulars, they were vanquished and dispirited in the arena of discussion and argument, and all of them recognized the virtue of ʿAli and said [switching to Arabic], "he brought [the evidence] that those before him were unable to bring."[109]

Hyperbolic as this statement may have been, and loath as Ghazzi may have been to admit defeat, Ghazzi himself recognized Kınalızade's virtues. Ibn Ayyub once heard him say that Kınalızade was the most learned chief judge that Damascus had ever had.[110]

Kınalızade was not the first Rumi scholar deeply versed in the Arabic literary tradition, nor the first to prevail over an Arab opponent in debate. However, his facility with Arabic and with the late Mamluk tradition was a sign of the times. Born in 1510, just a few years before the conquest, Kınalızade came of age in an environment in which the Arab world already seemed much closer to Anatolia. One of Kınalızade's most important teachers, Hoca Çivizade (d. 1547)—the father of the later chief judge in Damascus Çivizade Mehmed—had just returned from serving as judge in Cairo when he hired Kınalızade as his preceptor (*muʿid*) in 1538.[111] In the middle years of the sixteenth century, after Kınalızade had begun his own teaching career, many members of his inner circle were spending time in the Arab provinces, including his father Emrullah Efendi (d. 1559/60) as well as his former teachers Merhaba Efendi (d. c. 1543) and Maʿlul Efendi (d. 1555/6).[112]

With time, so many Rumis had gained this kind of expertise that it was no longer necessary for them to visit Arab lands to become experts on things Arabic. At least this is the point that Kınalızade's son made in

109. Kınalı-zade, *Tezkiretü'ş-Şuʿarâ*, 670.

110. Ibn Ayyūb, *Rawḍ*, 203b. Ghazzi apparently confirmed this verdict in his *ijaza* for Kınalızade. Ibn Ayyūb, "Dhayl," 329.

111. He was appointed in Cairo in 1530/1. Repp, *The Müfti of Istanbul*, 249. See also İpşirli, "Çivizâde Muhyiddin," 348–9.

112. Emrullah served as judge in Damascus and Aleppo. It is likely that he appears in Ibn Ayyub's account of the chief judges of Damascus as Hamid al-Rumi (since he was from the Hamidi family), who served 1549–50. Ibn Ayyūb, "Dhayl," 326; Kınalı-zade, *Tezkiretü'ş-Şuʿarâ*, 837. Merhaba Efendi served in Damascus from 1538–9. Ibn Ṭūlūn, *Quḍāt*, 320; Ṭaşköprīzāde, *Shaqāʾiq*, 491. For Maʿlul, see Ṭaşköprīzāde, *Shaqāʾiq*, 489–90; Mecdī, *Tercüme-i Şaḳaʾiḳ*, 484.

an anecdote he included in his father's biography. Once, when Kınalızade sat with the Damascene litterateur Abu al-Fath al-Maliki, conversation drifted to North Africa, where Maliki had spent his youth. Kınalızade offered an assessment of the region's natural environment and the manners of its people. Maliki turned to him and asked, "In what way did you see those lands, and how long did you stay at that time, that you could with full knowledge describe the particularities of its surroundings?" Kınalızade replied, "I saw those lands several times with history books; however I never saw them with the vision of the eye." Maliki, according to Hasan Çelebi, was "plunged in a sea of astonishment."[113]

Kınalızade represented a new generation of Rumi scholars who had benefited from decades of informal exchanges with their Arab colleagues. These exchanges had ironed out some of the discrepancies in the way that Turcophone and Arabophone scholars engaged with the Islamic intellectual tradition. The best of this new generation of centrally-trained scholars could participate in Arabic-language salons as fully and confidently as any homegrown one.

Writing

A salon is for an evening, but a book is forever. Just as Rumi scholars participated in live debates with their Arab colleagues, so too did they engage with their writings. Indeed, exchanges with Arab scholars prompted lasting transformations of the Ottoman written tradition. Over the course of the sixteenth century, scholars trained at the imperial center intensified their engagement with the Arabic-language intellectual canon, incorporating and appropriating a number of new genres that had previously been rare or even unknown.

One genre in which the Arabic influence surfaced was the biographical dictionary. The genre had long been one of the most favored forms for writing history in the Islamic tradition. Called *tarajim* ("biographies") or *tabaqat* (literally, "layers") in Arabic and *tazkira* ("aide-memoire") in Persian, the genre consisted of compilations of biographical sketches, each ranging from a few lines to several pages.[114] From the late ninth century

113. Kınalı-zade, *Tezkiretü'ş-Şu'arâ*, 668–9.

114. For just some of the vast scholarship on this genre, see Hirschler, *Medieval Arabic Historiography*; al-Qadi, "Alternative History"; Cooperson, *Classical Arabic Biography*; Robinson, *Islamic Historiography*; al-Qadi, "Biographical Dictionaries"; Khalidi, *Historical Thought*, 204–10; Gilliot, "Ṭabaqāt." For the Persian *tazkira*, see Hermansen and Lawrence, "Tazkiras," 156–9; Stewart-Robinson, "Tezkire," 63; Heinrichs et al., "Tadhkira."

onwards, across the increasingly vast Islamic world, a variety of thematic biographical collections emerged that profiled poets, hadith transmitters, calligraphers, grammarians, musicians, sages, Sufis, princes, prophets, lovers, lunatics, or gamblers.[115] The genre was particularly popular in late Mamluk lands, where new collections appeared with every generation and were written by such academic heavyweights as Ibn Hajar and Suyuti.[116]

But there was one place in the late medieval Islamic world where no locally produced biographical compilations could be found: Anatolia. The Seljuks of Anatolia, though eager to import other Islamic cultural forms, had never taken an interest in commissioning biographical compilations.[117] Nor are any such compilations known from the emerging Anatolian principalities of the fourteenth and early fifteenth centuries.[118] Glimmers of the tradition began to appear in Ottoman lands toward the end of the fifteenth century. The historian Aşıkpaşazade (d. 1494) included biographies at the end of each section of his chronicle of Ottoman history, and in the 1510s, when the Rumi poet Lamiʿi Çelebi (d. 1531/2) translated a well-known Persian biography of Sufis, he expanded it to include some thirty Ottoman mystics.[119] Still, until 1538, no free-standing biographical dictionary was devoted to leading Ottomans.

In that year, Sehi Bey (d. 1548) published the first compilation of biographies of Ottoman poets, entitled *Eight Heavens* (*Heşt Bihişt*). His dictionary was written in Ottoman Turkish in a deliberate effort to promote the language. Yet, tellingly, his inspiration came not from the Arabic-language tradition but rather from the Persian lands. As Sehi explained in his introduction, the idea of writing the book had come to him while reading the famous Timurid scholars ʿAbdurrahman Jami (d. 1492), Amir Dawlatshah (d. c. 1488), and ʿAli Shir Navaʾi.[120] True to his models, Sehi referred to his dictionary as a *tezkire* and restricted himself to profiling poets. He adduced the Persian literary tradition as the one to be emulated and exceeded. Arabic, meanwhile, occupied only a very marginal position in his work.

115. Cooperson, *Classical Arabic Biography*, 6–23; Gilliot, "Ṭabaqāt."

116. Ibn Ḥajar, *Durar*; Suyūṭī, *Ṭabaqāt*.

117. Peacock and Yıldız, *Islamic Literature*, 3.

118. Uzunçarşılı, *Beylikleri*, 260; İsen, *Sehî Bey*, 13–4.

119. Emecen, "Osmanlı Kronikleri ve Biyografi"; Alpay, "Lāmiʿī Chelebi," 78–9. Lamiʿi's work was a translation of ʿAbdurrahman Jami's biographical dictionary.

120. Sehī Bey, *Heşt Bihişt*, 76–9. For just some of the expansive scholarship on the *tezkire* tradition, see Kuru, "The Literature of Rum"; Aynur and Niyazioğlu, *Yazılar*; Tolasa, *Araştırma*; Andrews, "Latifi"; Stewart-Robinson, "Biographies."

Yet as the Arab influence in the Ottoman Empire grew, this novel biographical genre acquired a more Arabic flavor. The 1558 biographical dictionary of Ahmed Taşköprizade—who, as we have seen, had studied hadith with a Tunisian scholar—had little in common with the tradition launched just twenty years earlier by Sehi Bey. Instead of writing in Turkish, Taşköprizade wrote in Arabic. Instead of looking to the Persianate *tazkira*, he modeled his work on the Arabic *tarajim*. Like his models, Taşköprizade was interested in profiling scholars. Like them, his interest was in their teachers, works, and (thankfully!) their scholarly gatherings; he only rarely cited verses of poetry.[121] Though Taşköprizade was more coy about his inspiration than Sehi Bey had been, he acknowledged that he was working within a longer tradition: "While recent writers have recorded the virtues of the scholars and the notables . . . none of them devoted their attention to compiling accounts of the scholars of these lands."[122] ʿAşık Çelebi, who wrote a supplement to Taşköprizade's dictionary in 1568, was more explicit about his Arab predecessors:

> [Producing biographical works] was the usual path and the lasting practice for all: from the rightly-guided caliphs and the laboring [*mujtahid*] imams; to the scholars and learned men who followed their example in various realms; in the countries and towns; from the lands of the Arabs to their hills; from the cities of the Persians to the surrounding idyll—except for the king of Rum, who as the very best of the kings doth rule.[123]

By locating his book in the tradition of the first four caliphs and the Arab lands and hills, ʿAşık Çelebi signaled his debt to the Arabic-language tradition.

Even the Turkish biographical dictionaries of poets that continued to be written in the tradition inaugurated by Sehi Bey did not remain unaffected by intellectual contacts with Arab lands. This was especially visible in later contributions to the genre written by ʿAşık Çelebi and Hasan Çelebi Kınalızade, whose dictionaries were completed in 1568 and 1586, respectively. Both quoted much more Arabic-language poetry than Sehi Bey had.[124] Both allotted more space to evaluating the Arabic skills of

121. Taşköprīzade occasionally cited entire passages from the dictionaries of his Mamluk predecessors, including Suyuti and Ibn Hajar. Taşköprīzāde, *Shaqāʾiq*, 22, 23.

122. Taşköprīzāde, *Shaqāʾiq*, 5.

123. ʿĀşıḳ Çelebi, *Dhayl*, 36.

124. ʿAşık Çelebi even cited part of an Arabic treatise. ʿĀşıḳ Çelebi, *Meşâʿirü's-Şuʿarâ*, 1310–1.

those whom they profiled. We have already seen Hasan Çelebi emphasize his father's linguistic prowess, and can sense a similar enthusiasm for those who excelled in Arabic in ʿAşık's description of a poet appointed chief judge of Aleppo:

> In that family, knowledge of Arabic is a necessity, and young and old are devoted to study and knowledge. Newborns are put to sleep with the *Assemblies* [*Maqamat*] of Hariri, and when they cry they are consoled with *Platters of Gold* [*Atbaq al-Dhahab*] [two classics of Arabic literary prose]. The enslaved boys who serve them are taught Arabic before they are taught Turkish.[125]

Though ʿAşık Çelebi's aim was no doubt to celebrate Ottoman Turkish, he viewed familiarity with literary Arabic as an ineluctable part of the gentlemanly persona. Finally, both ʿAşık and Hasan Çelebi peppered their prose liberally with Arabic quotations and phrases, not only from the Qurʾan but also from proverbs or fragments of conversation, as we saw Hasan Çelebi do when quoting the praise of Arab scholars for his father.[126]

The growing importance of Arabic-language models in the Ottoman written tradition is visible in other genres as well. The interest in Arabic histories extended beyond the biographical tradition, and many scholars living and working in Anatolia set out to translate both newer Arabic chronicles and older classics into Turkish.[127] Others took inspiration from the tradition to write Arabic-language histories of their own.[128] In the field of geography, the influence of Arabic models was considerable as well. While Rumi scholars had taken little interest in Arabic geographies before 1550, the second half of the century saw both a growing number of Turkish translations of geographical works as well as new titles within the same tradition.[129] Around the same time, they began taking a greater interest in certain Mamluk-era treatises on political

125. This refers to ʿAbdü'l-ʿAziz Çelebi (d. 1545/6). ʿĀşıḳ Çelebi, *Meşâʿirü's-Şuʿarâ*, 1040–1, see also 979–82, 1309–11. Sehi Bey also emphasizes ʿAbdü'l-ʿAziz Çelebi's Arabic abilities, though with considerable less excitement. Sehī Bey, *Heşt Bihişt*, 158–9.

126. For some such Arabic-language citations, see Āşıḳ Çelebi, *Meşâʿirü's-Şuʿarâ*, 983, 1119, 1121, 1314, 1321. This was more rare in *Heşt Bihişt*.

127. Matrakçı Nasuh (d. c. 1564) was the first Ottoman scholar to translate the famous history of ʿAli al-Tabari (d. after 864) directly from Arabic into Turkish. Yurdaydın in Naṣūḥü's-Silāḥī, *Beyān*, 121–5. See also the histories of ʿAbdüssamed Diyarbekri (d. after 1542) and Mustafa ʿAli, both heavily indebted to older Arabic-language sources. Lellouch, *Les Ottomans en Égypte*, chapter 3; Fleischer, *Bureaucrat*, 68–9.

128. Baş, *Tarih Yazıcılığı*.

129. Emiralioğlu, *Geographical Knowledge*; Casale, *Exploration*, 186.

thought.[130] The Arabic literary influence even extended into the arena of erotica.[131]

The impact of Arab scholars was also felt in madrasa curricula. Of course, Arabic-language works had always featured prominently among the books assigned to Ottoman madrasa students. What appears to have changed is the greater incorporation of a distinctively Mamluk intellectual tradition. This is visible in a 1565 imperial rescript (*firman*) promulgated by Sultan Süleyman under the guidance of his chief mufti Ebu's Suʿud. The rescript laid out a list of suggested readings for high-level Ottoman imperial madrasas, an unprecedented show of educational centralization, as Shahab Ahmed and Nenad Filipovic point out in their analysis. In discussing the inclusion of a work by Jalal al-Din al-Suyuti, they also note "the receptiveness of the Ottoman canon to new works."[132]

The informal exchanges described here go a long way towards explaining this receptiveness. Suyuti was famous in his own lifetime across the Islamic world, as he himself liked to boast, including in Ottoman lands. Nonetheless, given how many students he had trained, in the post-conquest period, Rumis must have encountered his intellectual legacy far more frequently than they had previously. Ghazzi's license for Çivizade and ʿAbbasi's license for ʿAşık Çelebi both contained chains of transmission that passed through Suyuti, and Ghazzi, as we saw, included him in the list of teachers from whom he permitted Çivizade to transmit.[133]

Suyuti was not the only scholar from the Mamluk era who appeared in the 1565 guidelines. They also included an impressive range of works in the discipline of hadith, many of which stemmed from the golden era of hadith studies in Mamluk lands. This included the prodigious commentary on one of the canonical hadith collections by Ibn Hajar, who had taught Ghazzi's teacher Zakariyya al-Ansari and on whose authority Ghazzi transmitted hadith to Çivizade. The list also included a commentary on another canonical hadith collection written by Abu Zakariyya al-Nawawi, the Damascene scholar whose work of Shafiʿi law was the subject of one of Ghazzi's concluding sessions that Çivizade attended.[134] In

130. ʿAşık Çelebi prepared a translation of the Mamluk-era thinker Ibn Taymiyya's (d. 1328) work *Sharʿi Governance* (*al-Siyasa al-sharʿiyya*). Terzioğlu, "Ibn Taymiyya." See also Sariyannis, *Political Thought*, chapter 3.

131. Artan and Schick, "Pornotopia," esp. 157–9; Fleischer, *Bureaucrat*, 55.

132. Ahmed and Filipovic, "The Sultan's Syllabus," 210–1.

133. ʿĀşıḳ Çelebi, *Dhayl*, 109; Ghazzī, "Ijāza," 236b, 239a. Ghazzi issued Çivizade the license after this decree was issued, but it is likely that those he had issued to men like Kassabzade or Hacı Çelebi decades earlier were similar in content.

134. Ahmed and Filipovic, "The Sultan's Syllabus," 200, 202.

including Arabic authorities such as Suyuti and Ibn Hajar and placing a greater emphasis on hadith, the guidelines issued by the sultan responded to an evolving conversation within the empire.

The influence of live encounters on Ottoman intellectual priorities can be seen, albeit on a more modest scale, in the case of the reception of Ghazzi's oeuvre. At least nineteen manuscript copies of his works are found in collections across modern Turkey. Though many of these entered Turcophone lands well after his death, they very much reflect Ghazzi's travels and personal interactions with scholars. Several of the works found in Turkish collections were ones that he taught or even wrote while in Istanbul, including his commentaries on "The Mantle Ode," on *The Thousand-Line Poem*, and on a work by his host ʿAbbasi.[135] There are also two copies of the treatise he wrote following his debate with Kınalızade, and of course, a few copies of his Qurʾan commentary.[136] Then there is Ghazzi's Istanbul travel account and a copy of his *ijaza* for Çivizade.[137] These seven works account for fifteen of the nineteen copies in Turkish libraries today.[138] Other, equally contemporaneously popular, works that Ghazzi did less to promote to Rumi scholars are absent.

In-person exchanges between Arab and Rumi scholars left a lasting mark on the Ottoman written tradition. The importance of social gatherings in early modern Islamic scholarship meant that the Ottoman engagement with Arabic-language literature was highly mediated by Arab scholars. To be sure, in some instances Ottoman conquerors chose the titles they wanted from abandoned bookshelves, as in the citadel of Aleppo in 1517. But for the most part, Ottoman interaction with the Mamluk scholarly tradition was guided by scholars trained within it. In other words, Ottoman scholars received a library with a map, that is, a bibliography

135. There are two copies of *al-Zubda fi sharh al-Burda*: Süleymaniye Library, MS Laleli 3656, 201b–220b; Manisa İl Halk Kütüphanesi, MS 45 Hk 5256, 1b–7a. There is one copy of *Sharh al-Alfiyya li-l-Ghazzi*: Süleymaniye Library, MS Laleli 3265. There are four copies of Ghazzi's *Taqrib al-Maʿahid fi sharh al-shawahid*, a commentary on ʿAbbasi's *Maʿahid al-tansis fi sharh shawahid al-Talkhis* that Ghazzi wrote while at the scholar's house in Istanbul: Süleymaniye Library, MSS Yeni Cami 1036, Kılıç Ali Paşa 871, Laleli 2866; and Çorum Hasan Paşa İl Halk Kütüphanesi, MS 19 Hk 2384.

136. For the debate, see Ghazzī, "al-Durr al-thāmin," MS Mihrişah Sultan 39 and MS Manisa İl Halk Kütüphanesi, MS 45 Hk 177, 82b–92b. For the Qurʾan commentary, see notes 18 and 31 in this chapter.

137. Ghazzī, *Maṭāliʿ*, MS Fazıl Ahmed Paşa 1390; Ghazzī, "Ijāza."

138. Katib Çelebi mentioned several of Ghazzi's works in his bibliographical dictionary *Kashf al-zunun*: *"al-Durr al-thamin"* (1: 122–3, 730–1); *al-Burhan al-nahid* (1: 240); *Taqrib al-Maʿahid* (called *Takhsis*) (1: 279); *Tafsir* (1: 454); *Adab al-mufid* (1: 735); and *Sharh al-Burda* (2: 1332).

with annotations. This does not mean that Rumi scholars were not selective about what they did and did not assimilate; however, they were influenced by knowing guides.

Exchanging?

How reciprocal was this intellectual exchange? Arab scholars did read and reflect on the works of their Rumi colleagues. As early as 1517, the Damascene historian Ibn Tulun read an account of the Ottoman conquest of Egypt written by a scholar in the retinue of Sultan Selim; the Meccan scholar Nahrawali based his account of the Ottoman conquest of Yemen on a Turkish-language source.[139] In the early 1560s, Tibi the Elder, who had taught Kınalızade in Damascus, composed a treatise on one of Kınalızade's short poems (*maqtuʿ*); another Arab scholar wrote a reflection on the treatise Kınalızade composed following his debate with Ghazzi.[140] Around 1570, as we saw in Chapter 4, Syrian scholars gathered twice to hear Fevri Efendi gloss part of Baydawi's Qurʾan commentary, once in Damascus and once in Jerusalem. Although in Jerusalem the response to the work may have been tepid, in Damascus, things were different. Not only did all of the city's premier scholars attend the lecture, Fevri's friend Hamawi wrote a short treatise on it.[141] Ghazzi even wrote an endorsement (*taqriz*) of the gloss that circulated alongside it (see figure 5.3).[142]

As in the Ottoman center, such exchanges helped to transform the local Arabic written tradition. It seems possible, for example, that biographical dictionaries underwent a transformation in response to Rumi influence. Ibn Ayyub's *Sweet-Smelling Garden*, finished in 1590, at times seems to have more in common with ʿAşık Çelebi's Turkish-language *Senses of Poets* than it does with its Mamluk predecessors, especially in its interest in the elite social scene. Where the Mamluk versions were more tightly controlled and often focused on the academic vitae of their subjects, Ibn

139. The author whose account Ibn Tulun consulted was Idris the Rumi. Ibn Ṭūlūn, *Mufākaha*, 2: 59; Blackburn in Nahrawālī, *Journey*, xiv.

140. For the first, see Ibn Ayyūb, *Rawḍ*, 204b. For the second, see Fāriḍī, "Nukat." The latter, completed in 1571 (979), is not signed, but a later hand has identified its author as a certain al-Faridi.

141. Ḥamawī, *Ḥādī*, 32. For the treatise, see Ḥamawī, *Majmūʿa*, 154b–157a.

142. Būrīnī, *Tarājim*, 2: 97. For Fevri's gloss and Ghazzi's endorsement, see Fevrī Efendī, "Ḥāshiya," with the endorsement on 73a. For the genre of *taqriz*, see Bauer, "Network"; Rosenthal, "Blurbs." This interest may have been particularly prominent in the field of Hanafi jurisprudence; the Egyptian scholar Ibn Nujaym (d. 1562/3) cited the opinions of Ottoman jurists in his legal texts. Ayoub, *Law*, chapter 1.

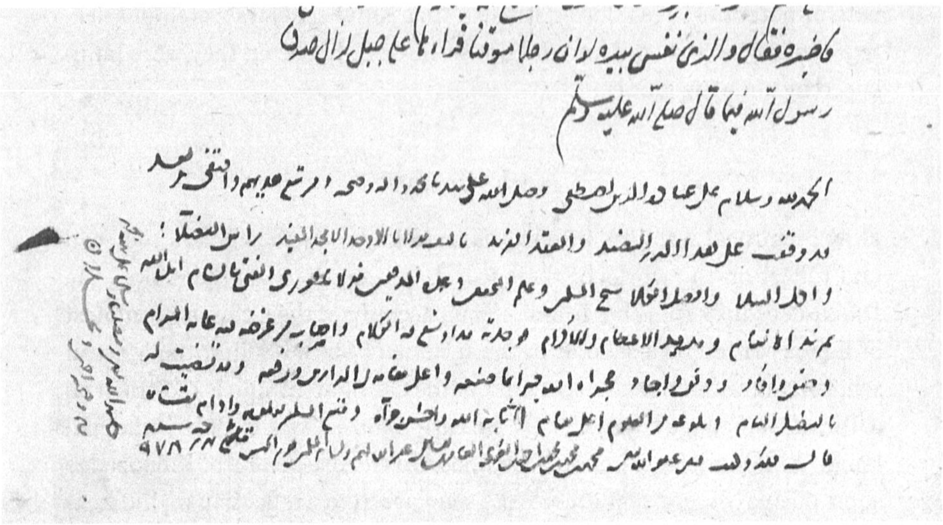

FIGURE 5.3. Badr al-Din al-Ghazzi's endorsement (*taqriz*) of Fevri Efendi's *Gloss on the Sura of the Believers (Hashiya ʿala surat al-muʾminin)*, a short work discussing one chapter of a famous Qurʾan commentary by Baydawi. The endorsement is written in Ghazzi's own hand. (Courtesy of Princeton University Library, Islamic Manuscripts, Garrett MS 3817Y, 73a.)

Ayyub, like ʿAşık Çelebi, frequently cited poetry and relayed salacious anecdotes.

Still, for much of the sixteenth century, the exchange between Arabs and Rumis does not seem to have been balanced. I have found no evidence of Arab scholars acquiring books on a large scale while in Istanbul, or even requesting copies of the works of Rumis who passed through their region. The only works Ghazzi acquired (or at least admits to having acquired) while in Istanbul were the ones written by his host, the Arab scholar ʿAbbasi; the only person from whom he borrowed books while in the Ottoman capital was the Syrian immigrant Ibrahim al-Halabi.[143] When Burini reviewed the chief judge Ahmed's collection in Damascus, the only books in which he showed any interest were Arabic-language classics. Similarly, although Damascene biographers did record biographies of Rumi visitors in their biographical dictionaries, they rarely mentioned scholarly works written by them.[144] Biographies of Kınalızade are a notable exception, though perhaps they are the exception that proves the rule. The only works of Kınalızade that Ibn Ayyub named in his biography were Kınalızade's

143. Ghazzī, *Maṭāliʿ*, 138; Tamīmī, *Ṭabaqāt*, 256–7.

144. The Meccan scholar Nahrawali did mention works by some such men, perhaps because of his knowledge of Turkish. Nahrawālī, *ʿIlām*, 306.

treatises on the pen and the sword, which, as Ibn Ayyub noted, were in the style of two fourteenth-century Syrian scholars.[145] Ghazzi's laudatory blurb for Fevri, moreover, is somewhat reserved. Though his praise for Fevri the man was lavish, of the work itself Ghazzi wrote only, "I found that he was very thorough, and totally achieved his purposes and goals. He was useful in every topic on which he dwelled, and whenever he singled out an issue he excelled."[146] This was certainly one of the more sober and terse examples of a genre that usually traded in hyperbole.[147]

The same asymmetry holds with regard to patterns of study. By his own telling at least, Ghazzi appears to have learned things from only two people while in Istanbul. One of them was his old friend Hacı Çelebi, though this transmission—of a single prayer—was very modest (and though Ghazzi did ask Hacı for an *ijaza* for his son Ahmad and for any future offspring).[148] The other person with whom Ghazzi studied was ʿAbbasi, himself educated in Arab lands. There is no evidence that Ghazzi studied with prominent scholars at more advanced points in their careers, men like Ebu's-Suʿud who was nearly ten years his senior. Nor is there any suggestion that Ghazzi ever studied anything under the guidance of the Rumi judges who took hadith or other lessons with him. To be sure, all of this could be put down to the unwillingness of Ghazzi or his Arab contemporaries to admit to Rumi intellectual influence. This began to change in the second half of the sixteenth century, as we will see in Chapter 6, as a new generation of Arab students began spending time studying in Istanbul. However, it seems that in the first half-century after the conquest, Arabs showed less interest in the Rumi scholarly tradition than Rumis did in the Arab one.

Conclusion

Informal gatherings shaped the intellectual life of the Ottoman Empire in fundamental ways. They featured centrally in the production of the written word. They figured prominently in its reception. There is no question that books were often written and read by men sitting silently in their studies, as Ghazzi's decision to retreat into his lone cell attests. That Ghazzi continued to convoke learned gatherings despite his supposed isolation also suggests just how important such gatherings were.

145. Namely Ibn Nubata (d. 1366) and Ibn al-Wardi (d. 1349). Ibn Ayyūb, *Rawḍ*, 204b.

146. Ghazzī in Fevrī Efendi, "Ḥāshiya," 73a.

147. C.f. Rosenthal, "Blurbs," 190–6.

148. Ghazzī, *Maṭāliʿ*, 263. This was a controversial practice with roots in the medieval period. Davidson, *Tradition*, 141–3.

Salons help to make visible the extent to which reading was embedded in human relationships. Interactions with others influenced not only which texts people read, but also how they understood those texts. Though Ebu' s-Suʿud no doubt judged Ghazzi's controversial verse commentary on its own merits when it came before him in Istanbul, he must have also been influenced by his impression of Ghazzi from their encounter years earlier. This highly contexualized form of reading helps us understand why biographical dictionaries were so popular: peculiarities of character, rivalries and friendships, and not least, in-person gatherings, formed the backdrop against which contemporaries read and evaluated written works. It is also why, nearly a century after the events, the Istanbul scholar Katib Çelebi included an account of the Ghazzi-Kınalızade debate in his bibliographical dictionary. As William Smyth has argued, for premodern Muslim scholars, the knowledge of in-person debates helped to "animate the discourse of commentary."[149] To our own generation of scholars, this suggests the perils of separating the history of ideas from that of the people; even the most arcane of treatises were written and received in a social—often emotionally charged—world.

Informal gatherings not only shaped the way that mature scholars engaged with the written record; they also were host to conventional forms of knowledge transmission from teacher to student. Conversations held in mosques, dervish lodges, and the domestic sphere often featured, or blended into, more formal modes of academic instruction, such as explanations of scholarly texts or the issuing of academic licenses. However important the madrasa was, contemporaries continued to teach in a variety of social and physical contexts. Indeed, there may have been benefits to such a mixed economy. Madrasas were highly regulated institutions, subject to the often-detailed stipulations of their founders or, increasingly, the meddling of the political class.[150] Scholars may well have welcomed a space for intellectual production that was not beholden to founders or to shifting political winds.

The relative freedom afforded by the salon took on a special significance following the conquest of Arab lands. In the wake of this event, two large and accomplished—but still largely separate—scholarly communities had to confront one another. Formally speaking, the two communities often remained separate: members were appointed to institutions in their respective regions and for the most part chose to study in their respective

149. Smyth, "Controversy," 595–6.
150. Atçıl, *Scholars*, 155–66.

regions. In this configuration of separate professional spheres, informal gatherings emerged as precious arenas in which intellectual exchange between the two groups could nonetheless occur.

Informal encounters thus help to make visible what the madrasa obscures, namely the extraordinary transfer of knowledge that occurred from the Arab lands to the Ottoman center. Rumis took great interest in the intellectual production of the Arab provinces, not just in long-accepted classics but likewise in the work of recent or contemporary scholars. Book acquisitions provide concrete evidence for this interest. So too do extant *ijazas*. Leading scholars like Çivizade and ʿAşık Çelebi were keen to join intellectual genealogies cultivated in late Mamluk lands. There is no doubt that the scholars who appear in these pages were exceptionally interested in the late Mamluk scholarly inheritance; plenty of Rumi learned men showed no such enthusiasm and hence did not even gain a mention in the dictionaries of Ibn Ayyub or Burini. However, those who did become interested set in motion a process whereby the Ottoman linguistic and written tradition became more Arabophone. They also fueled experimentation with a range of new literary genres. Like conquerors and imperialists in other times and places, the Ottomans learned as much from their subject populations as those populations did from them.

CHAPTER SIX

An Empire Polarized

BY THE 1570S, Badr al-Din al-Ghazzi was growing old. He had outlived many of his friends and colleagues, and, in 1576, he faced the singular sorrow of having to bury his own son. Still, he remained blessed with good health and a good temperament. In 1577, the year of his death, he could be heard reciting the following poem:

I have finally reached eighty years,
But never required an aid for my ears.[1]

Nevertheless, much had changed since 1530 when Ghazzi set out for Istanbul as an intrepid young man. Decades of interactions between Arabs and Rumis had made the two groups close as never before. Thanks in part to the vehicle of the salon and in part to new alliances struck between Rumi patrons and their Arab followers, information traveled across the empire more quickly than ever before. This facilitated governance on an imperial scale. Ghazzi, for one, had developed a network of connections so intricate and dense that when he faced a professional setback, all he had to do was wait for the problem to be resolved.

At the same time, broad social, cultural, and economic shifts had caused the dynamics between Arabs and Rumis to change. Rumis were more knowledgeable than ever about the society and culture of Arab lands, having become familiar with the region's inhabitants and assimilated many of their intellectual riches. Rumis had also brought to fruition a highly sophisticated and self-confident sociable world of their own, much of it grounded not in Arabic but in Ottoman Turkish. As a result, the knowledge that had made Arab scholars highly valued in the first decades

1. Būrīnī, *Tarājīm*, 2: 98.

of the century no longer carried the same weight. When the economic situation of the empire began to worsen in the 1570s, Arab scholars increasingly faced their own redundancy. Ottoman salons both reflected these changes and helped to reinforce them as Rumis used their gatherings as a means of regulating access to imperial patronage.

These shifts are refracted in the experiences of Ghazzi's student, Muhibb al-Din al-Hamawi, an Arabic speaker born in Hama in today's Syria in 1542. His two-part travel narrative, written in 1573–5, straddled the threshold between two eras. Part one documented Hamawi's journey to Cairo with his Rumi patron Çivizade Mehmed. It presented an imperial tableau as both men would have liked to imagine it: a seamlessly integrated world of Muslim gentlemen who exuberantly exchanged ideas and poems. In his descriptions of those interactions, Hamawi emphasized divisions between the educated and the unschooled rather than any ethnic boundaries that separated him from his Turcophone patron.

At the same time, part one of the travel account contained hints of the cynicism and desperation that flowered darkly in part two. In 1573, Hamawi was unexpectedly removed from his judgeship in Egypt. Just as his teacher Ghazzi had some four decades earlier, Hamawi packed his bags and headed to Istanbul in hopes of being reinstated. Yet unlike Ghazzi, Hamawi was unable to penetrate the circles of the imperial elite. Part two of Hamawi's travel account chronicled his difficulties in the Ottoman capital. Hamawi's frustrations caused him to adopt a searing tone, one that stands in stark contrast to that of Ghazzi's earlier account. This incivility reflected Hamawi's bitter disappointment, to be sure; but it also signaled the start of a new, more polemical era.

Empire of Salons

A motley, mobile crew assembled in the "Turcoman House," as Çivizade Mehmed Efendi's tent was called, even though none of its members would have identified with the nomadic Turkic tribesmen after which their temporary shelter was named. There was Çivizade himself, a high-born Rumi on his way to the Cairene judgeship; Fevri Efendi, an Albanian recruit of the child-levy system educated in the Topkapı Palace; Maʿlulzade, the vengeful heir to an Ottoman scholarly dynasty; and finally, Muhibb al-Din al-Hamawi, the son of a scribe, who was working furiously to make a place for himself in the Ottoman judicial and intellectual world. If many things divided the men, they were unified in their haughtiness toward the rural population that surrounded their tent that evening, as well as in their dedication to refined literary culture.[2] Indeed, their relationship exemplifies the extent to which, by the last quarter of the sixteenth century, gentlemen from all ends of the empire had come to share a common language, a common set of scholarly interests, and a common set of gatherings. Hamawi used his travel account to stress these commonalities, often at the expense of other social groups.

In a cocoon of colored walls and carpets, the four men warded off the cold and darkness of January with "sweet discussion and pleasant nightly banter."[3] It was 1571, and Maʿlulzade was traveling north, leaving his judgeship in Cairo for a new appointment in Bursa. Fevri, Çivizade, and Hamawi were all heading south. Çivizade was on his way to take up the Egyptian judgeship that Maʿlulzade was vacating, but he and his companions would make a stopover in Jerusalem where Christians had allegedly defaced a local mosque. The men crossed paths at a village near the town of Ramla, and they took advantage of the happy accident to gather in a special gathering (*al-majlis al-khass*), as Hamawi later called it.[4]

The gentlemen spent much of the evening discussing the scholars of Damascus and Cairo, and when Maʿlulzade mentioned four Egyptian students he found particularly promising, Hamawi recorded their names so that his patron Çivizade could treat them with special favor.[5] So congenial was the evening that, though they had never met before, Hamawi and Maʿlulzade reached a great level of intimacy and brotherhood.[6] Or so Hamawi believed until Maʿlulzade became chief military judge of Anatolia three years later. Thrilled to know the man who occupied such a powerful position, Hamawi wrote Maʿlulzade to ask to be promoted from his judgeship in the small Syrian town of al-Qadmus to a higher-ranking position. The letter he received in return informed Hamawi that he had instead been terminated.[7] But we get ahead of ourselves.

Born in 1542 in the small riverside town of Hama in today's Syria, Muhibb al-Din al-Hamawi lacked the scholarly genealogy that conferred

2. Reindl-Kiel speculates that a move away from Turcoman-style royal tents in the period 1550–1650 reflected a wish on the part of Ottoman sultans to distance themselves from these objects' nomadic associations. Reindl-Kiel, "Courtly Tents," 650–2. Çivizade had purchased his in Damascus. Ḥamawī, *Ḥādī*, 26.

3. Ḥamawī, *Ḥādī*, 25–6.

4. Ḥamawī, *Bawādī*, 153a.

5. Ḥamawī, *Ḥādī*, 25.

6. Ḥamawī, *Bawādī*, 153a.

7. Hamawi found out about the dismissal in Nov./Dec. 1573. Ḥamawī, *Bawādī*, 153b.

legitimacy and granted access to a man like Ghazzi.[8] Hamawi's father had been a scribe at a local law court who had managed, through a connection with a local Sufi shaykh, to set his son on a scholarly path. Completing his early studies in Hama, Hamawi did what an increasing number of Arab scholars did: he left his hometown for the imperial capital in his late teens or early twenties (likely in the early 1560s).[9] In Istanbul, he continued studying and "kept the company of some of its high-ranking leaders."[10] This social aspect was crucial to securing his future. Hamawi's great-grandson explained that his ancestor "entered Rum and mingled with all of its grandees. He praised them with exquisite odes and was appointed to the Qassaʿiyya Madrasa in Damascus."[11]

One such important person with whom Hamawi mingled was the rising Rumi scholar Çivizade Mehmed. In contrast to Hamawi, Çivizade Mehmed Efendi came from scholarly nobility.[12] His father, Hoca Çivizade, was a celebrated scholar who had served as chief judge of Egypt before advancing to the position of military judge and chief mufti of Istanbul.[13] When Çivizade junior met Hamawi in Istanbul in the 1560s, the former was already well along the path cut by his father. Çivizade Mehmed had spent the last decade or so teaching students at Istanbul's best colleges and was preparing to embark on a multiyear journey as chief judge in various provincial capitals.[14]

8. Najm al-Din al-Ghazzi, quoting Hamawi's son, dates his birth to 1544/5 (951). Burini writes 1542/43 (949). Ghazzī, *Luṭf*, 3: 115; Būrīnī, *Tarājim*, 175a. For more biographies of Hamawi, see Muḥibbī, *Khulāṣa*, 3: 322–32; Khafājī, *Rayḥāna*, 98–9; Elger, *Glaube*, 73–112; Brockelmann, "al-Muḥibbī"; Wüstenfeld, *Gelehrten-Familie*, 2–9.

9. Hamawi stayed in Hama until the death of his teachers, and since one of them died shortly before 1562/63, it is likely that Hamawi left his hometown in the early 1560s. On his way to Istanbul, he stopped in Aleppo to study. Būrīnī, *Tarājim*, 175a; Muḥibbī, *Khulāṣa*, 3: 323.

10. Būrīnī, *Tarājim*, 175a. Najm al-Din al-Ghazzi, who knew Hamawi personally, writes that he "learned from a group [of scholars] in Constantinople," though without specifying any names. Ghazzī, *Luṭf*, 116. Burini (who also knew him personally) and Muhibbi (his great-grandson) intimate that Hamawi went to Istanbul after completing his education. Būrīnī, *Tarājim*, 175a; Muḥibbī, *Khulāṣa*, 3: 324.

11. Muḥibbī, *Khulāṣa*, 3: 324. See also Ghazzī, *Luṭf*, 3: 115–6.

12. For biographies of Çivizade Mehmed, see Ibn Ayyub, *Rawḍ*, 259a–260b; Ghazzī, *Luṭf*, 3: 27–9; ʿAṭāʾī, *Ḥadāʾiḳ*, 292–4; İpşirli, "Çivizâde Mehmed Efendi," 346; Tunçay, *Çivizâde Ailesi*, 24–31.

13. Ṭaşköprīzāde, *Shaqāʾiq*, 446–7; Repp, *The Müfti of Istanbul*, 244–56; Tunçay, *Çivizâde Ailesi*, 16–23.

14. ʿAṭāʾī, *Ḥadāʾiḳ*, 292; İpşirli, "Çivizâde Mehmed Efendi"; Tunçay, "*Çivi-zade Ailesi*," 23–4.

Sometime before Çivizade left Istanbul, he accepted Hamawi into his household service. Najm al-Din al-Ghazzi, Badr al-Din's son who studied with Hamawi and became his close friend, wrote that Hamawi was "in constant contact with" Çivizade at this time.[15] Hamawi himself wrote of Çivizade's "protection" (*ẓill*) and "his abundant favors, for which I am incapable of thanking him."[16] So when Çivizade was appointed chief judge of Damascus in 1568, Hamawi traveled with him.[17] In Damascus, Hamawi taught and began to meet the great scholars of the city, including Badr al-Din al-Ghazzi, with whom he studied Qurʾanic exegesis and hadith.[18] However, Hamawi remained in Çivizade's orb, for when Çivizade was transferred to Cairo in 1571, Hamawi again traveled with him. In Egypt, he performed secretarial duties for his patron; he drafted letters on his behalf and was present when Çivizade received guests.[19] Not least, Hamawi made a record of their travels. This would become the first half of a two-part travel account, written in rhymed prose, whose first part would be entitled *The Navigator of the Challenging Paths to the Egyptian Lands* (*Hadi al-azʿan al-najdiyya ila al-diyar al-Misriyya*).[20]

Hamawi's travel account belonged to the travelogue (*rihla*) tradition of Ghazzi's earlier *Full Moon Rising*. Like his predecessor, Hamawi incorporated long excerpts from other literary works, including poems, biographies, and letters. Also like his predecessor, Hamawi was more interested in human encounters (especially with men of learning) than in the built environment or ethnographic description. However, Hamawi's account, especially part one, was much more closely tied to his patron than Ghazzi's ever was. Ghazzi did mention Süleyman briefly at the outset

15. Ghazzi used the verb *lazama*, which could also signal the close attachment of advanced students with their teachers. Ghazzī, *Luṭf*, 3: 116.

16. Ḥamawī, *Ḥādī*, quotations on 24 and 23, respectively.

17. Historians give different dates for Çivizade's appointment in Damascus, but it must have been around 1568 or 1569. Ibn Ayyūb, "Dhayl," 330; Ghazzī, *Kawākib*, 3: 27; Muḥibbī, *Khulāṣa*, 3: 324–5.

18. Būrīnī, *Tarājim*, 1: 99; Ghazzī, *Luṭf*, 3: 115; Muḥibbī, *Khulāṣa*, 3: 324. After Ghazzi's death, Hamawi wrote two treatises in defense of his teacher's versified commentary. Ḥamawī, "Sahm;" Muḥibbī, *Khulāṣa*, 1: 33. Hamawi must have entered the service of Ismaʿil al-Nabulusi in the late 1560s as well, since in 1570 he was writing letters on his behalf. Ḥamawī, *Majmūʿa*, 29b–31a.

19. For example, when news arrived that an Egyptian scholar had been promoted to a new position, Hamawi drafted the letter informing the scholar of that fact. Ḥamawī, *Ḥādī*, 59. For another letter, see Ḥamawī, *Majmūʿa*, 46a–b. For his presence when guests were received, Ḥamawī, *Ḥādī*, 44, 55, 58.

20. This first part of the travel narrative has been published as an edition by Muhammad Adnan Bakhit. Ḥamawī, *Ḥādī*. The work has been discussed most extensively by Elger, *Glaube*, chapter 2.

of his travelogue, and may have indeed intended to present it to the sultan, but overall his work has the mark of a fiercely independent scholar. Hamawi's *Navigator*, on the other hand, is so focused on Çivizade that it can be viewed as much a chronicle of Çivizade's travels as of Hamawi's.[21] However, although Hamawi wrote for a Rumi patron, nowhere did he mention that the two of them belonged to different linguistic groups. Though Çivizade's name and position would have made his background transparent to contemporary readers, Hamawi made no mention of his patron's place of birth nor of any divergences in their language, clothing, or habits.

Instead, many of the potential differences between himself and his patron were subsumed beneath the shared, universalizing idiom of Islam. Hamawi introduced Çivizade at the beginning of his account as a "blessed soul" who was "the head of the shaykhs of Islam, the king of the most learned ones, the pride of the lords most discerning, the leader of the meticulous men of learning, a sun around whom the religion, the world, and the faith keep turning."[22] Hamawi also advertised his patron's piety as it played out in practice. The two of them had first set out on their journey with Fevri in the service of an Islamic cause. Having heard that the monks of the Monastery of the Cross outside Jerusalem had expanded their building at the expense of a former mosque—illegal according to Ottoman law—Sultan Selim II (r. 1566–74) had ordered Çivizade and Fevri to investigate.[23] No sooner had they arrived in Jerusalem in Ramadan 1571 than the men called together a large group and headed towards the site. When their inspection unearthed remains of prayer niches allegedly proving that a mosque had indeed stood there previously, Çivizade ordered that the additions be demolished and the mosque be rebuilt.[24] The crowd, according to Hamawi, tore down the new structures on the spot. At the same time, they "subjected the infidels to the contempt and censure they deserved for their disgraceful behavior, confronting them fittingly—may

21. In fact, he introduces it as a description of his travels to Egypt with Çivizade. Ḥamawī, *Ḥādī*, 23.

22. Ḥamawī, *Ḥādī*, 23.

23. This was the famous Monastary of the Cross. Ḥamawī, *Ḥādī*, 35. For more on this incident, see Elger, *Glaube*, 83; Braude and Lewis, *Christians*, 50; Heyd, *Ottoman Documents*, 176–7.

24. In fact, local Muslims had made the same accusation against the monastary a decade earlier, but the judge of Jerusalem had found their claims to be groundless. Heyd, *Ottoman Documents*, 176. For the law and politics of church construction, see Gradeva, "Bottom Up," 144–5.

God punish them—and denouncing them unremittingly."[25] The Muslims rejoiced at the restitution of their sacred space. When the time for the afternoon prayer came, Çivizade led the people in worship. Hamawi finished his account by citing the Qurʾan: "It was a hard day for the faithless" (25:26). Such moments of collective zeal highlighted the bonds between the three travelers at the expense of the empire's Christians.[26]

Just as important as the religious sensibility that united Hamawi with his Rumi patron was their shared gentility. Hamawi portrayed both Çivizade and Fevri as embodying the ideal of the refined litterateur (*adib*). Hamawi praised his patron for "the delicacy of his manners" (*khaṣāʾis ādābihi*) and explained that they were tied to one another by "the bond of refinement" (*luḥmat al-adab*).[27] This bond found its most powerful expression in the many convivial evenings the two passed in one another's company. Looking back on those evenings later, Hamawi was reminded of the poem that read:

> Oh, those splendid nights, if only they could return
> As they once were—but what bygone nights ever return!
> I have not forgotten them since they were adjourned,
> No companionship since ever made me cease to yearn.[28]

As cultivated and genteel as Çivizade was, he may have even been outdone by Fevri, who had received his training in etiquette in the imperial palace (figure 6.1). Hamawi was effusive in his praise for the mufti, what with "the courteous manners with which God created him: his unblemished nature for which, by God, absolutely no one can rival him, his noble refinement—but what refinement!—and his great humility and disposition so enticing."[29] Fevri was the embodiment of the lines of the medieval poet Abu al-Tayyib al-Mutanabbi (d. 965), according to Hamawi: "His thought epitomizes knowledge, his speech epitomizes wisdom, his heart epitomizes religion, and his figure epitomizes elegance."[30]

25. Ḥamawī, *Ḥādī*, 35.

26. See likewise Ḥamawī, *Ḥādī*, 63. This was not the first such incident in the region. When the governor of Damascus discovered in 1560 that Christians had been building houses near the Great Mosque, he and his chief judge forced Christians and Jews alike to sell their properties to Muslims. *3 Numaralı Mühimme Defteri*, 690–1 (nos. 1556 and 1557); Bakhit, "Christian Population," 26–7.

27. Ḥamawī, *Ḥādī*, 23.

28. Ḥamawī, *Ḥādī*, 82, see also 86; Ḥamawī, *Majmūʿa*, 30a.

29. Ḥamawī, *Ḥādī*, 25.

30. Ḥamawī, *Ḥādī*, 25.

FIGURE 6.1. The mufti Fevri Efendi (left) meets with another scholar. From ʿAşık Çelebi, *Meşaʿirü's-şuʿaraʾ* (c. 1600). (Reproduced by permission from the Directorate of the Turkish Institution for Manuscripts, Millet Library Istanbul, MS Ali Emiri Tarih 772, 272b.)

Throughout the travel account, Hamawi stressed the three gentlemen's shared decorousness through a contrast with those he viewed as less polished. About two weeks into the trip to Jerusalem, the company arrived in Ludd in the subdistrict of Gaza.[31] Since the month of Ramadan had begun, Çivizade was holding magnificent evening meals for breaking the fast (*iftar*), as befitted a man of his station. Word spread of his munificence, and to believe Hamawi, soon madrasa students were streaming out

31. Bakhīt in Ḥamawī, *Ḥādī*, 99.

of every nearby village in hopes of currying favor with the powerful traveler.[32] Hamawi made no secret of his disdain for what he characterized as the rabble who attended these banquets: "They race down from every slope," he quoted the Qur'an as saying (21:96). His audience would have immediately known that the verse referred to Gog and Magog, the uncivilized brutes whom God threatened to send down upon humankind as a scourge.[33]

Though these villagers were obviously pursuing a higher education, Hamawi viewed them as ignorant and coarse. One day, the men paid tribute to the shrines of Zakariyya and Yahya near Nablus, where, according to some, the bodies of both saints were buried.[34] Fevri and Hamawi rode next to each other on their way home. They were blissfully exchanging stories and jokes when one of the most insistent of the villagers that trailed the travelers, an unnamed Egyptian student, spotted the two men and trotted over on his donkey to join them. The gentlemen were hardly keen on the student's company, but they did not dismiss him. Instead, they steered the conversation toward one of their favorite topics: competitive sparring over the virtues of some cities over others. In this case, the city in question was Damascus. Hamawi recited some lines by the medieval Syrian poet Ibn Nubata (d. 1366) in praise of the city's Great Mosque, called by its nickname *Jillaq*:

I see artistry concentrated in the *Jillaq* mosque,
Its façade is the epitome of beauty.
If people claim that their own mosques are better,
Say to them, "the door is open, go see!"[35]

No sooner had Hamawi finished when the student protested, accusing him of having mispronounced the mosque's nickname—it was *Jullaq*, not *Jillaq*! Calmly, Hamawi replied, "the matter is not as you misconceive, and what is correct is the opposite of what you perceive."[36] *Jillaq*, Hamawi insisted, was scholarly consensus. When the student protested that everyone pronounced it *Jullaq*, Hamawi replied, "Indeed, it is one of the mistakes made by commoners like you."[37]

32. Ḥamawī, *Ḥādī*, 27.
33. For this tradition, see Hagen, "Afterword," 222.
34. The following from Ḥamawī, *Ḥādī*, 28–9. See also Elger, *Glaube*, 86–7.
35. Ḥamawī, *Ḥādī*, 28.
36. Ḥamawī, *Ḥādī*, 28.
37. Ḥamawī, *Ḥādī*, 28.

Stung by the dual accusation of being both wrong and common, the student climbed down from his donkey, intent on defending his claims. However, to believe Hamawi, he only uttered more nonsense. Finally Fevri intervened. Addressing the student, he said:

> The words of my lord [Hamawi] are unobjectionably true. Take your donkey: the commoners pronounce it "*ḥumār*" with a "u," when in fact it is correct to call it "*ḥimār*" as the learned do. There are so many such common mistakes I could enumerate to you![38]

Thrilled by this explanation, Hamawi turned to Fevri and said, "My lord, may God keep you blessed as one of the most learned!"[39] When they saw that they had upset the student, they struck a conciliatory, albeit condescending, tone: "We treated him as those do who are generous [*ahl al-samāḥa*]." Maybe so, but Hamawi's summary of the encounter revealed their true feelings toward the student:

> He butted in on our conversation and got in our way, desperate to take part in our friendly parley. How we resented the interruption, his comments that were a constant disruption. We found his presence burdensome, and tried our best to stop him. But whenever he uttered an incorrect word, our corrections simply would not be heard. The rudeness of his company caused us to feel pain, and the situation was so bad that we nearly declared, "Just please go away!"[40]

Ultimately, Hamawi was dressing up elite prejudice as a violation of his sense of social and linguistic propriety. Doing so was common enough in the period, as we saw in Chapter 4.

Still, in this context Hamawi's chauvinism had additional functions. Hamawi may well have been acting out his own social anxieties. A small-town son of a scribe, Hamawi was likely at pains to differentiate himself from the first-generation rural college students that the travelers encountered along their way.[41] But even more importantly, such passages contributed to an argument about which axes of identity were decisive in defining societal faultlines: implicitly, Hamawi contended that the empire's inhabitants should be grouped not by ethnicity, but by gentility. A cultivated Arab had more in common with a cultivated Rumi than he did with an unpolished Arab.

38. Ḥamawī, *Ḥādī*, 29.
39. Ḥamawī, *Ḥādī*, 28–9.
40. Ḥamawī, *Ḥādī*, 28.
41. There was also a fair dose of Syrian-Egyptian rivalry.

Indeed, Hamawi portrayed his Rumi travel companions as fully assimilated into Arabic literary and conversational customs. This emerges most strongly from his account of their nightly gatherings with their host in Jerusalem, Ibn Jamaʿa. As we saw in Chapter 4, Fevri and Çivizade did not receive the respect they felt they deserved from the local scholar. However, this was mostly a reflection of Ibn Jamaʿa's own ignorance, as Hamawi made clear—in fact, the learned travelers were steeped in the Arabic literary tradition and superior in their connoisseurship of Arabic poetry. In one dispute, the four gentlemen discussed whether a certain unnamed Damascene poet was really as skilled as the host was making him out to be. The guests insisted that their host had overestimated him. When Ibn Jamaʿa retorted by reciting a magnificent ode the said scholar had supposedly composed to praise him, the travelers insisted that the ode had almost certainly been stolen. They had witnessed what the man was capable of. They recalled the words of the early Islamic poet Hassan Ibn Thabit (d. 674):

> Poetry reflects the mind of man: he presents
> It in gatherings with brilliance or stupidity.
> The truest verses that you could utter,
> Are those you utter sincerely.[42]

In other words, a man's poetic interjections in a gathering reflected his intellectual caliber. How was it possible that a man had composed only a single poem in his entire life, which just so happened to be so magnificent?[43] They recalled another poem about ʿAli Ibn al-Jahm (d. 863) well-known amongst the literati, which finished, "when he claims poetry, it makes me suspicious."[44] The men closed their case, but the intended effect of Hamawi's passage was clear. The conversation had exhibited both the literary discernment and scholarly network of the travelers. It showed off their mastery of polite conversation, and in particular their ability to quote the relevant classical poetry. It is often unclear from Hamawi's account who said what—the three guests' voices fuse into a single, collective "we." But that was precisely the point. "The whole time," Hamawi sighed, "[their host] was in one world and we were in another."[45]

42. Ḥamawī, *Ḥādī*, 33; see also note 10 on that page.
43. Ḥamawī, *Ḥādī*, 33.
44. The verse was written by Marwan Ibn Abi Hafsa (d. 798/9). Ḥamawī, *Ḥādī*, 34.
45. Ḥamawī, *Ḥādī*, 32.

Hamawi's account was certainly self-serving. It put him, a young and inexperienced provincial judge with few publications to his name, in the same category as some of the most powerful and esteemed men of the empire. But it also worked in the favor of the Rumis with whom he traveled. It portrayed them as fully assimilated into Arabic literary culture, able to recite Arabic poetry at the drop of a hat and hold their own in Arabic conversation against uppity local scholars who at first may have underestimated them. Indeed, the world Hamawi evoked aligns neatly with the one that emerges from near-contemporary biographical dictionaries, including Ibn Ayyub's *The Sweet-Smelling Garden* and Burini's *Biographies of the Notable Men*. These works portray Damascus as a unified society in which salons bringing Turcophone and Arab elites together were both frequent and frictionless. Thousands of casual interactions had culminated in a shared set of expectations and a shared sociability that, while it could not prevent misunderstanding completely, helped as much as did any navigator of challenging paths to move men across the empire.

Governance

By the 1570s, informal interactions held in homes and gardens across the Ottoman Empire had come to play a crucial role in the workings of imperial governance. Personal relations had been important in helping to stabilize Ottoman rule from the beginning, as we saw with Ghazzi and his father's efforts to offer their support for the new order. Since then, the wispy threads linking center and province had formed into a dense web of information and patronage networks crisscrossing the empire.

New and highly regularized patterns of mobility aided in the formation of these networks. Not only was it almost requisite for Arabs to make at least one visit to the capital during their lifetime (and usually more), new patterns of circulation had solidified for many Rumis as well, especially those who served as chief judges. These were usually appointed to a series of prominent judgeships across the empire, often rotating across Damascus, Aleppo, and Cairo before serving in Bursa and sometimes Edirne and finally Istanbul.[46] Back in the capital, the best of them would eventually become one of two of the empire's military judges, who together served as the head of the Ottoman judiciary. Not only Maʿlulzade, but Ghazzi's

46. The judgeships of the large Arab cities were incorporated into this rotational pattern in the 1530s. Atçıl, "Route," 502–7; Repp, *The Müfti of Istanbul*, 45–7.

friend Hasan Bey, his scholarly challenger Kınalızade ʿAli, and, as we will see, Çivizade all took this path.[47]

These patterns of circulation meant that an increasing number of officials in Istanbul could make decisions regarding the Arab provinces on the basis of firsthand experience. This was particularly useful for military judges, since they decided on madrasa and judgeship appointments under their jurisdiction. In the early years after the conquest, military judges often had to rely on scant information or on the wisdom of others to evaluate which candidate was worthy of a post in the Arab provinces. When Ghazzi approached Kadiri Çelebi, the chief military judge of Anatolia, in hopes of securing a position in the early 1530s, Kadiri had never served in Damascus and ultimately had to trust the recommendation of the vizier Ayas Pasha, who had.[48] Things had already begun to change by the late 1540s, when a growing number of men who served as military judges of Anatolia had spent time in Arab lands.[49]

This mobility, coupled with frequent stops in the empire's salons, facilitated the flow of information across the Ottoman Empire. Much of this information circulated orally, like Maʿlulzade's lobbying on behalf of the four Egyptian students during the assembly near Ramla. Clients with provincial roots played an important role in sustaining these channels of communication. On one occasion, Hamawi sought to convince Çivizade to improve the lot of Cairo's scholars, whose impoverishment he found pitiable (Çivizade promised that he would).[50] Hamawi continued to play a role as informant for his patron long after the two parted ways physically. When Hamawi bade Çivizade farewell in the fall of 1571, having been appointed to a town in Upper Egypt, Çivizade insisted that Hamawi "send long, detailed letters in service to his honorable majesty."[51] Hamawi complied, and would in fact continue to report back to Çivizade from the proverbial front years after his patron had returned to Istanbul.[52] In one especially long letter, sent while Çivizade was still judge in Cairo, Hamawi

47. Hasan Bey did not serve in Bursa or Edirne and served as military judge of Anatolia only (not of Rumelia). Many of these were also later appointed *şeyhülislam*.

48. İpşirli, "Hamidi," 240.

49. Atçıl, "Route," 504–5.

50. Ḥamawī, *Ḥādī*, 61–2.

51. Ḥamawī, *Ḥādī*, 66.

52. Ḥamawī, *Majmūʿa*, 91a–92a, 127a–128a. Ghazzi, too, had epistolary relations with Rumis he met in Damascus after they left, including the governor Ayas Pasha, as we saw in Chapter 2, as well as with Hasan Bey. Ghazzī, *Kawākib*, 3: 141–2.

informed his patron that certain local judges were misbehaving, relaying to him the complaints of residents about their injustices.[53]

Another passage in the same letter from Hamawi to Çivizade suggests just how well oiled these channels of communication had become by the 1570s. This passage summarized the contents of a second letter that the judge of Alexandria had shown to Hamawi. The latter letter was from ʿAbdurrahman Efendi detailing ʿAbdurrahman's return to Istanbul, probably following his four-year judgeship in Mecca.[54] The day after all of the high dignitaries of the capital had attended a reception in honor of ʿAbdurrahman's return, Hamawi reported to Çivizade, ʿAbdurrahman had gone to visit a vizier. There, ʿAbdurrahman had given the vizier a report on Çivizade's tenure as judge in Cairo:

> [ʿAbdurrahman] mentioned to [the vizier] some of your [i.e., Çivizade's] distinguished characteristics as he had witnessed them and heard about them from others. This increased [the vizier's] trust in you, and he was happy to hear that your work was going so well. Some time after that, Perviz Efendi [a scholar] met with his Highness the vizier, may God immortalize his days of fortune and protect his great honor. [The vizier] mentioned to him how ʿAbdurrahman Efendi had praised you and all that he had heard about your fine characteristics, and how this had increased [the vizier's] favor toward [you] and his trust in [you]. [The vizier] said, "Praise be to God, like father, like son." Some time after that reception, Hamid Efendi and Perviz Efendi went to the house of ʿAbdurrahman Çelebi and thanked him for having praised you.[55]

This was the entire content of ʿAbdurrahman's letter as Hamawi related it to Çivizade: that ʿAbdurrahman had reported good things about Çivizade to the vizier, who had in turn mentioned this to the judge Perviz Efendi, who had gone back to ʿAbdurrahman to thank him for the kind words on Çivizade's behalf.[56] ʿAbdurrahman, for whatever reason, had mentioned this series of exchanges in a letter to the judge of Alexandria, who had shown the letter to Hamawi, who had in turn relayed its contents back to

53. Ḥamawī, *Ḥādī*, 66–71.

54. This must have been ʿAbdurrahman ʿAli from Amasya (d. 1575), whose judgeship in Mecca ended in 1570. Ḥamawī, *Ḥādī*, 113n71; Atçil, "Route," 504. See ʿAlī ibn Bālī, *ʿIqd*, 476–8.

55. Ḥamawī, *Ḥādī*, 71.

56. Perviz Efendi (d. 1579) had also served as judge of Damascus in the early 1550s, between Hasan Bey's two terms. Ibn Ayyūb, "Dhayl," 327. Hamid Efendi (d. 1577) also had been chief judge in Damascus and in Egypt and was Çivizade's brother-in-law. Ḥamawī, *Ḥādī*, 113n72–3; Baltacı, "Hâmid Efendi," 460.

Çivizade. ʿAbdurrahman's praise for Çivizade thus became the subject of no less than six different exchanges, four of which took place in person, and two by letter. This leaves no doubt as to how important such oral testimonials could be for a man's reputation and career, and how quickly they could travel across the empire.

The reach of such networks of patronage and news had serious consequences for the practical matter of governing. In 1571, Maʿlulzade was appointed military judge of Anatolia. A descendant of the Prophet Muhammad and the son of a well-known scholar, Maʿlulzade, like Çivizade, was a child of privilege. After becoming first a sponsored candidate for office, and then the son-in-law, of Ebu's-Suʿud, Maʿlulzade began his teaching career, starting at a madrasa in Bursa and ending at one of the prestigious eight madrasas founded by Mehmed II in Istanbul.[57] In 1566, he was appointed chief judge in Aleppo; a year later he was transferred to Damascus.[58]

Maʿlulzade was not particularly loved in Syria. Shortly after his arrival, he picked a fight with the provincial governor.[59] Ibn Ayyub wrote that Maʿlulzade "was greedy and seized people's assets arbitrarily and ruthlessly. His tenure weighed heavily on the people, and they suffered under his harshness and violence."[60] No tears were shed when Maʿlulzade left for Cairo in 1569, nor when he left Cairo the next year. Thereupon he was appointed to Bursa (which he reached on a journey via Ramla, where he met our three travelers).[61] In May 1573, Maʿlulzade was finally transferred back to Istanbul. There, he assumed the position of military judge of Anatolia.[62]

When Hamawi heard of the news of Maʿlulzade's appointment as military judge, he rejoiced, and immediately took advantage of his close bond to Maʿlulzade to ask for a promotion.[63] Instead, Hamawi was removed from his judgeship entirely and left unemployed. Hamawi was not the only victim of Maʿlulzade's caprices. Around the same time, Ghazzi was relieved of his teaching position at the Taqawiyya Madrasa in Damascus as well. The removal of such an esteemed personage as Ghazzi caused a

57. ʿAṭāyī, *Hadāʾiḳuʾl-Haḳāʾiḳ*, 281; Özcan, "Mehmed Efendi, Mâlûlzâde," 456–7; Imber, *Ebu's-Suʿud*, 17.

58. Ibn Ayyūb, "Dhayl," 330; Özcan, "Mehmed Efendi, Mâlûlzâde," 456.

59. Winter, "Ottoman Qāḍīs," 99.

60. Ibn Ayyūb, "Dhayl," 330.

61. Özcan, "Mehmed Efendi, Mâlûlzâde," 456.

62. Ḥamawī, *Bawādī*, fols. 152b–153a; Özcan, "Mehmed Efendi, Mâlûlzâde," 456.

63. Ḥamawī, *Ḥādī*, 91.

scandal in the city; no less than three of the city's historians recorded the development.[64]

As unfortunate as these occurrences were for Hamawi and Ghazzi, to us they reveal the first-hand experience on which Maʿlulzade could draw as he made decisions over appointments. In removing Ghazzi, Maʿlulzade was settling old scores from his time in Damascus. He had never forgiven Ghazzi for refusing to pay him the visits chief judges had come to expect from local notables, nor for refusing to join the funeral cortège of his daughter.[65] Maʿlulzade likewise relied on his firsthand experience to select a replacement for Ghazzi; he awarded the position to a local scholar who had attached himself to Maʿlulzade in Damascus, an astrologer (and to believe some historians, a charlatan) called Muhammad al-Hijazi (d. 1611/2).[66] Both in removing Ghazzi and in appointing Hijazi, Maʿlulzade drew on relationships formed during his time in Damascus half a decade earlier.

The case of Hamawi's dismissal is even more telling. Bereft of his position, Hamawi soon set out for Istanbul to investigate what had happened. In the Ottoman capital, he learned that his alliance with Çivizade was to blame for his downfall. Maʿlulzade had a longstanding rivalry with Çivizade, and was exacting revenge by systematically having his followers removed from their positions.[67] So close-knit was the empire that these rivalries at the Ottoman center now reverberated in Syria. The empire-wide patronage structures that characterized politics in the seventeenth century were already taking shape in the sixteenth.[68]

The outcome of this episode likewise shows the reach of these patronage structures. In 1575, Maʿlulzade was dismissed from the position of military judge.[69] And who was to replace him but Çivizade Mehmed Efendi, former chief qadi of Damascus, patron of Hamawi, and loyal student of Ghazzi. On his first day in office, as Damascene historians report, Çivizade's assistant opened the file containing the list of the teaching positions at Taqawiyya Madrasa, and realized with horror that Maʿlulzade had dismissed Ghazzi. Outraged, Çivizade approached the recently enthroned

64. Būrīnī, *Tarājim*, 2: 99; Būrīnī, *Tarājim*, fols. 173b–174a; Ibn Ayyūb, *Rawḍ*, 108–9; Ghazzī, *Kawākib*, 3: 28–30.

65. Ghazzī, *Kawākib*, 3: 28–30; Būrīnī, *Tarājim*, 2: 99. See also Chapter 3.

66. Ibn Ayyūb, *Kitāb*, 108. For biographies of Hijazi, see Ibn Ayyūb, *Kitāb*, 107–9; Būrīnī, *Tarājim*, 173a–175a.

67. Ḥamawī, *Bawādī*, 161b–162a, 172b–174a.

68. For a similarly expansive patronage network in the sixteenth century, see Hoca Saʿdeddin (d. 1599) as discussed in Tezcan, "Ottoman Mevali," 15–21.

69. Ḥamawī, *Bawādī*, 180b; ʿAṭāʾī, *Ḥadāʾiḳ*, 281.

sultan, Murad III (r. 1574–95), explaining Ghazzi's stature as a scholar and urging him to have him reinstated. Çivizade informed Ghazzi of the decision in a personal letter to his former teacher.[70] He also increased Ghazzi's salary, and insisted—according to Damascene historians—that neither he nor the sultan wanted any gifts in return; the sultan merely asked to keep him in his prayers.[71] Burini viewed this as a response to the debt that Çivizade had incurred to Ghazzi in Syria; Çivizade honored Ghazzi in this way "because [Çivizade] transmitted hadith in Damascus on the authority of the shaykh when he was a judge there."[72] Hamawi likewise did well at Çivizade's hands, returning from Istanbul to greater Syria with an appointment as judge in Homs, the very step up the social ladder for which he had long hoped.

The mobility of Ottoman elites had enormous consquences for imperial governance. As they worked in different locales, men like Çivizade, Maʿlulzade, and even Ghazzi built up elaborate networks of personal contacts. Such networks allowed information to circulate not just more rapidly than ever before, but also more securely, with the bonds of allegiance that linked these individuals offering an insurance against misinformation. Indeed, what made these networks so effective is that they were held together by a sense of mutual obligation. Such obligations increasingly came to inform appointments made in the Arab provinces, as successive military judges used their power to reward loyalists, and, in some cases, punish those of their rivals. Çivizade on the whole may have been more fair-minded than Maʿlulzade (at least to believe our sources), but in both cases, the principle was the same: a promise made in Damascus would be upheld in Istanbul.

A New Order

Hamawi's account bears witness to how close relationships between Rumis and Arabs had become by the later sixteenth century. It also shows the ways in which these relationships had become strained. With the empire's economic downturn and Istanbul's increasing ability to assert itself in matters social, political, and intellectual, the standing of Arab elites began

70. Ibn Ayyūb, *Rawḍ*, 109; Būrīnī, *Tarājim*, 99. See also the letter Ḥamawī wrote to Ghazzi, and Burini's copy of it. Ḥamawī, *Majmūʿa*, fols. 77a–78b; Būrīnī, *Tarājim*, fols. 173b–174a.

71. Ibn Ayyūb, *Rawḍ*, 109; Ghazzī, *Kawākib*, 3: 28.

72. Būrīnī, *Tarājim*, 99.

to wane. Hamawi's path to his appointment in Homs was rough, and he would travel a good portion of it on his knees.

In the second half of the sixteenth century, the Ottoman Empire underwent major social and economic transformations. Around the middle of the century, it ceased its seemingly insatiable expansion, which had previously ensured a steady stream of new resources and new posts. This hiatus coincided with an influx of silver from the Americas, which depressed the purchasing power of currencies all across the old world. Between 1550 and 1580, the value of the silver akçe halved against the Venetian Ducat, the gold standard for much of the early modern Mediterranean.[73] Prices in the empire increased accordingly, though many wages did not.[74] Although imperial expenditures would only begin to outpace revenues at the end of the century, historians agree that the economic downturn began to be felt around the last quarter of the sixteenth century.[75] Elites employed by the government complained that their salaries no longer sufficed to support the sizeable retinues they were expected to maintain.[76]

One of the by-products of this economic stagnation was the increasing scarcity of teaching and administrative posts relative to the number of aspirants for them. If around the middle of the century the ongoing proliferation of such posts (coupled with increased insecurity in the Ottoman countryside) had encouraged many to enter the scholarly or bureaucratic track, by the 1570s, the number of qualified candidates for such posts far exceeded the positions available.[77] Although the Ottoman state sought to manage this problem by creating new positions and rotating appointees more frequently, even these measures could not keep up with demand.[78]

As the competition for positions became ever more fierce, those who won them came from an ever more slender subsection of the Ottoman elite. After 1570, men working at madrasas beyond a handful of cities

73. Darling, *Revenue-Raising*, 36. Though most of the data is from Anatolian cities, the level of economic integration in the empire meant that similar effects were often felt in other regions as well. Pamuk, *Monetary History*, 125.

74. Darling, *Revenue-Raising*, 36, 40–1; Rafeq, *ʿArab*, 124–48.

75. Çızakça, "Ottoman Government," 246–7; Pamuk, *Monetary History*, 131.

76. Fleischer, *Bureaucrat*, 90–1.

77. Atçıl, "Route," 508; Repp, *The Müfti of Istanbul*, 49. Kunt identifies a similar process in the 1570s and 1580s at the level of *sancakbeyi*. Kunt, *The Sultan's Servants*, 76, 310.

78. Atçıl argues that after 1570 limits on the length of office and new policies of promotion allowed more men to be employed in the highest four positions in the learned hierarchy. Atçıl, "Route"; Atçıl, *Scholars*, chapter 8.

around the imperial center were increasingly passed over for its top positions.[79] More and more often, leading offices were awarded to the sons of those who already occupied them, as the careers of both Çivizade and Maʿlulzade exemplify.[80] Newcomers who did manage to enter such spheres did so by forming alliances with those on the inside, a convention formalized through the *mülazemet* system that allocated appointments to the students of leading officials.[81] The armed student revolts that started in the 1570s in many Anatolian provinces signal the depth of despair felt by young scholars whom this system excluded.[82]

The Arab provinces were affected by the economic contraction as well. To be sure, scholars educated in Egypt or Syria had already ceased to be considered for top jobs at the imperial center by the early sixteenth century. However, now many key positions in the Arab provinces were awarded to centrally trained scholars as well. Among these were not just the chief judgeships of the major provincial capitals, but even some deputy judgeships in those cities as well as second-tier judgeships in provincial towns or in rural regions.[83] Other bureaucratic services in the provinces, such as the financial administration, were staffed by centrally trained elites as well.[84] In other words, while some of the surplus educated population from the Ottoman center could be sent out to be employed in the provinces, this measure came at the expense of provincial elites, who not only had few opportunities at the center but now also faced competition from Rumis at home.

At the same time, as Ottoman power both at the center and in the provinces was increasingly institutionalized, Arabs saw much of the soft

79. Atçıl, "Route," 501. Kunt observes a similar trend towards the appointment of centrally trained men to higher-level provincial positions (*beylerbeyi*, *sancakbeyi*) beginning in the 1570s, with lower-level position holders having few possibilities for promotion. Kunt, *The Sultan's Servants*, chapter 4, esp. 62–7.

80. Atçıl, "Route," esp. 494; Tezcan, "Ottoman *Mevali*." For a later period, see Zilfi, *The Politics of Piety*.

81. This system had become increasingly difficulty to circumvent in the second half of the sixteenth century. Atçıl, *Scholars*, 142–4.

82. Faroqhi, "Political Events," 415–6. Of course, there were other reasons for the unrest as well; population growth combined with an increased tax burden on peasants and the "little ice age" to push many people off the land into towns and cities. White, *Rebellion*; Kunt, *The Sultan's Servants*, 80. Discontent existed among qadis as well. Faroqhi, "Social Mobility," 217.

83. The judge of Tripoli in Greater Syria in the 1570s was a Turkish speaker. Saßmannshausen, "Reform in Translation," 105. For deputy judges, see Bakhit, *Ottoman Province*, 121; for rural regions, Ḥamawī, *Ḥādī*, 93–4.

84. This included not just the chief accountant (*defterdar*), but also the men that served below him (*muhasebeci*). Ḥamawī, *Ḥādī*, 93; Bakhit, *Ottoman Province*, 143–6.

power they had once enjoyed begin to dissipate. In part, they were simply victims of broader transformations in conceptions of elite status. As Richard Repp has argued, whereas in the fifteenth and early sixteenth centuries a scholar's knowledge and writings most contributed to his status in learned circles, by the seventeenth, the "scholar's chief interest—and the measuring rod of *his* success—was the attainment of the high learned offices and the power, salary and perquisites that went with them."[85] Such an attitude necessarily disadvantaged Arabs who were excluded from those positions. So too did the growing institutionalization of Ottoman governance in the provinces. Arab advice, so valuable as the state was building up its presence in the region, became less important after Ottoman institutions had taken root. This process was further accentuated as members of the imperial elite increasingly founded and managed imperial endowments—mosques, madrasas, soup kitchens—in the provinces. Usually supervised by officials from the Ottoman center, these institutions formed a new nexus for tying the center to the province, one routinized by the stipulations of their founders and overseen from Istanbul.[86]

Alongside their growing economic marginalization, the cultural and intellectual influence of Arab elites diminished as well. As we saw in Chapter 5, thanks in part to exchanges with men like Ghazzi, an expanding cadre of Rumis became conversant with Arabic literature and scholarship. In the long run though, an interest in Arabic scholarship did not require an interest in Arab scholars. Indeed, Arabic-language genres could just as easily be used—and indeed were used—to marginalize Arab scholars. Take the Arabic-language version of the biographical tradition, championed by Taşköprizade. His *Crimson Peonies* reflects the gradual exclusion of Arabophone scholars from the ranks of those associated with the Ottoman dynasty, the subject of his work. In the chapters of his book covering the fourteenth and fifteenth centuries, Taşköprizade featured many Arabs who spent time in Ottoman lands, whether or not they had been born or educated there; he memorialized five scholars from Syria and Egypt who spent time in Ottoman lands during Mehmed II's reign (of a total of sixty-three). By the sixteenth century, such men had all but disappeared from his account; only one (of 113) was mentioned by the

85. Emphasis in the original. Repp, *The Müfti of Istanbul*, 28.

86. Singer, *Beneficence*; Kafescioğlu, "'Image of Rūm,'" 78; Van Leeuwen, *Waqfs and Urban Structures*, chapter 3. For Egypt, see Behrens-Abouseif, *Egypt's Adjustment*.

time of Süleyman (1520–66), despite the torrent of Arab scholars hoping to find patronage in the capital.[87]

The great Rumi scholar Kınalızade ʿAli, curious about and respectful of the intellectual pursuits of Damascene scholars though he was, engaged in a similar exercise in the related genre of genealogies (*tabaqat*). This genre, which compiled biographies in such a way as to emphasize chains of transmission, also had its origins in the Arab lands.[88] The selection criterion Kınalızade applied in his work *The Generations of the Hanafi School* (*Tabaqat al-hanafiyya*), finished in 1558/9, was not affiliation with the Ottoman state but rather membership in the Hanafi legal school. Still, his genealogy followed largely the same trajectory as Taşköprizade's. Kınalızade began with Abu Hanifa (d. 767), the eighth-century founder of the Hanafi school in Kufa (today's Iraq), and ended with Kemalpaşazade (d. 1534), the influential Ottoman chief mufti. Many of the fourteenth- and early fifteenth-century jurists whom Kınalızade included in his book had worked in Mamluk centers of learning. By the second half of the fifteenth century, in contrast, almost all of the jurists listed were "of the learned men of Rum," to the exclusion of their counterparts in Arab domains—despite the fact that there continued to be prominent Hanafis who lived and worked there.[89] As Guy Burak has argued, this helped Kınalızade consolidate the authority of Ottoman scholars within the Hanafi school.[90] As with all canons though, this one relied on an act of selection. As sixteenth-century scholars aimed to establish intellectual genealogies commensurate with their world empire, they assimilated the intellectual heritage of the Arab provinces while excluding their Arab contemporaries.

Perhaps the most significant development behind the waning cultural influence of Arab scholars in the later sixteenth century was the precipitous rise in the status of Turkish.[91] As we saw, at the turn of the sixteenth century the language had enjoyed a status beneath that of Arabic or

87. Ökten, "Scholars and Mobility," 60, 64. Guy Burak has argued that this was part of an effort by Ottoman scholars to secure their position within the imperial hierarchy in the wake of imperial expansion. Burak, *Islamic Law*, 94–8.

88. Burak, *Islamic Law*, 118–9.

89. Ḳınalīzāde ʿAlī, *Ṭabaqāt*, 3: 15–54 vs. 65, 70–1, 74; Burak, *Islamic Law*, 77–8. A later work in the same genre by Süleyman Kefevi (d. 1582) follows a similar narrative strategy. Burak, *Islamic Law*, 80–8.

90. Burak, *Islamic Law*, 74–80.

91. Woodhead, "Ottoman Languages;" Darling, "Ottoman Turkish"; Kuru, "The Literature of Rum."

Persian, and still required defending for use in literature. However, the growing imperial muscle behind the language ensured that, by the second half of the sixteenth century, Turkish had taken its place among the languages of Islamic high culture.

These shifts conspired to alter the role of Arab scholars in Ottoman salons. Arab elites struggled to find a role for themselves in the Turkish-language gatherings that were becoming more important and more visible with each passing day. Ottoman biographical dictionaries reflect the growing importance of Istanbul's salon scene. Although early in the century Sehi Bey must have attended gentlemanly gatherings (and probably even collected much of his material there), his *Eight Heavens* rarely mentioned salons.[92] By the time of ʿAşık Çelebi, the biographical dictionary had become a full-fledged celebration of the Ottoman social and literary scene. We can measure the contrast in the successive biographies of İshak Çelebi, the litterateur who served as chief judge in Damascus in 1536–7. Although İshak was a direct contemporary of Sehi, the biographer only describes him briefly, recording İshak's origins in Skopje, his way with words, and a few lines of his poetry. The whole profile is just eleven lines long.[93] The biography written by Latifi about a decade later is more than double the length, and half of it describes İshak's social circle: "His whole life he was the leader of the single men and the chief of the circle of the bons vivants [*rindān*] in the world of bachelors."[94] ʿAşık Çelebi's biography of İshak is even longer and even more interested in his social life: his appointment as a boon companion (*musahib*) of Sultan Selim; his breach of etiquette at the latter's amicable gathering (*meclis-i üns*); the kind of company he kept during his time in Edirne (mostly disreputable types); his love (and then renunciation) of wine; his propensity to chase after young men.[95]

This greater attention to salons reflected a growing cultural confidence in the Ottoman capital. As Istanbul became the principal cultural trendsetter in the empire—or even in the Islamic world writ large—the city's elite and their lifestyles became of general interest as well.[96] At the

92. Many poets Sehi profiled were part of his inner social circle. Kut in Sehī Bey, *Heşt Bihişt*, 7–8.

93. Sehī Bey, *Heşt Bihişt*, 158.

94. Laṭīfī, *Teẕkire-i Laṭīfī*, 90.

95. ʿĀşıḳ Çelebi, *Meşâʿirü's-Şuʿarâ*, 328–41; Andrews and Kalpaklı, *The Age of Beloveds*, 307.

96. Andrews and Kalpaklı see in Aşık Çelebi's work a nostalgia for a bygone "age of beloveds" that was quickly fading in the light of harsh new economic and political realities. Andrews and Kalpaklı, *The Age of Beloveds*, chapter 10.

same time, the focus also reflected salons' increased power. The salon had always been a highly exclusive arena of patronage. However, the concentration of resources in the hands of the centralized elite amplified the salon's gatekeeping functions as growing numbers of aspirants vied for a seat.[97] More than ever, the road to appointments or commissions led through the salons of the powerful.[98]

Arabs, however, were by and large excluded from the assemblies that opened so many doors to those who attended them. As we saw in Chapter 4, Turkish-language salons, like Arabic-language ones, demanded immense literary and linguistic sophistication from participants. If, in the early decades of the sixteenth century, Arab gentlemen found that their mastery of Arabic traditions was a ticket into Ottoman salons, in the later decades this no longer compensated for their insufficient mastery of Turkish. To be sure, a growing number of Arab scholars did learn Turkish, including Hamawi.[99] However, a basic working knowledge of the language was hardly enough to cross the high threshold necessary to participate in literary soirées.[100] This was a direct reversal of the situation in which Rumis previously had found themselves when it came to Arabic-language circles. At a time when salons played an increased role in regulating access to imperial resources, many Arabs found their ability to partake in those salons circumscribed.

All of these shifts in Arab-Rumi relations are visible when we compare Hamawi's experiences with Ghazzi's a few decades earlier. The divergence begins with Hamawi's decision to study in Istanbul. Ghazzi, as we saw, was educated exclusively in Arab lands; so too was Ghazzi's son Ahmad, born in 1528, though he did possess the license from Hacı Çelebi that Ghazzi had obtained on his behalf in Istanbul.[101] By the generation of Hamawi—who was born in 1542—remaining in the provinces

97. Tezcan notes that due to the *mülazemet* system, "despite the high level of institutionalization achieved in the hierarchy of the ulema, the system was, in the final analysis, based on personal relations." Tezcan, "Ottoman *Mevali*," 6. Atçıl suggests that exposure to Ottoman culture determined access to higher-level positions. Atçıl, "Route," 490–1.

98. Mustafa ʿAli narrated attending the salon of Şemsi Pasha, one of Murad III's confidants and host to one of Istanbul's most important literary circles, to seek financial rewards. Fleischer, *Bureaucrat*, 74.

99. Both Hamawi and Nabulusi knew Turkish and Persian. Ghazzī, *Lutf*, 3: 119; Burīnī, *Tarājim*, 2: 68.

100. In the eighteenth century, Arab biographers did not take a knowledge of Turkish for granted. Rafeq, "Relations," 79.

101. For biographies of Ahmad, see Ibn Ayyūb, *Rawḍ*, 45b–48a; Ghazzī, *Kawākib*, 3: 100–9. Others of Ahmad's generation did already study in the center, e.g., Akmal al-Din Ibn Muflih (d. 1603). Blackburn in Nahrawālī, *Journey*, 60n162.

was hardly an option for a young scholar of ambition. Though local students still completed much or even most of their education in Syria, they eventually "followed the path of the Rumis" (*salaka ṭarīq al-arwām*), as contemporary Arab writers put it, spending a few months or years not merely socializing in the capital as Ghazzi had but studying there as well.[102] When ʿAşık Çelebi began writing his supplement to Taşköprizade's *Crimson Peonies* in the 1560s, it was perhaps hyperbolic but not entirely untrue to say that,

> because of the multitude of its scholars, the plenty of its learned men, its promise for the future, its capacity to exercise legal judgment, its esteem from all sides, its travelers from distant lands, and its students from every fortress and castle in all corners of the earth, Rum became the destination of students, the goal of seekers, the endpoint of travels, and a model for all. Riders are drawn to it from east and west to realize their desires and aims, [since] it outdoes all other countries in its ranks and positions. The kingdom of Rum has been the goal and the hope of the Arab and Persian scholars, who sometimes find protection in it from the oppression of foreigners [*aʿjām*], purifying their hearts and their minds; and sometimes coteries of Arabs come there to be educated and achieve their goals.[103]

By the eighteenth century, a third of Damascene scholars were educated at least in part in Istanbul, compared to a mere eight percent that went to Egypt for the same purpose.[104]

Hamawi's conversion to the Hanafi legal school from his original affiliation as a Shafiʿi is also reflective of these larger shifts in power dynamics. The Hanafi legal school served as a key instrument through which the central Ottoman elite exerted closer control over the empire's legal establishment.[105] Rather than force Arab scholars—who were rarely Hanafi—into the fold, the Ottoman elite simply provided incentives for them to join it by creating a growing number of positions available only to members of that legal school.[106] The effort worked, and, as Abdul-Karim Rafeq has shown through the example of towns in today's Palestine, the number of

102. This was especially common among Hanafis. Burak, *Islamic Law*, 114; Winter, "*Ashrāf*," 147–8; Rafeq, "Relations," 76.

103. ʿĀşıḳ Çelebi, *Dhayl*, 36. ʿAşık Çelebi continued working on his *Dhayl* until the year of his death in 1572. Barakāt in ʿĀşıḳ Çelebi, *Dhayl*, 30.

104. Thirty-four percent by Rafeq's count. Rafeq, "Relations," 76–7.

105. Burak, *Islamic Law*.

106. Masters, *Arabs*, 63–5; Elger, *Glaube*, 78; Winter, "Ottoman Qāḍīs," 101; Hathaway, *Beshir Agha*, 98–9.

Syrian scholars who adhered to the Hanafi school increased drastically from six percent in the late sixteenth century to over half in the late seventeenth.[107] The decision to do so was often a matter of convenience. Ghazzi's son Najm al-Din—who, like his father, always remained Shafiʿi—claimed that even after Hamawi's conversion, his heart stayed with the Shafiʿis. (Hamawi's great-grandson Muhibbi, who drew in part on Ghazzi's work, repeated this claim.[108])

The new state of affairs in the empire manifests most clearly in Hamawi's growing difficulties in securing a position—this in spite of all the precautions he had taken to make himself as employable as possible. The first part of Hamawi's travel account, which describes the events of the early 1570s, features him sailing smoothly from one provincial post to the next. After Maʿlulzade removed him from office in 1573, his situation worsened considerably. Hamawi spent more than a year in the Ottoman capital seeking to cajole Maʿlulzade into offering him a new position amidst a rising tide of internal despair: "It has been a year or more that I have persevered, since the door of generosity was shut to me. My sleep has been severely strained, as for my patience: it is all but feigned."[109] Even Hamawi's staunchest supporter Çivizade could not rectify the situation, in spite of Hamawi's letters beseeching him for support.

The declining soft power enjoyed by Arabs was reflected in Hamawi's experience of salons at the imperial center. For Hamawi as for earlier observers, the world of salons acted as a proxy for a man's professional success. He reported with palpable delight that the much-loathed astrologer Hijazi, who had usurped Ghazzi's job, was not well received in the capital city. Hijazi was "not taken into consideration by any of the grandees, and not respected by any of the learned men or local families. Amongst the people he had little visibility, and from them he won no agreement or amiability."[110] When Hijazi finally secured a meeting with the grand vizier, it lasted just moments. Ostracized and underappreciated, Hijazi departed, never to return.[111] However, Hamawi himself appears to have been only marginally more successful in gaining access to the local elite. Although he mentions attending the salons of the high-ranking men (*majalis*

107. Rafeq calculates that of those local scholars who died in the sixteenth and early seventeenth centuries, 85% were Shafiʿi and 6% Hanafi; by the end of the seventeenth century, 38% were Shafiʿi and 53% Hanafi. Rafeq, "Relations," 68–9.

108. Ghazzī, *Luṭf*, 3: 115; Muḥibbī, *Khulāṣa*, 323.

109. Ḥamawī, *Bawādī*, 187a.

110. Ḥamawī, *Bawādī*, 180a.

111. Ḥamawī, *Bawādī*, 180b.

al-mawali), he only offered the details of one such salon. Though it is difficult to make an argument out of silence, this does stand in sharp contrast to the detailed accounts of myriad assemblies that featured in part one of his account.[112] In any case, he failed with the one who mattered most, Maʿlulzade. Hamawi's strategy was simple enough: visit Maʿlulzade until he received what he wanted. "I kept returning to his house and kept being passed over until I left," Hamawi complained.[113] This went on for months. "Although I knew him, my situation worsened and I was treated like a stranger at his door; for nearly a year I've been stuck at his doorstep with nothing to do but beg and implore."[114] This protracted humiliation was a far cry from Ghazzi's swift and frictionless access to the sitting rooms of multiple members of the imperial divan in 1530–1.

Most redolent of the new power relations between Arabs and Rumis was Hamawi's self-abasement. When Ghazzi approached the vizier Ayas Pasha for help in finding a job in 1530, he did so as an old friend. Unequal as their stations were, their meetings were characterized by mutual respect and reciprocity. Forty years later, when Hamawi approached Maʿlulzade (who did not have the rank of a vizier), he was literally forced to grovel: "I prostrated myself in front of him, bowing and kissing the ground in front of him."[115] When the judge, in his contempt, did not acknowledge Hamawi's presence at all, "I departed like a falcon smarting from the sting, and hid my head under the cover of my wing."[116] Good relations, so Hamawi believed, depended on heightened deference, so when all else failed he began to "exhibit towards him complete submission and subjugation [*al-takhaḍḍaʿ wa-l-istirqāq*], so that perhaps he would express some sympathy or display some courtesy."[117] Instead, Hamawi finally realized, the more he abased himself, the more Maʿlulzade held him in contempt.[118] This desperate pleading—which occupies dozens of pages of Hamawi's travel account—simply has no parallel in Ghazzi's earlier narrative.

Hamawi's educational and professional experiences bring into sharp relief just how much the 1570s differed from earlier decades. To achieve

112. Hamawi does show immense interest in the affairs of the imperial elite, documenting various appointments, dismissals, and deaths. He mainly appears to have had contact with them through letters or, in one case, through a chance encounter on the street. For the latter, see Ḥamawī, *Bawādī*, 179b.

113. Ḥamawī, *Bawādī*, 160a.

114. Ḥamawī, *Bawādī*, 173a.

115. Ḥamawī, *Bawādī*, 160a.

116. Ḥamawī, *Bawādī*, 160a.

117. Ḥamawī, *Bawādī*, 162a.

118. Ḥamawī, *Bawādī*, 173a.

only a fraction of what Ghazzi achieved, Hamawi had to spend more time in the capital, make more intellectual concessions, and perform more emotional labor. To be sure, Hamawi did not enjoy Ghazzi's wealth and privilege, and some of the differences between their experiences surely can be traced to the positions from which they started. Still, the overall conditions in the empire had converged in such a way as to make life for Arab scholars considerably more difficult than it had once been.

A New Bitterness

With the slow erosion in the status of Arab elites, a sense of disillusionment set in among many. The new bitterness many felt is reflected in the tone of Hamawi's travel narrative, especially its second part. Like many of his contemporaries, Hamawi thought that he lived in a degenerate era when the learned were not sufficiently appreciated. Like a few of his peers, he began to interpret the inequities of his age in ethnic terms.

The charge that things were getting worse was not new. In the 1530s, Ghazzi pointed out what he saw as buildings or beliefs in a state of disrepair.[119] However, by and large, Ghazzi did not see his era as degraded, unfair, or corrupt, even though he watched the empire in which he had grown up stumble and fall.[120] Hamawi's travelogue, by contrast, featured such complaints with ever greater frequency as time progressed.[121] Hamawi announced his intentions at the very outset of the account's second half. In addition to describing his experiences and some daily occurrences, the work "included some complaints of our time, and addressed the pain of the scholars who are always last in line, as well as my sorrow about the misfortunes of the literati, who are unable to achieve the aims of that body."[122] This grief likely gave the book its lachrymose name: *The Nomads of the Crimson Tears in the Valley of the Rumi Lands* (*Bawadi al-dumuʿ al-ʿandamiyya bi-wadi al-diyar al-rumiyya*).

Compared to the first half of the travel account, the second half was characterized by an increasingly embittered tone. The more time Hamawi spent seeking and failing to retrieve his position, the more poisoned his outlook became, until he ultimately targeted Maʿlulzade himself. Having presented to the military judge a battery of praise poems and even a few

119. Elger, *Glaube*, 33–5.

120. For one exception, see Elger, *Glaube*, 105.

121. Ḥamawī, *Ḥādī*, 57, 61–2, 96; Ḥamawī, *Bawādī*, 160b, 163b, 173b, 177a; Elger, *Glaube*, 104–6.

122. Ḥamawī, *Ḥādī*, 96; Ḥamawī, *Bawādī*, 157a.

scholarly treatises, all to no avail, Hamawi gave up: "It became clear to me that in praising him I was just wasting my time, and I regretted expending effort addressing someone so asinine."[123] In his disappointment, Hamawi explained, "I saw that he was harsh and callous [*faẓẓan ghalīẓan*]," making reference to a Qurʾanic verse exhorting the faithful to be kind to one another (Q3:159).[124] By the end of the account, Hamawi was citing cruel epigrams marking the date of Maʿlulzade's accession as chief military judge.

May God fight Ibn Maʿlul
For his foolishness, his hatred for the brilliant,
And his ignorant nature.
Thus his date was "qadi of the ignorant."[125]

Using the Arabic alphanumerical system, the phrase "qadi of the ignorant" added up to 981, or 1573, the year of Maʿlulzade's appointment.

Occasionally, Hamawi formulated his frustrations using ethnically charged language. The man Maʿlulzade had appointed in his stead, it just so happened, was an ignorant Turcoman (*jahil turkmani*).[126] The pastoralist Turcomans had been the founding seed for the Ottoman state, and many sixteenth-century elites were their direct descendents. However, since then, many Turcomans had been transitioning into a more sedentary lifestyle, and many of their descendants began to distance themselves from their tribal roots.[127] Hamawi capitalized on popular perceptions of this group as being coarse and uneducated to discredit his opponent (and, by association, the man who had appointed him).[128] As far as Hamawi was concerned, this Turcoman judge—unnamed throughout—could not be outdone in terms of ignorance. One of Hamawi's friends in Istanbul "knew this ignoramus from head to toe," and recounted that when the said judge was serving in a village near Istanbul and got in a tussle with one of the local lords, he arrived in the capital to seek justice caked in three-day-old blood—not knowing that this evidence was not permissible in an Islamic court. The blood, then, Hamawi fumed, "was proof only of

123. Ḥamawī, *Bawādī*, 166a.
124. Ḥamawī, *Bawādī*, 165b.
125. Ḥamawī, *Bawādī*, 185a.
126. Ḥamawī, *Bawādī*, 173b.
127. Antov, *Wild West*, esp. 3–4; İnalcık, "The Yörüks"; Mengüç, "*Türk*"; Kasaba, *Moveable Empire*; Yıldırım, "Turkomans," chapter 3; İnalcık and Quataert, *Ottoman Empire*, 34–43.
128. Yıldırım, "Turkomans," 136–8; Kafadar, "Rome," esp. 11.

his ignorance and evidence for his stupidity, impiety, and lack of sense."[129] Nor did the Turcoman know basic Arabic: "He was well known by all for his ignorant folly, so much so that at the salon of a notability, one of the learned judges told me that he wrote *ʿAlī* with a hamza, that is, *Alī*."[130] This remark unsubtly drew attention to the judge's Turkish-language background, since Rumis did not pronounce the name ʿAli with the guttural *ʿayn* sound that characterized its Arabic pronunciation.

Hamawi's scorn for his Turcoman rival should not be mistaken for general anti-Turkishness, as his understanding of ethnicity—like that of his contemporaries—turned not only on a linguistic, but also on a social axis. Turcomans were seen as altogether distinct from the refined Rumis with whom Hamawi regularly associated and who constituted a potential audience for his work. After all, "Rumi" designated not simply members of a particular ethnic group, but of a sociocultural one, namely those socialized in and around urban centers.[131] In fact, in the last decades of the sixteenth century, Rumis themselves were decrying what they saw as the Turcoman infiltration of certain posts.[132] By denigrating Turcomen, Hamawi was engratiating himself with the Rumi elite, not alienating it.

Although Hamawi's understanding of what we would today call "Arabs" was equally stratified, on occasion he did reflect on what he viewed as their collective fate. As we have seen, Hamawi was more likely to deprecate his fellow Arabs than extol them, not only the Egyptian student on his donkey but also his fellow small-town judges. However, he did sometimes refer to Arabs as a collective. In one passage, he lamented the treatment of "the sons of the Arabs" (*abna᾽ al-ʿarab*), a category in which he counted himself. Writing to Maʿlulzade early on in his quest, he struck a hopeful tone: Why had he been treated differently from others of "the group of people who are the sons of the Arabs" (*ahl al-jins abnā᾽ al-ʿarab*)? After all, these enjoyed the favor of Maʿlulzade and his contemporaries.[133] In other passages, he was less optimistic. After describing one hopelessly inept Arabic-speaking judge in Damanhour, Hamawi remarked, "I regretted the

129. Ḥamawī, *Bawādī*, 160b. Hamawi's friend and informant on this matter was Baha᾽eddinzade, probably the following: Tamīmī, *Ṭabaqāt*, 4: 180–1. Normally plaintiffs could prove their claims only through witnesses or the admission of guilt by the defendant. Peters, *Crime*, 12–6.

130. Ḥamawī, *Bawādī*, 160b.

131. Kafadar, "Rome," 11.

132. Fleischer, *Bureaucrat*, 155–6, 256n7.

133. Ḥamawī, *Bawādī*, 163b.

declining fortune of the Arabs [*naqṣ haẓẓ abnāʾ al-ʿarab*]."[134] Whereas Ghazzi had positioned himself as largely blind to ethnic difference, by the time of Hamawi ethnicity was becoming an increasingly salient category through which social relations were understood.

Hamawi's ethnic polemic was intermittent, and carefully calculated not to ruffle the wrong feathers; however, it presaged a larger discursive shift that would ultimately end with the rampant interethnic disputes that shook the empire in the seventeenth and eighteenth centuries. There is no doubt that contemporaries had always perceived humankind as divided by ethnicity; different groups had different characteristics, and this was the most natural thing in the world.[135] However, beginning in the later sixteenth century, group affiliations seem to have become the basis for vituperative quarrels over everything from resources to ideas. Starting in the late 1560s, Egypt saw an increasing number of disputes between the local Arab military forces and Rumi ones, framed in those terms. After the latter's salaries were cut, they responded by demanding that the salaries of the Arab soldiers be slashed instead. Several similar conflicts followed, and by the 1620s, the term "sons of the Arabs" was increasingly used by Rumis to signify inferiority.[136]

Some Arab writers responded to such developments with full-fledged arguments for the intrinsic superiority of Arabs. Perhaps the most famous intellectual who engaged in this sort of polemic was ʿAbd al-Ghani al-Nabulusi (d. 1731), the great-grandson of Ghazzi's colleague and salon guest Ismaʿil.[137] In an essay of 1692 that offered a "Response to the Ignorant and Stubborn Rumi," Nabulusi rebuked "the uncivilized and sinister man" who had dared to challenge him on a technical point in theology despite being a member of an inferior ethnic group.[138] Nabulusi's rebuttal relied upon the work of an earlier author—the Damascus-based scholar Najm al-Din al-Ghazzi, youngest son of our Badr al-Din. In the earlier part of the seventeenth century, Najm al-Din had written an essay in which he enlisted prophetic traditions to demonstrate the primacy of Arabs over

134. Ḥamawī, *Ḥādī*, 70.

135. Far more research deserves to be done on this topic. Karateke et al., *Disliking Others*; Tezcan, "Ethnicity"; Tezcan, "Dispelling"; Haarmann, "Ideology."

136. Hathaway, "*Evlâd-i ʿArab*," esp. 213; Winter, "Egypt and Syria," 50–2.

137. Tamari, "National Consciousness"; Winter, "Polemical Treatise." For other examples, see Masters, *Arabs*, 111–2; Baer, "Egyptian Attitudes."

138. Tamari, "National Consciousness," 313.

other ethnic groups. Arabs, Najm al-Din maintained, were distinguished not only by their spirituality, but their speech and intellect:

> The more one's speech is clear and understood, the stronger one's intellect and the wiser one is. There is no doubt that the Arabs are the most eloquent of the peoples and that of all languages their language allows for the finest distinctions between meanings.[139]

That eloquence was prized was nothing new, as we have seen throughout this book. What was new was that Najm al-Din portrayed eloquence as characteristic of a single ethnic group. So too, by the end of the seventeenth century, was the prevailing tone. Nabulusi dispensed with all pretense of civility: if all that Arabs spoke turned to gold, for the Rumi in question, "if he spat, wine would come out of his mouth."[140] Would Ghazzi senior, ever the defender of a united Islamic world, have been dismayed to know that the hadiths he had transmitted to his son were being employed to such polemical ends? Perhaps. But times had changed.

Conclusion

By the late sixteenth century, the social world of Ottoman elites was more integrated than ever before. Rumis traveled to Arab lands as frequently as Arabs traveled to Anatolia. Building upon a common set of literary and historical references, many palace-trained Rumis could communicate effortlessly with provincial scholars from Hama or Jerusalem. More Rumis than ever before spoke sophisticated Arabic; more Arabs than ever before knew some Turkish. Both the general forms of elite sociability and their particular expression had come to be shared across vast portions of the empire.

All this eased communication across the imperial domain. We saw in Chapter 5 how quickly scholarly knowledge circulated. The same thing held for information of a more mundane sort regarding the conditions in particular locales or the performance of particular officeholders. As is well known, the health of early modern states relied on their ability to collect and move information.[141] In the Ottoman case, political communication was guaranteed not just through official channels like imperial edicts, but by a dense web of salons united by a common conversation culture.

139. Ghazzi as quoted in Tamari, "National Consciousness," 316.
140. Nabulusi as quoted in Winter, "Polemical Treatise," 94.
141. Ghobrial, *The Whispers of Cities*; Gürkan, "Espionage"; De Vivo, *Information*.

Underpinning this imperial system were sprawling networks of mutual obligation. Patronage had long been a key organizing principle in the Islamic world, just as it was in other premodern societies. However, what was remarkable in the Ottoman context of the later sixteenth century was that patronage networks routinely crossed the lines of ethnicity and spanned the entirety of the empire. In the 1530s, Ghazzi still had to go to Istanbul to lobby for an appointment. By the 1570s, this was no longer necessary; when he was removed from his position at the Taqawiyya, he simply had to wait for his man in Istanbul to be named military judge for the position to be restored.

Salons had a significant role to play in helping both to establish and to maintain such patronage relations—and, sometimes, in making them break down. Just how seriously contemporaries took salons can be seen from the fact that Hamawi expected Maʿlulzade to promote him simply on the basis of a single, congenial evening. Though this expectation turned out to be illusory, Hamawi's strategy in Istanbul—to claim the position he felt he was owed—still led through Maʿlulzade's salon. However, as Hamawi came to feel all too painfully, if salons could expand to include new populations, they could also contract to exclude them. Although high-ranking Rumis continued to participate in Arabic-language gentlemanly circles, Arabs did not enjoy the same access to Turkish-language gatherings. As the sixteenth century progressed, salons led by Rumis increasingly served to regulate and indeed limit elite Arabs' access to resources.

As Hamawi's repeated failures suggest, by the later sixteenth century many Arabs had come to play only a marginal role in the empire's affairs. With the routinization of Ottoman governance, Ottoman officials came to rely far less heavily on the informal support of Arab elites than they once had. Likewise, with the maturation of the Ottoman intellectual tradition, Ottoman scholars demonstrated less interest in the particular expertise of Arabs. By the middle of the century, the Ottoman educational system was as self-sufficient, confident, and competitive as the Mamluk learned hierarchy had been on the eve of the conquest. In some ways, Arab scholars had become victims of their own success. When ʿAbbasi and Ghazzi arrived in Istanbul in first third of the sixteenth century, they were welcomed as respected representatives of a venerable scholarly tradition. When Hamawi arrived in the last third, he was received as one more provincial scholar in need of a position.

This is not to say that Arabs were fully excluded from the workings of empire or that they played no role in intellectual or political life at the turn of the seventeenth century.[142] For one, Hamawi's fortunes increased swiftly after Çivizade was appointed military judge—and held, too. The appointment in Homs that Çivizade had helped him to secure was followed by a sequence of other judgeships in Greater Syria, just as Hamawi had always wanted.[143] In 1585, Hamawi finally settled in Damascus, working as a deputy judge in one of the city's main courts for several years before ultimately landing in the influential position of judge of the annual pilgrimage caravan to Mecca.[144] He taught at a number of madrasas, was appointed the city's Hanafi mufti, and frequently served as interim chief judge until the arrival of a new appointee.[145] Through Hamawi's union with the daughter of Isma'il al-Nabulusi, he helped sire an esteemed scholarly lineage that would survive into the eighteenth century and whose most celebrated member is the historian Muhammad Amin al-Muhibbi (d. 1699). These later generations would go on to enjoy unprecedented levels of local autonomy.

Yet these later generations would also engage in increasing interethnic polemic. Though Hamawi hinted at such a worldview, he would have never attacked Rumis wholesale, if only because his future depended on them. The more direct and virulent confrontations of the seventeenth century have often been taken as representative of the relationship between Arabs and Rumis (or even Arabs and Turks) writ large. The evidence presented in this book suggests that those polemics were the product of a historical development. For the better part of the sixteenth century, Arab and Rumi elites more often than not confronted one another with great courtesy, as members of a single Muslim community.

One of the last gatherings that Ghazzi attended was his eldest son's funeral. A kindly and withdrawn man, in the last years of his life Shihab al-Din Ahmad was plagued by migraines, so much so that he could not eat, and thus became emaciated and gaunt. So when a physician paid an unannounced visit to Ghazzi senior early one morning, he merely had to quote the Qur'an: "To God We belong, and to Him we return" (Q2:156). Ghazzi replied, "Shihab al-Din died?" "Yes," the doctor responded. Ghazzi said, "Have a grave dug for him close to his grandfather's, and have another one dug for me, for I will join him soon." And he turned away and wept.[146]

142. Shafir, "Road," esp. chapter 3; El-Rouayheb, *Intellectual History*; Akkach, *Nabulusi*; El-Rouayheb, "Opening."

143. Muḥibbī, *Khulāṣa*, 3: 327.

144. Muḥibbī, *Khulāṣa*, 3: 327; Winter, "Ottoman Qāḍīs," 102.

145. Muḥibbī, *Khulāṣa*, 3: 327.

146. Ibn Ayyūb, *Kitāb*, 16–7.

The funeral of Ghazzi's son was one for the history books. Judges, grandees, Sufis, ascetics—everyone came out to mourn the passing of a member of one of Damascus's most prominent scholarly families. A sea of men flooded the Great Mosque to honor the deceased, with his father at their head serving as imam. Together they kneeled, in unison, and stood. The throng carried the bier out to the grave where Ghazzi's father Radi al-Din already rested, and where Ghazzi knew that he himself soon would.

And so it was. Not a year passed but Ghazzi followed his son into the afterlife.[147] Everyone said that there had never been a funeral like it in Damascus, other than that of his son Ahmad. As the pallbearers carried Ghazzi to the family grave, a group of green birds lingered over the procession, protecting it. People said that they were angels, and indeed it seemed that it must have been so, for when they reached the summit by the burial tomb, the birds shaded the funeral cortege with clouds and showered it with a blessed rain.[148] The full moon of Damascus had finally set, his tongue laid to a firm, permanent rest. Yet his words and works lived on in all of the Ottoman scholars with whom he had, at one time or another, sat.

147. Ibn Ayyūb, *Kitāb*, 14.
148. Ghazzī, *Kawākib*, 3:10.

Conclusion

SALONS LAY AT THE HEART of early modern Ottoman politics, society, and culture. Bequeathed to the empire by previous generations, informal gatherings had long propelled ideas and culture across the Islamic ecumene. Long before the conquest of Greater Syria, Egypt, and the Arabian Peninsula in 1516–7—and long after—salons connected Ottoman inhabitants to the Islamic world at large. At the same time, although salons often served to soften political divides, they also reinforced the boundaries of the Ottoman polity: because salon culture relied upon domestic patterns of travel and patronage, the most regular and intense interactions occurred within imperial confines rather than across them.

As a result, salons were inseparable from the workings of empire. They aided political decision-making by providing spaces where men could negotiate and build alliances. They underpinned patronage networks, often informing decisions to commission books or to make appointments later confirmed in more formal arenas. Finally, salons facilitated the circulation of information and ideas, providing communication channels that ran in parallel to official ones. In all of these ways, salons helped the vast imperial domains to cohere.

Salons gained special significance in the era of imperial expansion, when they helped to integrate newly conquered populations into the Ottoman social and political world. Because the elite inhabitants of Syria and Egypt shared with Rumis from the central lands a basic conception of polite culture, salons performed this role especially effectively during the initial incorporation of these territories. Provincial elites were by and large excluded from the highest rungs of the imperial administration, but salons granted them the opportunity to participate informally in the workings of empire. In Damascus, Arab elites offered counsel and lobbied on behalf of local interests; in Istanbul, they offered advice on the qualifications of potential appointees. It was the indeterminate nature of salons that allowed for such involvement. The flexibility of salon conversation could be exploited to voice political opinions, its ambiguity of purpose to solicit appointments. Paying heed to informal occasions allows us to recognize that Arabs participated in the imperial project from the first moment they joined it, despite the fact that their involvement often flew under the radar of official documentation.

By drawing our attention to informal mechanisms of rule, salons afford a more capacious understanding of sixteenth-century Ottoman governance than has hitherto been common. Although studies of the seventeenth and eighteenth centuries have increasingly highlighted the variety of relationships that helped to sustain the Ottoman imperial order, understandings of sixteenth-century Ottoman statecraft often privilege formal institutions, especially the bureaucracy. Salons remind us that even in this period of remarkably centralized state control, political stability relied on "soft power," that is, on informal networks, shared norms, and common practices that encouraged cooperation and made social relations more predictable. This aligns with the workings of the Ottoman Empire's Eurasian contemporaries, and even with that supposed bastion of early modern absolutism, seventeenth-century France, where offices were distributed by royal favor and the bureaucracy was viewed as the personal property of elites.[1] Across the early modern world, just as administrative structures were forming, states continued to govern through households and patronage. In the Ottoman case, a focus on sixteenth-century salons reveals that the growing informality of governance in the seventeenth and eighteenth centuries was a shift in intensity, not in kind.

Whatever political role Arab elites might have enjoyed in early Ottoman salons, their power was greatest in the field of culture. Throughout the first half of the sixteenth century, the prestige of the Arabic language and the international acclaim of Mamluk scholarship earned individuals trained in Egypt and Syria the high regard of the Ottoman elite. Arabic speakers shone particularly brightly in gentlemanly conversation, which put a premium on eloquence and on displays of poetic virtuosity and scholarly knowledge. Salons allowed educated Arabs to acquire authority in the eyes of Ottoman audiences in an immediate and conspicuous way.

The prestige of Arabic culture was such that, at times, salons witnessed an inversion of the power relations that one might expect to obtain

1. Soll, *Information Master*, 29; Duindam, *Myths of Power*; Mettam, *Power and Faction*.

between conquerors and conquered. To be sure, Turcophone officials from the central lands took advantage of informal gatherings to wield power over provincial elites, flexing their imperial muscle by conferring or withholding material support. Still, focusing solely on state-sanctioned power elides the far more complex configurations of authority that face-to-face encounters engendered. Knowledge, eloquence, and piety each generated their own social hierarchies, hierarchies that existed alongside and sometimes in tension with the grades of official rank. In these domains, Arab elites sometimes outperformed their Rumi colleagues, especially in the early decades of the sixteenth century. Modern historians have often assumed that Arabs gained visibility in the Ottoman Empire only after the late seventeenth century, when the grip of the central state weakened and the provinces gained more leverage. The evidence compiled here suggests instead that Arab elites enjoyed considerable influence already in the earliest phases of the incorporation, at least in the social and cultural spheres.

Doubtless, the informal nature of the authority wielded by Arab elites had its drawbacks. Because it was not institutionalized, this power could be withdrawn as quickly as it had been granted. When the economy contracted at the end of the sixteenth century, and the number of available posts diminished, Arab scholars, like Rumi scholars educated outside the imperial center, saw their status and their employment options dwindle. As Rumis increasingly absorbed Arabic culture and transformed Turkish into a prestige language in its own right, educated Arabs struggled to maintain their former relevance.

Even so, by the end of the sixteenth century, decades of intense and sustained exchanges with Arabs had left an irreversible mark on Ottoman culture. Across the imperial domains, Arabic enjoyed greater currency than it had in earlier centuries, and the genres it had inspired remained influential for hundreds of years, all the way into the twilight of empire in the early twentieth century. Far more work has to be done before we can appreciate fully how Ottomans adopted and adapted the Arabic literary tradition. Nonetheless, it is clear that the openness of learned elites to new ideas led to the remarkable fusion of traditions so characteristic of, and indeed unique to, Ottoman culture.

The influence of Arab culture also underpinned one final social and cultural development in Ottoman lands, namely the growing attention to Islamic orthodoxy. The sixteenth century, especially its second half, has long been understood as a time in which various actors began to intensify their efforts to police religious belief and practice, a process recently referred to as "confessionalization" or "Sunnitization."[2] Modern scholars have often described this shift as resulting from a strategic effort led by Istanbul, as officials sought to oppose the threat of the neighboring Safavids, who professed Shiite Islam. No doubt this imperial rivalry pushed the Ottomans toward a more self-consciously Sunni political idiom. Still, the evidence presented here suggests that the transformation also had a distinct, internal cause, namely the intensified engagement of Ottoman elites with Syrian and Egyptian scholarship, a traditional bulwark of Sunni orthodoxy. As Rumi scholars spent more time with their Arab colleagues and absorbed new parts of the Islamic literary tradition, they also assimilated some of its pietistic vocabulary and concerns. As seen from the salon, this newfound confessionalism resulted not only from a coordinated program led by officials in Istanbul, but also from the diffuse and often informal influence of Arab scholars.[3]

As important as salons were to the functioning of empire and religion, they were also social institutions worth examining in their own right. Early modern men—and, as future research will hopefully show, women—spent a significant portion of their lives visiting and conversing with one another. Often enough, this was a means to an end, be that seeking an appointment or convincing a governor not to impose an additional tax. But conversation was also celebrated as an end in itself, as not only an art to be cultivated and a pleasure to be enjoyed, but also as a principal means through which the individual self could emerge. Scholars, judges, and even military men earned respect and advanced their careers not only by writing tracts, issuing judicial verdicts, or leading regiments, but also by delivering poems or debating ideas before an audience of cognoscenti.

In all of these ways, the salon did not merely reflect social relations, it also made them. The salon was not just the place where encounters between elite Arabs and Rumis happened to occur; it was a social matrix whose rules and practices shaped those very encounters. Both in the Arabic gatherings of Damascus and in the Turkish assemblies of Istanbul, the mix of polite parleying and serious discourse that characterized salon conversation set a high bar for participation. As such, salons excluded many whose family background or education had not prepared them for these demands.

2. See especially Krstić and Terzioğlu, *Sunni Islam*; Ivanyi, *Virtue*; Burak, "Faith"; Terzioğlu, "Catechism"; Terzioğlu, "Sunnitization"; Krstić, *Contested Conversions*; Dressler, "Inventing Orthodoxy"; Fleischer, "The Lawgiver as Messiah."

3. Pfeifer, "Hadith Culture."

However much salons contributed to social stratification, within the upper ranks of society they fostered a sense of community. The sociability salons nurtured crossed ethnolinguistic lines and bred feelings of familiarity and even brotherhood among men from different regions. Even so, participating in the salon never required individuals to suspend their ethnic identities; indeed, salons often heightened awareness of such identities. Salon sociability suited the Ottoman model of empire, which showed high tolerance for local diversity: it offered a shared language and social idiom that helped to bridge cultural differences without effacing them.[4]

Recognizing the role salons played in constructing elite identity also helps explain the salon's better-studied counterpart: the coffeehouse. Modern historians have often seen the emergence of Ottoman coffeehouses in the middle of the sixteenth century as effecting a break with traditional forms of sociability. In these accounts, the coffeehouse offered a new kind of social space more open to dialogue and less dominated by religious mores than the mosque or the home.[5] In many ways, salons instead affirm the continuities between domestic and coffeehouse sociability, what with their overlapping architectural features and shared conversational regimes.[6] Nevertheless, coffeehouses did diverge starkly from salons in one key respect: their inclusivity. Coffeehouses accommodated social groups that could never dream of stepping foot in a gentlemanly salon.[7] Indeed, learned critics of the coffeehouse decried the way it allowed non-elites to mimic elite sociability.[8] To be sure, instances of true social mixing across class lines remained rare. Nonetheless, by allowing new social groups to adopt aspects of the elite lifestyle, the coffeehouse did represent a departure from salon culture.

This book has focused on the sixteenth century, but salons remained vital laboratories of politics, culture, and society until the end of the empire. In the late seventeenth and eighteenth centuries, when power shifted away from the imperial palace, salons provided the base from which newly empowered provincial notables could operate. Leading Cairene families began to speak of holding an "open house" (*bayt maftuh*),

4. For this model, see Ágoston, "Flexible Empire."

5. Işın, "Coffeehouses," esp. 206.

6. Mikhail, "Heart's Desire," 146–51; Özkoçak, "Coffeehouses," 976–9; Hattox, *Coffee and Coffeehouses*, 98–100. For social hierarchy, see Artan, "Forms," 383. For hospitality, see Kafadar, "Night," 250. For architecture, see Watenpaugh, *Ottoman City*, 162–3; David, "Café."

7. Kafadar, "Night," 250–1; Özkoçak, "Coffeehouses," 975; Watenpaugh, *Ottoman City*, 164.

8. Mustafa ʿAli, *Description of Cairo*, 37.

which served as a particular mark of their power and influence.[9] At the same time, salons continued to afford coveted spaces for socializing and intellectualizing, especially in the natural-scientific domain.[10] Ottoman salons intersected with an increasingly mobile Islamic community to help form the globalizing sphere that, by the eighteenth century, had coalesced into what Ira Lapidus has called a "world system of Islamic societies."[11]

The importance of Ottoman salons did not abate in the nineteenth and early twentieth centuries, when Ottoman society transformed rapidly under the dual pressures of European hegemony and centralization. In this period, Ottoman salons, which were increasingly described with Francophone terms like *suvare* (from Fr. *soirée*) and *sosyete* (from Fr. *société*), gradually adapted to resemble their French counterparts, accommodating Enlightenment-era philosophy and sometimes admitting women.[12] Still, viewing modern salons from an early modern perspective highlights the continuities with earlier traditions of sociability. Elite gatherings continued to serve educational functions. In the early nineteenth-century Beşiktaş Society (*Beşiktaş Cemʿiyyet-i İlmiyesi*), a salon less formal than its name suggests, senior members offered instruction to younger ones, including many who would go on to play a leading role in the empire's reform project (*tanzimat*).[13] Salons continued to serve as arenas of politics, as suggested by government efforts to shut the same Society down.[14] Despite ongoing attempts to concentrate the administration of justice within the bureaucratized state, domestic gatherings continued to facilitate social mediation, and even hosted sessions of the Islamic court.[15] And, finally, salons retained their importance in generating and circulating ideas. When one considers the pride of place of language and literature at sixteenth-century gatherings, the late Ottoman salon's role in fostering the Arabic literary revival known as the "awakening" (*nahda*) comes

9. Ayalon, "Studies," 293–7.

10. For salons in the seventeenth and eighteenth centuries, see Liebrenz, "Library," 40; Sajdi, *Barber of Damascus*, 21–8; Winter, "*Ashrāf*," 146; Hanna, "Culture in Ottoman Egypt," 98–9; Akkach, *Nabulusi*, 26–9; Grehan, "Power of Words"; Hanna, *In Praise of Books*, 72–6; Reichmuth, "az-Zabīdī," 80; Kafadar, "Self and Others," 141. For the scientific sphere in particular, Reichmuth, "Wissenstransfer"; Tezcan, "Some Thoughts," 147–50; Murphy, "Improving the Mind," 131–2, 148–9; Brömer, "Scientific Practice."

11. Lapidus, *Islamic Societies*, 490. See also Reichmuth, "az-Zabīdī," 67, 83.

12. Hill, *Utopia*, 37–9; Khaldi, "Naḥdah"; Öztürk, "Kitaplar," 137; Strauss, "La Conversation," 284–93.

13. Mardin, *Genesis*, 229–47; Yetiş, "Beşiktaş Cemʿiyyet-i İlmiyyesi."

14. Mardin, *Genesis*, 230–1.

15. For the former, see Fahmy, *In Quest of Justice*; for the latter, see Saßmannshausen, "Reform in Translation," chapter 4.

to seem less surprising.[16] Even the legendary dinner parties of Mustafa Kemal Ataturk, the founder of modern Turkey, where history and politics were discussed and careers made and broken, bore more than a passing resemblance to early modern salons.[17] Reconnecting the nineteenth- and twentieth-century salon to its Ottoman forerunners reinforces the recent insight that Ottoman modernity was shaped not only by European models, but likewise from impulses indigenous to the region.[18] It was the recognizability of the French salon that allowed late Ottomans to embrace the institution so quickly and wholeheartedly.[19]

Despite these continuities, the nineteenth and twentieth centuries saw a growing discomfort with the overlap of social, cultural, and political functions so characteristic of the early modern salon. Increasingly, institutionalization converged with concerns over corruption to prompt the disaggregation of the different activities that had once converged in the salon. Politics moved to formal societies with charters, membership dues, and published transactions.[20] Poetry began its slow exit from everyday life into the separate realm of "literature" (Ar. *adab*, Tur. *edebiyat*).[21] *Majlis*es became what they still are in the Middle East today: parliaments, councils, and committees. Though circles of literati still meet regularly to discuss literature and verse, the fact that these gatherings serve primarily to entertain has caused them to lose much of their urgency. There are plenty of aspects of early modern Ottoman salons whose passage we need not lament, not least their role in buttressing elite, male privilege. Surely, however, we could do with more learning in our political culture and more poetry in our daily lives.

16. Zachs, *Syrian Identity*, 28–38.

17. Mango, *Atatürk*, chapter 26.

18. Anscombe, "Ottoman Reform"; Abu Manneh, "Islamic Roots."

19. Khaldi, "Naḥdah," esp. 263–5.

20. Hill, *Utopia*, chapter 1; Arsan, "Age of Associations." The salon of Mayy Ziyada (d. 1941) was celebrated as a space untainted by party politics. Khaldi, "Naḥdah," 281–2.

21. Petievich, *Assembly of Rivals*.

APPENDIX

Key Figures

ʿAbd al-Rahim al-ʿAbbasi (d. 1555)

No one navigated the Mamluk-Ottoman transition better than ʿAbd al-Rahim al-ʿAbbasi. Born in Cairo in 1463, he went on to become chancery secretary in Damascus and a disciple of Radi al-Din al-Ghazzi, Badr al-Din's father. When ʿAbbasi got mixed up with the wrong crowd in the late fifteenth century, he sought refuge in Istanbul, where he was welcomed by the Ottoman Sultan Bayezid II. After Selim I conquered Egypt and Syria in 1516–7, ʿAbbasi returned with him to Istanbul, where he quickly rose to the highest ranks of the Ottoman imperial elite.

Sharaf al-Din Ibn Ayyub al-Ansari (d. 1592)

Ibn Ayyub al-Ansari was a Damascene judge and socialite. He knew many of the key figures in this book, Rumi and Arab alike, and recorded his impressions of them in his 1590 Arabic-language biographical dictionary *The Sweet-Smelling Garden* (*al-Rawd al-ʿatir*).

Bayezid II (r. 1481–1512)

Sultan Bayezid II enters our story as a childhood friend of Müʾeyyedzade ʿAbdurrahman. He was a lifelong patron of knowledge, including of one work by the Egyptian scholar ʿAbd al-Rahim al-ʿAbbasi. Already in

Amasya, where Bayezid was stationed as a prince, he helped to cultivate a lively salon culture.

ʿAşık Çelebi (d. 1572)

ʿAşık Çelebi was a celebrated poet and scholar. He is most famous today for his 1568 biographical dictionary of Ottoman poets, *The Senses of Poets* (*Meşaʿirü's-şuʿaraʾ*), which describes the salon culture of the imperial elite in and around Istanbul. ʿAşık was also an acquaintance of ʿAbbasi, from whom he heard prophetic accounts (hadith).

Ayas Pasha (d. 1539)

Born into a peasant family in Albania, Ayas Pasha was recruited into palace service as a young boy. He served as commander of the janissary regiments during the Syrian and Egyptian campaigns of 1516–7, and returned to Syria in 1521 to help to quell the revolt of Janbirdi al-Ghazali. While stationed in Damascus, Ayas made friends with the Ghazzi family, a relationship that was rekindled during Badr al-Din's 1530–31 trip to Istanbul.

Hasan al-Burini (d. 1615)

Of humble origin, Hasan al-Burini would go on to become one of Ghazzi's most devoted students and a staple of the Damascus social scene. His Arabic-language biographical dictionary *Biographies of the Notable Men of the Age* (*Tarajim al-aʿyan min abnaʾ al-zaman*) is a record of that scene, attesting to the many elite gatherings that brought Rumis and Arabs together.

Çivizade Mehmed Efendi (d. 1587)

Çivizade Mehmed Efendi was born in Istanbul as the son of the great Hoca Çivizade. He served as chief judge in numerous cities of the Ottoman Empire, including Damascus in 1569. There, he made the acquaintance of Badr al-Din al-Ghazzi, from whom he heard prophetic accounts (hadith). When Çivizade was transferred to Egypt in 1571, he was accompanied by the Syrian scholar Muhibb al-Din al-Hamawi, who made a record of their journey. Though Çivizade would spend most of his adult life in the Ottoman center, he would never forget his obligations to his friends in Damascus.

Ebu's-Su'ud Efendi (d. 1574)

Ebu's-Su'ud was a revered scholar and the influential chief jurisconsult (*şeyhülislam*) during the reign of Sultan Süleyman. He crossed paths with Badr al-Din al-Ghazzi during the latter's visit to Istanbul in 1530–1, and would later help to exonerate him when Ghazzi's Qur'an commentary came under fire.

Fevri Efendi (d. 1571)

At the age of eight or nine, Fevri was captured in war and taken to the Ottoman Empire as a slave. He was educated and passed from elite family to elite family, until he was manumitted and began his own scholarly career. His literary talents caught the attention of Sultan Süleyman, whose poetry anthology Fevri helped to compile. In 1569, Fevri was appointed Hanafi mufti of Damascus, where he met Badr al-Din al-Ghazzi and where he ultimately died.

Badr al-Din al-Ghazzi (d. 1577)

Badr al-Din is the linchpin that holds this book together. Born in 1499 in Damascus, he was educated with the leading lights of Mamluk Cairo before starting his own scholarly career in Damascus at the age of sixteen. In 1530–1, he made a trip to Istanbul, which he described in one of the earliest Arabic-language travel accounts of the city, *Full Moon Rising: Waystations to Rum* (*al-Matali' al-badriyya fi al-manazil al-Rumiyya*). Ghazzi would become one of the most influential scholars of sixteenth-century Damascus, renowned for his exegetical work and sought after for his legal opinions (*fatwas*). He taught many Ottoman officials who spent time in Damascus.

Najm al-Din al-Ghazzi (d. 1651)

Najm al-Din al-Ghazzi was Badr al-Din's youngest and most famous son. Born in 1570, he was just seven when his father passed away. However, he did more than anyone else to preserve his father's legacy, speaking of him frequently in his monumental Arabic-language biographical dictionary of the scholars of the sixteenth century, *The Wandering Stars: The Notables of the Tenth Century* (*al-Kawakib al-sa'ira bi-a'yan al-mi'a al-'ashira*).

Radi al-Din al-Ghazzi (d. 1529)

Radi al-Din al-Ghazzi, Badr al-Din's father, was deputy Shafiʿi judge in Damascus for much of the late Mamluk period and an influential figure in the Qadiri Sufi order. He deftly navigated the transition to Ottoman rule; he quickly regained his position as judge and established close relationships with Ottoman officials.

Muhibb al-Din al-Hamawi (d. 1608)

Muhibb al-Din al-Hamawi was born in 1542 in the Syrian town of Hama. After receiving his earliest education in Syria, he traveled to Istanbul, where he continued his studies and entered the service of Çivizade Mehmed. When Çivizade was posted first to Damascus in 1569 and then to Cairo in 1570, Hamawi went with him. Hamawi left behind a two-part travel account and an expansive letter collection, both of which testify to the intensity of relations that linked Rumi and Arab scholars.

Hasan Bey (d. 1576)

Of German origin, Hasan Bey was captured on the battlefield, enslaved, and sold as a nine-year old to Rüstem Pasha, Süleyman's powerful vizier. Hasan studied with influential scholars at the imperial center before beginning his own career as a scholar and judge. In the 1550s, he served as chief judge in Damascus, becoming a close friend of Badr al-Din al-Ghazzi. He took a great interest in Arab culture and saw to it that his son Ahmed Efendi (d. 1586) would come to excel in the Arabic language and literature.

Kınalızade ʿAli (d. 1572)

Kınalızade ʿAli was one of the most important Ottoman scholars of the sixteenth century. Born in 1510 in Isparta, he held appointments at all the important madrasas in the Ottoman center before embarking on a career as judge. He spent four years in Damascus, becoming an eager student, close friend, and intellectual competitor of Badr al-Din al-Ghazzi.

Hasan Çelebi Kınalızade (d. 1604)

Hasan Çelebi Kınalızade was Kınalızade ʿAli's son and the author of an important Turkish-language biographical dictionary of poets.

Abu al-Fath al-Maliki (d. 1567/8)

Abu al-Fath al-Maliki was born in Tunisia and settled in Damascus as a young man. Once a serious student of Badr al-Din, he soon submitted to the temptations of wine and vernacular poetry, as Ghazzi himself and other historians observed with regret. Still, he managed to hold a career as a respected jurist and mufti. Maliki spent his days in the city's Yalbugha Mosque, where he received guests and delivered legal opinions.

Maʿlulzade Mehmed Efendi (d. 1585)

Maʿlulzade was a much-maligned judge from an important Istanbul learned family. He served as chief judge in a number of key provincial capitals, including Damascus from 1567–9, before becoming chief military judge of Anatolia in 1573. In Damascus, he did not leave behind a favorable impression, and would never forgive Badr al-Din al-Ghazzi for what Maʿlulzade perceived as the scholar's haughtiness.

Müʾeyyedzade ʿAbdurrahman (d. 1516)

Müʾeyyedzade ʿAbdurrahman was from a prominent Sufi family in Amasya with a history of government service. Müʾeyyedzade entered the entourage of prince Bayezid when Bayezid served as governor of Amasya. In the late 1470s, Müʾeyyedzade was forced to flee the city, spending time first in Aleppo and then in Shiraz. After his old friend Bayezid ascended the throne as Bayezid II, Müʾeyyedzade returned to Istanbul, where he acted as military judge and an influential patron of the literati.

Hacı Çelebi Müʾeyyedzade (d. 1538)

Hacı Çelebi was the younger brother of Müʾeyyedzade ʿAbdurrahman and the leader of one of the most important Sufi lodges in Istanbul. Sometime before 1529, he went on the annual hajj pilgrimage to Mecca. Stopping over in Damascus, he was warmly received by the Ghazzi family, and would later return the favor when Badr al-Din traveled to Istanbul.

ʿAlaʾ al-Din al-Shafiʿi (d. 1563)

A one-time student of Badr al-Din al-Ghazzi, ʿAlaʾ al-Din later became his nemesis, criticizing Ghazzi publicly for his rhymed Qurʾanic commentary. At a 1555 salon presided over by the Ottoman chief judge Hasan Bey, ʿAlaʾ al-Din made his distaste for his former teacher public.

Ahmed Taşköprizade (d. 1561)

Taşköprizade was a Bursa-born scholar and author of the first known Ottoman biographical dictionary of scholars, *The Crimson Peonies of the Scholars of the Ottoman State* (*al-Shaqaʾiq al- nuʿmaniyya fi ʿulamaʾ al-dawla al-ʿuthmaniyya*).

GLOSSARY

adab, Tur. edeb Connotes two distinct though interrelated things: first, proper etiquette, and second, literary and polite knowledge.

beylerbeyi Governor-general of a province, with commanding duties in the Ottoman army.

bezm A gathering for eating, conversing, and drinking, often with music and poetry.

diwan, Tur. divan A place for sitting, and by extension, the institutions in which people assembled in such a place; a council. Also, an anthology of poetry.

fatwa, Tur. fetva Nonbinding legal opinion issued by a mufti.

ghazal, Tur. gazel Love poetry, often recited in salons.

hadith, Tur. hadis Reports of the statements or actions of the Prophet Muhammad; an important source for Islamic law.

hajj The annual Islamic pilgrimage to Mecca.

imam A prayer leader, who might also be in charge of a mosque.

iwan, Tur. eyvan A hall open on one side and covered with a barrel vault.

kadıasker Military judge, of which there were two, one with jurisdiction in Anatolia, one in Rumelia. Head of the judiciary and member of the imperial council.

katib al-sirr Head of the chancery, key administrative figure in the Mamluk Sultanate.

khatib, Tur. hatip Preacher who delivers the Friday sermon (*khutba*) in a mosque.

majlis, Tur. meclis Literally "place where one sits," but also any occasion during which people sit together and converse.

mamluk Literally "the one who is owned." A slave, esp. one who plays a military or administrative role. Also refers to the ruling elite of the Mamluk Sultanate (1250–1517).

mawla, Tur. mevla High-ranking Ottoman judges and professors of law.

mufti, Tur. müfti A Muslim jurisconsult competent to issue legal opinions (*fatwas*).

mulazama, Tur. mülazemet Literally "constant companionship," often of the sort that allowed teachers to train advanced students. In the central lands, this was formalized into a system under which leading scholars could sponsor their students for new appointments.

musahib Trusted companion and giver of advice.

nadim, Tur. nedim Trusted friend, advisor, drinking companion.

qa'a Domed structure used as a reception hall in affluent residences. Consists of a lower entrance area and one or more elevated platforms where guests could be seated.

qasida, Tur. kaside Ode of praise.

Qur'an Central religious text of Islam, believed by Muslims to be a revelation from God through the archangel Gabriel (Jibril) to Muhammed.

sahn-ı seman Literally the "eight courtyards," referring to the prestigious eight madrasas in the mosque complex built by Mehmed II in Istanbul.

sayyid, Tur. seyyid One who claims descent from the Prophet Muhammad, an illustrious status that conferred great privilege.

şeyhülislam Chief jurisconsult, the head of the hierarchy of ulema.

shaykh, Tur. şeyh An honorific title given to a religious scholar or tribal head, connoting leadership and nobility. Also used for the leading figure in a Sufi order.

shaykh al-qurra' Qur'an reciter in a mosque.

subaşı Provincial administrator responsible for keeping law and order.

Sufism Path of Islam relying on experiential, mystical means. Sufis belonged to one of many different orders (*tariqas*).

taqriz A book endorsement, usually written by a senior scholar.

tezkire A compilation of biographies of key individuals, often poets.

waqf, Tur. vakıf An Islamic pious endowment.

zawiya, Tur. zaviye A Sufi lodge or small prayer house.

BIBLIOGRAPHY

Unpublished Manuscripts

al-ʿAbbāsī, ʿAbd al-Raḥīm. *Fayḍ al-bārī bi-sharḥ gharīb Saḥīḥ al-Bukhārī*. Süleymaniye Library, MS Hamidiye 299.

———. *Fayḍ al-bārī bi-sharḥ gharīb Saḥīḥ al-Bukhārī*. Süleymaniye Library, MS Ragıp Pasha 299.

———. *Fayḍ al-bārī bi-sharḥ gharīb Saḥīḥ al-Bukhārī*. Süleymaniye Library, MS Atıf Efendi 529.

———. *Kitāb shamārīkh al-jumān fī tārīkh sharīf al-khitān*. Süleymaniye Library, MS Yazma Bağışlar 3801.

———. *Kitāb maʿāhid al-tanṣīṣ*. Süleymaniye Library, MS Yeni Cami 1035.

———. *al-Maqāmāt al-ʿAbbāsiyya*. Süleymaniye Library, MS Reisülkuttab 916.

———. *Nathr al-durr al-thamīn fī ʿurs mawlānā Jaʿfar al-amīn*. Süleymaniye Library, MS Ayasofya 4325.

———. "Uns al-arwāḥ bi-ʿurs al-afrāḥ." Süleymaniye Library, MS Ragıp Paşa 1487, fols. 55b–100a.

ʿĀşıḳ Çelebi. *Meşāʿirüʾs-şuʿarāʾ*. Millet Library Istanbul, MS Ali Emiri Tarih 772.

al-Biqāʿī, Burhān al-Dīn. *ʿUnwān al-zamān bi-tarājim al-shuyūkh wa-l-aqrān*. Süleymaniye Library, MS Fazıl Ahmed Paşa 1119.

al-Burīnī, Ḥasan. *Tarājim al-aʿyān min abnāʾ al-zamān*. Staatsbibliothek zu Berlin, MS Wetzstein II 29.

al-Fāriḍī. "Nukat ʿalā mā waqʿa bayna al-qāḍī ʿAlī Çelebi wa ibn al-shaykh Raḍī al-Dīn." Royal Library of San Lorenzo de El Escorial, Escorial MS 1318, fols. 14b–33a.

Fevrī Efendī, Aḥmed. "Ḥāshiya ʿalā sūrat al-muʾminīn." Princeton University Library, Islamic Manuscripts, Garrett MS 3817Y, fols. 1b–73a.

al-Ghazzī, Badr al-Dīn. "al-Durr al-thāmin fī al-munāqasha bayna Abū Ḥayyān wa-l-Samīn." Süleymaniye Library, MS Mihrişah Sultan 39, fols. 64b–70b.

———. "Ijāza." Kastamonu Public Library, MS 970, fols. 231a–240b.

———. "Kitāb sharḥ al-Burda." Princeton University Library, Islamic Manuscripts, Garrett MS 1148H, fols. 142a–171b.

———. *al-Maṭāliʿ al-badriyya fī al-manāzil al-Rūmiyya*. British Library, MS Or. 3621.

———. *al-Maṭāliʿ al-badriyya fī al-manāzil al-Rūmiyya*. Princeton University Library, Islamic Manuscripts, Garrett MS 610Y, fols. 68b–73b.

———. *al-Maṭāliʿ al-badriyya fī al-manāzil al-Rūmiyya*. Süleymaniye Library, MS Fazıl Ahmed Paşa 1390.

———. *Sharḥ al-Alfiyya li-l-Ghazzī*. Süleymaniye Library, MS Laleli 3265.

———. *Tafsīr li-Badr al-Dīn al-Ghazzī*. Vol. 3. Süleymaniye Library, MS Fatih 632.

———. *al-Tafsīr al-manthūr*. Cadbury Research Library, University of Birmingham, Birmingham, MS Arabic Islamic 1374.

———. *Taqrīb al-maʿāhid fī sharḥ al-shawāhid*. Süleymaniye Library, MS Yeni Cami 1036.

———. *al-Taysīr fī al-tafsīr*. Vols. 1–2. Süleymaniye Library, MSS Ayasofya 98 and 99.

———. *al-Taysīr fī al-tafsīr*. Vols. 2–4. Süleymaniye Library, MSS Yeni Cami 39, 40, and 41.

———. *Taysīr al-bayān fī tafsīr al-Qur'ān*. Vols. 1–11. Süleymaniye Library, MS H. Hüsnü Paşa 11.

———. "Risāla ākhira fī al-muḥākama bayna Abī Ḥayyān wa Tilmīdhihi." Süleymaniye Library, MS Mihrişah Sultan 39, fols. 45b–70b.

———. "al-Zubda fī sharḥ al-Burda." Süleymaniye Library, MS Laleli 3656, 201b–220b.

al-Ghazzī, Raḍī al-Dīn. *al-Jawhar al-farīd fī ādāb al-ṣufī wa-l-murīd*. Princeton University Library, Islamic Manuscripts, Garrett MS 1041H, fols. 2a–44b.

al-Ḥamawī, Muḥibb al-Dīn. *Bawādī al-dumū'al-'andamiyya bi-wādī al-diyār al-Rūmiyya*. Süleymaniye Library, MS Ragıp Paşa 1474.

———. *Majmū'at inshāt* [*sic*] *wa murāsalāt wa adabiyyāt Muḥibb al-Dīn Efendī al-Ḥalabī*. Süleymaniye Library, MS Ragıp Paşa 1475.

———[Muḥibb al-Dīn al-Alwānī]. "al-Sahm al-mu'tariḍ fī qalb al-mu'tariḍ." Süleymaniye Library, MS Kemankeş 240, fols. 69b–78b.

Ibn Ayyūb, Sharaf al-Dīn. *al-Rawḍ al-'āṭir fī mā tayassara min akhbār ahl al-qarn al-sābi' ilā khitām al-qarn al-'āshir*. Staatsbibliothek zu Berlin, MS Wetzstein II 289.

Ḳınalizade, 'Alī. "Risāla fī al-muḥākama bayna Abī Ḥayyān wa tilmīdhihi al-Samīn." Süleymaniye Library, MS Mihrişah Sultan 39, fols. 45b–63b.

Muḥtasibzāde, Meḥmed Hākī. *Tercüme-i Şaḳā'iḳ-i nu'māniye*. Topkapı Saray Museum Library, MS H. 1263.

al-Tamīmī, Taqī al-Dīn. *Kitāb ṭabaqāt Taqī al-Dīn*. Süleymaniye Library, MS Ayasofya 3295.

Published Primary Sources

3 Numaralı mühimme defteri (966–968/1558–1560). Ankara: T.C. Başbakanlık Devlet Arşivleri Genel Müdürlüğü, 1993.

7 Numaralı mühimme defteri (975–976/1567–1569). Ankara: T.C. Başbakanlık Devlet Arşivleri Genel Müdürlüğü, 1999.

12 Numaralı mühimme defteri (978–979/1570–1572). Ankara: T.C. Başbakanlık Devlet Arşivleri Genel Müdürlüğü, 1996.

'Alī ibn Bālī. "*Al-'Iqd al-manẓūm fī dhikr afāḍil al-Rūm*." In *al-Shaqā'iq al-nu'māniyya fī 'ulamā' al-dawla al-'uthmāniyya, 336–503*. Beirut: Dār al-Kitāb al-'Arabī, [1395H] 1975.

Anonymous. *Konuşma Adabı (Âdâb-ı Makâl)*. Edited by Ahmet Kayasandık. Istanbul: Büyüyenay, 2012.

'Āşıḳ Çelebi, Pīr Meḥmed. *Dhayl al-Shaqā'iq al-nu'māniyya fī 'ulamā' al-dawla al-'uthmāniyya*. Edited by 'Abd al-Rāziq Barakāt. Cairo: Dār al-Hidāya, 2007.

———[Âşık Çelebi]. *Meşâ'irü's-Şu'arâ: inceleme-metin*. Edited by Filiz Kılıç. Istanbul: İstanbul Araştırmaları Enstitüsü, 2010.

al-'Asqalānī, Ibn Ḥajar. *Al-durar al-kāmina fī a'yān al-mi'a al-thāmina*. Hyderabad: Maṭba'at Majlis Dā'irat al-Ma'ārif al-'Uthmāniyya, [1348–1350H] 1929–1931.

———. *Inbā' al-ghumr bi-anbā' al-'umr. Vol. 3*. Edited by Ḥasan Ḥabashī. Cairo: al-Majlis al-A'lā li-l-Shu'ūn al-Islāmiyya, 1972.

ʿAṭāʾī, Nevʿīzāde. *Ḥadāʾiḳuʾl-ḥaḳāʾiḳ fi tekmiletiʾṣ-Şaḳāʾiḳ*. Edited by Abdülkadir Özcan. Istanbul: Çağrı Yayınları, 1989.

ʿAzzām, ʿAbd al-Wahhāb, ed. *Majālis al-Sulṭān al-Ghawrī: Ṣafaḥāt min tārīkh Miṣr fī al-qarn al-ʿāshir al-Hijrī*. Cairo: Maktabat al-Thaqāfa al-Dīniyya, 2010.

al-Būrīnī, Ḥasan. *Tarājim al-aʿyān min abnāʾ al-zamān*. Edited by Ṣalāḥ al-Dīn al-Munajjid. 2 vols. Damascus: al-Majmaʿ al-ʿIlmī al-ʿArabī bi-Dimashq, 1959–1963.

Caʿfer Efendi. *Risāle-i Miʿmāriyye: An Early Seventeenth-Century Ottoman Treatise on Architecture*. Edited and translated by Howard Crane. Leiden: Brill, 1987.

Çelebi, Asaf Hâlet, ed. *Dîvân Şiirinde Istanbul*. Ankara: Hece Yayınları, 2002.

Della Valle, Pietro. *The Pilgrim: The Travels of Pietro Della Valle*. Translated, abridged, and introduced by George Bull. London: Hutchinson, 1990.

al-Ghazzī, Badr al-Dīn. *Ādāb al-ʿishra wa-dhikr al-ṣuḥba wa-l-ukhuwwa*. Edited by ʿAlī Ḥasan ʿAbd al-Ḥamīd. Amman: al-Maktab al-Islāmī, 1987.

——. *al-Durr al-naḍīd fī ādāb al-mufīd wa-l-mustafīd*. Edited by Abū Yaʿqūb Nashʾat ibn Kamāl al-Miṣrī. [Giza, Egypt:] Maktabat al-Tawʿiyya al-Islāmiyya, 2006.

——. *al-Maṭāliʿ al-badriyya fī al-manāzil al-rūmiyya*. Edited by al-Mahdī ʿĪd al-Rawāḍiyya. Beirut: al-Muʾassasa al-ʿArabiyya li-l-Dirāsāt wa-l-Nashr, 2004.

——. *al-Murāḥ fī al-muzāḥ*. Edited by Bassām ʿAbd al-Wahhāb al-Jābī. Beirut: Dār Ibn Ḥazm, 1997.

——. *Risālat ādāb al-muʾākala*. Edited by ʿUmar Mūsā Pāshā. Rabat: Maktabat al-Maʿārif, 1984.

al-Ghazzī, Najm al-Dīn. *al-Kawākib al-sāʾira bi-aʿyān al-miʾa al-ʿāshira*. Edited by Jibrāʾīl Sulaymān Jabbūr. 3 vols. Beirut: Dār al-Āfāq al-Jadīda, 1979.

——. *Luṭf al-samar wa qaṭf al-thamar min tarājim aʿyān al-ṭabaqat al-ūlā min al-qarn al-ḥādī ʿashar*. Edited by Maḥmūd al-Shaykh. 2 vols. Damascus: Manshūrāt Wizārat al-Thaqāfa wa-l-Irshād al-Qawmī, 1981–82.

al-Ḥamawī, Muḥibb al-Din. *Ḥādī al-aẓʿān al-najdiyya ilā al-diyār al-Miṣriyya*. Edited by Muḥammad ʿAdnān Bakhīt. Jordan: Jāmiʿat Muʾta, 1993.

al-Ḥaṣkafī, Aḥmad and Shams al-Dīn Ibn Ṭūlūn. *Mutʿat al-adhhān min al-tamattuʿ bi-l-iqrān bayna tarājim al-shuyūkh wa-l-aqrān*. 2 vols. Edited by Ṣalāḥ al-Dīn Khalīl al-Shaybānī al-Mawṣilī. Beirut: Dār Ṣādir, 1999.

Ibn Ayyūb, Sharaf al-Dīn. "Dhayl Quḍāt Dimashq ḥattā sanat al-alf li-l-hijra." In *Quḍāt Dimashq: al-Thaghr al-bassām fī dhikr man wuliyya qaḍāʾ al-Shām*. Edited by Ṣalāḥ al-Dīn al-Munajjid, 323–336. Damascus: al-Majmaʿ al-ʿIlmī al-ʿArabī, 1956.

——[Ibn Aiyūb]. *Das Kitāb ar-rauḍ al-ʿaṭir des Ibn Aiyūb: Damaszener Biographien des 10./16. Jahrhunderts*. Edited by Ahmet Halil Güneş. Berlin: Klaus Schwarz Verlag, 1981.

——. *Nuzhat al-khāṭir wa bahjat al-nāẓir*. Edited by ʿAdnān Muḥammad Ibrahīm. Damascus: Wizārat al-Thaqāfa, 1991.

Ibn Baṭṭūṭa, Muḥammad. *Travels in Asia and Africa 1325–1354*. Edited and translated by H. A. R. Gibb. New York, NY: Robert M. McBride & Company, 1929.

Ibn al-Ḥanbalī, Muḥammad. *Durr al-ḥabab fī tārīkh aʿyān Ḥalab*. Edited by Maḥmūd al-Fākhūrī. 4 vols. in 2 parts. Damascus: Manshūrāt Wizārat al-Thaqāfa, 1972–1974.

Ibn al-Ḥimṣī, Aḥmad. *Ḥawādith al-zamān wa wafiyyāt al-shuyūkh wa-l-aqrān*. Edited by ʿAbd al-ʿAzīz Fayyāḍ Ḥarfūsh. Beirut: Dār al-Nafāʾis, 2000.

Ibn al-ʿImād, ʿAbd al-Ḥayy. *Shadharāt al-dhahab fī akhbār man dhahab*. Edited by ʿAbd al-Qādir al-Arnāʾūṭ and Maḥmūd al-Arnāʾūṭ. 10 vols. Damascus: Dār Ibn Kathīr, 1986–1995.

Ibn Iyās, Muḥammad. *Badāʾiʿ al-zuhūr fī waqāʾiʿ al-duhūr*. Vol. 5. Edited by Muḥammad Muṣṭafā. Cairo: al-Hayʾa al-Miṣriyya al-ʿĀmma li-l-Kitāb, 1984.

Ibn Taghrībirdī, Abu'l Maḥāsin. *al-Nujūm al-zāḥira fī mulūk Miṣr wa-l-Qāhira*. Edited by Muḥammad Ḥusayn Shams al-Dīn. 16 vols. Cairo: al-Muʾassasa al-Miṣriyya al-ʿĀmma li-l-Taʾlīf wa al-Ṭibāʿa wa-l-Nashr, 1963–1971.

Ibn Ṭūlūn, Muḥammad. *Iʿlām al-warā bi-man wulliya nāʾiban min al-atrāk bi-Dimashq al-Shām al-kubrā*. Edited by Muḥammad Aḥmad Duhmān. Damascus: Dār al-Fikr, 1984.

———. *Mufākahat al-khillān fī ḥawādith al-zamān*. Vol. 2. Edited by Muḥammad Muṣṭafā. Cairo: al-Muʿassasa al-Miṣriyya al-ʿĀmma li-l-Taʾlīf wa al-Anbāʾ wa-l-Nashr, 1964.

———. *Quḍāt Dimashq: al-Thaghr al-bassām fī dhikr man wulliya qaḍāʾ al-Shām*. Edited by Ṣalāḥ al-Dīn al-Munajjid. Damascus: al-Majmaʿ al-ʿIlmī al-ʿArabī, 1956.

al-Ibshīhī, Muḥammad. *al-Mustaṭraf fī kull fann mustaẓraf*. Beirut: Dār Maktabat al-Ḥayāt, 1992.

Karmī, Marʿī ibn Yūsuf. *Masbūk al-dhahab fī faḍl al-ʿarab wa-sharaf al-ʿilm ʿalā sharaf al-nasab*. Amman: Dār ʿAmmār, 1988.

Kātib Çelebi, Muṣṭafā. *Kashf al-ẓunūn fī asāmī al-kutub wa-l-funūn*. Edited by Muḥammad Sharaf al-Dīn Yāltaqāyā and Kilisli Muallim Rifat. 2 Vols. Beirut: Dār Iḥyaʾ al-Turāth al-ʿArabī, n.d. (199-).

Kaykāʾūs ibn Iskandar. *Das Qābusnāme: Ein Denkmal persischer Lebensweisheit*. Translated by Seifeddin Najmabadi in association with Wolfgang Knauth. Wiesbaden: Dr. Ludwig Reichert Verlag, 1988.

al-Khafājī, Aḥmad. *Hādhā kitāb rayḥānat al-alibbā wa-zahrat al-ḥayāt al-dunyā*. Cairo: al-Maṭbaʿa al-Wahbiyya, 1877.

Ḳınalızāde, ʿAlī [ʿAlāʾ al-Dīn ʿAlī ibn Amrallāh al-Ḥamīdī]. *Ṭabaqāt al-ḥanafiyya*. Edited by Muḥyī al-Sarḥān. Baghdad: Diwān al-Waqf al-Sunnī, 2005.

Kınalı-zade, Hasan Çelebi. *Tekiretü'ş-Şuʿarâ*. Edited by İbrahim Kutluk. Ankara: Türk Tarih Kurumu Basımevi, 1989.

Laṭīfī, Ḳasṭamonulu. *Tez̲kire-i Laṭīfī*. Istanbul: İḳdām Matbaʿası, 1896/7.

———[Latîfî]. *Latîfî: Tezkiretü'ş-Şuʿarâ ve Tabsiratü'n-Nuzamâ (İnceleme-Metin)*. Edited by Rıdvan Canım. Ankara: Atatürk Kültür Merkezi Başkanlığı, 2000.

al-Maqrīzī, Aḥmad. *Durar al-ʿuqūd al-farīda fī tarājim al-aʿyān al-mufīda*. Edited by Maḥmūd Jalīlī. 4 vols. Beirut: Dār al-Gharb al-Islāmī, 2002.

Mecdī, Meḥmed Efendi. *Tercüme-i Şaḳāʾiḳ li-Mecdī Efendī*. Istanbul: Maṭbaʿa-i ʿĀmire, 1852.

al-Muḥibbī, Muḥammad. *Khulāṣat al-athār fī aʿyān al-qarn al-ḥādī ʿashar*. Cairo: al-Maṭbaʿa al-Wahbiyya, [1284H] 1868.

al-Murādī, Muḥammad. *ʿArf al-bashām fī man waliya fatwā Dimashq al-Shām*. Edited by Muḥammad al-Ḥāfiẓ. Beirut: Dār Ibn Kathīr, 1988.

Muṣṭafā ʿĀlī [Gelibolulu Mustafa Âlî]. *Künhü'l-Ahbâr. Dördüncü Rükn: Osmanlı Tarihi. Tıpkıbasım*. Ankara: Türk Tarih Kurumu Basımevi, 2009.

———[Gelibolulu Mustafa ʿÂlî]. *Mevâʿidü'n-Nefâʾis fî Ḳavâʿidi'l Mecâlis*. Edited by Mehmed Şeker. Ankara: Türk Tarih Kurumu Basımevi, 1997.

——[*Muṣṭafā ʿÂlî*]. *Muṣṭafā ʿÂlî's Description of Cairo of 1599: Text, Transliteration, Translation, Notes.* Edited and translated by Andreas Tietze. Vienna: Verlag der Österreichischen Akademie der Wissenschaften, 1975.

——[Mustafa Âli]. *Mustafa Âli's Epic Deeds of Artists: A Critical Edition of the Earliest Ottoman Text about the Calligraphers and Painters of the Islamic World.* Edited and translated by Esra Akın-Kıvanç. Leiden: Brill, 2011.

——[Mustafa Âli]. *The Ottoman Gentleman of the Sixteenth Century: Mustafa Âli's Mevāʾidü'n-nefāʾis fī ḳavāʿidi'l mecālis (Tables of Delicacies Concerning the Rules of Social Gatherings).* Translated by Douglas Brookes. Cambridge, MA: Department of Near Eastern Languages and Civilizations, Harvard University, 2003.

al-Nahrawālī, Muḥammad. *Journey to the Sublime Porte: The Arabic Memoir of a Sharifian Agent's Diplomatic Mission to the Ottoman Imperial Court in the Era of Suleyman the Magnificent.* Edited and translated by Richard Blackburn. Würzburg: Ergon Verlag, 2005.

——[Muḥammad al-Nahrawānī]. *Kitāb al-iʿlām bi-aʿlām bayt Allāh al-ḥarām.* Edited by Hishām ʿAbd al-Azīz ʿAṭā. Mecca: Al-Maktaba al-Tijāriyya, 1996.

Naṣūḥü's-Silāḥī, Maṭrāḳçī. *Beyān-i Menāzil-i Sefer-i ʿIrāḳeyn-i Sulṭān Süleymān Ḫān.* Edited by Hüseyin Yurdaydın. Ankara: Türk Tarih Kurumu, 1976.

al-Nuwayrī, Shihāb al-Dīn Aḥmad. *Nihāyat al-arab fī funūn al-adab.* Edited by Ḥasan Nur al-Dīn. Vol. 3. Beirut: Dār al-Kutub al-ʿIlmiyya, n.d.

al-Sakhāwī, Shams al-Dīn Muḥammad. *al-Ḍawʾ al-lāmiʿ li-ahl al-qarn al-tāsiʿ.* 12 vols. Beirut: Dār Maktabat al-Ḥayāt, 1934–1936.

Sehī Bey [Sehī Beg]. *Heşt Bihişt: The Tezkire by Sehī Beg: An Analysis of the First Biographical Work on Ottoman Poets with a Critical Edition Based on Ms. Süleymaniye Library, Ayasofya, O. 3544.* Edited by Günay Kut. Cambridge, MA: Harvard University, 1978.

——[Sehî Bey]. *Sehî Bey Tezkiresi: Heşt Behişt.* Edited and translated by Mustafa İsen. Ankara: Akçağ Yayınları, 1998.

——[Edirneli Sehī]. *Tez̲kire-i Sehī.* Edited by Meḥmed Şükrü. Istanbul: Maṭbaʿa-i Āmedī, [1325H] 1907/8.

al-Shaʿrānī, ʿAbd al-Wahhāb. *al-Anwār fī ādāb al-ṣuḥba ʿinda al-akhyār.* Damascus: Maktabat Abī Ayyūb al-Anṣārī, 2007.

al-Shawkānī, Muḥammad. *al-Badr al-ṭāliʿ bi-maḥāsin man baʿd al-qarn al-sābiʿ.* 2 vols. Cairo: Maṭbaʿat al-Saʿāda, 1929–30.

al-Suyūṭī, Jalāl al-Dīn. *Bughyat al-wuʿāt fī ṭabaqāt al-lughawiyyīn wa-l-nuḥāt.* Edited by Muḥammad Ibrahīm. Vol. 2. [Cairo]: ʿIsā al-Bābī al-Ḥalabī, 1965.

——. *Naẓm al-ʿiqyān fī aʿyān al-aʿyān.* Edited by Philip Hitti. New York, NY: Syrian-American Press, 1927.

al-Tamīmī, Taqī al-Dīn. *al-Ṭabaqāt al-saniyya fī tarājim al-ḥanafiyya.* Edited by ʿAbd al-Fattāḥ Muḥammad al-Ḥulw. Cairo: al-Majlis al-Aʿlā li-l-Shuʾūn al-Islāmiyya, 1970.

Ṭaşköprīzāde. *al-Shaqāʾiq al-nuʿmāniyya fī ʿulamāʾ al-dawla al-ʿuthmāniyya.* Edited by Ahmed Subhi Furat. Istanbul: İstanbul Üniversitesi Edebiyat Fakültesi Yayınları, 1985.

al-ʿUlaymī, Mujīr al-Dīn. *al-Uns al-jalīl bi-tārīkh al-Quds wa-l-Khalīl.* Edited by Maḥmūd al-Kaʿābina. Vol. 2. Amman: Maktabat Dandīs, 1999.

Yıldız, Kenan, ed. *İstanbul Kadı Sicilleri: Üsküdar Mahkemesi 9 Numaralı Sicil (H. 940–942/M. 1534–1536).* Istanbul: İslam Araştırmaları Merkezi, 2010.

Secondary Sources

Abou-el-Haj, Rifaʿat A. *The 1703 Rebellion and the Structure of Ottoman Politics.* Leiden: Nederlands Historisch-Archeologisch Instituut te Istanbul, 1984.

———. "Aspects of the Legitimation of Ottoman Rule as Reflected in the Preambles to Two Early *Liva Kanunnameler.*" *Turcica* 21–23 (1991): 371–383.

———. *The Formation of the Modern State: The Ottoman Empire, Sixteenth to Eighteenth Centuries.* 2nd ed. Syracuse, NY: Syracuse University Press, 2005.

———. "The Ottoman vizier and Paşa Households 1683–1703: A Preliminary Report." *Journal of the American Oriental Society* 94 (1974): 438–447.

Abou-Khatwa, Noha. "An Ode to Remember: The Burda of al-Busiri in Cairene Ottoman Houses." In *Creswell Photographs Re-examined: New Perspectives on Islamic Architecture.* Edited by Bernard O'Kane, 43–70. Cairo and New York, NY: The American University in Cairo Press, 2009.

Abu-Husayn, Abdul-Rahim. *Provincial Leaderships in Syria, 1575–1650.* Beirut: American University of Beirut Press, 1985.

Abu Hussein, Tarek. "Social Dining, Banqueting, and the Cultivation of a Coherent Social Identity: The Case of Damascene ʿUlamaʾ in the Late Mamluk and Early Ottoman Period." In *Insatiable Appetite: Food as a Cultural Signifier.* Edited by Kirill Dmitriev, Julia Hauser, and Bilal Orfali, 11–26. Leiden: Brill, 2019.

Abu-Manneh, Butrus. "The Islamic Roots of the Gülhane Rescript." *Die Welt des Islams* 34, no. 2 (Nov. 1994): 173–203.

Adshead, S. A. M. *Central Asia in World History.* New York, NY: St. Martin's Press, 1993.

Ágoston, Gábor. "A Flexible Empire: Authority and Its Limits on the Ottoman Frontiers." *International Journal of Turkish Studies* 9, nos. 1–2 (2003): 15–31.

Ahmed, Shahab. *What is Islam? The Importance of Being Islamic.* Princeton, NJ: Princeton University Press, 2016.

Ahmed, Shahab, and Nenad Filipovic. "The Sultan's Syllabus: A Curriculum for the Ottoman Imperial *medreses* Prescribed in a *fermān* of Qānūnī I Süleymān, Dated 973 (1565)." *Studia Islamica* 98/99 (2004): 183–218.

Akkach, Samer. *Abd al-Ghani al-Nabulusi: Islam and the Enlightenment.* Oxford: One World Press, 2007.

Aksoy, Hasan. "Müeyyedzâde Abdurrahman Efendi." In *Türkiye Diyanet Vakfı İslâm Ansiklopedisi.* Vol. 31 (2006): 485–486.

———. "Derviş Şemseddin." In *Türkiye Diyanet Vakfı İslâm Ansiklopedisi.* Vol. 9 (1994): 197–198.

Alam, Muzaffar, and Sanjay Subrahmanyam. "Frank Disputations: Catholics and Muslims in the Court of Jahangir (1608–11)." *Indian Economic Social History Review* 46, no. 4 (2009): 457–511.

Ali, Samer. *Arabic Literary Salons in the Islamic Middle Ages.* Notre Dame, IN: University of Notre Dame Press, 2010.

Allen, Jonathan Parkes. "Up All Night Out of Love for the Prophet: Devotion, Sanctity, and Ritual Innovation in the Ottoman Arab Lands, 1500–1620." *Journal of Islamic Studies* 30, no. 3 (2019): 303–337.

Allen, Roger. *An Introduction to Arabic Literature.* Cambridge: Cambridge University Press, 2000.

Alpay, Günay Kut. "Lāmiʿī Chelebi and His Works." *Journal of Near Eastern Studies* 35, no. 2 (1976): 73–93.

Alvarez, Lourdes. "Muwashshaḥ." In *Encyclopedia of Arabic Literature*. Edited by Julie Scott Meisami and Paul Starkey. Vol. 2, 563–566. New York, NY: Routledge, 1998.

———. "Zajal, Medieval." In *Encyclopedia of Arabic Literature*. Edited by Julie Scott Meisami and Paul Starkey. Vol. 2, 818–819. New York, NY: Routledge, 1998.

Anay, Harun. "Devvânî." In *Türkiye Diyanet Vakfı İslâm Ansiklopedisi*. Vol. 9 (1994): 257–261.

Andrews, Walter. "Gardens—Real and Imagined—in the Social Ecology of Early Modern Ottoman Culture." In *Gardens and Imagination: Cultural History and Agency*. Edited by Michel Conan, 91–113. Washington, DC: Dumbarton Oaks Research Library and Collection, 2008.

———. "Literary Art of the Golden Age: The Age of Süleyman." In *Süleymân the Second and His Time*. Edited by Halil İnalcık and Cemal Kafadar, 353–368. Istanbul: The Isis Press, 1993.

———. *Poetry's Voice, Society's Song: Ottoman Lyric Poetry*. Seattle, WA: University of Washington Press, 1985.

———. "Speaking of Power: The 'Ottoman Kaside.'" In *Qasida Poetry in Islamic Asia and Africa*. Vol. 1: *Classical Traditions and Modern Meanings*. Edited by Stefan Sperl and Christopher Shackle. Leiden: Brill, 1996.

———. "The *Tezkere-i Suʿara* of Latifi as a Source for the Critical Evaluation of Ottoman Poetry." Unpublished Ph.D. Dissertation, University of Michigan, 1970.

Andrews, Walter, and Mehmet Kalpaklı. *The Age of Beloveds*. Durham, NC: Duke University Press, 2005.

Anooshahr, Ali. "Writing, Speech, and History for an Ottoman Biographer." *Journal of Near Eastern Studies* 69, no. 1 (2010): 43–62.

Anscombe, Frederick. "Islam and the Age of Ottoman Reform." *Past and Present* 208 (2010): 159–189.

Antov, Nicolay. *The Ottoman 'Wild West': The Balkan Frontier in the Fifteenth and Sixteenth Centuries*. Cambridge: Cambridge University Press, 2017.

Arsan, Andrew. "'This Age Is the Age of Associations': Committees, Petitions, and the Roots of Interwar Middle Eastern Internationalism." *Journal of Global History* 7, no. 2 (July 2012): 166–188.

Arsel, İlhan. *Arap Milliyetçiliği ve Türkler*. Ankara: Ankara Üniversitesi Hukuk Fakültesi Yayınları, 1975.

Artan, Tülay. "Forms and Forums of Expression: Istanbul and Beyond, 1600–1800." In *The Ottoman World*. Edited by Christine Woodhead, 378–406. London: Routledge, 2013.

Artan, Tülay, and İrvin Cemil Schick. "Ottomanizing Pornotopia: Changing Visual Codes in Eighteenth-Century Ottoman Erotic Miniatures." In *Eros and Sexuality in Islamic Art*. Edited by Francesca Leoni and Mika Natif, 157–207. Farnham: Ashgate, 2013.

Atasoy, Nurhan. "Türk Minyatürlerinden Üç Günlük Hayat Sahnesi." In *Sanat Tarihinde Doğudan Batıya: Ünsal Yücel Anısına Sempozym Bildirileri*. Edited by Nurhan Atasoy et al., 19–22. Istanbul: Güzel Sanatlar Matbaası, 1989.

———. *İbrahim Paşa Sarayı*. Istanbul: Edebiyat Fakültesi Basımevi, 1972.

Atçıl, Abdurrahman. *Scholars and Sultans in the Early Modern Ottoman Empire.* Cambridge: Cambridge University Press, 2017.

———. "Mobility of Scholars and Formation of a Self-Sustaining Scholarly System in the Lands of Rūm during the Fifteenth Century." In *Islamic Literature and Intellectual Life in Fourteenth- and Fifteenth-Century Anatolia.* Edited by Andrew C. S. Peacock and Sara Nur Yıldız, 315–332. Würzburg: Ergon Verlag, 2016.

———. "The Route to the Top in the Ottoman *Ilmiye* Hierarchy of the Sixteenth Century." *Bulletin of SOAS* 72, no. 3 (2009): 489–512.

Atıl, Esin. "Mamluk Painting in the Late Fifteenth Century." *Muqarnas* 2 (1984): 159–171.

Ayalon, David. "The End of the Mamlūk Sultanate (Why did the ottomans spare the mamlūks of egypt and wipe out the mamlūks of syria?)." *Studia Islamica* 65 (1987): 125–148.

———. "Mamluk Military Aristocracy during the First Years of the Ottoman Occupation of Egypt." In *The Islamic World from Classical to Modern Times.* Edited by Clifford Edmund Bosworth et al., 413–431. Princeton, NJ: Princeton University Press, 1989.

———. "Studies in al-Jabartī I. Notes on the Transformation of Mamluk Society in Egypt under the Ottomans (Continued)." *Journal of the Economic and Social History of the Orient* 3, no. 3 (1960): 275–325.

Ayaz, Kadir. "Hadis İlimlerinin Tedrîsâtı Açısından Osmanlı Dârulhadisleri." *Osmanlı Araştırmaları/Journal of Ottoman Studies* 47 (2016): 39–68.

———. "Molla Gürânî'nin *el-Kevseru'l-Cârî* Adlı Şerhinde Hadis İlimlerinde Dair Kaynakları." *Dini Araştırmalar* 19, no. 48 (2016): 153–178.

Aynur, Hatice. "Autobiographical Elements in Aşık Çelebi's Dictionary of Poets." In *Many Ways of Speaking About the Self: Middle Eastern Ego-Documents in Arabic, Persian, and Turkish (14th–20th Century).* Edited by Ralf Elger and Yavuz Köse, 17–26. Wiesbaden: Harrassowitz, 2010.

Aynur, Hatice, and Aslı Niyazioğlu. *Aşık Çelebi ve Şairler Tezkiresi Üzerine Yazılar.* Istanbul: Koç Üniversitesi Yayınları, 2011.

Ayoub, Samy. *Law, Empire, and the Sultan: Ottoman Imperial Authority and Late Hanafi Jurisprudence.* Oxford: Oxford University Press, 2020.

Baer, Gabriel. "Egyptian Attitudes Towards Turks and Ottomans in the 17th and 18th Centuries." *Contributions to Oriental Philology/Revue de Philologie Orientale (Prilozi za orijentalnu filologiju)* 30 (1980): 25–34.

Bağcı, Serpil et al. *Ottoman Painting.* Ankara: Ministry of Culture and Tourism Publications, 2010.

Bakhit, Adnan. *The Ottoman Province of Damascus in the Sixteenth Century.* Beirut: Librairie du Liban, 1982.

———. "The Christian Population of the Province of Damascus in the Sixteenth Century." In *Christians and Jews in the Ottoman Empire: The Functioning of a Plural Society.* Edited by Benjamin Braude and Bernard Lewis, 19–66. New York, NY: Holmes & Meier Publications, 1982.

Baldwin, James. *Islamic Law and Empire in Ottoman Cairo.* Edinburgh: Edinburgh University Press, 2017.

Baltacı, Cahid. *XV–XVI. Asırlarda Osmanlı Medreseleri.* Istanbul: M.Ü. İlahiyat Fakültesi Vakfı Yayınları, 2005.

——. "Hâmid Efendi, Çivizâde Damadı." In *Türkiye Diyanet Vakfı İslâm Ansiklopedisi*. Vol. 15 (1997): 460–461.

Barkey, Karen. *Empire of Difference: The Ottomans in Comparative Perspective*. Cambridge: Cambridge University Press, 2008.

Baş, Eyüp. *Dil-Tarih İlişkisi Bağlamında Osmanlı Türklerinde Arapça Tarih Yazıcılığı: XVI. ve XVII. Yüzyıl Örnekleriyle*. Ankara: Türkiye Diyanet Vakfı, 2006.

Bauer, Thomas. "Adab c) and Islamic Scholarship after the 'Sunnī Revival.'" In *Encyclopaedia of Islam*. 3rd ed. Edited by Kate Fleet, Gudrun Krämer, Denis Matringe, John Nawas, and Everett Rowson. Consulted online 30 September 2016. http://dx.doi.org/10.1163/1573-3912_ei3_COM_23652.

——. "'Ayna hādhā min al-Mutanabbī!' Toward an Aesthetics of Mamluk Literature." *Mamlūk Studies Review* 17 (2013): 5–22.

——. "How to Create a Network: Zaynaddīn al-Āṯārī and his *Muqarriẓūn*." In *Everything Is On the Move: The Mamluk Empire as a Node in (Trans-)Regional Networks*. Edited by Stephan Conermann, 205–222. Göttingen: V&R Unipress, 2014.

——. "Ibn Ḥajar and the Arabic Ghazal of the Mamluk Age." In *Ghazal as World Literature I: Transformations of a Literary Genre*. Edited by Thomas Bauer and Angelika Neuwirth, 35–56. Beirut: Ergon Verlag, 2005.

——. *Die Kultur der Ambiguität: Eine andere Geschichte des Islams*. Berlin: Insel Verlag, 2011.

——. "Literarische Anthologien der Mamlūkenzeit." In *Die Mamluken: Studien zu Ihrer Geschichte und Kultur. Zum Gedenken an Ulrich Haarmann (1942–1999)*. Edited by Stephan Conermann and Anja Pistor-Hatam, 71–122. Hamburg: EB-Verlag, 2003.

——. "al-Nawājī." In *Essays in Arabic Literary Biography, 1350–1850*. Edited by Joseph Lowry and Devin Stewart, 321–30. Wiesbaden: Harrassowitz Verlag, 2009.

——. "The Relevance of Early Arabic Poetry for Qur'anic Studies Including Observations on *Kull* and on Q 22:27, 26:225, and 52:31." In *The Qur'ān in Context: Historical and Literary Investigations into the Qur'ānic Milieu*. Edited by Angelika Neuwirth et al., 699–732. Leiden: Brill, 2010.

Bearman, P., et al. "al-Muʿawwidhatāni." In *Encyclopaedia of Islam*. 2nd ed. 1960–2004. Edited by P. Bearman, Th. Bianquis, C. E. Bosworth, E. van Donzel, and W. P. Heinrichs. Consulted online 7 April 2021. http://dx.doi.org/10.1163/1573-3912_islam_SIM_5283.

Behrens-Abouseif, Doris. *Egypt's Adjustment to Ottoman Rule: Institutions, Waqf, and Architecture in Cairo (16th and 17th Centuries)*. Leiden: Brill, 1994.

——. "The Fire of 884/1479 at the Umayyad Mosque in Damascus and an Account of Its Restoration." *Mamlūk Studies Review* 8, no. 1 (2004): 279–297.

——. "Sultan al-Ghawrī and the Arts." *Mamlūk Studies Review* 6 (2002): 71–94.

Bekar, Cumhur. "The Rise of the Köprülü Family: The Reconfiguration of Vizierial Power in the Seventeenth Century." Unpublished Ph.D. Dissertation, Leiden University, 2019.

Bencheneb, M. "Lughz." In *Encyclopaedia of Islam*. 2nd ed. 1960–2004. Edited by P. Bearman, Th. Bianquis, C. E. Bosworth, E. van Donzel, and W. P. Heinrichs. Consulted online 5 April 2021. http://dx.doi.org/10.1163/1573-3912_islam_SIM_4686.

Bennison, Amira. "Muslim Universalism and Western Globalization." In *Globalization in World History*. Edited by Antony G. Hopkins, 74–97. London: Pimlico, 2002.

Berkey, Jonathan. "Culture and Society During the Late Middle Ages." In *The Cambridge History of Egypt*. Vol. 1: *Islamic Egypt, 640–1517*. Edited by Carl F. Petry, 375–411. Cambridge: Cambridge University Press, 1998.

———. *The Formation of Islam: Religion and Society in the Near East, 600–1800*. Cambridge: Cambridge University Press, 2003.

———. *The Transmission of Knowledge in Medieval Cairo: A Social History of Islamic Education*. Princeton, NJ: Princeton University Press, 1992.

———. "'Silver Threads Among the Coal': A Well-Educated Mamluk of the Ninth/Fifteenth Century." *Studia Islamica* 73 (1991): 109–125.

Bevilacqua, Alexander. *The Republic of Arabic Letters*. Cambridge, MA: Harvard University Press, 2018.

Beyazit, Yasemin. "Efforts to Reform Entry into the Ottoman *İlmiyye* Career towards the End of the 16th Century: The 1598 Ottoman *İlmiyye Kanunnamesi*." *Turcica* 44 (2012–3): 201–218.

———. "Osmanlı İlmiyye Tarîkinde İstihdam ve Hareket: Rumeli Kadıaskerliği Ruznâmçeleri Üzerine Bir Tahlil Denemesi (XVI. Yüzyıl)." Unpublished Ph.D. Dissertation, Ankara University, 2009.

Bilge, Mustafa. *İlk Osmanlı Medreseleri*. Istanbul: Edebiyat Fakültesi Basımevi, 1984.

Binbaş, İlker Evrim. "A Damascene Eyewitness to The Battle of Nicopolis: Shams al-Dīn Ibn al-Jazarī (d. 833/1429)." In *Contact and Conflict in Frankish Greece and the Aegean, 1204–1453*. Edited by Nikolaos Chrissis and Mike Carr, 153–175. Farnham: Ashgate, 2014.

———. *Intellectual Networks in Timurid Iran: Sharaf al-Dīn ʿAlī Yazdī and the Islamicate Republic of Letters*. Cambridge: Cambridge University Press, 2016.

Blanning, Tim. *The Culture of Power and the Power of Culture*. Oxford: Oxford University Press, 2002.

Blecher, Joel. "*Ḥadīth* Commentary in the Presence of Students, Patrons, and Rivals: Ibn Ḥajar and *Ṣaḥīḥ al-Bukhārī* in Mamluk Cairo." *Oriens* 41 (2013): 261–287.

———. "In the Shade of the *Ṣaḥīḥ*: Politics, Culture and Innovation in an Islamic Commentarial Tradition." Unpublished Ph.D. Dissertation, Princeton University, 2013.

———. *Said the Prophet of God: Hadith Commentary across a Millennium*. Oakland, CA: University of California Press, 2018.

———. "'Usefulness without Toil': Al-Suyūṭī and the Art of Concise *Ḥadīth* Commentary." In *Al-Suyūṭī, a Polymath of the Mamlūk Period*. Edited by Antonella Ghersetti, 182–200. Leiden: Brill, 2016.

Bonebakker, Seeger A. "Adab and the Concept of Belles-Lettres." In *Abbasid Belles Lettres*. Edited by Julia Ashtiany et al., 16–23. Cambridge: Cambridge University Press, 1990.

Boqvist, Marianne. "Building an Ottoman City: The Complexes of Aḥmad Šamsī Pasha and Lālā Muṣṭafā Pasha and Their Role in the Establishment of New Urban and Social Contexts in 16th Century Damascus." *Bulletin d'Études Orientales* 61 (2012): 191–208.

Börner, Karla. "Wohnhausarchitektur in der Altstadt von Tripoli / Libanon: Bauhistorische Untersuchungen von Wohnhäusern in ihrem stadträumlichen, zeitgeschichtlichen und familienbezogenen Kontext." Unpublished Ph.D. Dissertation, Technische Universität Berlin, 2010.

Bosworth, Clifford Edmund. "A Janissary Poet of Sixteenth-Century Damascus: Māmayya al-Rūmī." In *The Islamic World from Classical to Modern Times: Essays in Honor of Bernard Lewis*. Edited by C. E. Bosworth et al., 451–466. Princeton: The Darwin Press, 1989.

——ed. *The Turks in the Early Islamic World*. London: Routledge, 2017.

Boyar, Ebru, and Kate Fleet. *A Social History of Ottoman Istanbul*. Cambridge: Cambridge University Press, 2010.

Braude, Benjamin, and Bernard Lewis, eds. *Christians and Jews in the Ottoman Empire: The Functioning of a Plural Society*. New York, NY: Holmes & Meier Publishers, 1982.

Bray, Julia. "Adab." In *Medieval Islamic Civilization: An Encyclopedia*. Vol. 1. Edited by Josef Meri, 13–14. New York, NY: Routledge, 2006.

——. "Starting Out in New Worlds. Under Whose Empire? High Tradition and Subaltern Tradition in Ottoman Syria, 16th and 19th/20th Centuries." *Annali di Ca' Foscari* 48, no. 3 (2009): 199–220.

Broadbridge, Anne F. "Academic Rivalry and the Patronage System in Fifteenth-Century Egypt: al-ʿAynī, al-Maqrīzī, and Ibn Ḥajar al-ʿAsqalānī." *Mamlūk Studies Review* 3 (1999): 85–107.

Brockelmann, Carl. "al-Muḥibbī." In *Encyclopaedia of Islam*. 2nd ed. 1960–2004. Edited by P. Bearman, Th. Bianquis, C. E. Bosworth, E. van Donzel, and W. P. Heinrichs. Consulted online 3 October 2015. http://dx.doi.org/10.1163/1573-3912_islam_SIM_5431.

Brömer, Rainer. "Scientific Practice, Patronage, Salons, and Enterprise in Eighteenth Century Cairo: Examination of Al-Gabarti's History of Egypt." In *Multicultural Science in the Ottoman Empire*. Edited by Ekmeleddin İhsanoğlu et al., 107–120. Turnhout: Brepols, 2003.

Brookshaw, Dominic Parviz. *Hafiz and His Contemporaries: Poetry, Performance and Patronage in Fourteenth-Century Iran*. London and New York, NY: I.B. Tauris, 2019.

——. "Palaces, Pavilions and Pleasure-gardens: the context and setting of the medieval *majlis*." *Middle Eastern Literatures* 6, no. 2 (2003): 199–223.

Brown, Jonathan. "Formalism vs. Realism and the Dynamism of Mullā Khusraw." In *Uluslararası Mollā Hüsrev Sempozyumu (18–20 Kasım 2011 Bursa): Bildiriler*. Edited by Tevfik Yücedoğru et al., 395–408. Bursa: Bursa Büyükşehir Belediyesi, 2013.

——. *Hadith: Muhammad's Legacy in the Medieval and Modern World*. Oxford: One World Publications, 2009.

Brown, Peter. "Late Antiquity and Islam: Parallels and Contrasts." In *Moral Conduct and Authority: The Place of* Adab *in South Asian Islam*. Edited by Barbara Daly Metcalf, 23–37. Berkeley, CA: University of California Press, 1984.

Brubaker, Rogers, and Frederick Cooper. "Beyond 'Identity.'" *Theory and Society* 29 (2000): 1–47.

Burak, Guy. "Dynasty, Law, and the Imperial Provincial Madrasa: The Case of al-Madrasa al-ʿUthmaniyya in Ottoman Jerusalem." *International Journal of Middle East Studies* 45 (2013): 111–125.

——. "Faith, Law and Empire in the Ottoman 'Age of Confessionalization' (Fifteenth-Seventeenth Centuries): The Case of 'Renewal of Faith.'" *Mediterranean Historical Review* 28, no. 1 (2013): 1–23.

———. *The Second Formation of Islamic Law*. Cambridge: Cambridge University Press, 2015.

Çaksu, Ali. "Janissary Coffee Houses in Late Eighteenth-Century Istanbul." In *Ottoman Tulips, Ottoman Coffee: Leisure and Lifestyle in the Eighteenth Century*. Edited by Dana Sajdi, 117–132. London: I.B. Tauris, 2007.

Canbakal, Hülya. "The Ottoman State and Descendants of the Prophet in Anatolia and the Balkans (c. 1500–1700)." *Journal of the Economic and Social History of the Orient* 52 (2009): 542–578.

———. "On the 'Nobility' of Provincial Notables." In *Halcyon Days in Crete V: A Symposium Held in Rethymno, 10–12 January 2003*. Edited by Antonis Anastasopoulos, 39–50. Rethymno, Greece: Crete University Press, 2005.

Casale, Giancarlo. *The Ottoman Age of Exploration*. Oxford: Oxford University Press, 2010.

Çavuşoğlu, Mehmet. "Kanunî Devrinin Sonuna Kadar Anadolu'da Nevâyi Tesiri Üzerine Notlar." *Gazi Türkiyat* 8 (2011): 23–35.

———. "Basîrî." In *Türkiye Diyanet Vakfı İslâm Ansiklopedisi*. Vol. 5 (1992): 105–106.

Çeltik, Halil. "Halep'te Kınalızade Hasan Çelebi'nin Şairler Meclisi." *Gazi Türkiyat* 1 (2007): 137–147.

Çetindağ, Yusuf. *Ali Şîr Nevâî'nin Osmanlı Şiirine Etkisi*. Ankara: T.C. Kültür ve Turizm Bakanlığı Yayınları, 2006.

Chamberlain, Michael. *Knowledge and Social Practice in Medieval Damascus, 1190–1350*. Cambridge: Cambridge University Press, 1995.

Chejne, Anwar G. "The Boon-Companion in Early ʿAbbāsid Times." *Journal of the American Oriental Society* 85, no. 3 (1965): 327–335.

Çizakça, Murat. "Ottoman Government and Economic Life: Taxation, Public Finance and Trade Controls." In *The Cambridge History of Turkey*. Vol. 2: *The Ottoman Empire as a World Power, 1453–1603*. Edited by Suraiya Faroqhi and Kate Fleet, 241–275. Cambridge: Cambridge University Press, 2013.

Çollak, Fatih and Cemil Akpınar. "Gazzi, Bedreddin." In *Türkiye Diyanet Vakfı İslâm Ansiklopedisi*. Vol. 13 (1996): 537–539.

Conermann, Stephan. "Ibn Aǧās (st. 881/1476), 'Taʾrīḫ al-Amīr Yašbak aẓ-Ẓāhirī': Biographie, Autobiographie, Tagebuch oder Chronik?" In *Mamlukica: Studies on the History and Society of the Mamluk Period*. Edited by Stephan Conermann, 157–212. Göttingen: V&R unipress, 2013.

Conermann, Stephan, and Gül Şen, eds. *The Mamluk-Ottoman Transition: Continuity and Change in Egypt and Bilād al-Shām in the Sixteenth Century*. Göttingen: V&R unipress, 2016.

Cooper, Frederick. "What Is the Concept of Globalization Good For? An African Historian's Perspective." *African Affairs* 100, no. 399 (2001): 189–213.

Cook, Michael. *Population Pressure in Rural Anatolia, 1450–1600*. Oxford: Oxford University Press, 1972.

Cooperson, Michael. *Classical Arabic Biography: The Heirs of the Prophets in the Age of al-Maʾmūn*. Cambridge: Cambridge University Press, 2004.

Cowan, Brian. "Public Spaces, Knowledge, and Sociability." In *The Oxford Handbook of the History of Consumption*. Edited by Frank Trentmann, 259–261. Oxford: Oxford University Press, 2012.

Daly Metcalf, Barbara, ed. *Moral Conduct and Authority: The Place of Adab in South Asian Islam.* Berkeley, CA: University of California Press, 1984.

Dankoff, Robert. "Turban and Crown: An Essay in Islamic Civilization." 2015. Unpublished essay. Accessed 15 July 2015. www.academia.edu/13435409/.

Darling, Linda T. "Investigating the Fiscal Administration of the Arab Provinces after the Ottoman Conquest of 1516." In *The Mamluk-Ottoman Transition: Continuity and Change in Egypt and Bilād al-Shām in the Sixteenth Century.* Edited by Stephan Conermann and Gül Şen, 147–176. Göttingen: V&R unipress, 2016.

———. "Ottoman Turkish: Written Language and Scribal Practice, 13th to 20th Centuries." In *Literacy in the Persianate World: Writing and the Social Order.* Edited by Brian Spooner and William L. Hanaway, 171–95. Philadelphia, PA: University of Pennsylvania Press, 2012.

———. *Revenue-Raising and Legitimacy: Tax Collection and Finance Administration in the Ottoman Empire, 1560–1660.* Leiden: Brill, 1996.

David, Jean-Claude. "Le café à Alep au temps des Ottomans: Entre le souk et le quartier." In *Cafés d'Orient revisités.* Edited by Hélène Desmet-Grégoire and François Georgeon, 113–126. Paris: CNRS Editions, 1997.

———. "Une grande maison de la fin du XVIe siècle à Alep." *Bulletin d'études orientales* 50 (1998): 61–96.

David, Jean-Claude, and Marie-Odile Rousset. "La *qaʿa* de la maison Wakil à Alep: Origine d'un nouveau modèle d'espace domestique." In *Angels, Peonies, and Fabulous Creatures: The Aleppo Room in Berlin.* Edited by Julia Gonnella and Jens Kröger, 55–69. Münster: Rhema Verlag, 2008.

Davidson, Garrett. *Carrying on the Tradition: A Social and Intellectual History of Hadith Transmission across a Thousand Years.* Brill: Leiden, 2020.

Davis, Natalie Zemon. *Trickster Travels: A Sixteenth-Century Muslim between Worlds.* New York, NY: Hill and Wang, 2006.

Değirmenci, Tülün. "Bir Kitabı Kaç Kişi Okur? Osmanlı'da Okurlar ve Okuma Biçimleri Üzerine Bazı Gözlemler." *Tarih ve Toplum* 13 (2011): 7–43.

———. "Osmanlı Sarayının Geçmişe Özlemi: Tercüme-i Şakâʾikû'n-nuʿmânîye." *Bilig* 46 (2008): 105–132.

Dekkiche, Malika. "New Source, New Debate: Re-evaluation of the Mamluk-Timurid Struggle for Religious Supremacy in the Hijaz (Paris, BnF MS ar. 4440)." *Mamlūk Studies Review* 18 (2014–5): 247–271.

De Vivo, Filippo. *Information and Communication in Venice: Rethinking Early Modern Politics.* Oxford: Oxford University Press, 2007.

DeWeese, Devin. "The Descendants of Sayyid Ata and the Rank of *Naqīb* in Central Asia." *Journal of the American Oriental Society* 115, no. 4 (1995): 612–634.

Dikici, Ayşe Ezgi. "Imperfect Bodies, Perfect Companions? Dwarfs and Mutes at the Ottoman Court in the Sixteenth and Seventeenth Centuries." Unpublished Master's Thesis, Sabancı University, Istanbul, 2006.

Dikmen, Melek. "Eşrefoğlu Rumi." In *Encyclopaedia of Islam.* 3rd ed. Edited by Kate Fleet, Gudrun Krämer, Denis Matringe, John Nawas, and Everett Rowson. Consulted online 16 April 2017. http://dx.doi.org/10.1163/1573-3912_ei3_COM_26232.

Doğan, Enfel. "Eski Anadolu Türkçesi Döneminde Yapılan Kabus-nâme Çevirileri Üzerine." *İÜEF Türk Dili ve Edebiyatı Dergisi* 43 (2011): 37–56.

Doumani, Beshara. *Rediscovering Palestine: Merchants and Peasants in Jabal Nablus, 1700–1900*. Berkeley, CA: University of California Press, 1995.

Dozy, R. "Majlis." In *Supplément aux dictionnaires arabes*. Vol. 1. Leiden: E.J. Brill-Maisoneuve Frères, 1927.

Dressler, Markus. "Inventing Orthodoxy: Competing Claims for Authority and Legitimacy in the Ottoman-Safavid Conflict." In *Legitimizing the Order: The Ottoman Rhetoric of State Power*. Edited by Hakan K. Karateke and Maurus Reinkowski, 151–173. Leiden: Brill, 2005.

Duindam, Jeroen. *Myths of Power: Norbert Elias and the Early Modern European Court*. Amsterdam: Amsterdam University Press, 1994.

Dursteler, Eric. "Speaking in Tongues: Language and Communication in the Early Modern Mediterranean." *Past and Present* 217 (2012): 47–77.

———. *Venetians in Constantinople: Nation, Identity, and Coexistence in the Early Modern Mediterranean*. Baltimore, MD: Johns Hopkins University Press, 2006.

Eckmann, János. "Die Kiptschakische Literatur." In *Philologiae Turcicae Fundamenta*. Vol. 2. Edited by Louis Bazin et al., 275–304. Wiesbaden: Steiner, 1964.

Eke, Nagehan. "Üsküplü İshak Çelebi Dîvânı'nda Klâsik Sanatlar." *Turkish Studies International Periodical for the Languages, Literature and History of Turkish or Turkic* 2, no. 4 (2007): 371–380.

El-Cheikh, Nadia, and C. E. Bosworth. "Rūm." In *Encyclopaedia of Islam*. 2nd ed. 1960–2004. Edited by P. Bearman, Th. Bianquis, C. E. Bosworth, E. van Donzel, and W. P. Heinrichs. Consulted online 8 May 2014. http://dx.doi.org/10.1163/1573-3912_islam_COM_0939.

El-Moudden, Abderrahmane. "The Ambivalence of Rihla: Community Integration and Self-Definition in Moroccan Travel Accounts, 1300–1800." In *Muslim Travellers: Pilgrimage, Migration, and the Religious Imagination*. Edited by Dale F. Eickelmann and James Piscatori, 69–84. London: Routledge, 1990.

El-Rouayheb, Khaled. *Before Homosexuality in the Arab-Islamic World, 1500–1800*. Chicago, IL: University of Chicago Press, 2005.

———. "Ḥasan b. Muḥammad al-Būrīnī (1556–1615)." Historians of the Ottoman Empire. Updated September 2008. Accessed 23 January 2011. https://ottomanhistorians.uchicago.edu/en/historian/al-burini-hasan-b-muhammad.

———. *Islamic Intellectual History in the Seventeenth Century: Scholarly Currents in the Ottoman Empire and the Maghreb*. Cambridge: Cambridge University Press, 2015.

———. "Opening the Gate of Verification: The Forgotten Arab-Islamic Florescence of the 17th Century." *International Journal of Middle East Studies* 38 (2006): 263–281.

Emiralioğlu, Pınar. *Geographical Knowledge and Imperial Culture in the Early Modern Ottoman Empire*. Farnham: Ashgate, 2014.

Ebied, Rifaat and M.J.L. Young. "Ibn Daḳīḳ al-ʿĪd." In *Encyclopaedia of Islam*. 2nd ed. 1960–2004. Edited by P. Bearman, Th. Bianquis, C.E. Bosworth, E. van Donzel, and W. P. Heinrichs. Consulted online 28 April 2014. http://referenceworks.brillonline.com/entries/encyclopaedia-of-islam-2/ibn-dakik-al-id-SIM_8644.

Elger, Ralf. "Badr al-Din Muhammad al-Ghazzi." In *Essays in Arabic Literary Biography, 1350–1850*. Edited by Joseph Lowry and Devin Stewart, 98–106. Wiesbaden: Otto Harrassowitz Verlag, 2009.

——. *Glaube, Skepsis, Poesie: Arabische Istanbul-Reisende im 16. und 17. Jahrhundert.* Würzburg: Ergon Verlag, 2011.

Emecen, Feridun. "Osmanlı Kronikleri ve Biyografi." *İslam Araştırmaları Dergisi* 3 (1999): 83–90.

Emre, Side. *Ibrahim-i Gulshani and the Khalwati-Gulshani Order: Power Brokers in Ottoman Egypt.* Leiden: Brill, 2017.

——. "İbrahim-i Gülşeni: Itinerant Saint and Cairene Ruler." Unpublished Ph.D. Dissertation, University of Chicago, 2009.

Enderwitz, Susanne. "Adab b) and Islamic Scholarship in the ʿAbbāsid Period." In *Encyclopaedia of Islam.* 3rd ed. Edited by Kate Fleet, Gudrun Krämer, Denis Matringe, John Nawas, and Everett Rowson. Consulted online 30 September 2016. http://dx.doi.org/10.1163/1573-3912_ei3_COM_23651.

Ergin, Nina, ed. *Bathing Culture of Anatolian Civilizations: Architecture, History, and Imagination.* Leuven: Peeters, 2011.

——. "Ottoman Royal Women's Spaces: The Acoustic Dimension." *Journal of Women's History* 26, no. 1 (2014): 86–111.

Ertuğ, Zeynep Tarım. "The Depiction of Ceremonies in Ottoman Miniatures: Historical Record or a Matter of Protocol?" *Muqarnas* 27 (2010): 251–275.

——. "Entertaining the Sultan: *Meclis*, Festive Gatherings in the Ottoman Palace." In *Celebration, Entertainment and Theater in the Ottoman World.* Edited by Suraiya Faroqhi and Arzu Öztürkmen, 124–144. Chicago, IL: Chicago University Press, 2014.

——. "Onaltıncı Yüzyılda Osmanlı Sarayı'nda Eğlence ve Meclis." *Uluslararası İnsan Bilimleri Dergisi* 4 (2007): 2–15.

Erünsal, İsmail. "Fethedilen Arap Ülkelerindeki Vakıf Kütüphaneleri Osmanlılar Tarafından Yağmalandı mı?" *Osmanlı Araştırmaları/Journal of Ottoman Studies* 43 (2014): 19–66.

——. *Ottoman Libraries: A Survey of the History, Development, and Organization of Ottoman Foundation Libraries.* Cambridge, MA: Department of Near Eastern Languages and Literatures, Harvard University, 2008.

Fahmy, Khaled. *All the Pasha's Men: Mehmed Ali, His Army and the Making of Modern Egypt.* Cambridge: Cambridge University Press, 1997.

——. *In Quest of Justice: Islamic Law and Forensic Medicine in Modern Egypt.* Oakland, CA: University of California Press, 2018.

Faroqhi, Suraiya. *Men of Modest Substance: House Owners and House Property in Seventeenth-century Ankara and Kayseri.* Cambridge: Cambridge University Press, 1987.

——. *Pilgrims and Sultans: The Hajj under the Ottomans, 1517–1683.* New York, NY: I.B. Tauris, 1994.

——. "The Principal Political Events." In *An Economic and Social History of the Ottoman Empire.* Vol. 2. Edited by Halil İnalcık and Donald Quataert, 413–432. Cambridge: Cambridge University Press, 1994.

——. "Social Mobility among the Ottoman ʿUlemâ in the Late Sixteenth Century." *International Journal of Middle East Studies* 4, no. 2 (1973): 204–218.

Fazlıoğlu, İhsan. "İlk dönem Osmanlı ilim ve kültür hayatında İhvânu's-safâ ve Abdurrahmân Bistâmî." *Dîvân İlmî Araştırmalar Dergisi* 2 (1996): 229–240.

———. "Osmanlı Döneminde 'Bilim' Alanındaki Türkçe Telif ve Tercüme Eserlerin Türkçe Oluş Nedenleri ve Bu Eserlerin Dil Bilincinin Oluşmasındaki Yeri ve Önemi." *Kutadgubilig: Felsefe-Bilim Araştırmaları* 3 (2003): 151–184.

Feldman, Walter. *Music of the Ottoman Court: Makam, Composition and the Early Ottoman Instrumental Repertoire.* Berlin: Verlag für Wissenschaft und Bildung, 1996.

Ferguson, Heather. *The Proper Order of Things: Language, Power, and Law in Ottoman Administrative Documents.* Stanford, CA.: Stanford University Press, 2018.

Fetvacı, Emine. "Others and Other Geographies in the Şehname-i Selim Han." *Osmanlı Araştırmaları/Journal of Ottoman Studies* 40 (2012): 81–100.

———. *Picturing History at the Ottoman Court.* Bloomington, IN: Indiana University Press, 2013.

Filipovic, Nenad. "Grand Vizier Sinan Paşa and the Ottoman Non-Muslims." Unpublished paper.

Fitzgerald, Timothy J. "The Ottoman Methods of Conquest: Legal Imperialism and the City of Aleppo, 1480–1570." Unpublished Ph.D. Dissertation, Harvard University, 2009.

Flemming, Barbara. "Literary Activities in Mamluk Halls and Barracks." In *Studies in Memory of Gaston Wiet.* Edited by Myriam Rosen-Ayalon, 249–260. Jerusalem: Institute of Asian and African Studies, Hebrew University of Jerusalem, 1977.

———. "Aus den Nachtgesprächen Sultan Ġaurīs." In *Folia rara: Wolfgang Voigt LXV. diem natalem celebranti ab amicis et catalogorum codicum.* Edited by Herbert Franke, Walther Heissig, and Wolfgang Treue, 22–3. Wiesbaden: Steiner, 1976.

———. "Šerīf, Sultan Ġavrī und die 'Perser.'" *Der Islam* 45, no. 1/2 (1969): 81–93.

Fleisch, Henri. "Al-Fīrūzābādī." In *Encyclopaedia of Islam.* 2nd ed. 1960–2004. Edited by P. Bearman, Th. Bianquis, C. E. Bosworth, E. van Donzel, and W. P. Heinrichs. Consulted online 3 September 2016. http://dx.doi.org/10.1163/1573-3912_islam_SIM_2383.

Fleischer, Cornell H. "Ancient Wisdom and New Sciences: Prophecies at the Ottoman Court in the Fifteenth and Early Sixteenth Centuries." In *Falname: The Book of Omens.* Edited by Farhad Massumeh and Serpil Bağcı, 231–243. Washington, D.C.: Ort Arthur M. Sackler Gallery, Smithsonian Institution, 2009.

———. *Bureaucrat and Intellectual in the Ottoman Empire: The Historian Mustafa Âli (1541–1600).* Princeton, NJ: Princeton University Press, 1986.

———. "The Lawgiver as Messiah: The Making of the Imperial Image in the Reign of Süleyman." In *Soliman le Magnifique et son Temps.* Edited by Gilles Veinstein, 159–177. Paris: La Documentation Française, 1992.

Frenkel, Yehoshua. "The Mamluks among the Nations: A Medieval Sultanate in Its Global Context." In *Everything Is On the Move: The Mamluk Empire as a Node in (Trans-)Regional Networks.* Edited by Stephan Conermann, 62–80. Göttingen: V&R unipress, 2014.

Fuess, Albrecht. "Sultans with Horns: The Political Significance of Headgear in the Mamluk Empire." *Mamlūk Studies Review* 12, no. 2 (2008): 71–94.

Gabrieli, Francesco. "Adab." In *Encyclopaedia of Islam.* 2nd ed. 1960–2004. Edited by P. Bearman, Th. Bianquis, C. E. Bosworth, E. van Donzel, and W. P. Heinrichs. Consulted online 8 May 2014. http://referenceworks.brillonline.com/entries /encyclopaedia-of-islam-2/adab-SIM_0293.

Gacek, Adam. "Technical Practices and Recommendations Recorded by Classical and Post-Classical Arabic Scholars Concerning the Copying and Correction of Manuscripts." In *Les Manuscrits du moyen-orient: Essais de codicologie et de paléographie*. Edited by François Déroche, 51–60. Istanbul: L'Institut Français d'Études Anatoliennes d'Istanbul, 1989.

Garcin, Jean-Claude. "The Regime of the Circassian Mamlūks." In *The Cambridge History of Egypt*. Vol. 1: *Islamic Egypt, 640–1517*. Edited by Carl F. Petry, 290–317. Cambridge: Cambridge University Press, 1998.

Geoffroy, Éric. "al-Suyūṭī." In *Encyclopaedia of Islam*. 2nd ed. 1960–2004. Edited by P. Bearman, Th. Bianquis, C. E. Bosworth, E. van Donzel, and W. P. Heinrichs. Consulted online 6 April 2018. http://dx.doi.org/10.1163/1573-3912_islam_COM_1130.

——. *Le soufisme en Égypte et en Syrie sous les derniers Mamelouks et les premiers Ottomans: Orientations spirituelles et enjeux culturels*. Damascus: Institut français de Damas, 1995.

Georgeon, François. "Présentation." In *Vivre dans l'Empire Ottoman: Sociabilités et Relations Intercommunautaires (XVIIe–XIXe siècles)*. Edited by François Georgeon and Paul Dumont, 5–20. Paris and Montreal: L'Harmattan, 1997.

Gharaibeh, Mohammad. "Brokerage and Interpersonal Relationships in Scholarly Networks: Ibn Ḥağar al-ʿAsqalānī and His Early Academic Career." In *Everything Is On the Move: The Mamluk Empire as a Node in (Trans-)Regional Networks*. Edited by Stephan Conermann, 223–268. Göttingen: V&R unipress, 2014.

Ghazi, Mhammed Ferid. "Un groupe social: 'Les Raffinés' (Ẓurafāʾ)." *Studia Islamica* 11 (1959): 39–71.

Ghobrial, John-Paul. *The Whispers of Cities: Information Flows in Istanbul, London, and Paris in the Age of William Trumbull*. Oxford: Oxford University Press, 2014.

Gilliot, Claude, ed. *Education and Learning in the Early Islamic World*. Farnham: Ashgate, 2012.

——. "Kontinuität und Wandel in der 'klassischen' islamischen Koranauslegung (II./VII.–XII./XIX. Jh.)." *Der Islam* 85 (2010): 1–155.

——. "Ṭabaqāt." *In Encyclopaedia of Islam*. 2nd ed. 1960–2004. Edited by P. Bearman, Th. Bianquis, C. E. Bosworth, E. van Donzel, and W. P. Heinrichs. Consulted online 8 May 2015. http://dx.doi.org/10.1163/1573-3912_islam_COM_1132.

Gökbulut, Hasan. "Al-Kafiyeci." In *Türkiye Diyanet Vakfı İslâm Ansiklopedisi*. Vol. 24 (2001): 154–155.

Gökçe, Ferhat. "Türkiye'de Memlükler Dönemi Hadis Çalışmaları." *Türkiye Araştırmaları Literatür Dergisi* 11, no. 21 (2013): 41–88.

Göktaş, Recep Gürkan. "On the Hadith Collection of Bayezid II's Palace Library." In *Treasures of Knowledge: An Inventory of the Ottoman Palace Library (1502/3–1503/4)*. Vol. 1. Edited by Gülru Necipoğlu, Cemal Kafadar, and Cornell H. Fleischer, 309–340. Leiden: Brill, 2019.

Gökyay, Orhan Şaik, and Şükrü Özen. "Molla Lutfî." In *Türkiye Diyanet Vakfı İslâm Ansiklopedisi*. Vol. 30 (2005): 255–258.

Goldgar, Anne. *Impolite Learning: Conduct and Community in the Republic of Letters, 1680–1750*. New Haven, CT: Yale University Press, 1995.

Gonnella, Julia, and Jens Kröger, eds. *Angels, Peonies, and Fabulous Creatures: The Aleppo Room in Berlin. International Symposium of the Museum für Islamische

Kunst—Staatliche Museen zu Berlin 12.–14. April 2002. Münster: Rhema-Verlag, 2008.
——. *Ein christlich-orientalisches Wohnhaus des 17. Jahrhunderts aus Aleppo (Syrien): Das "Aleppo-Zimmer" im Museum für Islamische Kunst, Staatliche Museen zu Berlin—Preußischer Kulturbesitz*. Mainz: Verlag Philipp von Zabern, 1996.
Goodman, Dena. *The Republic of Letters: A Cultural History of the French Enlightenment*. Ithaca, NY: Cornell University Press, 1994.
Goodman, Lenn E. *Islamic Humanism*. Oxford: Oxford University Press, 2003.
Goodwin, Godfrey. *A History of Ottoman Architecture*. Baltimore, MD: Johns Hopkins Press, 1971.
Gordon, Daniel. *Citizens without Sovereignty: Equality and Sociability in French Thought, 1670–1789*. Princeton, NJ: Princeton University Press, 1994.
Gradeva, Rossitsa. "From the Bottom Up and Back Again until Who Knows When: Church Restoration Procedures in the Ottoman Empire, Seventeenth–Eighteenth Centuries (Preliminary Notes)." In *Frontiers of Ottoman Space, Frontiers in Ottoman Society*. Edited by Rossitsa Gradeva, 135–163. Istanbul: The Isis Press, 2013.
——. "A *Kadi* Court in the Balkans: Sofia in the Seventeenth and Early Eighteenth Centuries." In *The Ottoman World*. Edited by Christine Woodhead, 57–71. London: Routledge, 2013.
Graf, Tobias. *The Sultan's Renegades: Christian-European Converts to Islam and the Making of the Ottoman Elite, 1575–1610*. Oxford: Oxford University Press, 2017.
Grafton, Anthony. "A Sketch Map of a Lost Continent: The Republic of Letters." In *Worlds Made by Words: Scholarship and Community in the Modern West*, 9–34. Reprint, Cambridge, MA: Harvard University Press, 2009.
Graham, William. "Traditionalism in Islam: An Essay in Interpretation." *Journal of Interdisciplinary History* 23, no. 3 (1993): 495–522.
Greene, Molly. *The Edinburgh History of the Greeks, 1453–1768*. Edinburgh: Edinburgh University Press, 2015.
——. *A Shared World: Christians and Muslims in the Early Modern Mediterranean*. Princeton, NJ: Princeton University Press, 2000.
Grehan, James. *Everyday Life and Consumer Culture in Eighteenth-Century Damascus*. Seattle, WA: University of Washington Press, 2007.
——. "Fun and Games in Ottoman Aleppo: The Life and Times of a Local Schoolteacher (1835–1865)." In *Entertainment among the Ottomans*. Edited by Ebru Boyar and Kate Fleet, 90–120. Leiden: Brill, 2019.
——. "The Mysterious Power of Words: Language, Law, and Culture in Ottoman Damascus (17th–18th Centuries)." *Journal of Social History* 37, no. 4 (2004): 991–1015.
Grotzfeld, Heinz. "Die Reisen des ʿAbdalġanī an-Nābulusī: Strukturen und Topoi Arabischer Wallfahrtsberichte." In *Beschreibung der Welt: Zur Poetik der Reise- und Länderberichte*. Edited by Xenja von Ertzdorff, 163–203. Amsterdam: Rodopi, 2000.
Gruendler, Beatrice. "Motif vs. Genre: Reflections on the *Dīwān al-Maʿānī* of Abū Hilāl al-ʿAskarī." In *Ghazal as World Literature*. Vol. 1: *Transformations of a Literary Genre*. Edited by Thomas Bauer and Angelika Neuwirth, 57–86. Beirut: Ergon Verlag, 2005.

———. "Qaṣīda: Its Reconstruction in Performance." In *Classical Arabic Humanities in Their Own Terms: Festschrift for Wolfhart Heinrichs on his 65th Birthday*. Edited by Beatrice Gründler with the assistance of Michael Cooperson, 325–393. Leiden: Brill, 2008.

Gürkan, Emrah Safa. "Espionage in the 16th Century Mediterranean: Secret Diplomacy, Mediterranean Go-Betweens and the Ottoman-Habsburg Rivalry." Unpublished Ph.D. Dissertation, Georgetown University, 2012.

Haarmann, Ulrich. "Arabic in Speech, Turkish in Language: Mamluks and their sons in the intellectual life of fourteenth-century Egypt and Syria." *Journal of Semitic Studies* 33 (1988): 81–114.

———. "Ideology and History, Identity and Alterity: the Arab Image of the Turk from the 'Abbasids to Modern Egypt." *International Journal of Middle East Studies* 20 (1988): 175–196.

Habermas, Jürgen. *Strukturwandel der Öffentlichkeit*. Suhrkamp: Frankfurt Am Main, 1990.

Hafteh, Georgina. "The Garden Culture of Damascus: New Observations Based on the Accounts of ʿAbd Allāh al-Badrī (d. 894/1489) and Ibn Kannān al-Ṣāliḥī (d. 1135/1740)." *Bulletin d'études orientales* 61 (2012): 297–325.

Hagen, Gottfried. "Afterword: Ottoman Understandings of the World in the Seventeenth Century." In *An Ottoman Mentality: The World of Evliya Çelebi*. Edited by Robert Dankoff, 215–256. Leiden: Brill, 2006.

———. "Mawlid, Ottoman." In *Muhammad in History, Thought, and Culture: An Encyclopedia of the Prophet of God*. Vol. 1. Edited by Coeli Fitzpatrick and Adam Walker, 369–373. Santa Barbara, CA: ABC-Clio, 2014.

———. "Ottoman Empire." In *Encyclopedia of Arabic Language and Linguistics*. Vol. 3: *Lat–Pu*. Edited by Kees Versteegh, 501–505. Leiden: Brill, 2008.

———. "Translations and Translators in a Multilingual Society: A Case Study of Persian-Ottoman Translations, Late Fifteenth to Early Seventeenth Century." *Eurasian Studies* 11, no. 1 (2003): 95–134.

Hallaq, Wael. *An Introduction to Islamic Law*. Cambridge: Cambridge University Press, 2009.

Hämeen-Anttila, Jaakko. "Adab a) Arabic, Early Developments." In *Encyclopaedia of Islam*. 3rd ed. Edited by Kate Fleet, Gudrun Krämer, Denis Matringe, John Nawas, and Everett Rowson. Consulted online 30 September 2016. http://dx.doi.org/10.1163/1573-3912_ei3_COM_24178.

Hanna, Nelly. "Culture in Ottoman Egypt." In *The Cambridge History of Egypt*. Vol. 2: *Modern Egypt, from 1517 to the End of the Twentieth Century*. Edited by M. W. Daly, 87–112. Cambridge: Cambridge University Press, 2008.

———. *Making Big Money in 1600: The Life and Times of Ismaʿil Abu Taqiyya, Egyptian Merchant*. Syracuse, NY: Syracuse University Press, 1998.

———. *In Praise of Books: A Cultural History of Cairo's Middle Class, Sixteenth to Eighteenth Century*. Syracuse, NY: Syracuse University Press, 2003.

Har-El, Shai. *Struggle for Domination in the Middle East: The Ottoman-Mamluk War, 1485–1491*. Leiden: Brill, 1995.

Has, Şükrü Selim. "A Study of Ibrāhīm al-Ḥalabī With Special Reference to the *Multaqā*." Unpublished Ph.D. Dissertation, Edinburgh University, 1981.

Hathaway, Jane. *The Arab Lands under Ottoman Rule*. Harlow: Pearson, 2008.
——. *Beshir Agha: Chief Eunuch of the Ottoman Imperial Harem*. Oxford: Oneworld Publications, 2005.
——. "The *Evlâd-i ʿArab* ('Sons of the Arabs') in Ottoman Egypt: A Rereading." In *Frontiers of Ottoman Studies I*. Edited by Colin Imber and Keiko Kiyotaki, 203–216. London: I.B. Tauris, 2005.
——. *The Politics of Households in Ottoman Egypt: The Rise of the Qazdağlıs*. Cambridge: Cambridge University Press, 1997.
Hattox, Ralph. *Coffee and Coffeehouses: The Origins of a Social Beverage in the Medieval Near East*. Seattle, WA: University of Washington Press, 1985.
Havemann, Axel. "The Chronicle of Ibn Iyās as a Source for Social and Cultural History from Below." In *Towards a Cultural History of the Mamluk Era*. Edited by Mahmoud Haddad et al., 87–98. Beirut: Ergon Verlag, 2010.
Havlioğlu, Didem. *Mihrî Hatun: Performance, Gender-Bending, and Subversion in Ottoman Intellectual History*. Syracuse, NY: Syracuse University Press, 2017.
——. "On the Margins and Between the Lines: Ottoman Women Poets from the Fifteenth to the Twentieth Centuries." *Turkish Historical Review* 1 (2010): 25–54.
Heinrichs, Wolfhart P. "ʿAbd al-Raḥīm al-ʿAbbāsī (al-Sayyid ʿAbd al- Raḥīm)." In *Essays in Arabic Literary Biography: 1350–1850*. Edited by Roger Allen, Joseph Lowry, and Devin Stewart, 12–21. Wiesbaden: Hassarowitz, 2009.
——and J.T.P de Bruijn and J. Stewart-Robinson. "Tadhkira." In *Encyclopaedia of Islam*. 2nd ed. 1960–2004. Edited by P. Bearman, Th. Bianquis, C. E. Bosworth, E. van Donzel, and W. P. Heinrichs. Consulted online 8 May 2014. http://dx.doi.org/10.1163/1573-3912_islam_COM_1140.
Heinzelmann, Tobias, and Henning Sievert, eds. *Buchkultur im Nahen Osten des 17. und 18. Jahrhunderts*. Bern: Peter Lang, 2010.
Hellman, Mimi. "Furniture, Sociability, and the Work of Leisure in Eighteenth-Century France." *Eighteenth-Century Studies* 32 (Summer 1999): 415–445.
Hermansen, Marcia, and Bruce Lawrence. "Indo-Persian Tazkiras as Memorative Communications." In *Beyond Turk and Hindu: Rethinking Religious Identities in Islamicate South Asia*. Edited by David Gilmartin and Bruce B. Lawrence, 149–175. Gainesville, FL: University Press of Florida, 2000.
Hess, Andrew. "The Ottoman Conquest of Egypt (1517) and the Beginning of the Sixteenth-Century World War." *International Journal of Middle East Studies* 4, no. 1 (1973): 55–76.
Heyberger, Bernard. "Inschriften und Malereien des Aleppo-Zimmers: Zeugnisse von Kulturangehörigkeit und konfessioneller Abgrenzung in Aleppo." In *Angels, Peonies, and Fabulous Creatures: The Aleppo Room in Berlin*. Edited by Julia Gonnella and Jens Kröger, 87–90. Münster: Rhema Verlag, 2008.
——. "Polemic Dialogues between Christians and Muslims in the Seventeenth Century." *Journal of the Economic and Social History of the Orient* 55, no. 2/3 (2012): 495–516.
Heyd, Uriel. *Ottoman Documents on Palestine, 1552–1615*. Oxford: Clarendon Press, 1960.
Hill, Peter. *Utopia and Civilization in the Arab Nahda*. Cambridge: Cambridge University Press, 2020.

Hirschler, Konrad. *Medieval Arabic Historiography: Authors as Actors*. London: Routledge, 2006.

——. *Medieval Damascus: Plurality and Diversity in an Arabic Library. The Ashrafīya Library Catalogue*. Edinburgh: Edinburgh University Press, 2016.

——. *The Written Word in the Medieval Arabic Lands: A Social and Cultural History of Reading Practices*. Edinburgh: Edinburgh University Press, 2012.

Hodgson, Marshall. *The Venture of Islam: The Gunpowder Empires and Modern Times*. Chicago, IL: The University of Chicago Press, 1974.

Homerin, Th. Emil. "al-Būṣīrī." In *Encyclopaedia of Islam*. 3rd ed. Edited by Kate Fleet, Gudrun Krämer, Denis Matringe, John Nawas, and Everett Rowson. Consulted online 3 October 2014. http://dx.doi.org/10.1163/1573-3912_ei3_COM_23124.

Hourani, Albert. "Ottoman Reform and the Politics of the Notables." In *The Emergence of the Modern Middle East*. Edited by Albert Hourani, 83–110. Berkeley, CA: University of California Press, 1981.

Howard, Douglas. "Genre and Myth in the Ottoman Advice for Kings Literature." In *The Early Modern Ottomans: Remapping the Empire*. Edited by Virginia Aksan and Daniel Goffman, 137–166. Cambridge: Cambridge University Press, 2007.

Humphreys, Stephen. "Egypt under the World System of the Later Middle Ages." In *The Cambridge History of Egypt*. Vol. 1: *Islamic Egypt, 640–1517*. Edited by Carl Petry, 445–461. Cambridge: Cambridge University Press, 1998.

Ibrahim, Laila ʿAli. "Residential Architecture in Mamluk Cairo." *Muqarnas: An Annual on Islamic Art and Architecture* 2 (1984): 47–59.

İhsanoğlu, Ekmeleddin. "Ottoman Educational and Scholarly-Scientific Institutions." In *History of the Ottoman State, Society and Civilization*. Vol. 2. Edited by Ekmeleddin İhsanoğlu, 361–518. Istanbul: IRCICA, 2002.

Imber, Colin. *Ebu's-Suʿud: The Islamic Legal Tradition*. Stanford, CA: Stanford University Press, 1997.

——. *The Ottoman Empire, 1300–1650: The Structure of Power*. New York, NY: Palgrave MacMillan, 2002.

İnalcık, Halil. *Has-Bağçede ʿAyş u Tarab*. Istanbul: Türkiye İş Bankası Kültür Yayınları, 2011.

——. "Klasik edebiyat menşei: İranî gelenek, saray işret meclisleri ve musâhib şâirler." In *Türk Edebiyatı Tarihi*. Vol. 1. Edited by Talât Sait Halman and Osman Horata, 253–267. Ankara: T. C. Kültür ve Türizm Bakanlığı Yayınları, 2006.

——. "Ottoman Methods of Conquest." *Studia Islamica* 2 (1954): 103–129.

——. "Rūmī." In *Encyclopaedia of Islam*. 2nd ed. 1960–2004. Edited by P. Bearman, Th. Bianquis, C. E. Bosworth, E. van Donzel, and W. P. Heinrichs. Consulted online 8 May 2014. http://dx.doi.org/10.1163/1573-3912_islam_SIM_6336.

——. *Şâir ve Patron: Patrimonyel Devlet ve Sanat Sisteminde Sosyolojik Bir İnceleme*. Ankara: Doğu Batı Yayınları, 2003.

——. "State, Sovereignty and Law." In *Süleymân the Second and His Time*. Edited by Halil İnalcık and Cemal Kafadar, 59–92. Istanbul: The Isis Press, 1993.

——. "The Yörüks: Their Origins, Expansion and Economic Role." *Cedrus* 2 (2014): 467–495.

İnalcık, Halil, and Donald Quataert, eds. *Economic and Social History of the Ottoman Empire*. Vol 1: *1300–1600*. Cambridge: Cambridge University Press, 1997.

İpekten, Haluk. *Divan Edebiyatında Edebî Muhitler*. Istanbul: Millî Eğitim Bakanlığı Yayınları, 1996.

Mehmet İpşirli. "Abdülkadir Hamîdî Çelebi." In *Türkiye Diyanet Vakfı İslâm Ansiklopedisi*. Vol. 1 (1988): 239.

——. "Çivizâde Mehmed Efendi." In *Türkiye Diyanet Vakfı İslâm Ansiklopedisi*. Vol. 8 (1993): 346.

——. "Çivizâde Muhyiddin Mehmed Efendi." In *Türkiye Diyanet Vakfı İslâm Ansiklopedisi*. Vol 8 (1993): 348–349.

——. "Fenârîzâde Muhyiddin Çelebi." In *Türkiye Diyanet Vakfı İslâm Ansiklopedisi*. Vol.12 (1995): 339–340.

——. "Kazasker." In *Türkiye Diyanet Vakfı İslâm Ansiklopedisi*. Vol. 25 (2002): 140–143.

——. "Osmanlı Devleti'nde Kazaskerlik (XVII. yüzyıla kadar)." *Belleten* 61 (1998): 597–700.

——. "Ottoman State Organization." In *History of the Ottoman State, Society and Civilization*. Vol. 2. Edited by Ekmeleddin İhsanoğlu, 133–285. Istanbul: IRCICA, 2001.

İsen, Mustafa. "Kınalızâde Ali Efendi." In *Türkiye Diyanet Vakfı İslâm Ansiklopedisi*. Vol. 25 (2002): 417.

Işın, Ekrem. "Coffeehouses as Places of Conversation." In *The Illuminated Table, the Prosperous House: Food and Shelter in Ottoman Material Culture*. Edited by Suraiya Faroqhi and Christoph Neumann, 199–208. Würzburg: Ergon Verlag, 2003.

Irwin, Robert. "Gunpowder and Firearms in the Mamluk Sultanate Reconsidered." In *The Mamluks in Egyptian and Syrian Politics and Society*. Edited by Michael Winter and Amalia Levanoni, 117–139. Leiden: Brill, 2004.

——. "Mamluk Literature," *Mamlūk Studies Review* 7, no. 1 (2003): 1–29.

——. "The Political Thinking of the 'Virtuous Ruler,' Qānṣūh al-Ghawrī." *Mamlūk Studies Review* 12, no. 1 (2008): 37–49.

Ivanyi, Katharina. *Virtue, Piety and the Law: A Study of Birgivī Meḥmed Efendī's* al-Ṭarīqa al-Muḥammadiyya. Leiden: Brill, 2020.

Kafadar, Cemal. "Between Amasya and Istanbul: Bayezid II, His Librarian, and the Textual Turn of the Late Fifteenth Century." In *Treasures of Knowledge: An Inventory of the Ottoman Palace Library (1502/3–1503/4)*. Vol. 1. Edited by Gülru Necipoğlu, Cemal Kafadar, and Cornell H. Fleischer, 79–153. Leiden: Brill, 2019.

——. *Between Two Worlds*. Berkeley, CA: University of California Press, 1995.

——. "How Dark Is the History of the Night, How Black the Story of Coffee, How Bitter the Tale of Love: The Changing Measure of Leisure and Pleasure in Early Modern Istanbul." In *Medieval and Early Modern Performance in the Eastern Mediterranean*. Edited by Arzu Öztürkmen and Evelyn Birge Vitz, 243–269. Turnhout: Brepols, 2014.

——. "The Myth of the Golden Age: Ottoman Historical Consciousness in the Post-Süleymanic Era." In *Süleymân the Second and His Time*. Edited by Halil İnalcık and Cemal Kafadar, 37–48. Istanbul: The Isis Press, 1993.

——. "A Rome of One's Own: Reflections on Cultural Geography and Identity in the Lands of Rum." *Muqarnas: An Annual on the Visual Culture of the Islamic World* 24 (2007): 7–25.

——. "Self and Others: The Diary of a Dervish in Seventeenth-Century Istanbul and First-Person Narratives in Ottoman Literature." *Studia Islamica* 69 (1989): 121–150.

Kafescioğlu, Çiğdem. "'In the Image of Rūm': Ottoman Architectural Patronage in Sixteenth-Century Aleppo and Damascus." *Muqarnas: An Annual on the Visual Culture of the Islamic World* 16 (1999): 70–96.

Kalpaklı, Mehmet. "Fevrî." In *Türkiye Diyanet Vakfı İslâm Ansiklopedisi*. Vol. 12 (1995): 504.

Kalpaklı, Mehmet, Walter G. Andrews, and Najaat Black, eds. *Ottoman Lyric Poetry: An Anthology*. Seattle, WA: University of Washington Press, 2006.

Kaplan, Cankat. "An Anti-Ibn ʿArabī (d. 1240) Polemicist in Sixteenth-Century Ottoman Istanbul: Ibrāhīm al-Ḥalabī (d. 1549) and his Interlocutors." Unpublished M. A. Thesis, Central European University, Budapest, 2019.

Kappert, Petra K. *Die osmanischen Prinzen und ihre Residenz Amasya im 15. und 16. Jahrhundert*. Istanbul: Nederlands Historisch-Archaeologisch Instituut, 1976.

Karataş, Hasan. "The City as a Historical Actor: The Urbanization and Ottomanization of the Halvetiye Sufi Order by the City of Amasya in the Fifteenth and Sixteenth Centuries." Unpublished Ph.D. Dissertation, University of California, Berkeley, 2011.

Karateke, Hakan, Erdem Çıpa, and Helga Anetshofer. *Disliking Others: Loathing, Hostility, and Distrust in Premodern Ottoman Lands*. Brighton, MA: Academic Studies Press, 2018.

Kartal, Ahmet. *Şiraz'dan İstanbul'a: Türk-Fars Kültür Coğrafyası Üzerine Araştırmalar*. Istanbul: Kurtuba Kitap, 2008.

Kasaba, Reşat. *A Moveable Empire: Ottoman Nomads, Migrants and Refugees*. Seattle: University of Washington Press, 2009.

Katz, Marion. *Prayer in Islamic Thought and Practice*. Cambridge: Cambridge University Press, 2013.

Kedar, Benjamin. "The Multilateral Disputation at the Court of the Grand Qan Möngke, 1254." In *The Majlis: Interreligious Encounters in Medieval Islam*. Edited by Hava Lazarus-Yafeh, Mark Cohen, Sasson Somekh, and Sidney Griffith, 162–183. Wiesbaden: Harrassowitz Verlag, 1999.

Kellner-Heinkele, Barbara. "Mīr ʿAlīšīr Nawāʾī—Eine Skizze zum historischen Hintergrund." In *Mīr ʿAlīšīr Nawāʾī: Akten des Symposiums aus Anlaß des 560. Geburtstages und des 500. Jahres des Todes von Mīr ʿAlīšīr Nawāʾī am 23. April 2001*. Edited by Barbara Kellner-Heinkele, 1–14. Würzburg: Ergon Verlag, 2003.

Khaldi, Boutheina. "Microcosming the Nahḍah: Mayy Ziyādah's Salon as a Hybrid Space." *Journal of Arabic Literature* 41, no. 3 (2011): 1–41.

Khalidi, Tarif. *Arabic Historical Thought in the Classical Period*. Cambridge: Cambridge University Press, 1994.

Khoury, Dina Rizk. "The Ottoman Centre versus Provincial Power-Holders: An Analysis of the Historiography." In *The Cambridge History of Turkey*. Vol. 3: *The Later Ottoman Empire, 1603–1839*. Edited by Suraiya Faroqhi, 133–156. Cambridge: Cambridge University Press, 2006.

——. *State and Provincial Society in the Ottoman Empire: Mosul, 1540–1834*. Cambridge: Cambridge University Press, 1997.

Kılıç, Rüya. *Osmanlıda Seyyidler ve Şerifler*. Istanbul: Kitap Yayınevi, 2005.

——. "The Reflection of Islamic Tradition on Ottoman Social Structure: The *Sayyids* and *Sharīfs*." In *Sayyids and Sharifs in Muslim Societies: The Living Links to the*

Prophet. Edited by Morimoto Kazuo, 123–138. London and New York, NY: Routledge, 2012.

Kilpatrick, Hilary. "Between Ibn Baṭṭūṭa and al-Ṭahṭāwī: Arabic Travel Accounts of the Early Ottoman Period." *Middle Eastern Literatures* 11, no. 2 (2008): 233–248.

———. "Socializing." In *Medieval Islamic Civilization: An Encyclopedia*. Vol. 2. Edited by Josef Meri, 762–763. New York, NY: Routledge, 2006.

Kim, Sooyong. *The Last of an Age: The Making and Unmaking of a Sixteenth-Century Ottoman Poet*. London and New York, NY: Routledge, 2017.

———. "An Ottoman Order of Persian Verse." In *Treasures of Knowledge: An Inventory of the Ottoman Palace Library (1502/3–1503/4)*. Vol. 1. Edited by Gülru Necipoğlu, Cemal Kafadar, and Cornell Fleischer, 635–656. Leiden: Brill, 2019.

Klein, Denise. "Mülazemet: Über den Werdegang osmanischer Ulema." In *Istanbul: Vom imperialen Herrschersitz zur Megapolis*. Edited by Yavuz Köse, 83–105. Munich: Martin Meidenbauer, 2006.

Klein, Lawrence. "Politeness and the Interpretation of the British Eighteenth Century." *Historical Journal* 45, no. 4 (Dec. 2002): 869–898.

Kömeçoğlu, Uğur. "The Publicness and Sociabilities of the Ottoman Coffeehouse." *Javnost–The Public* 12, no. 2 (2005): 5–22.

Korn, Lorenz. "Das Bait az-Zahrāwī in Homs: Ein Stadtpalast und seine Stellung in der syrischen Wohnarchitektur." *Damaszener Mitteilungen* 9 (1996): 263–280.

Kraemer, Joel. *Humanism in the Renaissance of Islam: The Cultural Revival during the Buyid Age*. Leiden: Brill, 1992.

Krstić, Tijana. *Contested Conversions to Islam: Narratives of Religious Change in the Early Modern Ottoman Empire*. Stanford, CA: Stanford University Press, 2011.

Krstić, Tijana, and Derin Terzioğlu, eds. *Historicizing Sunni Islam in the Ottoman Empire, c.1450–c.1750*. Leiden: Brill, 2020.

Kunt, Metin. "Royal and Other Households." In *The Ottoman World*. Edited by Christine Woodhead, 103–115. London: Routledge, 2013.

———. *The Sultan's Servants: The Transformation of the Ottoman Provincial Government, 1550–1650*. New York, NY: Columbia University Press, 1983.

———. "Turks in the Ottoman Imperial Palace." In *Royal Courts in Dynastic States and Empires: A Global Perspective*. Vol 1. Edited by Jeroen Duindam, Tülay Artan, and Metin Kunt, 289–312. Leiden: Brill, 2011.

Kurnaz, Cemal. "Osmanlı tarihinde iz bırakan Amasyalı bir aile: Müeyyedzâdeler." In *I. Amasya Araştırmaları (13–15 Haziran 2007)*. Vol. 2. Edited by Yavuz Bayram, 647–666. Amasya: T.C. Amasya Valiliği, 2007.

Kuru, Selim. "The Literature of Rum: The Making of a Literary Tradition (1450–1600)." In *The Cambridge History of Turkey*. Vol. 2: *The Ottoman Empire as a World Power, 1453–1603*. Edited by Suraya Faroqhi and Kate Fleet, 548–592. Cambridge: Cambridge University Press, 2012.

Kut, Günay. "Divan Edebiyatında Bezm, Âlât-ı Bezm ve Âdâb-ı Sohbet." *Osmanlı Kültür ve Sanat* 9 (1999): 616–629.

Kütükoğlu, Bekir. "Ayas Paşa." In *Türkiye Diyanet Vakfı İslâm Ansiklopedisi*. Vol. 4 (1991): 202–203.

Kütükoğlu, Mübahat. "Life in the *Medrese*." In *The Illuminated Table, the Prosperous House: Food and Shelter in Ottoman Material Culture*. Edited by Suraiya Faroqhi and Christoph Neumann, 209–217. Würzburg: Ergon Verlag, 2003.

——. "Minyatürlerde Divân-ı Hümâyûn ve Arz Odası." *Tarih Enstitüsü Dergisi* 16 (1998): 48–68.

Landolt, Herman. "Khalwa." In *Encyclopaedia of Islam*. 2nd ed. 1960–2004. Edited by P. Bearman, Th. Bianquis, C. E. Bosworth, E. van Donzel, and W. P. Heinrichs. Consulted online 7 November 2012. http://referenceworks.brillonline.com/entries/encyclopaedia-of-islam-2/khalwa-SIM_4178.

Lapidus, Ira. *A History of Islamic Societies*. 3rd ed. Cambridge: Cambridge University Press, 2014.

——. *Muslim Cities in the Later Middle Ages*. Cambridge: Cambridge University Press, 1984.

Lazarus-Yafeh, Hava, Mark Cohen, Sasson Somekh, and Sidney Griffith, eds. *The Majlis: Interreligious Encounters in Medieval Islam*. Wiesbaden: Harrassowitz, 1999.

Lekesiz, M. Hulûsi. "Osmanlı İlmî Zihniyetinde Değişme (Teşekkül-Gelişme-Çözülme XV–XVII. Yüzyıllar)." Unpublished M.A. Thesis, Hacettepe University, Ankara, 1989.

Lellouch, Benjamin. *Les Ottomans en Égypte: historiens et conquérants au XVIe siècle*. Paris: Peeters, 2006.

——. "Qu'est-ce qu'un Turc? (Égypte, Syrie, XVIe siècle)." *European Journal of Turkish Studies* (2013) [Online]. Accessed 10 December 2020. http://ejts.revues.org/4758.

Lellouch, Benjamin, and Nicolas Michel. *Conquête ottomane de l'Égypte (1517): Arrière-plan, impact, échos*. Leiden: Brill, 2013.

Lewicka, Paulina. *Food and Foodways of Medieval Cairenes: Aspects of Life in an Islamic Metropolis of the Eastern Mediterranean*. Leiden: Brill, 2011.

Lewis, Bernard. "ʿArūs Resmi." In *Encyclopaedia of Islam*. 2nd ed. 1960–2004. Edited by P. Bearman, Th. Bianquis, C. E. Bosworth, E. van Donzel, and W. P. Heinrichs. Consulted online 11 August 2020. http://dx.doi.org/10.1163/1573-3912_islam_SIM_0747.

Lewis, Franklin D. "Reading, Writing and Recitation: Sanāʾi and the Origin of the Persian Ghazal." Unpublished Ph.D. Dissertation, University of Chicago, 1995.

Liebrenz, Boris. "The Library of Aḥmad al-Rabbāṭ: Books and their Audience in 12th to 13th /18th to 19th Century Syria." In *Marginal Perspectives on Early Modern Ottoman Culture: Missionaries, Travellers, Booksellers*. Edited by Ralf Elger and Ute Pietruschka. *Orientwissenschaftliche Hefte* 32 (2013): 17–59.

Lilti, Antoine. "The Kingdom of Politesse: Salons and the Republic of Letters in Eighteenth-Century Paris." *Republic of Letters: A Journal for the Study of Knowledge, Politics, and the Arts* 1 (May 2009): 1–11.

——. *The World of the Salons: Sociability and Wordliness in Eighteenth-Century Paris*. Translated by Lydia Cochrane. Oxford: Oxford University Press, 2015.

Lowry, Heath. *Fifteenth Century Ottoman Realities: Christian Peasant Life on the Aegean Island of Limnos*. Istanbul: Eren, 2002.

MacLean, Derryl N. "Real Men and False Men at the Court of Akbar: The *Majalis* of Shaykh Mustafa Gujarati." In *Beyond Turk and Hindu: Rethinking Religious Identities in Islamicate South Asia*. Edited by David Gilmartin and Bruce Lawrence, 199–215. Gainesville, FL: University Press of Florida, 2000.

Madelung, Wilferd et al. "Madjlis." In *Encyclopaedia of Islam*. 2nd ed. 1960–2004. Edited by P. Bearman, Th. Bianquis, C. E. Bosworth, E. van Donzel, and W. P. Heinrichs.

Consulted online 25 September 2016. http://dx.doi.org/10.1163/1573-3912_islam_COM_0606.

——. "al-Taftāzānī." In *Encyclopaedia of Islam*. 2nd ed. 1960–2004. Edited by P. Bearman, Th. Bianquis, C. E. Bosworth, E. van Donzel, and W. P. Heinrichs. Consulted online 8 March 2014. http://dx.doi.org/10.1163/1573-3912_islam_SIM_7296.

Mahir, Banu. *Osmanlı Minyatür Sanatı*. Istanbul: Kabalcı Yayınevi, 2005.

Makdisi, George. *The Rise of Colleges: Institutions of Learning in Islam and the West*. Edinburgh: Edinburgh University Press, 1981.

Mango, Andrew. *Atatürk*. London: John Murray, 1999.

Manstetten, Paula. "Ibn ʿAsākir's *History of Damascus* and the Institutionalisation of Education in the Medieval Islamic World." Unpublished Ph.D. Dissertation, School of Oriental and African Studies, University of London, 2018.

Manz, Beatrice Forbes. *Power, Politics and Religion in Timurid Iran*. Cambridge: Cambridge University Press, 2007.

Marciniak, Przemysław. "Byzantine *Theatron*—A Place of Performance?" In *Theatron: Rhetorische Kultur in Spätantike und Mittelalter / Rhetorical Culture in Late Antiquity and the Middle Ages*. Edited by Michael Grünbart, 277–286. Berlin: De Gruyter, 2007.

Marcus, Abraham. *The Middle East on the Eve of Modernity: Aleppo in the Eighteenth Century*. New York, NY: Columbia University Press, 1989.

——. "Privacy in Eighteenth-Century Aleppo: The Limits of Cultural Ideals." *International Journal of Middle East Studies* 18, no. 2 (1986): 165–183.

Mardin, Şerif. *The Genesis of Young Ottoman Thought: Study in the Modernization of Turkish Political Ideas*. Syracuse, NY: Syracuse University Press, 2000.

Markiewicz, Christopher. *The Crisis of Kingship in Late Medieval Islam: Persian Emigres and the Making of Ottoman Sovereignty*. Cambridge: Cambridge University Press, 2019.

Marlow, Louise. "Advice and Advice Literature." In *Encyclopaedia of Islam*. 3rd ed. Edited by Kate Fleet, Gudrun Krämer, Denis Matringe, John Nawas, and Everett Rowson. Consulted online 10 January 2014. http://dx.doi.org/10.1163/1573-3912_ei3_COM_0026.

Marsh, Christopher. "Order and Place in England, 1580–1640: The View from the Pew." *Journal of British Studies* 44, no. 1 (2005): 3–26.

Masarwa, Alev. "Performing the Occasion: The Chronograms of Māmayya ar-Rūmi (930–985 or 987/1534–1577 or 1579)." In *The Mamluk-Ottoman Transition: Continuity and Change in Egypt and Bilād al-Shām in the Sixteenth Century*. Edited by Stephan Conermann and Gül Şen, 177–206. Göttingen: V&R unipress, 2016.

Masters, Bruce. *The Arabs of the Ottoman Empire, 1516–1918: A Social and Cultural History*. Cambridge: Cambridge University Press, 2013.

Matthee, Rudolph. "Alcohol in the Islamic Middle East: Ambivalence and Ambiguity." In *Intoxication and Early Modernity*. Edited by Phil Withington and Angela McShane. Oxford: Past & Present, supplement, nr. 9 (2014): 100–125.

Mauder, Christian. "Being Persian in Late Mamluk Egypt: The Construction and Significance of Persian Ethnic Identity in the Salons of Qāniṣawh al-Ghawrī (r. 906–922/1501–1516)." *Al-ʿUṣūr al-Wusṭā* 28 (2020): 376–408.

Mauder, Christian, and Christopher Markiewicz. "A New Source on the Social Gatherings (*Majālis*) of the Mamluk Sultan Qānṣawh al-Ghawrī." *Al-ʿUṣūr al-Wuṣṭā* 24 (2016): 145–148.

Meier, Astrid. "For the Sake of God Alone? Food Distribution Policies, *Takiyyas* and Imarets in Early Ottoman Damascus." In *Feeding People, Feeding Power: Imarets in the Ottoman Empire*. Edited by Nina Ergin, Christoph Neumann, and Amy Singer, 121–150. Istanbul: Eren, 2007.

———. "Perceptions of a New Era? Historical Writing in Early Ottoman Damascus." *Arabica* 51, no. 4 (2004): 419–434.

Melchert, Christopher. "The Etiquette of Learning in the Early Islamic Study Circle." In *Law and Education in Medieval Islam: Studies in Memory of Professor George Makdisi*. Edited by Joseph E. Lowry, Devin J. Stewart, and Shawkat M. Toorawa, 33–44. Cambridge: E. J. W. Gibb Memorial Trust, 2004.

———. *Hadith, Piety, and Law: Selected Studies*. Atlanta, GA: Lockwood Press, 2015.

Melville, Charles. "The Early Persian Historiography of Anatolia." In *History and Historiography of Post-Mongol Central Asia and the Middle East: Studies in Honor of John E. Woods*. Edited by Judith Pfeiffer and Sholeh A. Quinn, 135–165. Wiesbaden: Harrassowitz Verlag, 2006.

Mengüç, Murat. "The *Türk* in Aşıkpaşazâde: A Private Individual's Ottoman History." *Osmanlı Araştırmaları/Journal of Ottoman Studies* 30 (2014): 45–66.

Menzel, Th. "Muʾayyad-Zāde." In *Encyclopaedia of Islam*. 2nd ed. 1960–2004. Edited by P. Bearman, Th. Bianquis, C. E. Bosworth, E. van Donzel, and W. P. Heinrichs. Consulted online 13 March 2012. http://dx.doi.org/10.1163/1573-3912_islam_SIM_5286.

Meshal, Reem. "Antagonistic Sharīʿas and the Construction of Orthodoxy in Sixteenth-Century Ottoman Cairo." *Journal of Islamic Studies* 21, no. 2 (May 2010): 183–212.

Mettam, Roger. *Power and Faction in Louis XIV's France*. Oxford: Blackwell, 1988.

Mikhail, Alan. *God's Shadow: The Ottoman Sultan Who Shaped the Modern World*. London: Faber, 2020.

———. "The Heart's Desire: Gender, Urban Space, and the Ottoman Coffee House." In *Ottoman Tulips, Ottoman Coffee: Leisure and Lifestyle in the Eighteenth Century*. Edited by Dana Sajdi, 133–170. London: I.B. Tauris, 2007.

———. *Nature and Empire in Ottoman Egypt: An Environmental History*. Cambridge: Cambridge University Press, 2011.

Miura, Toru. *Dynamism in the Urban Society of Damascus: The Ṣāliḥiyya Quarter from the Twelfth to the Twentieth Centuries*. Leiden: Brill, 2015.

———. "The Salihiyya Quarter of Damascus at the Beginning of Ottoman Rule: The Ambiguous Relations Between Religious Institutions and *Waqf* Properties." In *Syria and Bilad al-Sham under Ottoman Rule: Essays in Honour of Abdul Karim Rafeq*. Edited by Peter Sluglett and Stefan Weber, 269–291. Leiden: Brill, 2010.

———. "The Ṣāliḥiyya Quarter in the Suburbs of Damascus: Its Formation, Structure, and Transformation in the Ayyūbid and Mamlūk Periods." *Bulletin d'études orientales* 47 (1995): 129–181.

———. "Transition of the ʿUlamaʾ Families in Sixteenth Century Damascus." In *The Mamluk-Ottoman Transition: Continuity and Change in Egypt and Bilād al-Shām in the Sixteenth Century*. Edited by Stephan Conermann and Gül Şen, 207–220. Göttingen: V&R unipress, 2016.

———. "Urban Society in Damascus as the Mamluk Era Was Ending." *Mamlūk Studies Review* 10, no. 1 (2006): 157–193.

Moin, Azfar. *The Millennial Sovereign: Sacred Kingship and Sainthood in Islam*. New York, NY: Columbia University Press, 2012.

Mollenhauer, Anne. "Private in Public or Public in Private: Representation Rooms in Manorial Courtyard Houses in Aleppo." In *Angels, Peonies, and Fabulous Creatures: The Aleppo Room in Berlin*. Edited by Julia Gonnella and Jens Kröger, 71–78. Münster: Rhema Verlag, 2008.

Montgomery, James. "Al-Jāḥiẓ on Misarticulation: *Bayān* 1.34.4–74.8." *Journal of Arabic Literature* 48 (2018): 1–22.

———. "Al-Jāḥiẓ's *Kitāb al-Bayān wa al-Tabyīn*." In *Writing and Representation in Medieval Islam: Muslim Horizons*. Edited by Julia Bray, 91–152. London: Routledge, 2006.

Moore, Robert. "Companionship." In *Encyclopaedia of Islam*. 3rd ed. Edited by Kate Fleet, Gudrun Krämer, Denis Matringe, John Nawas, and Everett Rowson. Consulted online 12 May 2017. http://dx.doi.org/10.1163/1573-3912_ei3_COM_24627.

Muhanna, Elias. "The Sultan's New Clothes: Ottoman-Mamluk Gift Exchange in the Fifteenth Century." *Muqarnas* 27 (2010): 189–207.

Murphey, Rhoads. *Exploring Ottoman Sovereignty: Tradition, Image and Practice in the Ottoman Imperial Household, 1400–1800*. London: Continuum, 2008.

Murphy, Jane. "Improving the Mind and Delighting the Spirit: Jabarti and the Sciences in Eighteenth-Century Ottoman Cairo." Unpublished Ph.D. Dissertation, Princeton University, 2006.

Musawi, Muhsin. al-. *The Medieval Islamic Republic of Letters: Arabic Knowledge Construction*. Notre Dame, IN: University of Notre Dame Press, 2015.

Muslu, Emire Cihan. "Ottoman-Mamluk Relations: Diplomacy and Perceptions." Unpublished Ph.D. Dissertation, Harvard University, 2007.

———. *The Ottomans and the Mamluks: Imperial Diplomacy and Warfare in the Islamic World*. London and New York, NY: IB Tauris, 2014.

Mutawallī, Aḥmad Fu'ād. *al- Fatḥ al-ʿuthmānī li-l-Shām wa-Miṣr wa-muqaddimātuhu min wāqiʿ al-watāʾiq wa-l-maṣādir at-turkiyya wa-l-ʿarabiyya al-muʿāṣira*. Cairo: al-Zahrāʾ li-l-Iʿlām al-ʿArabī, [1414H] 1995.

Naguib, Shuruq. "Guiding the Sound Mind: Ebu's-su'ūd's *Tafsir* and Rhetorical Interpretation of the Qur'an in the Post-Classical Period." *Osmanlı Araştırmaları/Journal of Ottoman Studies* 42 (2013): 1–52.

Nasser, Shady Hekmat. "(Q. 12:2) We have sent it down as an Arabic Qurʾān: Praying behind the Lisper." *Islamic Law and Society* 23 (2016): 23–51.

Necipoğlu, Gülru. *The Age of Sinan: Architectural Culture in the Ottoman Empire*. London: Reaktion Books, 2005.

———. *Architecture, Ceremonial, and Power: The Topkapı Palace in the Fifteenth and Sixteenth Centuries*. Cambridge, MA: MIT Press, 1991.

———. "Framing the Gaze in Ottoman, Safavid, and Mughal Palaces." *Ars Orientalis* 23 (1993): 303–342.

———. "A Kânûn for the State, a Canon for the Arts: Conceptualizing the Classical Synthesis of Ottoman Art and Architecture." In *Soliman le Magnifique et son Temps*. Edited by Gilles Veinstein, 195–215. Paris: Documentation Française, 1992.

——. "The Serial Portrait of Ottoman Sultans in Comparative Perspective." In *The Sultan's Portrait: Picturing the House of Osman*. Edited by Selmin Kangal, 22–61. Istanbul: Işbank, 2000.

——. "The Suburban Landscape of Sixteenth-Century Istanbul as a Mirror of Classical Ottoman Garden Culture." In *Theory and Design of Gardens in the Time of the Great Muslim Empires*. Edited by Attilio Petruccioli, 32–71. Leiden: Brill, 1997.

——. "Süleyman the Magnificent and the Representation of Power in the Context of Ottoman-Hapsburg-Papal Rivalry." *Art Bulletin* 71, no. 3, (1989): 401–427.

Netton, Ian Richard, ed. *Golden Roads: Migration Pilgrimage and Travel in Mediaeval and Modern Islam*. Richmond: Curzon Press, 1993.

——. "*Riḥla*." In *Encyclopaedia of Islam*. 2nd ed. 1960–2004. Edited by P. Bearman, Th. Bianquis, C. E. Bosworth, E. van Donzel, and W. P. Heinrichs. Consulted online 25 September 2016. http://dx.doi.org/10.1163/1573-3912_islam_SIM_6298.

Niyazioğlu, Aslı. *Dreams and Lives in Ottoman Istanbul: A Seventeenth-Century Biographer's Perspective*. Milton Park: Routledge, 2017.

——. "The Sixteenth-Century Ottoman Poet in Reclusion (*ʿUzlet*)." In *Poetry's Voice—Society's Norms: Forms of Interaction between Middle Eastern Writers and Their Societies*. Edited by Andreas Pflitsch and Barbara Winckler, 225–235. Wiesbaden: Reichert Verlag, 2006.

Nizri, Michael. *Ottoman High Politics and the Ulema Household*. Basingstoke: Palgrave MacMillan, 2014.

Ocak, Ahmet Yaşar. "Social, Cultural and Intellectual Life, 1071–1453." In *The Cambridge History of Turkey*. Vol. 1: *Byzantium to Turkey, 1071–1453*. Edited by Kate Fleet, 353–422. Cambridge: Cambridge University Press, 2009.

Oktay, A. S. *Kınalızâde Ali Efendi ve Ahlâk-ı Alâî*. Istanbul: İz Yayıncılık, 2005.

Ökten, Ertuğrul. "Scholars and Mobility: A Preliminary Assessment from the Perspective of Al-Shaqāyiq Al-Nuʿmāniyya." *Osmanlı Araştırmaları/Journal of Ottoman Studies* 41 (2013): 55–70.

Orhunlu, Cengiz. "Textes et images commentés, III: Recherches sur l'histoire du quartier de Fındıklı." In *Anatolia moderna/Yeni anadolu* 8 (1999): 114–129.

Ott, Claudia. "'Wer sich fürchtet, verliert—wer wagt, gewinnt': Neues zu den Inschriften des Aleppo-Zimmers." In *Angels, Peonies, and Fabulous Creatures: The Aleppo Room in Berlin*. Edited by Julia Gonnella and Jens Kröger, 81–85. Münster: Rhema Verlag, 2008.

Özbaran, Salih. *Bir Osmanlı Kimliği: 14.–17. Yüzyıllarda Rûm/Rûmi Aidiyet ve İmgeleri*. Istanbul: Kitap Yayınevi, 2004.

Özcan, Tahsin. "Mehmed Efendi, Mâlûlzâde." In *Türkiye Diyanet Vakfı İslâm Ansiklopedisi*. Vol. 28 (2003): 455.

Özkoçak, Selma. "Coffeehouses: Rethinking the Public and Private in Early Modern Istanbul." *Journal of Urban History* 33, no. 6 (2007): 965–986.

Öznurhan, Halim. "Abbâsî, Abdürrahîm." In *Türkiye Diyanet Vakfı İslâm Ansiklopedisi*. Suppl. 1 (2016): 5–6.

Öztürk, Zehra. "Eğitim Tarihimizde Okuma Toplantılarının Yeri ve Okunan Kitaplar." *Değerler Eğitimi Dergisi* 1, no. 4 (2003): 131–155.

——. "Osmanlı Döneminde Kıraat Meclislerinde Okunan Halk Kitapları." *Türkiye Araştırmaları Literatür Dergisi* 5, no. 9 (2007): 401–445.

Pamuk, Şevket. *A Monetary History of the Ottoman Empire*. Cambridge: Cambridge University Press, 2000.

Parmaksızoğlu, İsmet. "Üsküplü İshak Çelebi ve Selimnâmesi." *Tarih Dergisi* 3, no. 5–6 (1953): 123–43.

Parry, Vernon. "Ayās Pasha." In *Encyclopaedia of Islam*. 2nd ed. 1960–2004. Edited by P. Bearman, Th. Bianquis, C. E. Bosworth, E. van Donzel, and W. P. Heinrichs. Consulted online 18 February 2012. http://www.brillonline.nl/subscriber/entry?entry=islam_SIM-0895.

Peacock, Andrew C. S., and Sara Nur Yıldz, eds. *Islamic Literature and Intellectual Life in Fourteenth- and Fifteenth-Century Anatolia*. Würzburg: Ergon Verlag, 2016.

———. *The Seljuks of Anatolia: Court and Society in the Medieval Middle East*. London: I.B. Tauris, 2013.

Pedersen, John et al. "Madrasa." In *Encyclopaedia of Islam*. 2nd ed. 1960–2004. Edited by P. Bearman, Th. Bianquis, C. E. Bosworth, E. van Donzel, and W. P. Heinrichs. Consulted online 8 April 2017. http://dx.doi.org/10.1163/1573-3912_islam_COM_0610.

Peirce, Leslie. "Becoming Ottoman in 16th Century Aintab." In *Istanbul as Seen from a Distance: Centre and Provinces in the Ottoman Empire*. Edited by Elisabeth Özdalga et al., 59–72. Istanbul: Swedish Research Institute in Istanbul, 2011.

———. "The Material World: Ideologies and Ordinary Things." In *The Early Modern Ottomans: Remapping the Empire*. Edited by Virginia Aksan and Daniel Goffman, 213–232. Cambridge: Cambridge University Press, 2007.

———. *Morality Tales: Law and Gender in the Court of Aintab*. Berkeley, CA: University of California Press, 2003.

Pellat, Charles. "D̲jins." In *Encyclopaedia of Islam*. 2nd ed. 1960–2004. Edited by P. Bearman, Th. Bianquis, C. E. Bosworth, E. van Donzel, and W. P. Heinrichs. Consulted online 11 August 2015. http://dx.doi.org/10.1163/1573-3912_islam_SIM_2083.

Peters, Rudolph. *Crime and Punishment in Islamic Law: Theory and Practice from the Sixteenth to the Twenty-First Century*. Cambridge: Cambridge University Press, 2005.

Petersen, Andrew. *The Medieval and Ottoman Hajj Route in Jordan: An Archaeological and Historical Study* (Levant Supplementary Series, 12). Oxford: Oxbow Books, 2012.

Petievich, Carla. *Assembly of Rivals: Delhi, Lucknow, and the Urdu Ghazal*. Delhi: Manohar, 1992.

Petry, Carl. *The Civilian Elite of Cairo in the Later Middle Ages*. Princeton, NJ: Princeton University Press, 1981.

———. "A Paradox of Patronage during the Later Mamluk Period." *Muslim World* 73 (1983): 182–207.

———. "Travel Patterns of Medieval Notables in the Near East." *Studia Islamica* 73, no. 3–4 (1985): 53–87.

———. "'Travel Patterns of Medieval Notables in the Near East' Reconsidered: contrasting trajectories, interconnected networks." In *Everything Is On the Move: The Mamluk Empire as a Node in (Trans-)Regional Networks*. Edited by Stephan Conermann, 165–179. Göttingen: V&R unipress, 2014.

Pfeifer, Helen. "Encounter after the Conquest: Literary Salons in Sixteenth-Century Ottoman Damascus." *International Journal of Middle East Studies* 47 (2015): 219–239.

——. "Gulper and the Slurper: A Lexicon of Mistakes to Avoid While Eating with Ottoman Gentlemen." *Journal of Early Modern History* 24, no. 1 (2020): 41–62.

——. "A New Hadith Culture? The Role of Arab Scholars in Ottoman Confession-Building." In *Historicizing Sunni Islam in the Ottoman Empire, c.1450–c.1750*. Edited by Tijana Krstić and Derin Terzioğlu, 31–61. Leiden: Brill, 2020.

Pfeiffer, Judith, ed. *Politics, Patronage and the Transmission of Knowledge in 13th–15th Century Tabriz*. Leiden: Brill, 2014.

——. "Teaching the Learned: Jalāl al-Dīn al-Dawānī's *Ijāza* to Muʾayyadzāda ʿAbd al-Raḥmān Efendi and the Circulation of Knowledge between Fārs and the Ottoman Empire at the Turn of the Sixteenth Century." In *The Heritage of Arabo-Islamic Learning: Studies Presented to Wadad Kadi*. Edited by Maurice Pomerantz and Aram Shahin, 284–332. Leiden: Brill, 2016.

Philliou, Christine. *Biography of an Empire: Governing Ottomans in an Age of Revolution*. Berkeley, CA: University of California Press, 2011.

Phillip, Thomas. "The Economic Impact of the Ottoman Conquest on *Bilad al-Sham*." In *Syria and Bilad al-Sham under Ottoman Rule: Essays in Honour of Abdul-Karim Rafeq*. Edited by Peter Sluglett and Stefan Weber, 101–114. Leiden: Brill, 2010.

Phillips, Amanda. *Everyday Luxuries: Art and Objects in Ottoman Constantinople, 1600–1800*. Dortmund: Verlag Kettler, 2016.

Pollock, Sheldon. *The Language of Gods in the World of Men*. Berkeley, CA: University of California Press, 2006.

al-Qāḍī, Wadād. "Biographical Dictionaries: Inner Structure and Cultural Significance." In *The Book in the Islamic World: The Written Word and Communication in the Middle East*. Edited by G. N. Atiyeh, 93–122. Albany, NY: State University of New York Press, 1995.

——. "Biographical Dictionaries as the Scholars' Alternative History of the Muslim Community." In *Organizing Knowledge: Encyclopaedic Activities in the Pre-Eighteenth Century Islamic World*. Edited by Gerhard Endress, 23–76. Leiden: Brill, 2006.

Qutbuddin, Tahera. "Books on Arabic Philology and Literature: A Teaching Collection Focused on Religious Learning and the State Chancery." In *Treasures of Knowledge: An Inventory of the Ottoman Palace Library (1502/3–1503/4)*. Vol. 1. Edited by Gülru Necipoğlu, Cemal Kafadar, and Cornell Fleischer, 607–634. Leiden: Brill, 2019.

Rafeq, Abdul Karim. "ʿAbd al-Ghani al-Nabulsi—Religious Tolerance and 'Arabness' in Ottoman Damascus." In *Transformed Landscapes: Essays on Palestine and the Middle East in Honor of Walid Khalidi*. Edited by Camille Mansour and Leila Fawaz, 1–18. Cairo and New York, NY: American University in Cairo Press, 2009.

——. *Al-ʿArab wa-l-ʿUthmāniyyūn, 1516-1916*. Damascus: Maktabat Atlas, 1974.

——. "Diversion and Pleasure in Damascus during the Ottoman Period." In *Divertissements et loisirs dans les sociétés urbaines à l'époque moderne et contemporaine*.

Edited by Robert Beck and Anna Madœuf. Tours: Presses universitaires François-Rabelais, 2005. http://books.openedition.org/pufr/632.

——. *The Province of Damascus, 1723–1783*. Beirut: Khayats, 1966.

——. "Relations between Syrian 'Ulamā' and the Ottoman State in the Eighteenth Century." *Oriente Moderno* 18, no. 79 (1999): 67–95.

——. "Social Groups, Identity and Loyalty, and Historical Writing in Ottoman and Post-Ottoman Syria." In *Les Arabes et l'histoire creatrice*. Edited by Dominique Chevallier, 79–93. Paris: Université de Paris Sorbonne, 1995.

——. "The Syrian *'Ulamā*, Ottoman Law and Islamic *Sharī'a*." *Turcica* 26–27 (1994–95): 9–32.

Raymond, André. *Arab Cities in the Ottoman Period: Cairo, Syria and the Maghreb*. Aldershot: Ashgate, 2002.

——. *Artisans et commerçants au Caire au XVIIIe siècle*. 2 vols. Cairo: IFAO IFEAD, 1999.

——. "The Ottoman Conquest and the Development of the Great Arab Towns." *International Journal of Turkish Studies* 1 (1979–80): 84–101.

Reichmuth, Stefan. "Mündlicher und literarischer Wissenstransfer in Ägypten im späten 18. / frühen 19. Jahrhundert—Arabische Gelehrte und ihr Zugang zu europäischer Naturwissenschaft." In *Buchkultur im Nahen Osten des 17. und 18. Jahrhunderts*. Edited by Tobias Heinzelmann and Henning Sievert, 27–52. Bern: Peter Lang, 2010.

——. "Murtaḍā az-Zabīdī (d. 1791) in Biographical and Autobiographical Accounts: Glimpses of Islamic Scholarship in the 18th Century." *Die Welt des Islams* 39, no. 1 (1999): 64–102.

Reilly, James. *A Small Town in Syria: Ottoman Hama in the Eighteenth and Nineteenth Centuries*. Oxford: P. Lang, 2002.

Reindl-Kiel, Hedda. "Ottoman Courtly Tents and Turkic Tradition." In *CIÉPO Interim Symposium: The Central Asiatic Roots of Ottoman Culture*. Edited by İlhan Şahin, Baktıbek İsakov, and Cengiz Buyar, 641–655. Istanbul: İstanbul Esnaf ve Sanatkarlar Odaları, 2014.

Repp, R. C. *The Müfti of Istanbul: A Study in the Development of the Ottoman Learned Hierarchy*. London: Ithaca Press, 1986.

——. "Mulāzim." In *Encyclopaedia of Islam*. 2nd ed. 1960–2004. Edited by P. Bearman, Th. Bianquis, C. E. Bosworth, E. van Donzel, and W. P. Heinrichs, 545–546. Consulted online on 7 April 2021. http://dx.doi.org/10.1163/1573-3912_islam_SIM_5486.

Reynolds, Gabriel Said. *The Emergence of Islam: Classical Traditions in Contemporary Perspective*. Minneapolis, MN: Fortress Press, 2012.

Rice, David Storm. *The Unique Ibn al-Bawwāb Manuscript in the Chester Beatty Library*. Dublin: Walker, 1955.

al-Rīḥāwī, 'Abd al-Qādir. "Jāmi' Yalbughā fī Dimashq." *Les Annales Archaeologiques Arabes Syriennes* 24 (1974): 125–150.

Robinson, Chase. *Islamic Historiography*. Cambridge: Cambridge University Press, 2003.

Rogan, Eugene. *The Arabs: A History*. New York, NY: Basic Books, 2009.

Roper, Geoffrey, ed. *The History of the Book in the Middle East*. Farnham: Ashgate Publishing, 2013.

Rosenthal, Franz. "'Blurbs' (*Taqrīẓ*) from Fourteenth-Century Egypt." *Oriens* 27–28 (1981): 177–196.

——. "al-Kāfiyadjī." In *Encyclopaedia of Islam*. 2nd ed. 1960–2004. Edited by P. Bearman, Th. Bianquis, C. E. Bosworth, E. van Donzel, and W. P. Heinrichs. Consulted online 19 September 2014. http://dx.doi.org/10.1163/1573-3912_islam_SIM_3779.

Rothman, Natalie. *Brokering Empire: Trans-Imperial Subjects between Venice and Istanbul*. Ithaca, NY: Cornell University Press, 2012.

Rouget, François. "Academies, Circles, 'Salons,' and the Emergence of the Premodern 'Literary Public Sphere' in Sixteenth-Century France." In *Making Publics in Early Modern Europe: People, Things, Forms of Knowledge*. Edited by Bronwen Wilson and Paul Yachnin, 53–67. London and New York, NY: Routledge, 2011.

Saba, Elias. *Harmonizing Similarities: A History of Distinctions Literature in Islamic Law*. Berlin: De Gruyter, 2019.

Sahillioğlu, Halil. "Arûs Resmi." In *Türkiye Diyanet Vakf İslâm Ansiklopedisi*. Vol. 3 (1991): 422–423.

Şahin, Kaya. *Empire and Power in the Reign of Süleyman*. Cambridge: Cambridge University Press, 2013.

——. "Staging an Empire: An Ottoman Circumcision Ceremony as Cultural Performance." *American Historical Review* 123, no. 2 (2018): 463–492.

Sajdi, Dana. *The Barber of Damascus: Nouveau Literacy in the Eighteenth-Century Ottoman Levant*. Stanford, CA: Stanford University Press, 2013.

——. "The Dead and the City: The Limits of Hospitality in the Early Modern Levant." In *Hosting the Stranger: Between Religions*. Edited by Richard Kearney and James Taylor, 123–132. New York, NY: Continuum, 2011.

Saleh, Marlis. "Al-Suyūṭī and His Works: Their Place in Islamic Scholarship from Mamluk Times to the Present." *Mamlūk Studies Review* 5 (2001): 73–89.

Saleh, Walid A. "The Gloss as Intellectual History: The *Ḥāshiyahs* on *al-Kashshāf*." *Oriens* 41, nos. 3–4 (Jan. 2013): 217–259.

Salzmann, Ariel. "An Ancient Regime Revisited: 'Privatization' and Political Economy in the Eighteenth-Century Ottoman Empire." *Politics & Society* 21, no. 4 (1993): 393–423.

Sariyannis, Marinos. *A History of Ottoman Political Thought up to the Early Nineteenth Century*. Leiden: Brill, 2019.

——. "Prostitution in Ottoman Istanbul, Late Sixteenth–Early Eighteenth Century." *Turcica* 40 (Dec. 2008): 37–65.

Saßmannshausen, Christian. "Reform in Translation: Family, Distinction, and Social Mediation in Late Ottoman Tripoli." Unpublished Ph.D. Dissertation, Freie Universität Berlin, 2013.

Savaş, Hamdi. "İshak Çelebi, Kılıççı-zâde." In *Türkiye Diyanet Vakfı İslâm Ansiklopedisi*. Vol. 22 (2000): 528–9.

Schmidt, Jan. "Poets and Poetry in Mid-17th-Century Istanbul: Additions to the *Dīvān* of Fā'iżī by the Copyist Yaḥyā Efendi and Others in the John Rylands University Library MS Turkish 81 (Manchester)." *Arabic and Middle Eastern Literatures* 3, no. 2 (2000): 165–178.

Şeşen, Ramazan. "Eski Araplar'a Göre Türkler." *Türkiyat Mecmuası* 15 (1968): 11–36.

Shafir, Nir. "In an Ottoman Holy Land: The Hajj and the Road from Damascus, 1500–1800. *History of Religions* 60, no. 1 (2020): 1–36.

———. "The Road from Damascus: Circulation and the Redefinition of Islam in the Ottoman Empire, 1620–1720." Unpublished Ph.D. Dissertation, University of California, Los Angeles, 2016.

Sharkas, Ahmad. "Badr al-Dīn al-Ghazzī (904/1499–984/1577) and His Manual on Islamic Scholarship and Education 'al-Durr al-Naḍīd.'" Unpublished Ph.D. Dissertation, Harvard University, 1976.

Shaw, Stanford. *History of the Ottoman Empire and Modern Turkey*. Cambridge: Cambridge University Press, 1976–7.

Shoshan, Boaz. "On the Marital Regime in Damascus, 1480–1500." In *History and Society during the Mamluk Period (1250–1517)*. Edited by Stephan Conermann. 7–27. Göttingen: Bonn University Press, 2016.

Sievert, Henning. "Eavesdropping on the Pasha's Salon: Usual and Unusual Readings of an Eighteenth-Century Ottoman Bureaucrat." *Osmanlı Araştırmaları/Journal of Ottoman Studies* 41 (2013): 159–195.

———. *Zwischen arabischer Provinz und Hoher Pforte: Beziehungen, Bildung und Politik des osmanischen Bürokraten Rāġıb Meḥmed Paşa (st. 1763)*. Würzburg: Ergon Verlag, 2008.

Simmel, Georg, trans. Everett Hughes. "The Sociology of Sociability." *American Journal of Sociology*, 55, no. 3 (1949): 254–61.

Singer, Amy. *Constructing Ottoman Beneficence: An Imperial Soup Kitchen in Jerusalem*. Albany, NY: SUNY Press, 2002.

———. *Palestinian Peasants and Ottoman Officials: Rural Administration Around Sixteenth-Century Jerusalem*. Cambridge: Cambridge University Press, 1994.

Smyth, William. "Controversy in a Tradition of Commentary: The Academic Legacy of al-Sakkākī's Miftāḥ al-ʿUlūm." *Journal of the American Oriental Society* 112, no. 4 (1992): 589–597.

Sohrweide, Hanna. "Dichter und Gelehrte aus dem Osten im osmanischen Reich (1453–1600): Ein Beitrag zur türkisch-persischen Kulturgeschichte." *Der Islam* 46 (1970): 263–302.

Soll, Jacob. *The Information Master: Jean-Baptiste Colbert's Secret State Intelligence System*. Ann Arbor, MI: The University of Michigan Press, 2009.

Sternberg, Giora. *Status Interaction during the Reign of Louis XIV*. Oxford: Oxford University Press, 2014.

Stetkevych, Suzanne Pinckney. *The Mantle Odes: Arabic Praise Poems to the Prophet Muḥammad*. Bloomington, IN: Indiana University Press, 2010.

Stewart-Robinson, J. "The Ottoman Biographies of Poets." *Journal of Near Eastern Studies* 24, no. 1/2 (1965): 57–74.

———. "The Tez̠kire Genre in Islam." *Journal of Near Eastern Studies* 23, no. 1 (1964): 57–65.

Stilt, Kristen, and Roy Mottahedeh. "Public and Private as Viewed through the Work of the *Muhtasib*." *Social Research* 70, no. 3 (Fall 2003): 735–748.

Stowasser, Karl. "Manners and Customs at the Mamluk Court." *Muqarnas* 2 (1984): 13–20.

Strauss, Johann. "La Conversation." In *Vivre dans l'Empire Ottoman: Sociabilités et Relations Intercommunautaires (XVIIe-XIXe siècles)*. Edited by François Georgeon and Paul Dumont, 251–318. Paris and Montreal: L'Harmattan, 1997.

Stripling, George William Frederick. *The Ottoman Turks and the Arabs: 1511–1574*. Urbana, IL: University of Illinois Press, 1942.

Stroumsa, Sarah. "Ibn al-Rāwandī's *sū' adab al-mujādala*: The Role of Bad Manners in Medieval Disputations." In *The Majlis: Interreligious Encounters in Medieval Islam*. Edited by Hava Lazarus-Yafeh, Mark Cohen, Sasson Somekh, and Sidney Griffith, 66–83. Wiesbaden: Harrassowitz Verlag, 1999.

Sturmberger, Hans. "Das Problem der Vorbildhaftigkeit des türkischen Staatswesens im 16. und 17. Jahrhundert und sein Einfluss auf den europäischen Absolutismus." In *Actes et rapports du XIIe Congrès international des sciences historiques IV (30 Août, 3–4 Septembre 1965)*. Edited by the Comité International des Sciences Historiques, 201–209. Vienna: Ferdinand Berger and Söhne, 1965.

Subrahmanyam, Sanjay, and Muzaffer Alam. "Frank Disputations: Catholics and Muslims in the Court of Jahangir (1608–1611)." *Indian Economic Social History Review* 46, no. 4 (2009): 457–511.

Subtelny, Maria. "Art and Politics in Early 16th Century Central Asia." *Central Asiatic Journal* 27, no. 1/2 (1983): 121–148.

———. "Scenes from the Literary Life of Tīmūrid Herāt." In *Logos Islamikos: Studia Islamica in Honorem Georgii Michaelis Wickens*. Papers in Mediaval Studies. Vol. 6. Edited by Roger Savory and Dionisius Agius, 137–155. Toronto: Pontifical Institute of Mediaeval Studies, 1984.

Subtelny, Maria, and Anas Khalidov. "The Curriculum of Islamic Higher Learning in Timurid Iran in the Light of the Sunni Revival under Shāh-Rukh." *Journal of the American Oriental Society* 115, no. 2 (1995): 210–236.

Süreyya, Mehmed. *Sicill-i ʿOs̱mānī*. Constantinople: Maṭbaʿa-i ʿĀmire, 1893–4.

Szombathy, Soltan. "Ridiculing the Learned: Jokes About the Scholarly Class in Mediaeval Arabic Literature." *al-Qanṭara* 25, no. 1 (2004): 93–117.

Szuppe, Maria. "The Female Intellectual Milieu in Timurid and Post-Timurid Herāt: Faxri Heravi's Biography of Poetesses, *Javāher al-ʿAjāyeb*." *Oriente Moderno* 76, no. 2 (1996): 119–137.

Talib, Adam. *How Do You Say "Epigram" in Arabic? Literary History at the Limits of Comparison*. Leiden: Brill, 2014.

Tamari, Steve. "Arab National Consciousness in Seventeenth- and Eighteenth-Century Syria." In *Syria and Bilad al-Sham under Ottoman Rule: Essays in Honour of Abdul-Karim Rafeq*. Edited by Peter Sluglett and Stefan Weber, 309–322. Leiden: Brill, 2010.

Taner, Melis. *Caught in a Whirlwind: A Cultural History of Baghdad as Reflected in Its Illustrated Manuscripts*. Leiden: Brill, 2019.

Tanındı, Zeren. "Transformation of Words to Images: Portraits of Ottoman Courtiers in the 'Dîwâns' of Bâkî and Nâdirî." *Anthropology and Aesthetics* 43 (2003): 131–145.

Tarte, Kendall. *Writing Places: Sixteenth-Century City Culture and the Des Roches Salon*. Newark, DE: University of Delaware Press, 2007.

Terzioğlu, Derin. "How to Conceptualize Ottoman Sunnitization: A Historiographical Discussion." *Turcica* 44 (2012–3): 301–338.

——. "Ibn Taymiyya, al-Siyāsa al-Shar'iyya, and the Early Modern Ottomans." In *Historicizing Sunni Islam in the Ottoman Empire, c.1450–c.1750*. Edited by Tijana Krstić and Derin Terzioğlu, 101–154. Leiden: Brill, 2020.

——. "Where *'İlm-i Ḥāl* Meets Catechism: Islamic Manuals of Religious Instruction in the Ottoman Empire in the Age of Confessionalization." *Past and Present* 220 (2013): 79–114.

Tezcan, Baki. "Dispelling the Darkness: The Politics of 'Race' in the Early Seventeenth-Century Ottoman Empire in the Light of the Life and Work of Mullah Ali." In *Identity and Identity Formation in the Ottoman World: A Volume of Essays in Honor of Norman Itzkowitz*. Edited by Baki Tezcan and Karl Barbir, 73–95. Madison, WI: University of Wisconsin Press, 2007.

——. "Ethnicity, Race, Religion and Social Class: Ottoman Markers of Difference." In *The Ottoman World*. Edited by Christine Woodhead, 159–170. London: Routledge, 2013.

——. "The Ottoman *Mevali* as 'Lords of the Law.'" *Journal of Islamic Studies* 20, no. 3 (2009): 1–25.

——. *The Second Ottoman Empire*. Cambridge: Cambridge University Press, 2010.

——. "Some Thoughts on the Politics of Early Modern Ottoman Science." In *Beyond Dominant Paradigms in Ottoman and Middle Eastern/North African Studies*. Edited by Donald Quataert and Baki Tezcan, 135–156. Istanbul: Center for Islamic Studies [İSAM], 2010.

Tietze, Andreas. "Ethnicity and Change in Ottoman Intellectual History." *Turcica* 23 (1991): 385–395.

——. "Muṣṭafā 'Ālī on Luxury and the Status Symbols of Ottoman Gentlemen." In *Studia Turcologica Memoriae Alexii Bombaci Dicata*. Edited by Aldo Gallotta and Ugo Marazzi, 585–90. Naples: Istituto Universitario Orientale, 1982.

Tolasa, Harun. *Sehî, Lâtîfi, ve Âşık Çelebi Tezkirelerine Göre 16. Yüzyılda Edebiyat Araştırma ve Eleştirisi*. Izmir: Ege Üniversitesi Matbaası, 1983.

Touati, Houari. *Islam and Travel in the Middle Ages*. Translated by Lydia Cochrane. Chicago, IL: University of Chicago Press, 2010.

Tunçay, Şerafettin. "Çivi-zade Ailesi." Unpublished Undergraduate Thesis, Istanbul University, 1950.

Turan, Ebru. "The Sultan's Favorite: İbrahim Pasha and the Making of the Ottoman Universal Sovereignty in the Reign of Sultan Süleyman." Unpublished Ph.D. Dissertation, University of Chicago, 2007.

Uludağ, Süleyman. "Sohbet." In *Türkiye Diyanet Vakfı İslâm Ansiklopedisi*. Vol. 37 (2009): 350–351.

Uzunçarşılı, İsmail Hakkı. *Anadolu Beylikleri ve Akkoyunlu, Karakoyunlu Devletleri*. Ankara: Türk Tarih Kurumu Basımevi, 1969.

——. *Osmanlı Devletinin İlmiye Teşkilâtı*. Ankara: Türk Tarih Kurumu, 1988.

van Gelder, Geert Jan. "Arabic Banqueters: Literature, Lexicography and Reality." In *Banquets d'Orient (Res Orientales IV)*. Edited by Rika Gyselen, 85–93. Bures-sur-Yvette: Peeters, 1992.

——. "Shihāb al-Dīn, Al-Khafājī." In *Essays in Arabic Literary Biography, 1350–1850*. Edited by Joseph Lowry and Devin Stewart, 251–262. Wiesbaden: Otto Harrassowitz Verlag, 2009.

———. "A Muslim Encomium on Wine: *The Racecourse of the Bay (Ḥalbat al-Kumayt)* by al-Nawāǧī (d. 859/1455) as a Post-Classical Arabic Work." *Arabica* 42 (1995): 222–234.

———. "Poetry for Easy Listening: *Insijām* and Related Concepts in Ibn Ḥijjah's *Khizānat al-Adab*." *Mamlūk Studies Review* 7, no. 1 (2003): 31–48.

Van Leeuwen, Richard. *Waqfs and Urban Structures: The Case of Ottoman Damascus*. Leiden: Brill, 1999.

Varlık, Nükhet. *Plague and Empire in the Early Modern Mediterranean World: The Ottoman Experience, 1347–1600*. Cambridge: Cambridge University Press, 2015.

Vatin, Nicolas. "Arabes et Turcs au Maghreb dans les années 1513–1520 d'après les *Ġazavât-ı Ḫayrü-d-dîn Paşa*." *Osmanlı Araştırmaları/Journal of Ottoman Studies* 40 (2012): 365–398.

Veinstein, Gilles. "L'administration ottomane et le problème des interprètes." In *Études sur les villes du Proche-Orient XVIe–XIXe siècles: Hommage à André Raymond*. Edited by Brigitte Marino, 65–79. Damascus: IFEAD, 2001.

———. "Le serviteur des deux saints sanctuaires et ses mahmal: Des Mamelouks aux Ottomans." *Turcica* 41 (2009): 229–246.

Walker, Paul. "Fatimid Institutions of Learning." *Journal of the American Research Center in Egypt* 34 (1997): 179–200.

Walsh, John. "Fenārī-Zāde." In *Encyclopaedia of Islam*. 2nd ed. 1960–2004. Edited by P. Bearman, Th. Bianquis, C. E. Bosworth, E. van Donzel, and W. P. Heinrichs. Consulted online 3 February 2015. http://referenceworks.brillonline.com/entries/encyclopaedia-of-islam-2/fenari-zade-SIM_2350.

———. "Gūrānī, Sh͟araf (or Sh͟ihāb or Sh͟ams) al-Dīn Aḥmad b. Ismāʿīl b. ʿOt͟hmān." In *Encyclopaedia of Islam*. 2nd ed. 1960–2004. Edited by P. Bearman, Th. Bianquis, C. E. Bosworth, E. van Donzel, and W. P. Heinrichs. Consulted online 27 March 2014. http://www.brillonline.nl/subscriber/entry?entry=islam_SIM-2564.

Watenpaugh, Heghnar. *The Image of an Ottoman City: Imperial Architecture and Urban Experience in Aleppo in the 16th and 17th Centuries*. Leiden: Brill, 2004.

Weber, Stefan. "The Creation of Ottoman Damascus: Architecture and Urban Development of Damascus in the 16th and 17th Centuries." *ARAM* 9–10 (1997–8): 431–470.

———. "An Egyptian *Qa'a* in 16th Century Damascus: Representative Halls in Late Mamluk and Early Ottoman Residential Architecture in Syria and Lebanon." In *From Handaxe to Khan: Essays Presented to Peder Mortensen on the Occasion of His 70th Birthday*. Edited by Kjeld von Folsach et al., 265–296. Aarhus: Aarhus University Press, 2004.

———. "Walls and Ceilings." In *The Future of the Past: The Robert Mouawad Private Museum*. Edited by Robert Mouawad and John Carswell, 242–265. Beirut: The Robert Mouawad Private Museum, 2004.

Weintritt, Otfried. "Concepts of History as Reflected in Arabic Historiographical Writing in Ottoman Syria and Egypt (1517–1700)." In *The Mamluks in Egyptian Politics and Society*. Edited by Thomas Philipp and Ulrich Haarmann, 188–195. Cambridge: Cambridge University Press, 2007.

Wensinck, A. J. "K͟huṭba." In *Encyclopaedia of Islam*. 2nd ed. 1960–2004. Edited by P. Bearman, Th. Bianquis, C. E. Bosworth, E. van Donzel, and W. P. Heinrichs. Consulted online 8 May 2014. http://dx.doi.org/10.1163/1573-3912_islam_SIM_4352.

White, Sam. *The Climate of Rebellion in the Early Modern Ottoman Empire*. Cambridge: Cambridge University Press, 2011.

Wilkins, Charles. "Masters, Servants and Slaves: Household Formation among the Urban Notables of Early Ottoman Aleppo." In *The Ottoman World*. Edited by Christine Woodhead, 291–306. London: Routledge, 2013.

Winter, Michael. "The *ashrāf* and the *naqīb al-ashrāf* in Ottoman Egypt and Syria: A comparative analysis." In *Sayyids and Sharifs in Muslim Societies: The Living Links to the Prophet*. Edited by Morimoto Kazuo, 139–157. London and New York, NY: Routledge, 2012.

———. "The Conquest of Syria and Egypt by Sultan Selim I, According to Evliyâ Çelebi." In *The Mamluk-Ottoman Transition: Continuity and Change in Egypt and Bilād al-Shām in the Sixteenth Century*. Edited by Stephan Conermann and Gül Şen, 127–146. Göttingen: V&R Unipress, 2016.

———. "Egypt and Syria in the Sixteenth Century." In *The Mamluk-Ottoman Transition: Continuity and Change in Egypt and Bilād al-Shām in the Sixteenth Century*. Edited by Stephan Conermann and Gül Şen, 34–56. Göttingen: V&R Unipress, 2016.

———. "Al-Ġazzī, Najmuddīn Muḥammad b. Muḥammad (b. 1570, d. 1651)." Historians of the Ottoman Empire. Edited by Cemal Kafadar, Hakan Karateke, and Cornell H. Fleischer. Accessed online 23 January 2011. https://ottomanhistorians.uchicago.edu/en/historian/al-gazzi.

———. "The judiciary of late Mamluk and early Ottoman Damascus: The administrative, social and cultural transformation of the system." *ASK Working Paper* 5 (2012): 1–25.

———. "Ottoman Qāḍīs in Damascus during the 16th–18th Centuries." *Law, Custom, and Statute in the Muslim World*. Edited by Ron Shaham, 87–109. Leiden: Brill, 2007.

———. "A Polemical Treatise by ʿAbd al-Ghani al-Nabulusi against a Turkish Scholar on the Religious Status of the *Dhimmis*." *Arabica* 35 (1988): 92–103.

———. *Society and Religion in Early Ottoman Egypt: Studies in the Writings of ʿAbd al-Wahhab al-Shaʿrani*. New Brunswick, CT: Transaction Books, 1982.

———. "Sufism in the Mamluk Empire (and in early Ottoman Egypt and Syria) as a focus for religious, intellectual and social networks." In *Everything is On the Move: The Mamluk Empire as a Node in (Trans-)Regional Networks*. Edited by Stephan Conermann, 145–164. Göttingen: V&R unipress, 2014.

Winter, Stefan. *The Shiites of Lebanon under Ottoman Rule, 1516–1788*. Cambridge: Cambridge University Press, 2010.

Wollina, Torsten. "Sultan Selīm in Damascus: The Ottoman Appropriation of a Mamluk Metropolis (922–924/1516–1518)." In *The Mamluk-Ottoman Transition: Continuity and Change in Egypt and Bilād al-Shām in the Sixteenth Century*. Edited by Stephan Conermann and Gül Şen, 221–246. Göttingen: V&R unipress, 2016.

———. "Ibn Ṭawq's *Taʿlīq*. An Ego-Document for Mamlūk Studies." In *Ubi sumus? Quo vademus? Mamluk Studies—State of the Art*. Edited by Stephan Conermann and Gül Şen, 337–361. Göttingen: V&R unipress, 2013.

Woodhead, Christine. "Ottoman Languages." In *The Ottoman World*. Edited by Christine Woodhead, 143–158. London: Routledge, 2013.

Wüstenfeld, Ferdinand. *Die Gelehrten-Familie Muḥibbí in Damascus und ihre Zeitgenossen im XI. (XVII.) Jahrhundert*. Göttingen: Dieterich, 1884.

Yalçïn, Mehmet. "'Dîvan-ï Qânṣūh al-Ğûrî': A critical edition of Turkish poetry commissioned by Sulṭan Qânṣûh al-Ğûrî (1501–1416)." Unpublished Ph.D. Dissertation, Harvard University, 1993.

Yaşar, Ahmet, ed. *Osmanlı Kahvehaneleri: Mekan, Sosyalleşme, İktidar*. Istanbul: Kitap Yayınevi, 2009.

———. "Osmanlı Şehir Mekânları: Kahvehane Literatürü." *Türkiye Araştırmaları Literatür Dergisi* 3, no. 6 (2005): 237–256.

Yavuz, Kemâl. "XIII–XVI. Asır Dil Yadigarlarının Anadolu Sahasında Türkçe Yazılış Sebepleri ve Bu Devir Müelliflerinin Türkçe Hakkındaki Görüşleri." *Türk Dünyası Araştırmaları* 27 (1983): 9–57.

Yavuz, Salih Sabri. "Kestelî." *Türkiye Diyanet Vakfı İslâm Ansiklopedisi*. Vol. 25 (2002): 314.

Yérasimos, Stéphane. "Dwellings in Sixteenth-Century Istanbul." In *The Illuminated Table, the Prosperous House: Food and Shelter in Ottoman Material Culture*. Edited by Suraiya Faroqhi and Christoph Neumann, 275–300. Würzburg: Ergon Verlag, 2003.

Yetiş, Kazım. "Beşiktaş Cemʿiyyet-i İlmiyyesi." *Türkiye Diyanet Vakfı İslâm Ansiklopedisi*. Vol. 5 (1992): 552–553.

Yıldırım, Rıza. "Turkomans between Two Empires: The Origins of the Qizilbash Identity in Anatolia (1447–1514)." Unpublished Ph.D. Dissertation, Bilkent University, 2008.

Yıldız, Sara Nur. "Aydinid Court Literature in the Formation of an Islamic Identity in Fourteenth-Century Western Anatolia." In *Islamic Literature and Intellectual Life in Fourteenth- and Fifteenth-Century Anatolia*. Edited by Andrew Peacock and Sara Nur Yıldız, 197–242. Würzburg: Ergon-Verlag, 2016.

———. "From Cairo to Ayasuluk: Hacı Paşa and the Transmission of Islamic Learning to Western Anatolia in the Late Fourteenth Century." *Journal of Islamic Studies* 25, no. 3 (2014): 263–297.

———. "A Hanafi law manual in the vernacular: Devletoğlu Yūsuf Balıḳesrī's Turkish verse adaptation of the *Hidāya-Wiqāya* textual tradition for the Ottoman Sultan Murad II (827/1424)." *Bulletin of SOAS* 80, no. 2 (2017): 283–304.

———. "A *Nadīm* for the Sultan: Rāwandī and the Anatolian Seljuks." In *The Seljuks of Anatolia: Court and Society in the Medieval Middle East*. Edited by Andrew Peacock and Sara Nur Yıldız, 91–112. London: I.B. Tauris, 2013.

———. "Ottoman Historical Writing in Persian, 1400–1600." In *Persian Historiography*. Edited by Charles Melville and Ehsan Yarshater, 436–502. London: I.B. Tauris, 2012.

Yılmaz, Fikret. "What About a Bit of Fun? Wine, Crime and Entertainment in Sixteenth-Century Western Anatolia." In *Celebration, Entertainment and Theatre in the Ottoman World*. Edited by Suraiya Faroqhi and Arzu Öztürkmen, 145–172. Chicago, IL: University of Chicago Press, 2014.

Yılmaz, Hüseyin. *Caliphate Redefined: The Mystical Turn in Ottoman Political Thought*. Princeton, NJ: Princeton University Press, 2018.

Yosef, Koby. "Ethnic Groups, Social Relationships and Dynasty in the Mamluk Sultanate (1250–1517)." *ASK Working Paper* 6 (2012): 1–12.

Zachs, Fruma. *The Making of a Syrian Identity: Intellectuals and Merchants in Nineteenth-Century Beirut*. Leiden: Brill, 2005.

Zecher, Carla. "The Çengî: Descriptions of Professional Female Performers in French and Italian Accounts of Travel to the Middle East, 1550–1650." *L'esprit créateur* 60, no. 1 (Spring 2020): 148–158.

Ze'evi, Dror. *An Ottoman Century: The District of Jerusalem in the 1600s*. Albany, NY: SUNY Press, 1996.

Zildzic, Ahmed. "Friend *and* Foe: The Early Ottoman Reception of Ibn ʿArabī." Unpublished Ph.D. Dissertation, University of California in Berkeley, 2012.

Zilfi, Madeline. *The Politics of Piety: The Ottoman Ulema in the Postclassical Age (1600–1800)*. Minneapolis, MN: Bibliotheca Islamica, 1988.

———. "Women, Minorities and the Changing Politics of Dress in the Ottoman Empire, 1650–1830." In *The Right to Dress: Sumptuary Laws in Global Perspective, c. 1200–1800*. Edited by Giorgio Riello and Ulinka Rublack, 393–415. Cambridge: Cambridge University Press, 2020.

INDEX

Page numbers in *italics* indicate figures and tables.

ʿAbbasi, ʿAbd al-Rahim al-, 70; background of, 241; *Bounty of the Creator*, 39; *Clusters of Pearls*, 80, *81*; encounters in Istanbul, 79–80, 82–5, 87; *Frequented Places for Clarification*, 34, 85, 142n45; Ghazzi and, 138–9, 143, 144, 169, 180; Ghazzi family and, 25, 131; hadith accounts, 183; in Istanbul, 24–5; lineage, 120; Müʾeyyedzade and, 29–30, 33–4, 37–40; origin of, 29; reciting poems, 139; refuge in Istanbul, 241; travels of, 17

ʿAbdurrahman Efendi, Çivizade and, 213–4

Abu Hanifa, 220

Abu Nuwas, 180

adab, edeb: books of etiquette, 11; command of, 135; concept of, 130; contrasting ʿilm and, 136n13, 143; as etiquette, 108, 164; principles of, 135. *See also* etiquette

adib (litterateur), 136, 206

Ahmed, Shahab, madrasa curriculum, 193

Ahmed Efendi, 168; knowledge of Arabic, 178, 184; library of, 175, 175nn36–7

Ahmedi, poet, 40n74, 42n85, 80n110

Ahmed Pasha, 42n85

ʿajam, ʿacem. *See* Persian

Aleppo, 5, 25, 32, 38, 42n80, 47, 59, 67, 77, 82, 109, 127, 150, 155, 162, 168, 180, 192, 194, 211, 214; Janbulat house, *102*; map, *14*, *28*

Aleppo Chamber, *5*, 87; Christians and Muslims mingling in, 7; wall paneling in, *88*

ʿAli, Mustafa, 108–9, 169; *Tables of Delicacies*, 108

Ali, Samer, on Abbasid salons, 3n1

Amasya, 25, 29, 30, 35n45, 63, 103, 213n54; map, *14*, *28*

Ankara, *14*, *28*, 104

Ansari, Zakariyya al-, 91, 182, 193

Aqquyunlu Sultanate, 29, 49n123, 51n135; map of, *28*

Aqsaraʾi, Amin al-Din al-, 31, 31n21, 46

Arabic language: books, 168, 174–5, 196; education, 40, 153, 162–63, 166; eloquence, 15, 21, 134, 160, 184, 230; grammar, 30, 32, 47, 136, 153, 162, 177; in Mamluk lands, 43; poetry, 40, 51, 191; prestige of, 235; Rumis and, 19, 20, 38, 39–40, 51–52, 54, 67, 151–6, 163–5, 199, 219, 222, 231; salons, 137, 160, 189; writing, 189–94. *See also* language; poetry

Arabophone, 43, 145, 189, 199, 219

Arabs, 15–17; access to appointments, 39, 44, 52–3, 82–3, 93–4; awlad al-ʿarab, evlad-i ʿarab, 16, 45, 228–9; interest in writings of Rumis, 42–3, 195–7; marginalization, 52–3, 82–3, 154, 216–26; prestige of culture, 21, 43–6, 235–7; role in governance, 68–78, 83–4, 94–6, 212–13, 235–6; role in knowledge transmission, 39–40, 166–7, 176–84, 193–4; role of salons in constructing identity, 238

ʿAşık Çelebi, 119, 144, 150, 199, 242; hadith transmission, 183; *Senses of Poets*, *4*, *86*, *92*, 169, 191–2, 195–6, *207*, 221; *Supplement to the Crimson Peonies*, 191, 223

Aşıkpaşazade, 190

ʿAsili, Nur al-Din al-, 141

Ataturk, Mustafa Kemal, 240

Authentic Collection (Bukhari), 39; ʿAbbasi's commentary, 39; public readings, 112n62; transmission, 183

awlad al-ʿarab, evlad-i ʿarab (the sons of the Arabs), 16, 45, 66, 115n75, 157, 228–9

Ayas Pasha, 71, 136; background of, 242; commissions for Ghazzi, 90–1, 169, 171; Ghazzi and, 89–91, 93, 94, 95, 116, 225; Radi al-Din and, 71–6

Azhar, al-, 43
ʿAzm palace in Damascus, *110*

Babarti, Akmal al-Din al-, 40n74
Baghdad, 27, 52; map, *14*, *28*
Baki, *4*, 82
banquets. *See* salon(s)
Basiri, 49, 49n123
Basra, map, *14*, *28*
Bawwab, Ibn al-, 90
Baydawi, ʿAbdallah al-, Qurʾan commentary, 161, 179, 195, *196*
Bayezid I: scholars from Arab lands and, 42n81, 44, *48*, 48n117; scholars from Persian lands and, *48*, 48n118
Bayezid II, 30, 32, 38, 44, 80, 116, 241–2; ʿAbbasi and, 38, 39, 39n71; Müʾeyyedzade and, 31–2, 34–5; salon in Amasya, 34–5; scholars from Arab lands and, 40n73, 41n78, *48*, 48n117; scholars from Persian lands and, *48*, 48n118
Bayqara, Husayn, 46
Belgrade, *14*, *28*, 76
Beşiktaş Society, 239
bezm. *See* salon(s)
bezm ü rezm (feast and fight), 34
Bidlisi, İdris, 49n125, 51n135
biographical dictionaries, 75, 151, 164, 189–90, 195–6, 198; ʿAşık Çelebi's, *4*, *86*, *92*, 169, *170*, 195–6, *207*, 221; Burini's, 100, 100n12, 105, 199, 211; Ibn Ayyub's, 107n44, 123, 211; Ibn Khallikan's, 175; Najm al-Din al-Ghazzi's, 20, 20n61, 149; Persian tazkira 189, 190; tabaqat, 189, 220; tarajim, 11; Taşköprizade's, 31n23, 36, 41nn78–9, 55, *48*, 48nn117–18, 82, 98, 107, 121, 129, 191, 219, 223; Turkish tezkire, 11, 190–2
Biographies of the Notable Men of the Age (Burini), 100, 100n12, 105, 199, 211
Birr, Ibn ʿAbd al-, commentary on Tirmidhi's *Compilation*, 159
Bistami, ʿAbd al-Rahman al-, 40
Book of Healing (Ibn Sina), 143
Book of Kabus (Kaykaʾus ibn Iskandar), 51, 52, 106, 137
books: acquisition, 175, 199; Arabic, 51–2, 175–6; commissioning, 42, 169, 174–5, 190, 234; endowment to madrasas, 43–4; as gifts, 23, 90; launches, *112*, 171–2, 181, 186; Persian, 51; reading, 168–76; recitation, 139, 179, 200, 210
boon companions (nadim, nedim), 10, 49
Bostanzade Mehmed, 175, 178
Brookshaw, Dominic, on salons, 3n1
Bukhari, Muhammad al-, 39. See also *Authentic Collection*
Bunani, Thabit al-, 180
Burak, Guy: authority of Ottoman scholars, 220, 220nn87, 89; jurisprudence, 154
Burini, Hasan al-, 20, 146, 148, 184; *Biographies of the Notable Men of the Age*, 100, 199, 211; Ghazzi and, 105, 115, 168
Bursa, *14*, 63, 124, 142, 147, 183, 202, 211, 212n47, 214

Cairo, 13, 21, 26–7, 31–3, 36–7, 42–5, 56, 59–60, 63, 140, 146, 149, 154, 168, 187, 202, 211, 214; ʿAbbasi, 24–5, 29–30, 42, 53, 80, 180; Badr al-Din, 57, 79, 83; Çivizade, 181–2, 188, 201, 204, 212–13; Ibn al-Jazari, 44; Kınalızade, 163; Mamluk, 27, 31, 43; map, *14*, *28*
Canon of Medicine (Ibn Sina), 143
Cezeri Kasim Pasha, 35n45
chief mufti (şeyhülislam), 44, 212n47
Christians, 6n10, 27, 111, 202, 206, 206n26; cultural tradition, 166; Muslims and, 7n13, 21–2, *88*; origins, 125–6; owner of Aleppo Chamber, 5, 7
Çivizade, Hoca, 188, 203
Çivizade Mehmed Efendi, 19, 129, 159–61, 178–9, 201–7, 210, 218; Ghazzi granting ijaza to, 181–3; imperial governance, 212–16
Clusters of Pearls (ʿAbbasi), 80, *81*
coffeehouses, 2–3, 101, 101n19, 238
Commentary on the Throne Verse (Ghazzi), 90, 177
confessionalization, 237
conquest: of Constantinople, 13; of Mamluk Sultanate, 2, 13, 21–2, 59, 71
councils (divan): imperial, 32, 68, 91, *92*, 93, 118n85, 147, 225; provincial, 68
courts: judicial, 6, 68–9; Mamluk royal, 80; Ottoman princely, 53; Ottoman royal, 34, 37, 131
Crimson Peonies Concerning the Scholars of the Ottoman State (Taşköprizade), 36, *48*, 55, 98, 115n75, 121, 129, 148n75, 149n80, 191, 219–20, 246; Arabic, 153,

191; hadith, 180; Ottoman scholars studying abroad, 31, 41; salons in, 98, 107, 121; scholars from Arab lands, *48*, 48n117, 82, 219–20; scholars from Persian lands, *48*, 48n118; sources for, 148n75, 149n80; supplement to, 223

Damascus, 2, 6, 10, 13, 18–19, 22, 27, 43–4, 59–61, 69–72, 74, 76–80, 98, 105, 113, 119, 122, 128–9, 132, 134, 136, 145–6, 151, 155–60, 162–4, 168–9, 184–5, 195–6, 214, 221, 234, 237; ʿAbbasi, 30, 32–3, 38–9, 42, 95, 180, 196; ʿAzm palace in, *110*; Ghazali, 67–8; Ghazzi, 20, 56, 57, 62–3, 65, 82–4, 89, 94–5, 99–100, 107, 109, 173, 175, 177–8, 181, 186–8, 212, 215–16, 229, 233; Hamawi, 202–4, 208, 211, 215, 232; map, *14*, *28*
Dawadari, Sanjar al-, 34n36
Dawani, Jalal al-Din al-, 47, 49
Dawlatshah, Amir, 190
Delicacies of Conversation (Ghazzi, Najm al-Din), 149
Derviş Pasha, Ghazzi and, 128–29
Derviş Şemşeddin, 49n125

Ebu's-Suʿud Efendi, 160, 193, 243; ʿAbbasi and, 82; Ghazzi and, 84–5, 174, 197, 198; Hasan Bey and, 104–5; Maliki and, 137; scholarly gathering, 113, *114*
edeb. *See* adab, edeb
Edirne, *14*, *28*, 32, 38n64, 211, 212n47, 221
Eight Heavens (Sehi Bey), 190, 221
Emancipation of the Slave, 140
Emrullah Efendi, 188, 188n112
endowments, 63–4, 219; to madrasas, 43–44
Erzurum, *14*, *28*
Essence of Commentary on the Mantle Ode (Ghazzi), 90–1, 94, 177, 182, 194n135
ethnicity, 15–17, 131, 209, 228–9, 231, 238
etiquette: adab, edeb, 108, 135; adab and ʿilm, 143; in Arab vs. Rumi lands, 50, 52, 88, 108, 134–5; art of conversation, 134–4, 143; books of, 10–11, 52, 79, 101, 106, 108, 137, 147, 148n72; social status, 135–6, 176. *See also* adab, edeb
Etiquette of Teaching and Learning (Ghazzi), 108n48, 176
Evliya Çelebi, 11, 180

Fatimids, 43
Fenari, ʿAlaʾeddin ʿAli, 48
Fenari, Şemseddin, 31, 37, 37n56, 40n74, 46n105
Fenari, Zeynüddin, 61–5, 74, 77, 92, *112*, 156
Fenarizade Muhyiddin, 91–3
Fevri Efendi, 136, 141, 159, 160–2, 172, 195, 201–2, *207*; background of, 243; gentleman and litterateur, 206–11; Ghazzi and, 159, 178, 178n57, 195–7; *Gloss on the Sura of the Believers*, 161, 195, *196*, 197; Hamawi and, 195, 208–10; and Monastery of the Cross, 205–6
Filipovic, Nenad, madrasa curriculum, 193
Firuzabadi, Muhammad al-, 135
food, 63
Frequented Places for Clarification (ʿAbbasi), 34, 34n39, 85
Full Moon Rising (Ghazzi), 78–9, 88, 148, 162, 169, 182, 204
Furfur, Wali al-Din Ibn al-, 62, 63, 67, 82

garden(s), 8, 33n35, 37, 68n53, 93, 111, 140; of companionship, 84; royal pavilions, 87
gazels, ghazals, 140n35, 141
Generations of the Hanafi School (Kınalızade ʿAli), 220
Gharnati, Abu Hayyan al-, Qurʾan commentary, 186
Ghawri, Qansawh al-, 33, 36, 42
Ghazali, Janbirdi al-, 60; rebellion, 67–8, 71, 76
Ghazzi, Badr al-Din al-: ʿAbbasi and, 83–8, 138–9, 143, 144; ʿAlaʾ al-Din al-Shafiʿi and, 97, 122–5, 132; Ayas Pasha and, 89–91; background of, 243; birth of, 2, 56; Çivizade and, 181–83; *Commentary on the Throne Verse*, 90, 177; death of, 200, 204n18; death of son, 200; education, 104, 176; *Essence of Commentary on the Mantle Ode*, 90–91, 94, 177, 182, 194n135; etiquette books, 11; *Etiquette of Teaching and Learning*, 176; father Radi al-Din, 18, 33, 55–6; Fevri and, 159, 178, 178n57, 195–97; *Full Moon Rising* travelogue, 78–9, 88, 94, 148, 204; Hacı Çelebi and, 84–5; Hamawi and, 19, 20, 201;

Ghazzi, Badr al-Din al- (*continued*)
Hasan Bey and, 100–1, 116–17, 122–4; job for, 89–94; Kınalızade ʿAli and 178–9, 185–8; loss of teaching position, 78, 214; Maliki and, 133–4; poetry of, 87, 103, 140–1, 171, 200; *Qurʾanic Exegesis Made Simple*, 90, *112*, 172–4, *174*; retreat of, 127–30, 197; *Rules of Conviviality*, 101, 108; stutter, 2, 150; *Table Manners*, 103; withdrawal from salons, 6, 127–30; women and, 7
Ghazzi, Najm al-Din al-, 20; on Arabs, 229–30; background of, 243; Bostanzade and, 175; *Delicacies of Conversation*, 149; Derviş Pasha and, 128–9; son of Badr al-Din, 88, 128, 132; *Wandering Stars*, 20, 178–9n57, 243
Ghazzi, Radi al-Din al-, 32–3; ʿAbbasi and 32–3, 34, 40n70; Ayas Pasha and, 71–6; background of, 244; death of, 78; father of Badr al-Din, 18, 55–6, 79; Hacı Çelebi and, 70, 84, 177; influence of, 32–4, 95–6; poetry of, 74–6; relationships with Ottomans, 69–71; role in judicial system, 33, 62
glossary, 247–8
Gloss on the Sura of the Believers (Fevri Efendi), 161, 195, *196*, 197
governance, 23; Arabs and, 211–16; salons and, 58, 68–78, 95–6, 211–16
Great Mosque of Damascus, 6, 61, 66, 77, 78, 99, 111, *112*, 125, 133, 135, 156, 171, 181, 233
Grehan, James, 137n18
Gülşeni, İbrahim-i, 154
Gürani, Ahmed, 37, 40, 42n81, 55, 106n38

Habermas, Jürgen, public sphere, 2
Hacı Çelebi: background of, 245; Badr al-Din and, 84–5; brother of Müʾeyyedzade ʿAbdurrahman, 70; Radi al-Din and, 70, 84, 177
hadith, 19, 30, 39, 45, 80, 85n134, 152, 154, 162, 167, 179–83, 193–4, 216, 230. *See also* ijaza
Hafiz, 50, 141
hajj pilgrimage, 27, 41n78, 60, 64, 66
Halabi, al-Samin al-, commentary, 186
Halabi, Ibrahim al-, 54n147, 81n41, 82, 196
Hama, 10, *14*, 59, 67, 203
Hamawi, Muhibb al-Din al-, 19, 195, 201; Arabic grammar and, 155–6; background of, 244; Çivizade and, 212–13; Ghazzi and, 19, 20, 149, 222–3, 224–6; Maʿlulzade and, 226–9; scholarly path of, 201–11; travel account, 151, 201, 202, 204–5, 224, 226–7
Hamdullah, Shaykh, 35n45
Hanafi legal school, 42n81, 47, 61, 65, 66, 67, 220, 223–24
Hasan Bey, 100–1, 175n37, 184; appearance, 115; background of, 244; entry into elite circles, 104–5; Ghazzi and, 107–8, 128, 212; reception in Damascus, 107–8, 116–18, 122–6, 132; son Ahmed, 178
Hathaway, Jane, on Arabs, 16
Hızır Bey, 37
Hocazade Muslihuddin Efendi, 119–21
Homs, *14*, 59, 67, *111*, 113n66, 145n58, 216–17, 232
hospitality, 3, 7–8, 12, 85, 90, 101, 130, 138

Ibn ʿArabi, 61, 66, 71, 85n134
Ibn Ayyub, Sharaf al-Din, 98, 175n32, 185, 188; background, 241; *Sweet-Smelling Garden*, 98, 111, 195, 199, 211
Ibn Daqiq al-ʿId, 139
Ibn Hajar, 90, 99, 183, 186, 194
Ibn Hanbal, 180
Ibn al-Hanbali, 150
Ibn Iyas, 59, 60, 66n41
Ibn al-Jahm, ʿAli, 210
Ibn Jamaʿa, 160–1, 160n128, 210
Ibn al-Jazari, 42n81, 44n97
Ibn Khallikan, 175
Ibn Malik, *Thousand-Line Poem*, 177, 182, 194
Ibn Nubata, 197n145, 208
Ibn Qutayba, 90
Ibn Shawr, al-Qaʿqaʿ, 138
Ibn Sina, 143
Ibn Taghribirdi, 45
Ibn Thabit, Hasan, 210
Ibn Tulun, 20, 64, 66n41, 154, 157, 158
Ibshihi, Shihab al-Din al-, 79n105
ijaza (academic license), 10, 178, 179, 181–4, 194, 197, 199
imam, 6, 65n39, 66, 99
imperial council (divan-i hümayun), 67
İnalcik, Halil, on imperial integration, 57–8

intoxicants, 35; wine, 21, 34–5, 50, 54, 138, 140, 221, 230
İshak Çelebi, 157–8, 221
İskender Çelebi, 49
Islamic community, 53–4
Islamic Republic of Letters, 25, 41, 54
Istanbul, 10, 22, 48, 60, 71–2, 74, 76, 95, 98, 113, 119, 132, 137, 160, 175, 176, 198, 211–16, 219, 221–3, 235, 237; ʿAbbasi, 24–5, 39n70, 55, 70, 80, *81*, 82–3, 85, 138–9, 142, 144, 162, 171, 178; encounters in, 78–88; Ghazzi, 17, 19–21, 57–58, 66–8, 85–9, 94, 99, 105, 107, 109, 116, 121–2, 129, 142, 144, 148–50, 155, 169, 174, 177, 180, 182, 194, 196–7, 200–1, 203, 231; Gürani, 37; Hamawi, 201, 203–4, 203n10, 207, 212–16, 222–3, 227; Ibn al-Jazari, 42n81; map, *14*, *28*; Müʾeyyedzade, 32, 36, 38n64, 49
Izmit, *14*, 67, 85, 155, 177

Jami, ʿAbdurrahman, scholar, 190
Janbulat house in Aleppo, *102*
Jazzar, Yahya al-, 79n105
judges: chief (qadi al-qudat), 19, 61–3, 69, 74, 85, 94, 100, 106, 107–8, 129, 156, 159, 160, 163, 167, 168, 174–5, 178–9, 181, 184, 187, 188, 192, 203, 211, 215, 218, 221, 232; deputy (naʾib), 33, 61–62, 218; military (kadiasker), 32, 38n64, 44, 91, 136, 211–12, 212n48, 245
jurisconsults (muftis), 99
jurisprudence (fiqh), 30, 40, 56, 122, 154, 166, 179, 182
Jurjani, al-Sayyid al-Sharif al-, 46, 156, 187

kadiasker. *See* judges
Kadiri Çelebi, 91, *92*, 93, 104–5, 118, 119, 212
Kafiyaji, Muhyi al-Din al-, 31, 31n21, 46
Kallasa Mosque (Damascus), 76
Kars, map of, *14*, *28*
Kasım Pasha, 93
Kassabzade, 86–7, 177–8
Katib Çelebi, 143
Kaykaʾus ibn Iskandar, 51n135. See also *Book of Kabus*
Kayseri, *28*, 31, 101n19
Kemalpaşazade, 220
Kestelli, Molla, 36, 40
Key to the Disciplines (Sakkaki), 30n18
Kınalızade, ʿAli, 19, 119n84, 169, 181, 212; Arabic books and, 174–5; background of, 244; biographies of, 196–7; chief judge, 169, 178–9; excelling in Arab learned circles, 163, 168, 184–9, 195, 197–8; *Generations of the Hanafi School*, 220; Ghazzi and, 19, 128, 168, 178–9, 185–8; hadith studies, 181, 183
Kınalızade, Hasan Çelebi: background of, 244; *Biographies of Poets*, 163, 185, 188, 189, 191–2
knowledge transmission, 166–8, 197–9; reading, 168–76; reciprocity, 195–7; results of, 184–9; teaching, 176–84; writing, 189–95
Konya, *28*, 31, 42n84
Kutbi Pasha Çelebi, 35n45

Lamiʿi Çelebi, 190
language: eloquence, 15, 21, 137–8, 163, 185, 230, 236; grammar, 134, 136–7, 155–56, 159–60, 162–3; learning Arabic, 30, 32, 152–3; in Mamluk circles, 29, 52; in Ottoman circles, 51–2; speaking, 135–44; tool for exclusion, 165, 209. *See also* Arabic language, Turkish language
Lapidus, Ira, on Islamic globalization, 239
Latifi, 146
legal opinions (fatwas), 99, 153
lineage, 18, 29, 126, 130, 131; ʿAbbasi, 29, 37–8, 120; Fenari, 62–3; Müʾeyyedzade, 29; prominent seat, 98, 119–20, 126; sayyids and sharifs, 29, 38, 115n70, 120, 131n137; scholarly, 181–2, 232
Lutfi, Molla, 143, 145, 149

madhhabs (Islamic legal schools), 22, 61, 99. *See also* Hanafi legal school; Shafiʿi legal school
madrasas, 3, 30; appointments, 104, 122, 167, 212; al-Azhar, 43; books in, 42, 43–4; competition for posts in, 19, 217–18; curriculum, 31, 42, 193–4; eight, 84, 85n131, 174, 214; endowments to, 19, 43–4, 219; Ghazzi's appointments at, 99; institutionalization of learning in, 142, 167, 198; Mamluk, 43, 46; more than 280, 43;

madrasas (*continued*)
Nasiriyya, 33; Ottoman, 27, 30n18, 31–4, 42–4, 52–3, 167, 193, 217, 219; Qassaʿiyya, 203; Seljuks, 31n20; students, 31, 208; of Sultan Bayezid, 39, 53; Taqawiyya, 214, 215, 231
majlis, term, 7–9, 25. *See also* salon(s)
Maliki, Abu al-Fath al-, 82, 100; background of, 245; Ghazzi and, 133–4; litterateur, 145–6, 189
Maʿlul Efendi, 188
Maʿlulzade Mehmed Efendi, 129; 202, 211–16, 218, 225; background of, 245; chief military judge, 226–8
mamluk (slave), 15, 27, 247
Mamluk Sultan, 33, 45
Mamluk Sultanate, 2, 13, 25, 26–7, 29, 37, 41, 53, 55, 57, 59, 60; map of, *28*
Mani (painter), 26
Manisazade Muhyiddin, 40n76
Manstetten, Paula, on higher education, 167n2
Mantle Ode (Busiri), 90–1, 94; Ghazzi's commentary on, 90–1, 94, 177, 182, 194
marriage tax, 64–5, 77
masculinity, 7
Mayli, Shihab al-, 100
Mecca, 13, 27, 38, 60, 64, 77, 118, 155n106, 177, 182, 213, 232; map, *14*, *28*. *See also* hajj pilgrimage
Medina, 13, 27, 64, 182; map, *14*, *28*
Mehmed I: scholars from Arab lands and, 41n78, *48*, 48n117; scholars from Persian lands and, *48*, 48n118
Mehmed II, 32, 35, 36–7, 40, 46n101, 122n98, 124, 141, 146n64, 219; education of, 44; mosque complex of, 44n40, 84; reign of, 41n78; scholars from Arab lands and, 41n78, *48*, 48n117; scholars from Persian lands and, *48*, 48n118
merchants, 5, 46, 59, 67n48, 105, 147
Merhaba Efendi, 188
Mesihi, 44
Mihri Hatun, 35n45, 103
mosques: Great Mosque of Damascus, 6, 61, 66, 77, 78, 99, 111, *112*, 125, 133, 135, 156, 171, 181, 233; Yalbugha Mosque, 133, 146, 147
Müʾeyyedzade, ʿAbdurrahman, 17; ʿAbbasi and, 29–30, 33–4, 37–40; background of, 245; Bayezid and, 31–2, 34–5; death of, 70; education of, 30; travels of, 17, 25, 53
Müʾeyyedzade, Hacı Çelebi. *See* Hacı Çelebi
Muhammad, Prophet, 19, 66, 90; hadiths, 30, 167; lineage, 120; poetry and, 172–3; Radi al-Din's dream of, 73
Muhibbi, Muhammad Amin al-, 224, 232
Muhyiddin Mehmed Çelebi, 160
Muhyi Efendi, 155
Muʿidzade, Mehmed, 159n122, 178
Murad I: scholars from Arab lands and, 41n78, *48*, 48n117; scholars from Persian lands and, *48*, 48n118
Murad II, 34; scholars from Arab lands and, 41n78, *48*, 48n117; scholars from Persian lands and, *48*, 48n118
Murad III, 68n53, 216, 222n98
Mutanabbi, Abu al-Tayyib al-, 206
Muttalib, ʿAbbas ibn ʿAbd al-, 29

Nablus, *14*, 105, 208
Nabulusi, ʿAbd al-Ghani al-, superiority of Arabs, 229–30
Nabulusi, Ismaʿil al-: 115, 139, 140, 146, 150n83, 151, 185; Ghazzi and, 139, 159; Hamawi's union with daughter of, 232
Nahrawali, Qutb al-Din al-, 90n151, 99, 152n357, 160, 195, 197n144; on Ghazzi's Qurʾan commentary, 173
Nasiriyya Madrasa, 33
Navaʾi, ʿAli Shir, 145, 190
Navigator of the Challenging Paths (Hamawi), 201, 202, 204–5, 224
Nawawi, Abu Zakariyya al-, scholar, 175, 181, 193
Nomads of the Crimson Tears (Hamawi), 201, 224, 226–7

occult sciences (al-ʿulum al-ghariba), 37
Orhan, Sultan: scholars from Arab lands and, *48*, 48n117; scholars from Persian lands and, *48*, 48n118
Osman I, Sultan, House of, 46; scholars from Arab lands and, *48*, 48n117; scholars from Persian lands and, *48*, 48n118
Ottomanization, 21

patronage, 10, 12, 13, 18, 19, 27, 94, 130, 201, 211, 214, 216–6, 231, 234, 235; lazama, mülazemet, 93, 105, 204n15,

218, 222n97; of learning, 43, 46; Mamluk, 43, 60
Persian: ʿajam, ʿacem, 46, 187; culture, 26, 27, 29, 46–52; influence in Ottoman salons, 46–52; language, 49–50; Mamluks and, 29, 36, 45–6; poetry, 49–51; migrants to Ottoman lands, 47–8; Safavids, 55; Seljuks, 46; Timurids, *28*, 46. *See also* poetry
Petry, Carl, on scholarly travel, 31n21, 41n79, 42n80
Philliou, Christine, on governance, 23
poetry: 12, 13, 54, 136n12, 138, 240; anthologies (diwan, divan), 42, 50, 51–2, 141, 175; Arabic, 40, 51–2, 146, 151–4, 162, 173, 184–5, 191, 210, 211; discussion of, 48, 142, 144–51, 208–10; epigrams (maqtuʿ), 74, 75, 87, 133, 139, 227; gatherings for, 9, 85, 93, 138; gazel, ghazal, 140n35, 141, 141n40; Ghazzi's, 57, 65, 87, 103, 139, 140–1, 177, 200; impromptu recitation of, 1, 34–5, 139, 140–2, 184; inscriptions of, 87; Kınalızade's, 185, 195; languages, 153–54; literature and, 240; memorization, 30, 34, 75, 139, 143, 151, 164, 172, 178, 180, 184; Müʾeyyedzade's, 35; odes (qasida, *kaside*), 40, 76n89, 90, 135, 139, 141n40, 142, 148, 160, 203; for Ottoman officials, 40, 74–6, 82, 87, 95, 135, 203, 226; Ottoman, 42, 140; Persian, 49–51, 158; quintet genre (khamsa), 50; recitation, 75, 138–42, 145–6, 148, 171; relationships and, 138–9; seating in gathering, 119, 121; Turkish, 20, 151; zajal, 51, 146, 162. *See also* biographical dictionaries
Pollock, Sheldon, on cosmopolitan language, 152
prepubescent boys, 9, 34, 138
provincial councils (divans), 67
provincial governors (beylerbeyi), 35, 60, 71, 128, 169, 214, 218n79. *See also* Ayas Pasha
public sphere, 2–3, 12

qadi al-qudat. *See* judges
Qadiri Sufi order, 70
Qari, Taqi al-Din al-, 65–6, 76–7
Qassaʿiyya Madrasa, 203
Qaytbay, Ashraf, 42n85
Qurʾan, 30, 56, 67, 76, 90, 94; Arabic as sacred language, 152; Ghazzi reading, 150; reading and memorizing, 153; reciters, 99; rhymed verse in, 172–3. *See also* Qurʾanic exegesis
Qurʾanic exegesis, 30, 47, 84, 162n133, 171, 182, 183n83, 204; Baydawi, 161, 179, 195, *196*; commentary, 172; Gharnati, 186; Ghazzi (Throne Verse), 90, 177; Zamakhshari, 156–7, 179, 187. See also *Qurʾanic Exegesis Made Simple*
Qurʾanic Exegesis Made Simple (Ghazzi), 90, *112*, 172–4, *174*
Qutbuddin, Tahera, on Arabic books 51

Rafeq, Abdul-Karim, on conversion to Hanafism, 223
Rashid, Harun al-, 142
rational sciences (al-ʿulum al-ʿaqliyya), 47
reception areas, 8, 87, 101–3, *102*, 108–15; courtyard, 109, *111*, 113, 147; domed hall, *5*, 7, *88*, *110*, 113, 116n76; indoor, *5*, *88*, *110*, 113, *114*, 116, 118, 147; outdoor, 109, 111; pavilions, 109, 147; private, 8, 69, 101; public, 8, 69, 101–3, 111–12, *112*; soffa, 117–18
Repp, Richard, on scholar's status, 219
Republic of Letters, 25, 41, 54
Revealer (Zamakhshari), 156–7, 179, 187
riddles (uhjiyya), 49n120, 85, 87n138, 139, 144, 148
rihla. *See* travel accounts
Rukh, Shah, 46
Rules of Conviviality (Ghazzi), 11n38, 101, 108
Rumi, Mamaya al-, poet, 145–6, 162, 175
Rumis, 16–17; access to appointments 52–3, 83, 167, 216–18, 222; Arabic language, 19, 20, 38, 39–40, 51–2, 54, 67, 151–6, 163–5, 199, 219, 222, 231; in Arabic salons, 151–63; clothing, 115; culture, 109; influence of Arab scholars on, 176–84, 189–95; influence on Arab scholars, 42–3,195–7; lineage, 131; reception of Persian culture, 46–52
Rüstem Pasha, 125; Hasan Bey and, 104, 107; Mihrimah and, 80

Saʿdi Çelebi, 82, 85, *86*, 87, 169
Safavid Empire, 55
Sakhawi, Muhammad al-, 40n74, 41n79

Sakkaki, Yusuf al-, *Key to the Disciplines*, 30n18
Saleh, Walid, on Kınalızade ʿAli, 187
salon(s): Arabic-dominated, 137, 160, 163, 189; Arabic culture, 39–40, 51–2; banquets (diyafa, ziyafet), 6, 9, 11, 20, 103, 119, 124, 128, 140–1, 171, 208; bezm, 9, 34; concluding sessions (majlis khatm), 111n62, *112*, 171–2, 181, 186; culture, 33–5, 54–5; definition, 7; domain of Muslim gentlemen, 7; dress, 113, 115; empire of, 201–11; etiquette, 50–2, 88, 106, 108, 134–5, 164, 206–9, 221; exchange of resources, 58–9, 68–76, 89–94; flexibility, 9, 235; in France, 13, 239, 240; importance, 11–12, 234–40; judging, 144–51; layout, 113, *114*, 117–18; mahfil, mehfil (soirées), 9, 149, 163; majlis, term, 7–9, 25; majlis adab, meclis-i suʿaraʾ (literary gathering), 7, 9–10, 25, 34n36, 138; majlis ʿilm (scholarly gathering), 9–10, 25, 34n36, 142–3, 150, 176–84, 186–7, 191, 198; Mamluk, 34–5; meclis-i ʿişret (drinking party), 9; in modern era, 239–40; in paintings, *4*, 11, *86*, *114*, *207*; patronage, 12, 13, 18, 19, 89–94, 130, 201, 211–16, 222, 231; Persian, 48; Persian culture, 46–52; political functions, 17–18; scholarly disputation, 11, 35, 142–3, 144, 145; seating arrangements, 18, 116–24, 130–1, 145, 181; social status, 18, 97–8, 99–107, 108–9, 116–22, 130–2; storytelling, 34, 49, 142; term, 12; Turkish, 29, 152, 200–201, 221–2, 231; welcoming reception (majlis salam), 107, 116–26; withdrawal from, 127–30; women in, 7, 12, 35n45, 103–4, 134, 237, 239. *See also* governance; language; reception areas
sayyids. *See* lineage
Schmidt, Jan, on responsive genres, 141
Sehi Bey, 190, 221; biography of İshak, 157–9; *Eight Heavens*, 50n133, 154n101, 190–2, 221
Selim, Sultan, 59, 61, 63, 64, 67, 73, 76, 80, 111, 154, 158, 161, 195, 221
Selim II, Sultan, 205
Seljuks, 40n75
Şemseddin Mehmed Şemsi Çelebi, 84, 139
Senses of Poets (ʿAşık Çelebi), *4*, *86*, *92*, 169, 191–2, 195–6, *207*, 221, 242. *See also* ʿAşık Çelebi
servants, 7–8, *86*, *92*, 104, 108, *114*, 119–21, 147, 164
Shafiʿi, ʿAlaʾ al-Din al-, 82; background, 246; Ghazzi and, 97, 122–5, 127–8, 132, 173; Hasan Bey and, 122, 124–6
Shafiʿi legal school, 22, 33, 61–2, 65
sharifs. *See* lineage
Shiraz, 25, *28*, 32, 46–7, 50
Simmel, Georg, on sociability, 9
slaves, 7, 15, 27, 71–2, 104–5, 143, 147, 159, 181, 192
Smyth, William, on in-person debates, 198
sociability, 2, 8n21, 9, 12–13, 18, 40, 47, 58, 101, 211, 230, 238–9; cultures of, 25; elite, 2, 12, 18, 21, 101, 230, 238; Persian influence, 47; similarities across Middle East, 25, 33–7, 40–1, 58, 206–11
sohbet (intimate conversation), 9, 51, 134–5
Sternberg, Giora, on status interactions, 97–8
Subtelny, Maria, on majlis, 3n1
Sufis, 10–11, 70n63, 76, *117*, 127, 131, 147, 154, 190, 203
Sufism, 70, 71, 84; Ayas Pasha and 70–1, 76; basis for bond, 70–1, 73, 84; Ghazzi and, 56, 79, 84; Müʾeyyedzade and, 29; Qadiri Sufi order, 70; Radi al-Din and, 33, 70–1, 79, 131; sociability, 6, 11, 101, 127; sultans and, 76, 107. *See also* Ibn ʿArabi
Süleyman, Sultan, 67n53, 80, 82, 161, 204
Sunni Islam, 17, 22, 25, 46, 54, 183, 236–7
Sunnitization, 237
Suyuti, Jalal al-Din al-, 45, 99, 157, 180, 182, 193, 194; ʿAbbasi and, 53; Ghazzi and, 182
Sweet-Smelling Garden (Ibn Ayyub), 98 195–7, 211, 241. *See also* Ibn Ayyub

tabaqat. *See* biographical dictionaries
Table Manners (Ghazzi), 103, 104
Tables of Delicacies (Mustafa ʿAli), 108
Taci Bey, 35n45
Taftazani, Saʿd al-Din al-, 46, 120n93, 121n96, 124, 156, 157, 187

Tanukhiyya, Fatima bint al-Munajja al-, 139, 143
Taqawiyya Madrasa, 214, 215, 231
taqriz (book endorsement), 39n70, 195, *196*, 197
tarajim. *See* biographical dictionaries
Taşköprizade, Ahmed, 36; background, 246; *Crimson Peonies*, 36, 55, 98, 107, 115n75, 219–20, 223, 246; defense of scholars, 121, 129–30; hadith, 183, 191. See also *Crimson Peonies*
tezkire. *See* biographical dictionaries
Thousand Line Poem (Ibn Malik), 177, 194; Ghazzi's commentary, 182, 194
Tibi, Sharaf al-Din al-, 156, 157, 187
Tibi, Shihab al-Din al- (the Elder), 127n122, 175, 179n59, 181n71, 183n83, 195; pilgrimage manual, 175
Timurids, 29, 46, 47, 49, 156, 187, 190; map of, *28*
Topkapı Palace, 10, 68, 117, 201; library, 39n70, 40, 50, 51, 52n144, 80, *81*, 90n155
travel accounts (rihla), 11, 204. See also *Full Moon Rising*; *Navigator of the Challenging Paths*; *Nomads of the Crimson Tears*
travel and migration: Arabs, 48, 78, 82–3, 153, 201, 204, 207–8, 219–20, 226, 230; on hajj, 27, 41n78, 60, 64, 66; Persians, 47, 48; Rumis, 31, 41, 154n105, 168, 180, 196, 200, 205, 210–11, 230; salons and, 25, 58, 59, 234
Tripoli, *14*, 145n58, 218n83
Tunisi, Shihab al-Din Ahmad al-, poet, 139
Turcomans, 27, 47, 55, 201, 227–8
Turkish language, 16, 19–20, 29, 152; Arabs and, 18, 20, 151–2, 154, 222, 231; biographical dictionaries, 11, 190–2, 195–6; conversation, 134, 137, 141–2, 149, 222; eloquence, 2, 138; literature, 42, 43n86, 50, 154, 195; in Mamluk lands, 27, 42–3, 52; prestige, 152, 220–1, 236; salons, 17, 18, 19, 29, 137, 152, 200, 220, 221, 222, 231; translations into, 42, 50–1, 52, 153, 154n101. *See also* poetry

al-ʿulum al-ʿaqliyya (rational sciences), 47
Umayyad Mosque. *See* Great Mosque of Damascus
Urmawi, Siraj al-Din al-, 42n84

waqf (Islamic endowments), 27, 63–4, 219

Yahya ibn Zakariyya (John the Baptist) shrine, 111, *112*, 186, 208
Yalbugha Mosque, 133, 146, 147
Yılmaz, Hüseyin, on political thought, 154

Zahrawi residence, *111*, 145n58, 147
Zamakhshari, Abu'l Qasim al-. See *Revealer*
Zarkashi, Muhammad al-, 140n36, 180

A NOTE ON THE TYPE

THIS BOOK has been composed in Miller, a Scotch Roman typeface designed by Matthew Carter and first released by Font Bureau in 1997. It resembles Monticello, the typeface developed for The Papers of Thomas Jefferson in the 1940s by C. H. Griffith and P. J. Conkwright and reinterpreted in digital form by Carter in 2003.

Pleasant Jefferson ("P. J.") Conkwright (1905–1986) was Typographer at Princeton University Press from 1939 to 1970. He was an acclaimed book designer and AIGA Medalist.

GPSR Authorized Representative: Easy Access System Europe - Mustamäe tee 50, 10621 Tallinn, Estonia, gpsr.requests@easproject.com

www.ingramcontent.com/pod-product-compliance
Lightning Source LLC
Chambersburg PA
CBHW031757220426
43662CB00007B/443
9780691224947